The Philosophy of Human Rights

MORTON E. WINSTON
Trenton State College

Wadsworth Publishing Company
Belmont, California
A Division of Wadsworth, Inc.

For the prisoners of conscience

Philosophy Editor: Kenneth M. King
Editorial Assistant: Cheri Peterson
Production Editor: Stacey C. Sawyer
Interior Design: Donna Davis
Print Buyer: Randy Hurst
Compositor: TypeLink, Inc.
Cover: Albert Burkhardt
Signing Representative: Jeff Wilhelms

Printed in the United States of America

1 2 3 4 5 6 7 8 9 10—93 92 91 90 89

Library of Congress Cataloging-in-Publication Data

The Philosophy of human rights.

Bibliography: p.
1. Human rights—Philosophy. 2. Civil rights—Philosophy. I. Winston, Morton Emanuel.
JC571.P477 1988   323.4'01   88-27809
ISBN 0-534-10020-1

Contents

Preface

Hardly a day goes by without mention of human rights in the world news. The term itself has gained nearly universal acceptance and is used by people of widely differing political beliefs and ideologies to denote the highest moral standards that governments and individuals alike should strive to uphold and protect. Unfortunately, despite its currency, few people seem to really understand what human rights are and why they are so important.

My own interest in the topic dates from 1977, the first year of the Carter administration's emphasis of human rights as a cornerstone of U.S. foreign policy and also the year in which Amnesty International, the oldest nongovernmental human rights organization, was awarded the Nobel Prize for Peace. I had recently become an active member of Amnesty International USA, and at that time it seemed that the topic of human rights was on everyone's lips. In subsequent years, as my involvement with human rights issues grew, I came to feel that much of the talk about human rights involved more "lip-service" than critical understanding. I felt that the meaning of the term might be obscured by its being too shallowly and too broadly employed and that its value in political and moral discourse would be debased by its being used for narrow political purposes. Consequently, I began to feel the need to place this topic before students, and the general public, in a way that was understandable without being oversimple.

This book grew out of my own attempts to explain the doctrine of human rights to myself and to my students. In 1983 I was awarded a small curriculum development grant from the New Jersey Department of Higher Education to develop a course on human rights for my college's honors program. While reviewing the literature I discovered that, despite the great number of books and articles dealing with aspects of the subject of human rights, there were relatively few college texts that provided up-to-date philosophical treatments of the topic. Of most use to me at that time were a course outline developed by Henry Shue for his course on human rights and U.S. foreign policy at the University of Maryland at College Park and a 1981 bibliography on the teaching of human rights edited by Julian R. Friedman and Laurie Wiseberg of Human Rights Internet; the bibliography contained sample syllabi for a variety of courses on human rights that were then being taught. My own course, which I subsequently taught at Trenton State College and at The Johns Hopkins University School of Continuing Studies, owes a debt to suggestions contained in these works, as well as to the work of many others who have contributed to our better understanding of human rights.

This text is intended to be used in undergraduate and graduate courses in ethics, political theory, or international law that deal solely with the topic of human rights, or in other courses that treat this topic as part of a larger curriculum. Because there are so many approaches to the subject of human rights, I have narrowed the focus of the collection to philosophical theories of human rights— mainly those mainstream articles published since 1970. The selections have been grouped into sections that correspond to the major philosophical issues concerning human rights and are arranged in a logical progression through the central issues. The introductory essay, "Understanding Human Rights," is intended to provide students with an overview of the major contours of the concept of human rights, to introduce important issues and distinctions, and to provide brief expositions of the individual selections.

I would like to express my gratitude to a number of individuals and organizations that have supported my work in the area of human rights over the past decade: to the Faculty Research Committee of Trenton State College for continuing support; to Ann Costanzo and Michelle Schooley for their assistance in preparing the manuscript; to Louis Pojman and James Sterba for their advice; to James Nickel, University of Colorado, George Sher, Institute for Advanced Study, and Carl Wellman, Washington University, who served as reviewers; to my editor, Ken King, for his support and encouragement; to Jack Healey, Suzanne Riveles, and my other fellow human rights activists for their enthusiasm and commitment; but most of all, to my wife, Sally, without whose assistance I could not continue to be a "prisoner of conscience" to the cause of human rights.

M. E. Winston

Introduction

Understanding Human Rights

They came on January 4, in the morning. There were at least three of them: the captain, the sergeant, and one whose rank was kept secret. Perhaps he was unranked. From the outset they were uncompromising. I was forced to sit on an imaginary chair, then to rest on my clenched fists on the floor, with my legs stretched backwards. I was forced to stand on my head, my legs raised, pushed against the wall. In this position I received kicks from all angles. I was forced to lie on my back, raise my legs, then open them. The captain kicked my genitals. I rolled in pain, excruciating pain. "I am determined," he said, "to destroy your manhood, those dirty testicles that make you feel like a small bull." They threw me into the air and let me fall on the concrete floor several times. They lifted me into the air by my hair. They pulled off my beard and hair. They banged me against the wall, hit me with sticks and chairs. Punches landed on my head, stomach, chest, ears, everywhere. It was a total onslaught. Karate chops and judo kicks took their toll. During this nightmarish experience I bled profusely and lost consciousness several times.

Toward evening, I was forced to clean the blood on the floor and to use the same cloth to wipe the blood on my body and face. I was badly injured and swollen. My head was swollen, my nose and mouth bleeding, and my eyes were so swollen I could hardly see. I was bleeding and breathing through the ears: my eardrums were punctured. The wounds in my knees were so deep I could put in the tips of my fingers.

They dragged me from the torture room. I was thrown into a pickup truck, handcuffed to the bars, and covered with a blanket. "If you are alive tomorrow morning," shouted the captain self-assuredly, "then we don't know our job."

T. S. Farisani[1] (reprinted by permission of Fortress Press)

The moral revulsion one feels when confronted with such accounts of brutality directed against a fellow human being is the starting point for understanding human rights. Torture, slavery, arbitrary arrest and imprisonment, extrajudicial execution, and genocide are, for most people, so clearly morally wrong that it seems almost perverse to inquire into the reasons why human beings should not be treated in these ways. However, our modern moral sensibilities were not, we know, universally shared by our ancestors, and in the present century we have witnessed atrocities taking place within what were thought to be highly civilized societies. When we are pressed for reasons that will justify our moral feelings we will usually say that such things are wrong because they are against the law. But what can we say when the laws of a particular polity permit and even condone such actions? To what can we appeal when such practices are carried out by duly appointed agents of the state in execution of national policies? Is there some higher ethical standard to which we can appeal to judge the performance of governments and the justice of their laws?

In the twentieth century the answer most often given to these questions is that such practices as torture or slavery are wrong because they violate a person's human rights. But what are human rights? Can there be "rights" that transcend national borders and competing political ideologies? How did the idea of universal human rights evolve?

What goods or interests ought to be protected by such rights? How do we know that such rights really exist? And what is the meaning and significance of this philosophical conception for the future of civilization?

The Historical Development of the Idea of Human Rights

The idea of "rights"—specifically, "human rights"—is of fairly recent vintage. There is no explicit mention of "rights" in the works of Plato and Aristotle, nor does this concept appear anywhere in the Bible, nor in the ancient writings in philosophy and religion of India, China, or other major cultures. What are now called "human rights" were referred to by Enlightenment philosophers such as Locke and Rousseau as "natural rights," and the classical eighteenth-century conception of the "Rights of Man" traces its philosophical lineage to the Scholastic doctrine of natural law, which, in turn, finds its intellectual origins in the thought of Aristotle and the Greek Stoics and in the moral teachings of Judaism and Christianity.[2]

In the *Nichomachean Ethics* (ca. 340 B.C.), Aristotle argued that in political affairs "justice" is to be "found among men who share a common life in order that their association bring them self-sufficiency, and who are free and equal. . . ."[3] Aristotle's society was, however, stratified into classes, including slaves, so not all humans were regarded as free and equal. However, for those who were regarded as equals, "justice" was determined by the natural and universal ends of human society—freedom, self-sufficiency, and human flourishing—so that "what is by nature just has the same force everywhere and does not depend on what we regard or do not regard as just."[4] Although some of the laws by which people govern themselves exist only by agreement or convention, Aristotle held that because human nature is universal "there is only one constitution that is by nature the best everywhere."[5]

The idea of a "natural law" governing human relations in society exerted considerable influence on subsequent thinkers from the Greek Stoics to the Christian Scholastics. St. Thomas Aquinas (1224–1274) believed that "natural law" is that which "everyone is aware of and through which everyone become conscious within himself of what is right and wrong." For St. Thomas, "God directs rational creatures by instilling in them certain natural inclinations and capacities that enable them to direct themselves as well as other creatures." These inclinations or natural capacities represent the eternal law of God in us.[6]

Probably the first philosopher to use the concept of a "right" (*ius*) in anything like the modern sense was William of Ockham (1290–1349), who thought of "natural right" as a personal "power" to "conform to right reason, without an agreement or pact."[7] The term *ius* is related to the word "justice" and had previously been used to express the notion of what is just or "right" in this sense. Later thinkers, such as the Renaissance humanist Pico Della Mirandola (1463–1494), rejected the Aristotelian idea of a fixed, eternal human nature and held instead that man's essence was precisely that he was protean; through the gifts of reason and free will man was capable of shaping his own nature and destiny. The Renaissance's humanistic ideal of human creativity and self-creativity, combined with the older doctrine of natural law and the emerging doctrine of "rights" as powers, helped form the basis of the modern belief in individual autonomy—the right of the individual to control his or her own life free from the interference of society. Richard Hooker's (1554–1600) *Laws of Ecclesiastical Polity* (1593) defended the Thomistic doctrine of a natural law discoverable by human reason whose observance justified the authority of the secular state. Also influential was the work of Dutch humanist Hugo Grotius (1683–1645), who thought of *ius* as concerning the natural law that prescribes rules of conduct for nations as well as individuals.

However, the notion of "natural rights" did not gain wide acceptance until it was employed in the works of major figures of the European Enlightenment, such as Thomas Hobbes (1588–1679), John Locke (1632–1704), and Jean Jacques Rousseau (1712–1778). According to the Enlightenment Doctrine of the Rights of Man, individual human beings possess certain inherent or "natural" rights in a hypothetical "state of nature" prior to the formation of governments. The legitimate powers of governments are derived from these antecedent natural rights by means of a social contract or agreement. When the ideas of natural law and natural rights were combined in this way with the social contract theory of the state, the idea of natural rights emerged as a necessary presupposition of the theory of the state and as marking both the origins and limits of all legitimate governmental authority.

For Hobbes the "right of nature" included a right of self-preservation which, unlike other natural powers in the state of nature, could not be traded away for security under the rule of a sovereign in civil society. Locke's *Two Treatises of Government*, published anonymously in 1690, declared the state of nature to be "a state of perfect freedom to order [one's] actions and dispose of [one's] possessions and persons as [one] thinks fit, . . . [and] a State also of equality, wherein all the power and jurisdiction is reciprocal, no one having more than another. . . ."[8] Locke defended the view that man has natural rights to life, liberty, and private property, ". . . in all he could effect with his labor—all that his industry could extend to, to alter from the state nature had put it in. . . ."[9] Unlike Locke, who defended slavery, Rousseau argued that no man has the power to "alienate" his own natural liberty or that of his children because " . . . they are born free men; their liberty belongs to them, and no one has the right to dispose of it except themselves."[10]

Revolutionaries of the eighteenth century, such as Thomas Jefferson, adopted these philosophical theses and declared the truth of the idea of natural rights to be "self-evident" and held that it was not only permissible but morally required to overthrow tyrannies that violate these principles of "natural equity and justice." Similarly, the authors of the French Declaration of the Rights of Man and Citizen (1789) asserted that the rights of "liberty, property, security, and resistance to oppression" are "natural, inalienable, and sacred." The decision to incorporate a formal Bill of Rights into the Constitution of the United States of America (1791) extended the tradition of constitutional law deriving from the Magna Carta (1215) and earlier bills of rights and gave explicit political recognition to the eighteenth-century doctrine of the rights of man.

The phenomenal political success that the philosophical theory of natural rights enjoyed in the eighteenth century provoked a variety of critical responses in the nineteenth century. The English philosopher Jeremy Bentham (1748–1832) rejected the French declaration as meaningless nonsense—"nonsense upon stilts"—believing instead that "There are no such thing as rights anterior to the establishment of government." According to Bentham, "Reasons for wishing there were such things as rights, are not rights—hunger is not bread." He also feared that the loose talk of "natural rights" would raise the "spirit of insurrection, or anarchy" to the status of a virtue and that the enshrinement of these "rights" in national constitutions would "enslave" future generations to the will of their ancestors.

The early feminist author Mary Wollstonecraft (1759–1797) launched a different sort of critique against the eighteenth-century doctrine of the rights of man. In her *Vindication of the Rights of Women* (1792) she argued that it was only because of lack of education and custom that women were commonly thought to be the intellectual inferiors of men and that "by nature" women were also "rational creatures." Because the possession of "reason" was then commonly thought to be the universal human characteristic on which human dignity and hence human rights was based, if women are also rational creatures, she reasoned, then women should enjoy the same rights as men. In her own time, Wollstonecraft's view was satirized by Thomas Taylor in his *Vindication of the Rights of Brutes,* who insisted that by the same argument we should soon extend natural rights to animals—a conclusion that he regarded as absurd.

But probably the most influential nineteenth-century critique of the "liberal" doctrine of natural rights came from the pen of Karl Marx (1813–1883), who argued that the revolutions of the previous century were incomplete in that, although they abolished class privileges based on hereditary title and nobility, they retained class privileges based on economic, sexual, and racial distinctions. These inequalities could, he thought, be overcome only in a "classless" society in which not only political but also economic justice and equality were fully realized. Marx and Engels also held that the philosophical idea of "natural rights" was "itself a historical product, the creation of which required definite historical conditions which in turn themselves presuppose a long previous historical development. It is therefore anything but an eternal truth."[11] They believed that the particular manifestation of the idea of natural rights in eighteenth-century France and America reflected the interests of the emerging capitalist class, the bourgeoisie, just as their own theory of economic rights reflected the interests of the proletariat. Lenin (1870–1924), like earlier revolutionaries inspired by the idea of universal rights, transformed Marxist philosophy into political reality with the Bolshevik revolution of 1917.

In the latter half of the twentieth century the primary impetus for the development of the contemporary doctrine of human rights has been the Second World War, especially the post-war revelation of the atrocities that the Nazis committed during the Holocaust. In response to these crimes against humanity, and in the hope of creating an international framework for preserving world peace, on December 10, 1948, the United Nations adopted the *Universal Declaration of Human Rights*.[12] In this document the Member States of the newly formed United Nations committed themselves to the "promotion of universal respect for and observance of human rights and fundamental freedoms." Recognizing that "a common understanding of these rights and freedoms is of the greatest importance for the full realization of this pledge," they proclaimed that both individuals and governments should "strive by teaching and education to promote respect for these rights and freedoms and by progressive measures, national and international, to secure their universal and effective recognition and observance."[13]

In the forty years since this declaration was made, there has been significant progress in implementing the United Nations' pledge: Human rights are now generally regarded as providing the fundamental moral standard by which to measure the performance of governments; the belief in human rights has demonstrated its appeal to peoples all over the world; and many specific rights have been recognized in international treaties and covenants that now have the force of international law.[14]

Despite the widespread belief in human rights, and the *de facto* recognition that these rights are given by most governments, many human rights, including some of the most basic, are too often still grievously violated. The failure of present-day political societies to effectively implement and adequately protect human rights is due partly to a lack of political will, partly to an absence, in most cases, of any effective mechanisms for enforcing international human rights standards, and partly to a scarcity of resources. In addition to these problems of implementing human rights, however, fundamental philosophical questions remain about the nature and basis of human rights, and different conceptions and interpretations exist that continue to divide international opinion.

Major Human Rights Questions.   The major contemporary philosophical questions concerning human rights include:

1. What are rights in general, and, specifically, what are human rights? How do rights differ from goals, duties, interests, needs, and claims? What is distinctive and important about human rights as opposed to these other moral notions?
2. What kinds of goods, benefits, and interests do human rights protect, and what specific human rights are there? Do all of the rights mentioned in documents such as the *Universal Declaration of Human Rights* have equal stature? Do the so-called economic rights, such as the rights to rest and leisure, reasonable working hours, and periodic holidays with pay (Article 24), have equal standing with more traditional liberty and security rights such as the right not to be held in slavery (Article 4)?
3. Does the having of such rights entail correlative duties, and, if so, to whom can these duties be ascribed? Are such duties borne only by governments, or are all persons responsible for fulfilling, enforcing, and protecting such rights? What conditions suffice for the effective protection or fulfillment of a right? Who may be held responsible for failing to fulfil, protect, or enforce the right?
4. What is the "weight" of a human right? Are there any absolute rights, or, if not, under which specific conditions can human rights be limited, abridged, suspended, or alienated? In cases where one human right conflicts with other rights,

which right takes priority? In cases where individual rights conflict with considerations of general social utility, how does one decide how far to protect individual rights and how far to promote the general interests of society?

5. How is it possible to answer the charge that the doctrine of human rights is merely a projection of the Western philosophical and political tradition? Does the fact that there are different understandings of human rights within different cultures invalidate the claim that they represent a universal moral standard?

6. What ultimately justifies the claim that there are human rights? What is the basis for the central claim that such rights belong to human beings or persons as such—that is, simply in virtue of their humanity? What features of human beings, in particular, justify the claim that we possess intrinsic rights? Do the particular grounds provided as justification adequately explain the particular features of human rights—for example, their universality, equality, their contents, addressees, and their weights?

7. What justifies the claim that certain rights are possessed universally and equally by all individual human beings or persons, as opposed to nonhuman animals, groups, or supra-individual entities like corporations? Is it, in fact, true that all human beings qualify for having these rights? Might different human individuals have some rights in varying degrees? In particular, do embryos, fetuses, young children, the mentally ill, the comatose, or members of future human generations also possess full human rights?

It is essential that we understand these philosophical controversies if we are to understand human rights. The remainder of this introduction will summarize major contemporary theories of human rights that provide answers to these questions. Students interested in exploring these issues further should consult the selected bibliography in Appendix B. The *Universal Declaration of Human Rights* and two International Human Rights Covenants are in Appendix A.

The Nature of Human Rights

We generally understand "human right" to mean a kind of universal moral right that belongs equally to all human beings simply by virtue of the fact that they *are* human beings. This statement bears close scrutiny, because it states conditions that are normally deemed to be essential to the idea of human rights.

First, human rights are *moral* rights, as opposed to *legal* or *civil* rights—that is, rights that are recognized and protected by the laws of a particular polity or government. In the United States and Canada and many other countries, national constitutions contain specific "Bills of Rights" that recognize certain moral rights of citizens and protect their exercise under law. Citizens of such states are said to have or enjoy these civil rights. Having civil rights normally means that the legal system of the state can be invoked to protect rights in cases in which individual right-holders believe that their rights have been violated. However, persons who live in countries without similar civil laws do not thereby lack human rights; it is crucial to the modern idea of human rights that persons can *have* these rights, in some sense, even though the particular civil laws enforced by their own governments may not recognize or protect them.

Moral rights, in general, are not always protected by law, even in countries that do recognize and protect the subset of moral rights known as human rights. For instance, it might be argued that parents have a moral right to their grown children's care should they become old or infirm or for some reason are unable to care for themselves. Most people would acknowledge some validity to such a right-claim and would hold that the children of such parents have a moral *duty* to aid their infirm parents. In this example we have a *moral* right that entails a correlative *duty* or obligation on the parts of some others, which is *not* explicitly recognized or protected by law. If a child refuses to care for his or her sick parent, the parent cannot go to a police officer or judge to complain and attempt to redress the wrong; however, if there were civil laws requiring the discharge of such filial obligations, the parent would have such recourse. In any case, the fact that such civil recourse does not exist does not demonstrate that there is no such *moral* right!

The example of filial obligation serves to illustrate several other points. In the case of parental rights, the group that has these rights, or the class of *right-holders,* is a limited set of persons. Not all persons are parents, and therefore those persons who never had or raised children themselves cannot claim parental rights. Rights involving restricted classes of right-holders are termed *special rights,* whereas rights held by all persons, regardless of their particular qualities or stations, are termed *general,* or *universal rights.*

The individuals who owe duties to the holders of special rights are only a special subset of persons—in this case, the right-holding parents' own children; children of other parents are not responsible for providing care. Individuals who have duties that arise from the rights of others are often termed the *objects,* or *addressees,* of the rights. In the case of a special right, both the right-holders and the addressees of the right are a subset of the class of all persons restricted in a particular way—in our example, by being related to one another as parents and children.

The parents' moral right to receive their children's care exists, in some sense, latently, until it is *triggered* by certain conditions—in this case, when the parents become ill and are no longer able to care for themselves—at which point the moral right in question becomes an actual right and can provide the basis for a *moral* claim by parents against their children.

Human rights, in contrast, are *universal* rights: All persons are the holders of human rights, and the class of human right-holders is not restricted by any special characteristics, abilities, properties, or status. The universality of human rights is the feature that accounts for the claim that human beings have such rights whether or not they are recognized and protected under the laws of a particular government, because citizenship or nationality is a special status. Civil rights can be restricted to only those persons who are citizens of a country or who reside within its boundaries. Human rights have no boundaries.

Because the class of right-holders of human rights includes all human beings, it seems appropriate to suggest that the class of addressees of these rights is also universal and that all persons have duties to respect and protect the human rights of all other persons. However, some controversy exists on this point, because, traditionally, governments have been seen as the primary addressees of human rights. One way to reconcile this apparent disagreement is to suggest that whereas individual persons are the primary addressees of human rights, when individuals enter into the social compacts by which governments are created, they in effect deputize their governments to discharge their duties to protect human rights on their behalves. This would explain why it is customary to treat governments as the addressees of human rights, but also why, when governments fail to fulfill their roles in protecting these rights, the responsibility to see that they are protected devolves on individuals.

To say that human rights are *equal* means that persons have the same rights irrespective of their particular characteristics as individuals—that is, their race, nationality, religion, language, gender, ethnic origin, property, relations, or other status. Differences among individual characteristics should not make any difference in the respect we accord each person's rights: If any person has a particular human right, then all persons must have the same right. Human beings are thought to have these equal, universal moral rights simply because they are *human* or because they are *persons*. Being a human person is thought to carry with it a special moral status, a quite different moral status than we accord to inanimate objects, plants, and members of other species of animals. Human persons have what is called "dignity," or intrinsic worth, and we have these moral characteristics *inherently,* by our very natures. Human dignity, and the special moral status it confers, is thought to ground the ascription of those universal and equal rights that we call *human rights.* The ideas of human dignity and equality are the core ideas in the contemporary concept of human rights.

Finally, human rights are *rights*; to claim something as one's right is not the same as to express a wish, announce a goal, or ask for a favor; it is to make an authoritative, emphatic demand. Fundamental human rights, such as the rights not to be held in slavery, not to be tortured or killed, and not to be arbitrarily imprisoned, have a preemptory character; they express powerful moral constraints that take precedence over most other moral and nonmoral reasons for action. To claim something as a human right is to recognize it as supremely important and to imply that failure to respect it constitutes a grave injustice.

The philosophical problem of understanding human rights arises when we reflect that several aspects of the concept are not entirely self-evident. For instance, the proposition "x is human; therefore, x has rights" is far from being self-evident, say, in the way that the statement "x is a bachelor; therefore, x is unmarried" can be said to be self-evident. The assertion that "all human beings have equal rights" is not a bare tautology; quite the contrary, it makes a substantive, nontrivial, moral claim. However, the claim that all humans have rights is not easily construed as a statement of a natural fact such as, for example, "all human beings have opposable thumbs," because one cannot determine the possession of properties such as "rights" by observation or experiment. But if rights-statements are neither truths of logic nor truths of fact, what kind of truths are they?

The claim that all humans have equal moral rights, if it is true, must express a *moral* truth. But what kind of things are rights, in general, and what specifically are human rights? Contemporary theorists who have attempted to answer this question have described rights variously as grounds of duties to benefit the interests of others, as claims or entitlements, as entitlements having institutional or social recognition, as constellations of powers, immunities, liberties, and claims, and as "trumps" against considerations of general social utility.[15]

Rights and Interests.   Joseph Raz, in the first reading selection in this book, attempts to frame a general definition of "rights" that will capture, in a theoretically neutral way, how the term is used in legal, political, and moral discourse. Raz offers the following definition: "'x has a right' if and only if x can have rights, and other things being equal, an aspect of x's well-being (his interest) is a sufficient reason for holding some other person(s) to be under a duty." For an individual to be capable of having rights, his or her well-being must have "ultimate value" or intrinsic worth; that is, his or her well-being must be an "end-in-itself." The only exception concerns "artificial persons," such as corporations that are accorded some legal rights—for instance, the power to enter into contracts.

Raz goes on to distinguish *core* rights from *derivative* rights: A core right is "based on the interest which figures essentially in the justification of the statement that the right exists," whereas a derivative right is grounded on a core right (or rights) as the "conclusion of a sound argument (nonredundantly) including a statement of the existence of the core right." Core rights are often abstract—for instance, a right to "freedom of expression"—whereas derivative rights might specify rights to political expression, commercial expression, or artistic or scientific expression as flowing from this core right. However, specific rights such as these may also be independently grounded, and the general right of freedom of expression can be derived from the more specific cases by generalization.

Next Raz discusses the thesis of the correlativity of rights and duties: He rejects the strong correlativity thesis that holds that "x has a right to P against y if and only if y is under a duty to x concerning P" on the grounds that not all duties entail corresponding rights. He does, however, accept the weaker thesis that all rights *ground* duties— that is, that x's possessing a right to P provides a reason for holding y to be under an obligation, all other things being equal. He cautions that the duties grounded on rights are *prima facie* obligations that can sometimes be overridden by conflicting rights and duties and, therefore, that having a right may not actually guarantee that an object or interest is secured to the right-holder; that not all of the duties associated with a right can always be waived by the right-holder; and that a single right may be the ground of a number of different duties, and new duties may be created depending on the changing circumstances under which a right is exercised. Rights in this view have a "dynamic" aspect that precludes there being any exhaustive enumeration of all of the duties for which it may serve as ground. He illustrates these points for the right to promise, noting that several distinct duties are grounded on this right, whose core protects "the interests of persons to be able to forge normative bonds with others."

Raz points out that his definition of rights "does not settle the issue of who is capable of having rights beyond requiring that right-holders are creatures who have interests." He mentions in passing that there is a significant controversy concerning this issue between those who hold a "reciprocity thesis" according to which only members of "the same moral community" can have rights and those who would enlarge the class of possible right-holders to include all moral agents, or even all sentient beings. The distinction that he believes is crucial to settling this question is the difference between an *instrumental* and an *intrinsic,* or *ultimate,* value: For something to be ultimately valuable it must be valuable in its own right, apart from its possible use to satisfy the interests of others. Plants such as corn, which have a use-value as a food crop, are instrumentally valuable because of their relation to human interests but lack any intrinsic value. Sentient nonhuman creatures, such as dogs, should, in some views, be treated as lacking any ultimate value; their values derive from their relationship to human well-being and hence are not ultimate. Others hold that the well-being of sentient nonhuman animals should be seen as also having ultimate value. Raz does not attempt to resolve this dispute but argues that "only those whose well-being is of ultimate value can have rights. . . ."[16]

This is so, in his account, because the peculiar function that "rights-talk" has in practical discourse is to focus attention on benefits of aspects of individuals' well-being that function as grounds of the duties of others: "Rights ground requirements for action in the interest of other beings." Rights, in this view, "are intermediate conclusions in arguments from ultimate values to duties." Additional premises are needed to demonstrate that the existence of a right follows from the existence of an interest that has ultimate value, and still further premises are needed to show what duties follow from the existence of the right. These additional premises are needed to identify the specific class of right-holders, the class of addressees of the right, and its specific contents—that is, the range of duties it serves to ground, its weight, and its scope.[17]

Raz concludes by responding to an objection to his account that says that his definition of rights as based on interests rules out the possibility that "rights" are a fundamental feature of morality, in the sense of being underived from ultimate interests. He responds by noting that it is possible, in his account, that we may have some rights because we have "an interest in having those same rights." This is, he argues, not viciously circular, because we may hold that "it serves the right-holder's interest in having that right inasmuch as that interest is considered to be of ultimate value." But what interest is served by having rights? Could we possibly conduct our moral affairs without recourse to rights at all, or is there some distinctive and ultimately valuable interest that having rights serves?

Rights As Claims.   In a selection in this volume, Joel Feinberg argues that rights make it possible to engage in a particular and valuable kind of linguistic performance: "making claims." He writes, "To have a right is to have a claim to something and against someone, the recognition of which is called for by legal rules or, in the case of moral rights, by the principles of an enlightened conscience."[18] To "have a claim" is to be in a position to make a claim *to* or to claim *that*. What is central to the having of rights, according to Feinberg, is being in a position to *act* in a certain way, that is, to make claims:

> it is claiming that gives rights their special moral significance. . . . Having rights enables us to "stand up like men," to look others in the eye, and to feel in some fundamental way the equal of anyone. To think of oneself as the holder of rights is not to be unduly but properly proud; to have that minimal self-respect that is necessary to be worthy of the love and esteem of others. Indeed, . . . what is called "human dignity" may simply be the recognizable capacity to assert claims.

Feinberg illustrates the distinctive functions of rights-as-claims by means of a thought-experiment involving an imaginary land called "Nowheresville." Nowheresville is just like our own world except that no one in it has any rights. The denizens of Nowheresville have other moral qualities in abundance; they are compassionate, dutiful, forgiving, and deserving of various goods. What they lack is the power to claim something as their right. In particular, they cannot make a claim to something against someone else that will be recognized as valid under a system of rules.

In Feinberg's view, rights must have at least four elements: (1) a *content*—that is, some good that is the object of a claim; (2) a *holder*—that is, someone who has the right; (3) an *addressee*—that is, someone toward whom one's claim to the good is addressed or directed; and (4) a *source of validation*—that is, something to which one can appeal to justify one's claim as valid. Feinberg terms a claim that lacks an addressee and a source of validation a *manifesto right*; for instance, "A natural need for some good as such, like a natural desert, is always a reason in support of a claim to that good. . . . Such claims, based on need alone, are 'permanent possibilities of rights,' the natural seeds from which rights grow," but they are not yet actual rights. Actual rights are, for Feinberg, valid claims—that is, claims, to something against others, that are justified under a system of governing rules.

To use a homely example: Under the rules of Monopoly if a player's piece lands on a square owned by another player, the owner may demand payment of a rent determined by the number of houses and hotels built on that property. We can say, in precisely Feinberg's sense, that the Monopoly property owner "has a right" to be paid rent because he is in a position to make a claim to a certain good, the rent, against the player who was unfortunate enough to land on his property, and, moreover, he is in a position to justify his claim by referring to the system of rules that govern the game of Monopoly.

Although Feinberg's analysis seems to go a good way toward clarifying legal or civil rights—that is, those rights that are explicitly guaranteed by the laws of a state and for which there exist institutional mechanisms for promotion and enforcement—it is not clear that it serves also as an explication of moral and, specifically, *human* rights. Against whom are such rights claimed? What systems of rules justify such claims?

Rights As Recognized Entitlements.   Rex Martin argues that although it is possible to consider a moral claim as fully valid whether it is responded to or not, "a human right is defective, not as a claim but as a right, in the absence of appropriate practices of recognition and maintenance." For Martin, human rights are claims plus something else—namely, the appropriate form of social recognition: "A human rights claim which lacks such recognition is still a claim, and may even be a morally valid one, but it cannot qualify as a human right." This is so, Martin argues, because what is distinctive about human rights, as opposed to other universal moral rights, is that the primary addressees of these rights are governments. Human rights require that particular societies recognize and protect certain moral claims under civil laws: "In a society which has no civil rights (for example, a caste society, in particular, one with a slave caste) there are no human rights" but only "a moral claim (presumably valid) that something should be a civil right." It follows from this Benthamite view that "If there are any human rights at all, . . . there are civil rights at least in some countries."

Martin's view suggests that there is a developmental pattern in the evolution of rights: Rights begin as what Feinberg calls "manifesto rights," when a human need or good is recognized as requiring special social protection, and such protection is claimed by some persons as a moral entitlement. At this stage the right in question is validated only by the dictates of "enlightened conscience," perhaps the consciences of only a small minority of the population. One can imagine this once to have been the status of the now universally recognized human right not to be held in slavery. In the second stage, the right-claim gains wider social recognition and acceptance as more and more people come to believe that the right-claim is indeed a morally valid one, because the interest that it serves to protect really is an ultimately valuable one. In this stage there may arise political or social movements whose goal is to secure explicit recognition and protection of the right and to end what they take to be violations of the right. In the third stage, the right in question is formally recognized in civil or international law, and appropriate procedures for the protection and recognition of rights-claims are instituted. Only when a claim reaches this last stage of explicit social recognition does it become, in Martin's view, an actual or positive right.

Rights As Clusters of Hohfeldian Elements.   Recent work drawing on the theory of legal rights developed earlier in this century by Wesley Hohfeld distinguishes four elements that can be signified by any legal right: (1) a claim, (2) a liberty, (3) a power, or (4) an immunity. A *liberty* of x to do a certain thing, A, is the absence of x's duty not to do A, matched by other people's lack of any claim that x refrain from doing A. For instance, I am at liberty to paint my bedroom green in that I have no duty not to, and others have no claim against me not to. A *power* to do A consists of a legal competence to act in a way that will bring consequences to bear on another and is matched by a liability to be acted on. For instance, a judge has the power to sentence a convicted criminal to prison, and the convicted criminal is liable to being sentenced. An *immunity* to A signifies a lack of power or disability on the parts of others to prevent me from doing A, as when we say "No one has the right to prevent me from practicing my religion." Finally, a *claim* correlates with a legal duty of some second party.[19] Only this last variety of right, claim rights, are clearly recognized within Feinberg's theory.

Carl Wellman argues that this Hohfeldian pattern of correlated "advantages" and "disadvantages" can be found in moral as well as legal rights. In "A New Conception of Human Rights" (this volume) Wellman applies this model of rights to understanding human rights.[20] He takes the Hohfeldian conception of a legal right as a "cluster of legal liberties, claims, powers, and immunities" as his model and develops an analogous concept of an *ethical* right as "a complex system of ethical advantages, a cluster of ethical liberties, claims, powers, and immunities." Just as in the case of legal rights, several of these elements can function as the *core* of the right, its essential content. Finally, Wellman defines a human right as "a cluster of ethical liberties, claims, powers, and immunities that together constitute a system of ethical autonomy possessed by an individual as a human being vis-a-vis the state."

Wellman illustrates this approach with respect to the right of privacy that has been invoked controversially by the U.S. Supreme Court in recent years.[21] A human right to "privacy" would claim privacy as a kind of good which ought to be protected in all persons. But what specifically is the content of such a right? Is it a liberty to "be private;" a claim that others have a duty to refrain from invading a person's privacy; a power to control others' access to one's personal or private affairs? Or is it an immunity from laws that would restrict or invade one's autonomy? Wellman argues that the right of privacy contains three distinct elements in its core: "a claim to freedom from invasions of one's privacy," "a claim to legal protection from invasions of one's privacy by the state or other individuals," and "the ethical claim of the individual against the state that it sustain the conditions necessary for the existence of privacy for the individual." He agrees with Martin that governments are the primary addressees of human rights and goes on to propose that similar analyses can be given for other human rights.

Rights As "Trumps".   Wellman's analysis of moral rights as consisting of clusters of ethical advantages helps to make sense of the idea that rights function in political discourse in much the same way as "trumps" function in card games such as bridge. Ronald Dworkin, who is credited with this insightful analogy, argues that governments frame social policies to promote the general welfare of society, to maximize the common good, or to satisfy the preferences of the majority. In a society that did not recognize individual rights at all, such as Feinberg's Nowheresville, individuals and minorities would have no guarantee that their dignity and equality would not be sacrificed to promote some general social good or to satisfy the preferences of the majority.

For example, suppose that a particular society is beset with civil unrest, protest demonstrations, riots, and occasionally violent killings at the hands of mobs. The government believes (perhaps correctly) that it is in the best interest of the society as a whole to stop the unrest and prevent more killings. Officials of the government decide that the most effective way to prevent further killings is to "make an example" of several individuals who it believes may have participated in a riot in which a local official was murdered by a mob. But, rather than trying the accused fairly in a court of law to determine whether they were in fact guilty of the crime, the government officials decide to arrest several people who were alleged by government informants to have been present at the time of the killing and to execute them immediately with only a "show" trial, so that the example would have maximum effect.

Without strong legal rights that guarantee due process of law before an accused individual can be convicted of a crime and punished, individuals would be threatened by such arbitrary imprisonment and punishment. Rights exist precisely to protect individuals from being used indiscriminately as means to achieve general social or political ends: Having a right to due process gives the individual a legal or ethical claim against being turned into an unwilling instrument of social policy. In cases such as these, no mere consideration of social utility ought to override the rights of individuals to a fair trial; the individual's right "trumps" the good of society as a whole.

Saying this, however, does not commit one to the view that rights are *absolute* and may never be overridden under any circumstances. Dworkin explains this point as follows:

> Someone who claims that citizens have a right against the government need not go so far as to say that the State is *never* justified in overriding that right. He might say, for instance, that although citizens have a right to free speech, the Government may override that right when necessary to protect the rights of others, or to prevent a catastrophe, or even to obtain a clear and major public benefit (though if he acknowledged this last as a possible justification he would be treating the right in question as not among the most important or fundamental). What he cannot do is to say that the Government is justified in overriding a right on the minimal grounds that would be sufficient if no such right existed. He cannot say that the government is entitled to act on no more than a judgment that its act is likely to produce, overall, a benefit to the community. That admission would make his claim of a right pointless, and would show him to be using some sense of "right" other than the strong sense necessary to give his claim the political importance it is normally taken to have.

The position that most or perhaps all rights may justifiably be limited in certain circumstances is often expressed by saying that rights embody *prima facie* moral claims. A prima facie claim is one that implies a strong initial presumption that the right in question is to be respected, unless a competing right or other strong moral justification can be presented showing why the right should be limited in a particular case. We know of several standard cases in which a right may be abridged; for instance, the right of free speech does not cover the right of an individual to yell "Fire!" as a prank in a crowded theatre. Here the rights of other individuals to have their personal safety protected conflict with the individual's right of free speech. In this case, most everyone will readily agree that other people's collective rights to safety outweighs the individual's interest in yelling "Fire!" and thereby justifiably limits his right of free speech.

However, other possible conflicts among particular rights and between rights and important social interests may not be so easily resolved, and the problem of deciding when a reason is strong enough to justify limiting or suspending a particular right is one that causes reasonable people to disagree. Particularly troublesome are cases in which different "weighty" rights conflict. For instance, the debate concerning abortion is often portrayed as a conflict between a fetus's right to life and a woman's right to control the reproductive uses of her body. In such cases, the problem is to balance the competing claims exerted by each right and to decide which right should prevail when both cannot prevail. We speak of the strength or *weight* of a right as a measure of its "rank or importance in relation to other norms."[22] A weighty right will take precedence over a less weighty right when the two rights conflict. An *absolute* right would be one with so great a weight that no combination of competing rights or other moral claims would suffice to override it. Few if any of our rights are absolute in this sense, because any particular right may come into conflict with many other rights and other moral considerations, each of which expresses *prima facie* constraints on action.

We also speak of the *scope* of a right and distinguish it from weight and content: Scope refers to the class of particular cases to which the right applies. In cases such as the yelling of "Fire" we limit the scope of a right to exclude cases that constitute justified exceptions to the general core right protecting free speech. In other cases, we may extend the scope of a right to include derivative rights, as for instance when the U.S. Supreme Court interpreted the right of privacy to protect a woman's decision to have an abortion. Questions of scope are particularly important in relation to *abstract* rights, such as a right to fair treatment or equal consideration, in which it is necessary to determine whether and how the right applies to specific cases. *Concrete* rights, such as, say, the right to enter a theatre, which is conferred by an individual having bought a ticket to a particular performance, do not generally involve similar problems of scope.[23]

In this book's selection, Dworkin considers several cases in which significant rights conflict with important social interests. He argues that the balancing metaphor used with dealing with conflicts *among* rights is not appropriate when the conflict is one between rights and general social interests, because it is precisely here that rights are most important. Rights function primarily as claims against governments and are designed to protect individuals from being used as expedient instruments of government policy. If a government adjudicates cases in which the interests of the government conflict with those of individuals or minorities so as to fail to recognize rights in such critical cases, it will become difficult to believe that the government really takes rights seriously at all. But governments cannot allow the scopes of all individual rights to be extended so far as to seriously damage the collective good of society, and so it must in some cases draw the line clearly between instances that are protected by a right and those that are not; that is, it must sometimes delimit the scope of a right.

A case in point is the law regarding conscientious objection to military service in time of war or national emergency. Should anyone be allowed to claim him- or herself as an exception to the draft laws? If so, should exceptions be granted only to those who object to all wars on religious grounds or also to those who may object to a particular war for particular moral reasons? Such "line drawing" problems are always difficult and cannot be answered in general, any more than problems of balancing competing rights can be answered in general. Although he acknowledges the need to consider such problems on a case-by-case basis, Dworkin presents a compelling argument for the conclusion that the rule of law requires respect for the law, and law will not be respected if the dignity and the equality of individuals and minorities are not protected in precisely those cases where it matters most to say that they have rights.

Problems of balancing competing rights or of limiting or extending rights in relation to social goods arise only when there are at least some rights that are recognized by governments. But which rights, in general, ought governments to recognize? What interests ought to be protected by human rights? A fundamental problem for the contemporary doctrine of human rights is to determine what the *content* of human rights should be. Significant disagreements about this issue continue to divide international political opinion.

The Content of Human Rights

People nowadays invoke many different rights: We speak of rights to health care, to education, to social security, to fair wages, to a clean environment, to smoke-free offices, to abortion, to child-care, and to sick leave. We also speak of the rights of the poor as against those of the rich, parents against children, tenants against landlords, believers against atheists, women against men, gays against straights, citizens against the police, the developing nations against the developed nations, and the list goes on and on. How are we to decide which interests deserve the protection of civil rights in one's own society? Even more difficult is this question: How are we to decide which rights are to be included among the list of human rights to which all persons are entitled?

The drafters of the *Universal Declaration of Human Rights* faced a problem that had not been encountered previously in the history of the development of the doctrine of human rights: Previously, when "Bills of Rights," such as the first ten amendments to the Constitution of the United States of America, had been drawn up, their intended use was to serve as the expression of the fundamental political values and moral principles of a particular society or state and as the governing principles of a single sovereign nation. In 1947, however, the newly formed United Nations' agency UNESCO was given the task of drafting an *international* bill of human rights whose purpose was to state a conception of human rights that could accommodate the differing political beliefs, economic systems, and cultures of the member states of the United Nations. UNESCO responded to this challenge by establishing a Committee on the Philosophic Principles of the Rights of Man, whose charge was to examine the "changes of intellectual and historical circumstances between the classical declarations of human rights which stem from the eighteenth century and the bill of rights made possible by the state of ideas and the economic potentials of the present."[24] The committee prepared a questionnaire that it sent out to distinguished scholars and diplomats, and met from June 26 to July 2, 1947 to consider the replies and to draft a report on "The Grounds of an International Declaration of Human Rights."

In the opening words of this report the committee wrote that "An international declaration of human rights must be the expression of a faith to be maintained no less than a programme of actions to be carried out." The report goes on to record the committee's decision not to try to resolve all philosophical disagreements or to attempt to arrive at a doctrinal consensus concerning human rights, but instead "to discover the intellectual means to secure agreement concerning fundamental rights and to remove difficulties in their implementation such as might stem from intellectual differences."[25] In carrying out this strategy the committee recommended that, for pragmatic reasons, the definitions of certain key terms such as "rights," "liberty," and "democracy" be left intentionally ambiguous. It went on to express a core of agreement among the members of the committee on the importance of human dignity and to develop a list of fifteen specific rights that it grouped under three headings: (1) rights to live, (2) rights to live well, and (3) rights to social participation. This historic compromise was based on the general agreement that the claims protected by human rights derive from the requirements of "human dignity," but it largely left open the question of what human dignity requires and how best to secure it.

Customary Categories of Rights.   Following the adoption of the *Universal Declaration of Human Rights,* the United Nations' Commission on Human Rights began drafting international conventions that were intended to raise the status of the rights mentioned in that document to that of international law. The committee, however, soon ran into difficulty. One problem was that some nations objected to the very idea of international law as an unwarranted infringement on national sovereignty. This problem was compounded by the fact that different nations adhering to different political ideologies placed differing emphases on different historically influential categories of rights.

Proponents of so-called "first-generation" rights stress the priority of individual liberties and powers that protect the autonomous choices of individuals free from interference by governments. In such accounts, rights such as freedom of religion and freedom of speech are given great weight, whereas economic rights are given lesser weights or are not recognized as rights at all. In contrast, defenders of "second-generation" rights, the socialist or economic rights, stress rights that are intended to provide individuals with protection against deprivation of the basic material necessities of life. In some cases, proponents of this view place greater weight on economic rights than on traditional "first-generation" liberty rights and often believe that civil liberties can be justifiably suspended when they conflict with the general economic well-being of society. In this century, there has been added a "third generation" of rights dealing with the rights of groups and "peoples" to political self-determination, cultural participation, and economic development.[26]

The division of rights into first-, second-, and third-generation rights roughly corresponds to the conventional division of nations into first-world nations (liberal, democratic, developed), second-world nations (socialist, authoritarian, developed), and third-world nations (mixed economy and ideology, but developing). The first-world conception of human rights is rooted in the classical, liberal doctrine of the

Rights of Man, which conceived of a person as "an autonomous individual possessed of individual rights." In the socialist, or second, world the dominant conception of human rights is based on the Marxist view of human nature and society according to which the idea of the "autonomous individual" is a myth. There is no fixed "human nature"; instead, a person's nature is as a social or communal being whose particular characteristics are formed by the social, economic, and historical conditions of his or her society. In this conception, there are no "natural rights" prior to and independent of civil society, but the state "grants" rights to its citizens. In third-world countries, whose modern histories have often been ones of colonial domination by European cultures, the emphasis is generally on so-called "group rights" and rights of national or ethnic "self-determination." Rights, in this view, are neither the natural possession of individuals nor are they historically conditioned goods granted by states; rather, they derive from the relationship between individuals and the cultures they inhabit and from the interaction between them. Because these societies have traditionally defined themselves in terms of ethnic, racial, tribal, or linguistic communities, great emphasis is placed on the individual's relation to traditionally defined communal groups and the "rights" of these groups to cultural self-determination.

The upshot of these political and philosophical controversies has been to conventionally distinguish between two general categories of rights: civil and political rights on the one hand, and economic, social, and cultural rights on the other. This division of rights has become customary largely because it reflects a kind of "all-purpose" view of government that combines the classical "liberal" view of rights as inherent liberties or powers of individuals that impose limitations on the legitimate powers of governments, with the "socialist" view emphasizing the duty of governments to guarantee economic security and equality to their citizens. A major innovation of the United Nations declaration was to combine these two traditional categories while also giving prominence to a third category of rights—cultural rights—that had not previously been mentioned in major human rights documents.

Cultural Relativism and Human Rights. Insight into the reasons why cultural rights were considered important to the drafters of the *Universal Declaration of Human Rights* can be gained from the Statement on Human Rights issued by the American Anthropological Association, which has been reprinted for this volume. The basic problem confronting the Commission on Human Rights was to find a formulation of the notion of human rights that could be accepted as truly universal, not merely "a statement of rights conceived only in terms of the values prevalent in the countries of Western Europe and America." Because many of the member states of the United Nations were newly formed, many having previously been colonies of the great powers before the world wars, special sensitivity was needed to avoid the suggestion that Western cultural and political values alone would receive recognition.

The American Anthropological Association statement asserts that the rights of human individuals "must be based on a recognition of the fact that the personality of the individual can develop only in terms of the culture of his society" and, therefore, urges that "respect for cultural differences" be a guiding principle in formulating any statement of human rights. The statement goes on to suggest that because anthropology, the science of human culture, has not been able to discover any "technique of qualitatively evaluating cultures" and that its studies have shown that ethical "standards and values are relative to the culture from which they derive," it concludes that any attempt to judge the values of one culture against those of another will be counterproductive and will tend to undermine the validity of the idea of universal human rights. Rather than imposing a single, rigid standard of ethical and political values, the statement, in effect, proposes that ethical relativism, pluralism of values, and cultural tolerance be adopted as the universal standard.

Real and Supposed Rights.   The solution just described to the problem of the cultural relativism of moral values, has, in the opinion of some critics, created an even more serious problem. The admission of the existence of a plurality of basic values and basic moral conceptions and the recognition of a variety of these goods and interests as protected by human rights have led to a rapid inflation in the number of human rights! The inflation of rights is viewed in some quarters as a serious problem because it is held to devalue the meaning of human rights while also creating seemingly endless problems of determining the weights and scopes of particular rights in relation to one another.

An early and influential statement of this view is contained in the article by Maurice Cranston, "Human Rights, Real and Supposed." Cranston argues that the inclusion of second- and third-generation economic and cultural rights, along with first-generation civil and political rights, "does not make sense" and, moreover, that "circulation of a confused notion of human rights hinders the effective protection of what are correctly seen as human rights." He reviews the history of the development of this customary, late twentieth-century view of rights and then proposes a classification of legal and moral rights that, he argues, enables us to develop some tests of a right's authenticity.

The first test he proposes is that of practicability: One cannot have a right to something that the addressees of one's right cannot possibly provide. Second, he proposes that genuine rights be such as can be "readily secured by legislation," or easily protected under law. These provisions would in his view rule out such things as "the right to social security" or "periodic holidays with pay" as universal moral rights because many governments are simply too poor to be able to provide such goods to all of their citizens. Third, he argues that real human rights must be truly universal, not special rights that apply only to a restricted class of individuals, such as those who are employed. Finally, he argues that the most important test of a genuine human right is that it protects something that is of ultimate value and that may rightfully be demanded as an essential component of human dignity and well-being, rather than something that would merely be nice to have in utopia. The status of "human rights" should be reserved for just those things "of which no one may be deprived without a grave affront to justice." The language of human rights should not be used to express ideals or aspirations, however worthy; we must restrict universal moral rights to cover only "those deeds which should never be done," those "freedoms which should never be invaded," in short, to only those human goods that are "supremely sacred."

As can be seen from this brief discussion, a major problem for the theory of international human rights is to adequately specify the content of these rights. Although documents such as the *Universal Declaration of Human Rights* enumerate specific "manifesto rights," the hard work comes when we try to forge an international consensus on the particular weights and scopes of individual rights and assign responsibility for enforcing those rights to particular addressees.

It is therefore somewhat misleading to think of particular human rights as existing separately from the entire *system* of human rights. The system of human rights provides a theoretical blueprint for how human societies ought to be structured by specifying which important human interests ought to be specifically protected by national governments. However, different societies finding themselves in differing historical, social, and economic circumstances, may seek to adapt these standards to their own needs and capabilities. Determining the extent to which national governments ought to be free to impose their own interpretation on these standards remains a major unsolved problem for the international human rights movement.

Rights Under International Law. During the past forty years the effort to transform "manifesto-rights" into real rights and to implement effective social guarantees for human rights has taken the form of international treaties and covenants, which when ratified by sovereign nations acquire the status of international law. Louis Henkin discusses the idea of "international human rights" as a movement attempting to induce states to insure that all human individuals should be entitled to enjoy certain goods as civil rights under the constitutional and legal systems of their societies. Failures of national governments to secure these rights, either through failure to enact appropriate legislation, or through failure to adequately enforce it, places the government in a position of noncompliance with its international obligations and exposes it to international criticism and, in extreme cases, stronger economic and political sanctions.

The major instruments for the international protection of human rights are the *International Covenant on Civil and Political Rights* (1966) and the *International Covenant on Economic, Social, and Cultural Rights* (1966).[27] These treaties spell out not only specific rights to which citizens ought to be entitled, but also specific conditions in which a government may be justified in derogating or limiting certain rights and specific mechanisms for enforcing compliance. Among the rights protected by the *Covenant on Civil and Political Rights* are the right to life; the right not to be subjected to torture or to cruel, inhuman, or degrading treatment or punishment; the right not to be held in slavery; the right against arbitrary arrest; the right to travel; and the rights of freedom of conscience and religion, of speech, and association. The *Covenant on Economic, Social, and Cultural Rights* protects, among other rights, the right to work; the right to fair wages; the right to form unions; the right to paid maternity leave; the right to "an adequate standard of living for himself and his family, including adequate food, clothing, and housing" (Article 11); the right to free education; and the right of "all members of the human family," regardless of "race, color, sex, language, religion, political or other opinion, national or social origin, property, birth, or other status," to take part in social life and enjoy the benefits of scientific progress.[28]

Although many rights are now formally recognized and protected under international law, there is no universally shared interpretation of what signing and ratifying such covenants commits a nation to. Henkin discusses three possible interpretations. One view has it that such agreements create rights and obligations among nations in which national governments are obligated to other nations' governments to behave as they have promised and that individual human beings living under these governments are only the "incidental beneficiaries" of the rights and duties existing among the state parties. Under this view, individuals have no international human rights themselves and are dependent on other nation states to see that their own governments adhere to their international obligations.

A second view is that such treaties also give individuals rights under international law, so that individuals whose rights are being violated may appeal directly to international bodies, such as the European Human Rights Commission, for remedies.

A third view would be that in signing and ratifying these treaties the state parties somehow create human rights and give them a status as "affirmative independent values." Each new right that is affirmed in this way is "legitimized" and granted social recognition, which is the first step toward guaranteeing that the substance of the right will be protected and universally enjoyed. That all of the rights mentioned in these documents are not in fact universally protected and enjoyed, does not, in this view, mean that they do not exist as rationally justified moral claims or even as "rights" so long as they are recognized and effectively protected by the civil laws of at least some nations.

In Martin's and Henkin's view national governments function as the primary addressees of human rights; however, it is widely believed that all persons have a duty to uphold and protect human rights. This is so not only because in democratic societies individual citizens bear ultimate responsibility for the actions of their governments, but more fundamentally because the interests protected by human rights can be grievously harmed or significantly benefitted by the actions of individuals or nongovernmental groups. Torture is no more justifiable when it is carried out by individuals acting on their own than it is when carried out by agents of the state. To say that all humans have a right not to be tortured imposes a general ethical duty on all other moral agents to refrain from torture, as well as a special responsibility on governments to protect individuals against such abuse. In cases where an individual's rights are being violated and the responsible government does not act effectively to protect his or her rights, the responsibility for protecting the human rights of others devolves on individuals, nongovernmental human rights organizations, and, under international law, other governments.

A notable development in the international protection of human rights has been the emergence in recent years of nongovernmental human rights monitoring organizations, such as Amnesty International and the Watch Committees, whose role is to alert world public opinion to human rights abuses so that individuals and governments can act more effectively to ensure that human rights are protected by all of the world's governments. Although these nongovernmental organizations (NGOs) can impose no sanctions against offending governments, other than moral condemnation, they have come to play an increasingly effective role in alerting world public opinion to the existence of human rights abuses and in galvanizing public opinion to oppose them.

The Justification of Human Rights

Although there is no doubt that historical and cultural circumstances can powerfully condition one's view of human rights, there remains the philosophical problem of determining which view is the best. Perhaps, as is sometimes argued, there is no "best" view of human rights; the diverse conceptions of human rights simply reflect the differing economic and political values of different societies. This "relativistic" conception of human rights sometimes leads people to draw the conclusion that there is and can be no rational method for choosing among these alternative conceptions: Each is valid in its own way, for the society which holds it, and thus one's attitude toward these differing conceptions ought to be one of tolerant understanding. Because there is no Archimedean point outside of history or culture from which any of us can judge, no one is in a position to say which view of these moral norms is correct. So it seems to follow that persons or governments cannot legitimately criticize the moral beliefs of other people or other cultures.

This line of reasoning, called "prescriptive relativism," argues from the facts of cultural relativism and moral diversity to the conclusion that a particular moral norm—universal toleration of moral beliefs different from one's own—ought to be accepted. Although there is clearly some virtue in tolerance, like most things, tolerance can be carried too far. Are we to "tolerate" it when a foreign government decides to commit genocide against the members of an ethnic minority living in its midst? Are we to tolerate slavery and torture if we believe that the folks who are practicing them are sincerely convinced of the correctness of their own moral opinions?

What, in particular, does a prescriptive relativist (PRian) say about the culture that does not accept the moral belief that she should tolerate the moral beliefs of other cultures (call them anti-PRians) and believes instead that all PRians should be put to death? Either (1) the PRian tolerates the beliefs of the anti-PRians, in which case she is committed to holding that (weakly) she should not criticize or attempt to alter the beliefs of the anti-PRians, or (strongly) that anti-PR is "true for" the anti-PRians and also that PR is "true for" her—that is, that both PR and anti-PR are true, which is a contradiction. Or (2) she does not tolerate this belief, in which case she violates her own principle of moral toleration (PR) and is likewise inconsistent.

Arguments such as this have convinced most philosophers that prescriptive relativism cannot serve as an adequate ethical theory. If we reject this extreme relativistic view, however, we are still left with the problem of justifying moral norms such as those expressed by human rights.

Approaches toward justifying human rights can be classified into several varieties. *Conventionalist* approaches suggest that the moral norms embodied in human rights, like other social norms, exist only by custom or social convention. Where the appropriate social agreements have been reached, rights exist, but not elsewhere. *Prudentialist* theories of rights emphasize that individuals enter into the sorts of social agreements in which rights are created in order to advance their self-interests. A conventional, prudentialistic theory of human rights would hold that it is reasonable for individuals to accept and comply with the norms embodying human rights because doing so is the best way to protect their own fundamental interests in the long run. Such an approach to justifying rights is taken by Gilbert Harman in a selection in this book.

Deontological approaches to justifying human rights, deriving largely from the philosophy of Immanuel Kant (1724–1804), contrast with conventionalist views in holding that human rights are based on a universal feature of human nature; they are not, therefore, merely products of social convention. Alan Gewirth develops such an approach and attempts to derive the existence of basic rights to freedom and well-being from the necessary requirements of rational human agency.

Utilitarian approaches toward justifying human rights attempt to show that the moral norms embodying human rights represent important, high-priority rules for regulating human behavior whose general observance promotes the greatest happiness for the greatest numbers of people over the long run. This approach derives from the philosophy of John Stuart Mill (1806–1873) and is represented in this volume by an article by David Lyons.

In contrast, an *interdependency* theorist, such as Henry Shue, attempts to justify the existence of "basic" rights to liberty, security, and well-being, by showing that they are necessary for the enjoyment of all other rights. In his view, accepting the existence of any rights commits one to the view that these basic rights must also exist.

It is worth mentioning that some contemporary philosophers are *skeptics* and doubt that any of these philosophical approaches succeed in providing a philosophically sound justification for the belief in human rights. A brief selection from Alasdair MacIntyre's influential book *After Virtue* represents this position.

On the other hand, many people believe that secular, philosophical justifications for the belief in human dignity and human rights such as those offered by conventionalists, deontologists, utilitarians, and interdependency theorists are supported by *religious* teachings that ground the existence of human rights on the sacredness of human life and other moral doctrines associated with Judaism, Christianity, and other major faiths. Whether one arrives at the idea of human rights through faith or through reason, the conviction that human rights are things that matter can unite people whose belief in human rights flows from widely disparate perspectives.

Conventionalism and Human Rights.   Gilbert Harman, a defender of the conventionalist approach, argues that not only are certain kinds of moral relativism not inconsistent with the belief in universal human rights, they, in fact, provide a plausible foundation for this belief. The form of relativism that he defends does not claim that "what is right is what people say is right or that the moral conventions of a group are beyond criticism," but it does claim that "morality has its source in convention." By this he means that moral norms, including the norms embodied in the idea of human rights, come about through a process of "implicit bargaining" among individuals and groups in a society. According to this view, the norms that come to exist result from a process of negotiation and compromise in which everyone attempts to secure universal observance of those norms that advance his or her own self-interests.

He applies this theory of justification to explaining why, in some interpretations of human rights, there is a strong "negative" duty not to directly harm others—for example, to refrain from directly killing or torturing other human beings—correlating with strong "negative" human rights against torture and murder, but only a weak "positive" duty to help others avoid harm—for instance, protect others who are vulnerable to such harms even though one is not oneself the source of the harm—correlating with weak "positive" rights such as a right to subsistence. According to Harman:

> A duty to prevent harm to others favors the interests of the poorer and weaker members of society over the richer and more powerful members. The richer and more powerful members of society have less need of outside help in order to avoid being harmed than the poorer and would end up doing most of the helping, given a strong symmetrical duty to help people avoid harm. The rich and powerful would do best with a strong duty not to harm others and no duty not to help others. The poor and weak would do best with equally strong duties of both sorts. Implicit bargaining should therefore yield as a compromise a strong duty not to harm others and a weaker duty to help others avoid harm; it should in other words yield a natural right not to be harmed, which is what we have.

There is, however, nothing in Harman's account that requires that the conditions under which the bargaining take place be fair or that everyone gets an equal chance to participate in the negotiations. Although many people might agree with Harman that our actual, social morality is conventional, it does not follow that there are no universal principles for determining what our moral conventions *ought* to be. Harman's argument also seems to assume that natural rights correlate only with what are called "negative duties"—that is, duties requiring others to refrain from or omit certain actions—and do not involve so-called "positive duties"—that is, duties to provide protection for the enjoyment of a good.[29] This is a view often held by many defenders of the classical or "libertarian" view of rights, which emphasizes individual liberties and powers—so-called negative rights—as the primary and only genuine ones. Other theories sharply reject this assumption and suggest that the distinction between "positive" and "negative" rights and duties is illusory because the enjoyment of all genuine rights requires both actions and omissions on the parts of their addressees.

Basic Rights. Henry Shue defends the view just described. He argues that the customary division of rights into "positive" and "negative" rights, corresponding roughly to the division of rights into social, economic, and cultural rights (positive) and civil and political rights (negative), is highly misleading. Shue defines a moral right as "(1) the rational basis for a justified demand (2) that the actual enjoyment of a substance be (3) socially guaranteed against standard threats." By emphasizing that rights require that the "actual enjoyment" of a substance be socially guaranteed against "standard threats," Shue agrees with Martin in thinking that adequate social recognition and enforcement is a necessary element of a right: "A proclamation of a right is not the fulfillment of a right, anymore than an airplane schedule is a flight." What is required for rights to be fulfilled, for Shue, is the creation of social arrange-ments that will effectively protect people's enjoyment of those goods that they have a right to enjoy. To be effectively protected does not mean that no violations of a person's right will ever occur; that is an unattainable goal in any society. However, it does mean that social institutions have been established under which the right is recognized, that measures have been implemented to prevent violations of the right, and that individuals who feel that their rights have been violated may appeal to society to have such wrongs redressed.

Shue argues that the supposed division into "negative" rights that require only that others omit or refrain from certain actions and "positive" rights that require that others act to provide certain goods is largely illusory, because *protecting* any right requires both positive and negative actions. For instance, "it is impossible to protect anyone's rights to physical security without taking, or making payments toward the taking of, a wide range of positive actions. . . . police forces; criminal courts, penitentiaries, schools for training police, lawyers, and guards; and taxes to support an enormous system for the prevention, detection, and punishment of violations of personal security."[30] Along with Raz, Shue thinks there are no simple "one-to-one" pairings of particular rights and particular duties involving specific acts or omissions; rather, the fulfillment of any right requires the performance of multiple kinds of duties. There are, he argues, basically three kinds of duties implied by the core of any right: (1) duties to avoid depriving people of their rights, (2) duties to protect people against deprivations of their rights, and (3) duties to aid those whose have been deprived of their rights.[31]

But what goods do human rights protect? And how are we to justify the claim that these particular goods are entitled to social protection? In the selection in this volume, Shue outlines a theory of what he calls "basic rights." Basic rights represent "everyone's minimal reasonable demands upon the rest of humanity." They are "the morality of the depths" and specify "the line beneath which no one is to be allowed to sink." Put another way, the goods provided for by basic rights are the necessary minimum requirements of self-respect and human dignity.

Shue describes three categories of basic rights: (1) security rights, (2) liberty rights, and (3) subsistence rights. *Security rights* include traditional civil and polit-ical rights such as the rights not to be subjected to murder and torture; his category of *liberty rights* includes, among others, traditional freedoms such as rights to thought, opinion, religion, speech, and political participation. His third category, *subsistence rights,* includes some of the newer second- and third-generation rights that serve to protect an individual's "minimal economic security" by providing for "unpolluted air, unpolluted water, adequate food, adequate clothing, adequate shelter, and minimal preventive health care." This classification challenges the conventional division of rights into civil and political rights on the one hand and economic and social rights on the other, by emphasizing that at least some rights from each category are properly regarded as "basic."

According to Shue, what is crucial to rights being "basic" is that the "enjoyment of them is essential to the enjoyment of all other rights. . . . This is what is distinctive about a basic right. When a right is genuinely basic, any attempt to enjoy any other right by sacrificing the basic right would be quite literally self-defeating, cutting the ground from beneath itself. Therefore, if a right is basic, other, nonbasic rights may be sacrificed, if necessary, in order to secure the basic right."

Consider the right to physical security: Suppose we had a society that claimed to recognize rights such as freedom of speech and freedom of assembly, but in actual fact, whenever opponents of the government met to discuss their grievances, their meetings were broken up by the police and the participants taken away and tortured. In such a case, can one really enjoy one's other rights and liberties? According to Shue, "No one can fully enjoy any right that is supposedly protected by society if someone can credibly threaten him or her with murder, rape, beatings," and so on. If so, then, "If any right is to be exercised except at great risk, physical security must be protected," thus showing that physical security qualifies as a basic right. It is basic because part of the meaning of having a right is being able to enjoy or exercise the right, and no right can be enjoyed unless the person's physical security is protected.

Shue provides a similar argument for his claim that subsistence is also a basic right by noting that "No one can fully, if at all, enjoy any right that is supposedly protected by society if he or she lacks the essentials for a reasonably healthy and active life." By combining this argument with his classification of duties, it follows that there is a universal human right to subsistence that requires that governments avoid deprivations of subsistence, protect persons against such deprivations, and aid those who have been deprived of subsistence. Shue also argues that certain traditional liberty rights, such as freedom of speech and freedom of political participation, also qualify as basic rights, because these rights provide the only effective guarantee that all of one's other rights will not be usurped by tyrannies.[32]

Shue's argument, if it is accepted, provides a scheme for assigning weights to rights in which fulfilling all of the basic rights has a higher priority than fulfilling any other nonbasic rights, and fulfilling all nonbasic rights has a higher priority than the "enrichment of culture" and the "satisfaction of preferences."[33] However, Shue denies that there can be any priorities among basic rights, because each basic right is necessary for the exercise of all other rights; "the absence of any of these basic rights is sufficient normally to allow the thwarting of the enjoyment of any other rights. . . ."[34] Shue's analysis also suggests that both the first-world view, which emphasizes the importance of individual liberties, and the second-world view, which emphasizes the importance of economic security, are correct in holding that their own most cherished rights deserve top priority, but both are wrong in thinking that *only* their own most cherished rights deserve this weight; liberty rights do not trump economic rights, nor do economic rights trump liberty rights, nor are either of these two categories of basic rights trumped by basic rights guaranteeing personal security. All three kinds of basic rights deserve equal weight because all are equally necessary to the enjoyment of all other rights.

Shue's theory also leads to an interesting argument for justifying basic rights:

1. Everyone has a right to something.

2. Some other things are necessary for enjoying the first thing as a right, whatever the first thing is.

3. Therefore, everyone also has rights to the other things that are necessary for enjoying the first as a right.

According to this argument, if there are any rights at all, then there must be "basic rights," because basic rights are just those rights that are necessary for the enjoyment of any other rights. Shue's interdependency approach toward justifying rights-claims and his method of determining the weights of basic rights seem promising as ways of resolving differences among various leading interpretations of human rights. However, does a theorist such as Shue have an argument against the skeptic who doubts that there are any human rights at all?

Skepticism About Human Rights.   Alasdair MacIntyre is one such skeptic. In his selection in this book, MacIntyre judges the post-Enlightenment attempt to discover a rationally compelling foundation for the belief in universal human rights to be a failure. There have, he argues, been two main approaches to this problem: The utilitarian, or teleological, approach attempts to derive moral norms from human goods such as pleasure and happiness, whereas the Kantian, or deontological, approach attempts to ground the authority of moral norms in the requirements of practical reason. He takes Bentham and J. S. Mill as representatives of the former tack, and he sees Gewirth as a contemporary exponent of the Kantian approach.

MacIntyre argues that the utilitarian approach has failed because the ends of pleasure and happiness are too polymorphous to provide any real guidance as to the specific content of rights or any reliable method for determining the priorities and weights of particular rights:

> For there are too many different kinds of enjoyable activity, too many different modes in which happiness is achieved. . . . The pleasure-of-drinking-Guinness is not the pleasure-of-swimming-at-Crane's Beach, and the swimming and drinking are not two different means for providing the same end state. The happiness which belongs peculiarly to the way of life of the cloister is not the same happiness that belongs peculiarly to the military life. For different pleasures and different happinesses are to a large degree incommensurable: There are no scales of quality or

quantity on which to weigh them. Consequently, appeal to criteria of pleasure will not tell me to drink or swim, and appeal to those of happiness cannot decide for me between the life of a monk and the life of a soldier.

Because forms of pleasure and happiness are diverse and incommensurable, any attempt to employ these ends to ground claims concerning the rational necessity and universality of moral norms is doomed to failure. Sensing this problem, philosophers working in the tradition have, MacIntyre says, retreated to intuitionism and emotivism, doctrines that deny that moral norms possess any objective validity.

Against the Kantian approach, MacIntyre questions the step in Gewirth's argument from the claim that all purposive agents need or want freedom and well-being in order to function successfully as agents to the conclusion that they have *rights* to these goods. According to MacIntyre, in making this step Gewirth has "illicitly smuggled in" a conception of the rational agent functioning within a social context in which the notions of entitlement and having a right are intelligible ones: "Lacking any such social form, the making of a claim to a right would be like presenting a check for payment in a social order that lacked the institution of money." Consequently, MacIntyre believes that Gewirth fails to provide a non-question-begging justification for there being institutions under which such claims signify entitlements and correlate with the duties of others.

The skeptical conclusion to which MacIntyre is then drawn is that the belief in human rights is, in fact, rationally groundless: "There are no human rights, and belief in them is one with belief in witches and unicorns." Human rights are, he thinks, "moral fictions" that serve useful purposes in political polemics and protests as records of our considered moral judgments, values, and preferences, but they are not demonstrable moral truths.

Rights and Human Agency. Alan Gewirth, whose views MacIntyre attacks, believes that it is possible to provide a rational justification for the existence of human rights that derives these rights from fundamental facts about human agency. Gewirth begins by reviewing several familiar strategies for justifying the claim that there are human rights, but finds them wanting on the grounds that they tend to beg the question of supplying an independent moral foundation for human rights by presupposing moral notions such as human dignity and equality. He then provides a definition of morality as "a set of categorically obligatory requirements for actions that are addressed at least in part to every actual or prospective agent and that are intended to further the interests, especially the most important interests, of persons or recipients other than or in addition to the agent or speaker." Because all moral norms presuppose and address the "context of human action," Gewirth argues that the foundation of the universal moral norms known as human rights is to be found in "the proximate necessary conditions of human action."

According to Gewirth, each human agent regards his or her own purposive actions as good according to "whatever criteria (not necessarily moral ones) are involved in his acting to fulfill them." But all purposive actions presuppose the agent's freedom and well-being, because "without these conditions he either would not be able to act for any purposes or goods at all or at least would not be able to act with any chance of succeeding in his purposes." Thus, from the point of view of a purposive agent, each person must regard "his freedom and well-being as necessary goods," because they characterize the generic requirements of all successful action.

But how does treating freedom and well-being as necessary goods entail that persons have rights to freedom and well-being? Gewirth's argument at this point is rather complex, but it repays careful study. Basically, he argues that the transition from "necessary goods" to "rights" is accomplished by "dialectical necessity" when we adopt the agent's own perspective and advocate or will that each of us, as agent, "must have freedom and well-being in order to act." This act of will, says Gewirth, transforms the necessary goods of freedom and well-being into prudential prescriptions having "normative necessity"; that is, each person *qua* rational agent must claim these goods as necessary for attainment of his or her own ends. Each actual or prospective rational agent must take this step, because "any agent who denies that he has rights to freedom and well-being contradicts himself."

Thus far, however, the argument serves only to establish the individual agent's prudential claim to be allowed to act to achieve his or her own ends without interference; a further argument is needed to show that "each agent must admit that all other humans also have these rights" to reach the conclusion that freedom and well-being are universal human rights. This further conclusion is reached by accepting the generalization that "if some predicate P belongs to some subject S because S has the quality Q (where the 'because' is that of sufficient reason or condition), then it logically follows that every subject that has Q has P." If P as the predicate "has generic rights to freedom and well-being," S is "human beings," and Q is the quality of "being a prospective purposive agent," then the generalization principle logically entails that all human beings *qua* prospective purposive agents have generic rights to freedom and well-being.

If one assumes that all human beings are prospective purposive agents (see the article by Husak for a critique of this assumption), then this argument provides a rational basis for the belief in equal and universal human rights to freedom and well-being. This basic right, Gewirth claims, serves to ground universal duties that "every person ought to refrain from interfering with the freedom and well-being of all other persons" and also that "under certain circumstances every person ought to assist other persons to have freedom and well-being, when they cannot have these by their own efforts. . . ." Put in other terms, Gewirth argues that the Principle of Generic Consistency (PGC)—*Act in accord with the generic rights of your recipients as well as yourself*—is the supreme principle of morality that every prospective moral agent must accept "on pain of self-contradiction."

In the later part of his article, Gewirth goes on to derive several other interesting consequences from the PGC having to do with the content of these basic rights to freedom and well-being, the claims of children and other "potentially purposive agents" to these rights, their *prima facie* character, and methods of resolving conflicts among basic rights. Gewirth's approach, combining features of a prudentialism and Kantian theories of morality, purports to provide a way of grounding the belief in universal human rights in a basic fact about human nature—the fact that humans are rational, purposive beings.

Human Rights and the General Welfare.   MacIntyre's skeptical arguments attack both deontological approaches toward justifying human rights, such as Gewirth's, and utilitarian approaches, such as found in the work of David Lyons. Lyons attempts to rebut the presumption that a commitment to the utilitarian belief that moral norms are justified by their serving as effective means of advancing the general welfare of society is in conflict with the belief in rights, including universal human rights. Certainly this presumption is made by many authors, and, as we earlier observed, some thinkers, such as Ronald Dworkin, tend to conceive of "rights" as things that are, in some sense, fundamentally opposed to considerations of social utility.

Lyons develops his argument by means of a close reading of the works of the most famous utilitarian thinker, John Stuart Mill (1806–1873). Most modern versions of utilitarianism make a distinction between "act utilitarianism" and "rule utilitarianism." In the former, we are supposed to judge the rightness or wrongness of particular actions directly on the basis of the Principle of Utility, which says that that action is right that tends to produce the greatest happiness of the greatest number of people. In the latter view, the "greatest happiness principle" is invoked to justify specific moral rules or norms, the general observance of which will tend, in the long run, to maximize the general welfare of society. Particular actions are to be judged not by appealing directly to the Principle of Utility, but rather as specific instances within the scopes of moral rules whose general observance will tend to promote the general welfare of society.

As Lyons interprets him, Mill was a kind of rule-utilitarian who believed that certain moral obligations ought to be performed because they are the most important means for protecting and promoting the general welfare of society. Failures to perform these obligations count as moral wrongs, which is to say, in Mill's account, that punishment of some kind would be justified. Punishment can range from self-imposed pangs of guilt issuing from the agent's own conscience, to forms of social disapproval, to legal sanctions imposed by society on persons judged guilty of wrongful behavior. These distinctions imply that to show that an act is wrong, it is not enough to show merely that it is "inexpedient," that is, that it fails to maximize the general happiness; one must also be prepared to argue that punishment of some kind would be justified for those who commit such acts. Only when this condition is met is it appropriate to establish a moral rule prohibiting such acts and to compel compliance with this rule by means of social or legal sanctions.

Rights, in Mill's view, correspond to those moral obligations that concern justice. There can be wrongs that are not unjust, and there can also be acts that are inexpedient but not wrong. For Mill, "When we call anything a person's right, we mean that he has a valid claim upon society to protect him in the possession of it, either by the force of law or by that of education and opinion." Put another way, someone has a moral right when another person or persons are under a beneficial moral obligation toward her or him. The obligations entailed by rights are formulated in terms of high-priority moral rules that have "weight" when opposed to transient considerations of utility and other categories of moral rules, because, as Mill writes, they "concern the essentials of human well-being more nearly, and are therefore of more absolute obligation, than any other rules for the guidance of life." The rules that serve to protect the interests of justice will "generally take precedence over other moral rules"; and hence the infringement of rights "will not easily be justified."

This account of Mill, Lyons says, explains why utilitarians can "take rights seriously." Critics of utilitarianism, such as Ronald Dworkin, have suggested that when rights conflict with considerations of social utility, rights should "trump" them. As Lyons interprets him, Mill would appear to agree that certain types of moral obligations, those concerning justice, should take priority over considerations of utility and other kinds of moral obligations. In fact, Mill's own conclusion that strong rights to freedom of thought and opinion and to security of the person could be justified on the grounds of the general welfare standard seems consistent with this interpretation.

Although the approaches toward justifying human rights developed by Shue, Gewirth, and Lyons are quite different, they all seem to converge on the conclusion that there are some human rights that are properly regarded as basic: Each person can justifiably claim that his or her freedom, personal security, and access to the means of well-being are goods the enjoyment of which ought to be protected by society. It could, of course, turn out that more than one of the approaches toward justifying human rights that we have reviewed can succeed in establishing this conclusion. However, perhaps skeptics such as MacIntyre are right in doubting that any of the theories that have thus far been advanced can provide a cogent justification for the belief in human rights. In the concluding section of this essay (*Human Rights Now and in the Future*) I will outline an *historical* justification of human rights that may help to allay such doubts.

The Holders of Human Rights

Perhaps the most perplexing challenge in recent years to the idea of human rights concerns the question of whether human rights do in fact belong to all human beings, and if so why. Although it is certainly true that all human beings are members of a particular biological species—*homo sapiens sapiens*—why is it that belonging to this species qualifies individual humans for inherent and inalienable rights? If species membership alone is the ground of the attribution of rights to human beings, then why don't members of other species also enjoy similar rights? Is our belief in human rights based on an unargued and irrational preference for those of "our own kind"? Conversely, if mere species membership is not the basis for rights but some other characteristic of human beings is the ground of these rights, what is this characteristic and how does its possession serve as the basis for attributing rights? Is there, in fact, any characteristic of human beings that is truly universal and can serve as the basis for human rights?

In Gewirth's account, human rights to freedom and well-being are thought to be grounded on the universal human capacity for rational, purposive agency. In this sort of account a particular capacity or characteristic functions as criterial for the possession of certain rights. We can usefully refer to such accounts as "C-type" theories of rights, because they depend on identifying some characteristic or capacity C that (1) belongs to all members of a group of holders of the right R, (2) does not belong to others who are not holders of R, and (3) can serve as a rational basis for attribution of R to individuals having C.

C-type theories can be criticized on three sorts of grounds. First, they can be too narrow in that they fail to attribute an R-based-on-C to some individuals who intuitively ought to hold R; for instance, grounding a right to freedom of speech on, say, high intelligence, would exclude humans with low intelligence from having this right. Second, C-type theories can be too broad and attribute R to individuals who intuitively ought to lack R; for instance, grounding the right to life on being alive and hence being vulnerable to being killed would imply that nonhuman animals and plants, including bacteria and microorganisms, have rights to life equal to ours. Third, the connection between C and R can be unintelligible or inappropriate in that possession of C provides no rational basis for the attribution of R. As an example of the last failing consider the claim that all human beings have an inalienable right to life (R) because they have opposable thumbs (C). Although it is true that all and only human beings have this characteristic, it is difficult to see why having the ability to touch the tips of one's thumb and index finger is an intrinsically valuable characteristic serving as the ground for the right to life.

Inalienable Rights.   A C-type theory of human rights is developed and defended by Diana Meyers in her selection in this volume. Meyers argues that four inalienable rights—the right to life, the right to personal liberty, the right to benign treatment, and the right to satisfaction of basic needs—should be attributed to human beings because of the human capacity for moral agency. For Meyers, moral agency is more specific than purposive, rational agency: It is capacity to deliberate and act as a morally responsible agent—that is, to reason about moral duties and rights, to make judgments based on moral considerations, and to be held morally accountable for one's actions. A developed capacity for moral agency makes it possible to have a moral system in which individual moral agents act and interact in accordance with moral norms and in which their self-chosen actions can be held subject to moral evaluation. The particular rights that she mentions function as the minimum conditions necessary for sustaining such a community of moral agents.

Meyers argues that these four rights are *inalienable*—that is, that once someone is a member of the moral community he or she has these rights and cannot lose them, forfeit them, or have them revoked, because to do so would make the moral system that permitted this"self-rescinding" and "self-defeating." Her argument is developed in greater detail in the book from which her selection is taken.[35] However, the basic idea of her account is that human rights exist precisely in order to enable moral agents to sustain moral communities in which moral agents can function. To function as a moral agent, one must be able to act on moral reasons to achieve moral purposes and to be held accountable for one's moral judgments and actions. To permit individual right-holders or others to alienate the rights that make such communities possible would therefore render the moral system that contains these rights self-defeating by undermining the conditions of its own existence.

Meyers' argument seems to avoid the objection that C, in this case, the capacity for moral agency, does not provide a rational basis for attributing rights, because a capacity for moral agency is obviously relevant to an individual's having "moral standing"—that is, being the sort of being to whom moral duties and correlative rights can be appropriately ascribed. However, is it true, in fact, that all human beings have this capacity? Do all humans have it to the same degree? What about nonhuman animals, young children, and adults suffering from conditions that prevent them from functioning as responsible moral agents? Are they also entitled to equal inalienable rights?

Meyers acknowledges that young children are not responsible moral agents but argues that because they have the *potential* to become moral agents, they ought to be "treated as if (they) qualified for rights to life and satisfaction of basic needs" in order to further their "moral education." All children, she believes, have an inalienable right to moral education—that is, to the special sort of training that develops a child's innate capacity to function as a moral agent. If a moral system denied this right it would soon enough result in its own destruction and so would be as self-defeating as one that permitted the arbitrary killing of moral agents. But what if we provided adequate moral education only to some children—might not the moral community survive nonetheless?

To circumvent this objection Meyers discusses an ingenious, but rather bizarre, "thought-experiment" devised by Robert Nozick. In this fantasy certain children are selected to be reared in tanks connected to machines that simulate real-life experiences and their results. These tanks provide a comfortable environment but one that systematically deprives their occupants of any real moral interaction and hence any moral education. In her analysis of this case, Meyers finds that the objector is mistaken in believing that placing children in these tanks renders them no longer the holders of inalienable human rights; even tank children will have to be treated as if they had equal inalienable rights because someone on the outside ". . . cannot discern the difference between a person with an inalienable right and a tank manifestation with a pseudo-right, they must respect all of these claims indiscriminately to avoid violating genuine rights."

Nonhuman animals, however, do not enjoy the same status on Meyers' account. Animals may indeed be vulnerable to having their vital interests harmed in the same ways as human beings, but because protecting individual animals is "not necessary to maintain an environment that supports moral communities, a moral system that denies these rights would not be self-defeating." This does not imply that human moral agents are permitted to do anything to animals that they please: Many non-humans may have a kind of "moral standing" that would entail that moral agents have certain duties toward them—say, a duty to treat sentient animals benignly and not subject them to cruel or wanton suffering. However, saying that moral agents may have duties toward animals is different than saying that animals have equal and inalienable rights. The difference between being the beneficiary of another's duty and being the holder of a right is accounted for in Meyers' theory by the fact that humans can, whereas animals cannot, sustain moral communities in which they interact as responsible moral agents.

Humans and Persons.   Meyers attempts to defend the doctrine of human rights by offering a C-type account based on the notion of moral agency. However, skeptics, such as Douglas Husak, doubt that any C-type account is ever likely to succeed. The reason he adduces for this conclusion is that it seems likely that whatever empirical characteristic C we choose on which to ground human rights, it will likely turn out that at least some individual human beings lack C. At this point the defender of human rights has two options: Either she can claim that the possession or absence of C does not really matter to the ascription of human rights, in which case she is thrown back on the purely biological criterion of species membership, or she can admit that some humans lack equal rights because they lack C. The problem with the latter reply, as Husak notes, is that "it threatens to undermine what is largely believed to be attractive about the concept of human rights," namely, the idea that "all human beings possess [these] rights, regardless of whatever contingent properties they might happen to have."

As a case in point Husak invites us to consider Karen Anne Quinlan, the young woman who fell into a deep coma following an automobile accident. In this condition, Karen Anne Quinlan qualified as a human *nonperson*; that is to say, she remained a member of the biological species *homo sapiens,* but she lost all of the psychological capacities associated with personhood: consciousness, self-consciousness, moral agency, language ability, rationality, purposiveness, and sentience. Moreover, unlike young children who lack one or more of these capacities but who have the potential to develop them, Karen Anne Quinlan's loss of these characteristics was irreversible; saving a miracle, there was no hope that she would ever recover her "personhood."

Husak regards cases of this kind as posing a challenge to C-type accounts, such as Gewirth's and Meyers', because they show that not all humans can be reasonably said to have a capacity for purposive or moral agency or the potential for such agency and hence that the rights that are claimed to be based on possession of these characteristics are not in fact universally shared by human beings. The challenge he issues to defenders of the doctrine of human rights is to produce some characteristic C that can meet the conditions of universality, and relevancy, or else admit that the claim that all human beings possess equal natural rights cannot be defended.

Given the difficulty of establishing any acceptable C-type theory and the further doubts about the possibility of a deontological or a utilitarian justification for human rights adduced by critics like MacIntyre, Husak believes it is reasonable to wonder why moral philosophers have not abandoned the quest for a philosophical foundation for human rights altogether. There are, he thinks, three reasons why many good philosophers, as well as many other people, continue to believe in human rights. First, to deny that all humans have equal rights would appear to put one in the company of Nazis, slave-owners, and torturers in allowing that some human lives are less valuable than others. Second, it would open the door to a pernicious relativism in which invoking human rights in criticizing barbaric practices would appear nothing more than shallow propaganda. Third, asserting that some humans are nonpersons and hence do not possess equal rights would invite the conclusion that it is morally permissible to treat such individuals in any way we please.

Husak believes that none of these consequences would in fact follow from our frankly admitting that no philosophically adequate theory of human rights has yet been forthcoming and that, in most all cases that concern us, the moral standards associated with human rights would still apply because the individuals concerned would be undoubted *persons*. In other cases, such as that of Karen Anne Quinlan, Husak argues, we would be mistaken to assume that such humans had exactly equal rights to those of undoubted persons. He invites us to consider, for instance, if one had to choose whether to give a single life-saving transfusion to Karen Quinlan or to an undoubted person, if it would be a matter of moral indifference which one selected. Or whether it would be morally acceptable to "harvest" the vital organs of someone in a deep and irreversible coma to save the lives of five undoubted persons? These are test cases for Husak's theory because "If one is willing to allow Karen Quinlan to be sacrificed to achieve a net savings of lives, while resisting that result when it is unquestionable that a person is involved, one has come a long way toward acceptance of the thesis that there are no human rights."

Human Rights Defended.   In responding to Husak's critique, Alan Gewirth offers some valuable clarifications of his theory. Husak's line of objection mistakenly takes Gewirth to have asserted that all human individuals capable of purposive agency have equal rights, whereas Gewirth contends that his argument is a dialectical one from the point of view of the prospective agent himself: "Humans do not," he says, "have human rights in the way they have legs or feelings." But, each prospective agent must grant that "he and all other actual or prospective agents have rights—that is, justified claims or entitlements—to the necessary conditions of actions and successful action in general." So that, although the justification for human rights is "agent-relative," it is nonetheless valid because "it has been shown to be normatively necessary and universal within the whole relevant context"—namely, the context of human action.

In response to the objection based on the Quinlan case, Gewirth draws attention to "The Principle of Proportionality" according to which agents must recognize that when human individuals (and also nonhuman animals) possess in "lesser degree the practical abilities to enter into agency, . . . [they] also have rights in correspondingly lesser degrees." According to Gewirth, Karen Quinlan still has the generic rights of other human persons though she lacks any realized practical ability for agency because she is still a "prospective" agent—medical research may restore her agency—and because she "was a human agent, and is still a living human, she has the right to life and to any other goods that are a condition of agency which she is capable of having." However, because her practical ability to exercise agency is destroyed, and because the purpose of human rights, for Gewirth, is to protect agency, "Husak is correct in thinking that in the case he supposes [the transfusion case], the 'person's' life should be saved rather than Quinlan's," under the Proportionality Principle.

Finally, Gewirth attempts to cast doubt on Husak's suggestion that we ground rights on criteria for "personhood" rather than on human agency. One question is which criteria do we employ—that is, "Aristotle's, Nietzsche's, Kant's, Bentham's, Spencer's, Schweitzer's"? Each set of criteria would yield different classes of "persons." A second problem he sees concerns whether an approach such as this could ever succeed in providing a noncircular account of the possession of human rights. Gewirth doubts it could and views his own dialectical account as offering a solution to this problem.

Human Rights Now and in the Future

If after examining these issues and reading the selections in this book, you are still left with unanswered questions and uncertainties about the reality of these things we call "human rights," that is good. The theory of human rights is the product of a living philosophical tradition, not a dead relic of past theorizing and, as such, is still undergoing growth and revision. If the belief in the value and importance of human rights is to remain strong, it must not be grounded on unreasoned dogma or shallow political rhetoric, but instead, on the enlightened understanding of thoughtful, concerned individuals. Each generation must appropriate the concept of human rights for itself and adapt it to the conditions of its own time if progress is to be made in realizing the moral standards that this idea presents for human societies. As with any evolving body of belief, there will always be internal tensions, disagreements, and unresolved problems with which one must contend. In reviewing the historical development of the idea of rights and the contemporary understanding of human rights, I have noted several such problems. I would now like to take the opportunity to speculate a bit on the future of the concept of human rights.

In reviewing the historical development of the doctrine of human rights it seemed reasonable to suggest that rights "evolve" from manifesto rights to socially guaranteed protections against threats to basic human interests. The human rights we now recognize have evolved in response to perceived threats to basic human values and interests as they have arisen in definite historical, political, and economic circumstances. Philosophical conceptions of human rights have emerged from thoughtful people reflecting on their historical experience, determining what were the most significant threats to basic human values, and then attempting to frame policies and norms that would forestall or defeat these threats. One of the earliest of rights, the right of *habeus corpus,* was a response to the threat of arbitrary and secret imprisonment; the rights of the Enlightenment were in large part responses to the experience of tyranny and to the sad history of religious persecution in Europe; economic rights can be seen as responses to threats to livelihood caused by the economic dislocations of the Industrial Revolution; the cultural rights of the twentieth century are intended to forestall and repair the deleterious effects of colonialism; and other recent rights, such as the right of peoples not to be subjected to genocide, are quite obviously responses to the atrocities of the Holocaust.

The purpose of human rights is to avert, as far as possible, the social conditions and practices that history teaches us inevitably lead to human suffering and misery—political tyranny and injustice, economic exploitation, discrimination, and domination by other cultures—and to create as far as possible the social conditions that are most conducive to human well-being, happiness, and flourishing. The doctrine of human rights must be considered as an evolving whole in relation to the changing political and economic conditions of human society, and, in this light, the idea of human rights can be understood as a description of a political *ideal*; it is a partial blueprint for the building of just and peaceful human societies and for creating a stable world order in which all persons may lead fulfilling and dignified human lives.

As moral ideals, human rights are, in one sense, "fictions," because the social conditions that they describe need not and in most cases do not actually exist. But, they are not mere fictions, they are *moral* fictions, and useful ones at that. Moral fictions are like the "theoretical fictions" of a perfect vacuum or a frictionless surface that are needed to correctly and succinctly state the fundamental laws of nature. Moral fictions and ideals are likewise needed in ethics to state our best approximation to the moral truth. Like other theoretical fictions, human rights will survive to the extent to which the theories of human nature and human society of which they are parts succeed in attaining their goals. However, unlike theories in the physical sciences whose goals are to explain and predict the behavior of physical objects, ethical and political theories aim to provide a plan for organizing and regulating human life in societies. The truth of such theories can be adequately tested only by the judgment of history: Indeed, it is not an exaggeration to say that the past two hundred years of human history have been a grand experiment designed to test the adequacy of this particular theory of human society.

If modern history is a laboratory for testing ethical and political theories such as the theory of human rights, then we must ask: Has our historical experience shown that in societies where human rights are respected and uniformly protected people are less likely to suffer and human potential less likely to be squandered than in those in which rights have been neglected or systematically abused? Does observance of the moral norms that embody the theory of human rights promote the development of stable and progressive societies where greater numbers of human individuals can lead productive, fulfilling, and peaceful lives, and does failure to observe these standards tend to promote social conflict and war? If we think the answer to these questions is "yes" then we have some basis for thinking that the theory of human rights is a good one and that the moral standards that this theory proposes ought to be universally respected and protected. Admittedly, this sort of justification is less satisfying than ones that would deduce the existence of universal human rights from natural law or divine commandment; however, such a justification may be the best that we can reasonably hope for, and it may be as good a justification as we really need.

The warrant provided for the belief in human rights through this kind of historical argument does not guarantee the universal and eternal validity of the standards in which they are embodied. Nor does it imply that the theory of human rights is a finished and consistent whole. The plan is in constant need of revision and readjustment: Fundamental values must be balanced to maintain equilibrium, and as the conditions of human society change, so too do the threats that we face.

In the late twentieth century new threats loom on the historical horizon—pollution and degradation of the global environment, overpopulation, the depletion of natural resources, international terrorism, and the threat of a global nuclear war engulfing all of humanity and potentially destroying all of the achievements of human civilization. In turning to face these new threats we must ask whether the theory of human rights can be adapted and revised to meet these new dangers without sacrificing the protection to individuals provided by traditional rights. Can the doctrine of human rights provide an adequate framework for organizing human societies in an increasingly insecure and interdependent world, a world in which the collective survival of the human race is at stake?

If the idea of human rights is to survive and to succeed, it must adapt itself to meet these new threats. Answering the question of how the theory of human rights should respond to these challenges is the work of future philosophers. This problem, however, should not delay our taking steps to implement the rights we have. In our own time the most urgent task for the human moral community is to implement effective mechanisms for the universal enjoyment of these basic human rights that are no longer controversial—that no one should be tortured or enslaved; that no one should be imprisoned for his or her beliefs; that no one should be allowed to starve to death when ample food is available. That all persons should enjoy the equal protection of such basic rights as these, should be, and is, beyond dispute.

For the present, it seems that despite our doubts and disagreements and the challenges that we face, we ought to hold firmly onto our belief in human rights. The theory of human rights represents the distillation of our accumulated historical wisdom and our best approximation to the moral truth about the human condition. It is, thus, also our best hope for the future of humankind.

M. E. Winston

Notes

1. Tshenuwani Simon Farisani, *Diary from a South African Prison*. (Philadelphia: Fortress Press, 1987).

2. For accounts of the historical development of the doctrines of natural law and natural rights cf. Richard Tuck, *Natural Rights Theories: Their Origin and Development*. (Cambridge: Cambridge University Press, 1979); Kenneth Minoque, "The History of the Idea of Human Rights," in *The Human Rights Reader*, Walter LaQueur and Barry Rubin (Eds.). (New York: New American Library, 1977), pp. 3–17; Richard McKeon, "Philosophy and History in the Development of Human Rights,"

in *Ethics and Social Justice,* Howard E. Kiefer and Milton K. Munitz (Eds.), (Albany, NY: State University of New York Press, 1968), pp. 300–323; and M. P. Golding, "The Concept of Rights: An Historical Sketch," in *Bioethics and Human Rights,* B. Bandman and E. Bandman (Eds.). (Boston: Little, Brown, 1978), pp. 44–50.

3. *Nichomachean Ethics,* Book Five, Chapter 6, 25–31.

4. *Ibid.,* Book Five, Chapter 7, 1134b 18–20.

5. *Ibid.,* 1135a 4–5.

6. *Treatise on Law and Justice,* Question 91, Article 2.

7. Cf. Martin P. Golding, "The Concept of Rights: A Historical Sketch," in *Bioethics and Human Rights. op. cit.*

8. John Locke, *Second Treatise of Civil Government.* Chapter 2, 10, 4.

9. *Ibid.,* Chapter 5, 46.

10. Jean Jacques Rousseau, *The Social Contract* (1762), in *The Human Rights Reader,* Walter LaQueur and Barry Rubin (Eds.). (New York: New American Library, 1979), p. 70.

11. Frederick Engels, "Anti-Duhring" (1878). In *Reader in Marxist Philosophy,* Howard Selsam and Harry Martel (Eds.). (New York: International Publishers, 1963), p. 260.

12. See Appendix A for the text of this document. For a discussion of the drafting of this document see: *Human Rights: Comments and Interpretations,* a symposium edited by UNESCO with an introduction by Jacques Maritain. (London: A. Wingate, 1949); and Richard McKeon, "Philosophy and History in the Development of Human Rights," in *Ethics and Social Justice,* Howard E. Kiefer and Milton K. Munitz (Eds.). (Albany: State University of New York Press, 1968, 1970), pp. 300–322. December 10th is celebrated as International Human Rights Day.

13. *Universal Declaration of Human Rights.* Preamble.

14. Cf. The European Convention on Human Rights (1950); Convention on the Prevention and Punishment of Crimes of Genocide (1948); The Slavery Convention (1926, amended 1953) and the Supplementary Convention on the Abolition of Slavery, the Slave Trade, and Institutions and Practices Similar to Slavery (1956); Convention Relating to the Status of Refugees (1951); Convention Relating to the Status of Stateless Persons (1954); Convention on the Elimination of All Forms of Racial Discrimination (1966); International Covenant on Civil and Political Rights (1966); Covenant on Economic, Social, and Cultural Rights (1966); American Convention on Human Rights (1970); African Charter on Human and People's Rights (1986). See Ian Brownlee (Ed.), *Basic Documents on Human Rights.* (Oxford: Clarendon Press, 1971).

15. For useful surveys of the major issues in the theory of rights and human rights in the contemporary philosophical literature see: Rex Martin and James W. Nickel, "Recent Work on the Concept of Rights," *American Philosophical Quarterly,* Vol. 17, No. 3 (1980): pp.165–180; and Tibor R. Machan, "Some Recent Work on Human Rights Theory," *American Philosophical Quarterly,* Vol. 17, No. 2 (1980): pp. 103–115.

16. Fuller discussions of this issue can be found in the selections by Meyers and Husak included in this volume.

17. The question of the additional premises needed to establish the existence of human rights is covered in the articles by Alan Gewirth included in this volume; discussions of the concepts of weight and scope as they apply to human rights appear in the section on rights as "trumps," p. 144 ff.

18. Joel Feinberg, "The Rights of Animals and Unborn Generations," in *Philosophy and Environmental Crisis,* William T. Blackstone (Ed.). (Athens, GA: University of Georgia Press, 1974). Reprinted in *Ethics: Theory and Practice,* M. Velasquez and C. Rostankowski (Eds.). (Englewood Cliffs, NJ: Prentice-Hall, 1985), p. 467.

19. Cf. Wesley Hohfeld, *Fundamental Legal Conceptions As Applied in Judicial Reasoning,* Walter Wheeler Cook (Ed.). (New Haven: Yale University Press, 1966).

20. For more detailed analyses of the Hohfeldian conception of rights see; Carl Wellman, *A Theory of Rights: Persons Under Laws, Institutions, and Morals.* (Totowa, NJ: Rowman & Allanheld, 1985), especially Chapters 2 and 6; and L. W. Sumner, *The Moral Foundations of Rights.* (Oxford: Clarendon Press, 1987), especially Chapter 2.

21. E.g., in *Griswold v. Connecticut* and *Roe v. Wade.*

22. James Nickel, *Making Sense of Human Rights.* (Berkeley: University of California Press, 1987), p. 14.

23. There is, unfortunately, some disagreement in the literature on the meaning of the notion of "scope"; Sumner distinguishes scope and content, as I do, but says that "The scope of a right consists of the class of things whose normative positions are stipulated by a right" and explains this by saying that scope decomposes into two classes: the objects and the subjects of the right (L. W. Sumner, *The Moral Foundations of Rights, op. cit.,* p. 11.). My definition of scope follows that employed by Nickel, who writes "To be exceptionless is a matter of scope, and to be absolute is a matter of weight. But it is often difficult to know whether the failure of a right to outweigh competing considerations and to dictate the result that should be followed, all things considered, in a particular case is best described as an instance of its containing an implicit qualification (scope) or as an instance of its being overridden (weight)." (James Nickel, *Making Sense of Human Rights, op. cit.,* p. 49.)

24. *Human Rights: Comments and Interpretations, op. cit.,* p. 262.

25. *Ibid.,* p. 263.

26. These so-called "third-generation" rights are found in the most recent international human rights covenant, *The African Charter of Human and People's Rights,* which came into force on October 21, 1986. See Claude E. Welch, Jr., "Human Rights As a Problem in Contemporary Africa," in *Human Rights and Development in Africa,* Claude E. Welch, Jr. and Ronald I. Meltzer (Eds.). (Albany, NY: State University of New York Press, 1984), pp. 7–31.

27. See Appendix A for the texts of these documents.

28. For a summary of the countries that have ratified these covenants and the particular rights that are protected under the civil laws of the world's sovereign nations see: Charles Humana, *World Human Rights Guide.* (New York: Pica Press, 1984). The United States has signed both covenants, but they have never been ratified by the Senate.

29. This use of the term "positive right" is different from that employed by Cranston, who uses it in a more traditional sense to mean actual, recognized, or legally protected rights. In the present context, a positive right contrasts with a negative right and correlates with a positive duty. This use of the term is now more common and derives, I believe, from its employment by D. D. Raphael, who distinguished between "rights of action" and "rights of recipience": "When a man has a right to liberty, the obligation against those whom he has the right is a *negative* obligation, an obligation to leave him alone, to leave him free to do as he thinks fit. But when he is said to have a right to participate in government, or a right to work, and even more when he is said to have a right to social security, the obligation of those against whom he has the right is a *positive* obligation, an obligation to provide him with something which he could not achieve by himself." In *Political Theory and the Rights of Man,* D. D. Raphael (Ed.). (Bloomington, IN: Indiana University Press, 1967), p. 60.

30. Henry Shue, *Basic Rights.* (Princeton, NJ: Princeton University Press, 1979), Chapter 2, pp.37–38.

31. *Ibid.,* p. 52.

32. See Henry Shue, *Basic Rights. op. cit.,* Chapter 3.

33. *Ibid.,* p. 118.

34. *Ibid.,* p. 86.

35. Diana T. Meyers, *Inalienable Rights: A Defense.* (New York: Columbia University Press, 1985).

Part I

The
Nature of
Human Rights

On the Nature of Rights

JOSEPH RAZ

The nature of rights is one of the perennial topics of practical philosophy. One would have expected that interest in it would grow in times when rights are perceived to be central to morality or to political theory. This article is motivated by an interest in the importance of rights in morality and political theory. But that interest will here be kept in the background. My present purpose is to offer an outline of an account of the nature of rights and to leave the examination of its moral consequences for another occasion.[1]

The first section outlines an account of rights. The others explain it. Sections 2–5 are concerned with relatively technical points. Sections 6–9 touch on the philosophically significant aspects of the account here offered: the capacity to have rights and the relations between rights, duties, and interests.

I. The Outline of an Account of Rights

Is the "ulterior" purpose of assessing the importance of rights in morality and politics in danger of infecting an account of the nature of rights with an illegitimate bias? One danger of prefacing a discussion of the importance of rights with a definition of rights

1. I have pursued some aspects of this question in "Right-Based Moralities" in R. Frey (Ed.), *Rights and Utility.* (University of Minnesota Press, 1984).

Joseph Raz, "On the Nature of Rights," *Mind,* 93 (1984), pp. 194–214. Reprinted by permission of Oxford University Press.

is that one may end with a definition according to which rights are not important but which is not acceptable to those who claim that they are.

An opposite danger is of proving the importance of rights by calling anything of value a right. Both dangers exemplify the vice of spuriously arguing for a moral or a political view by surreptitious verbal legislation. Both dangers result from the fact that a philosophical definition of "a right" like those of many other terms, is not an explanation of the ordinary meaning of a term. It follows rather the usage of writers on law, politics, and morality who typically use the term to refer to a sub-class of all the cases to which it can be applied with linguistic propriety.

Philosophical definitions of rights[2] attempt to capture the way the term is used in legal, political, and moral writing and discourse. They both explain the existing tradition of moral and political debate and declare the author's intention to carry on the debate within the boundaries of that tradition. At the same time they further that debate by singling out certain features of rights, as traditionally understood, for special attention, on the grounds that they are the features which best explain the role of rights in moral, political, and legal discourse. It follows that while a philosophical definition may well be based on a particular moral or political theory (the theory dictates which features of rights, traditionally understood, best explain their role in political, legal and moral discourse), it should not make that theory the only one which recognizes rights.[3] To do so is to try to win by verbal legislation. A successful philosophical definition of rights illuminates a tradition of political and moral discourse in which different theories offer incompatible views as to what rights there are and why. The definition may advance the case of one such theory but if successful it explains and illuminates all. In this spirit, I shall first propose a definition of rights and then explain various features of the definition and criticize some alternative definitions.

Definition: "x has a right" if and only if x can have rights, and other things being equal, an aspect of x's well-being (his interest) is a sufficient reason for holding some other person(s) to be under a duty.[4]

The Principle of Capacity to have Rights: An individual is capable of having rights if and only if either his well-being is of ultimate value or he is an "artificial person" (e.g., a corporation).

---

2. I refer of course to what philosophers most commonly do, whether they know this or not. I do not wish to deny that some understand their enterprise in other ways.

3. Though a consideration of notions such as "chastity," "honour," "chivalry" shows that not all political or moral theories have room for all normative concepts. Some theories may not recognise rights. For an argument that utilitarianism is incompatible with the existence of rights see D. Lyons, "Utility and Rights", *Nomos* **24** (1982).

4. The definition draws on several elements of analyses of rights which stem from Bentham's beneficiary theory. It has much in common with R. M. Dworkin's explanation in *Taking Rights Seriously* (London: Duckworth, 1977), p. 100 (but not with his more well-known "trump" theory), and with D. N. MacCormick's "Rights in Legislation," in P. M. S. Hacker and J. Raz (Eds.), *Law, Morality and Society*. (Oxford, 1977). Most of all I have been influenced by K. Campbell's ideas in his *The Concept of Rights,* 1979, an Oxford D.Phil. thesis.

Note that since "a right" is a very general term, one rarely asserts that someone has a right without specifying what rights he has, just as one does not normally mention that a person is subject to a duty without saying something more about what duty it is. Sometimes one may state of another that he has rights in order to indicate that he is the kind of creature who is capable of having rights. For example, one may say that slaves have (legal or moral) rights, or that partnerships have rights, or that foetuses have them. (Similarly one may say that the monarch has duties, etc.) The fact that assertions of rights *tout court* are rare does not invalidate the definition, nor does it detract from its value as the key to the explanation of all rights. It is true that there is much about statements of rights which cannot be learned from my definition alone. One needs to distinguish a right to act from a right in an object, and that from a right to an object, and that from a right to a service or a facility, and that again from "a right to . . ." where the dots stand for an abstract noun. A right to use the highway, for example, is a liberty right to use the highway or a right to have that liberty. A right in a car may be a right of ownership in the car, or some other right in it. Detailed explanations of rights are in part linguistic explanations (a right to a car differs from a right in a car) but in part they depend on political, legal, or moral argument. (Does a right to free speech include access to the mass media or to private premises?) The proposed definition is meant to be neutral concerning all such detailed questions. At the same time, it aims to encapsulate the common core of all rights, and thus to help to explain their special role in practical thought.

The definition is of rights *simpliciter.* Some discourse of rights is of rights as viewed from the point of view of a certain system of thought, as when one compares Kantian rights with Utilitarian rights. Prefixing an adjective to "rights" is one way to indicate that the speaker does not necessarily accept the existence of the right and is merely considering the implications of a system of thought. (On other occasions such adjectives identify the contents of the rights, e.g., economic rights, or their source, e.g., promissory rights, or both.)

Rights are grounds of duties in others. The duties grounded in a right may be conditional.[5] Consider the duty of an employee to obey his employer's instructions concerning the execution of his job. It is grounded in the employer's right to instruct his employees. But it is a conditional duty, i.e., a duty (in matters connected with one's employment) to perform an action if instructed by the employer to do so. When the condition which activates the duty is an action of some person, and when the duty is conditional on it because it is in the right-holder's interest to make that person able to activate the duty at will, then the right confers a power on the person on whose behaviour the duty depends.[6] Thus the employer's right over the employees is a

5. Throughout this essay I draw no distinction between duties and obligations. Nor will I indicate how to distinguish a future duty which will exist if a condition is satisfied (If . . . then one has a duty to . . .) from a presently existing conditional duty (One has a duty to . . . if . . .). I will assume that only conditional duties can be conditioned on the exercise of powers to impose them.
6. For a clarification of the notion of a normative power cf. my *Practical Reason and Norms.* (London: Hutchinson, 1975), Sec. 3.2. By extending the same reasoning rights can be shown to be grounds of immunities and liberties: They are reasons for not subjecting individuals to duties or to the power of others.

ground for his power to instruct them. This power is one aspect or one consequence of his right. But the very same right also endows him with a power to delegate his authority to others. It can, if he chooses to delegate authority, become the source of a power in one of his subordinates. In that case the employee will have a duty to obey the person in whom power was vested and that duty as well as the power of the delegated authority are grounded in the right of the employer. To simplify I shall not dwell specifically on rights as the grounds of powers.

2. Core and Derivative Rights

Some rights derive from others. Just as rights are grounds for duties and powers so they can be for other rights. I shall call a right which is grounded in another right a derivative right. Non-derivative rights are core rights. The relation between a derivative right and the core right (or any other right) from which it derives is a justificatory one. The statement that the derivative right exists must be a conclusion of a sound argument (non-redundantly) including a statement entailing the existence of the core right. But not every right thus entailed is a derivative one. The premises must also provide a justification for the existence of the derivative right (and not merely evidence or even proof of its existence). To do so their truth must be capable of being established without relying on the truth of the conclusion. An example may illustrate the point.

Let us assume that I own a whole street because I bought (in separate transactions) all its houses. My ownership of a house in the street does not derive from my ownership of the street as a whole, even though the statement that I own a house in the street is entailed by the statement that I own the street. For in attempting to provide a normative justification for my rights I have to refer to the individual transactions by which I acquired the houses. Therefore my right in the street derives from my rights in the houses and not the other way round. Had I inherited the whole street from my grandfather the situation would have been reversed.

Without grasping the relation between core and derivative rights one is liable to fall into confusion. My right to walk on my hands is not directly based on an interest served either by doing so or by others having duties not to stop me. It is based on my interest in being free to do as I wish, on which the general right to personal liberty is directly based. The right to walk on my hands is one instance of my general right to personal liberty. The right to personal liberty is the core right from which the other derives. Similarly with my right to make the previous statement, which is a derivative of the core right of free speech, and my right to spoil the cigarette I am holding at the moment, which derives from my ownership in it, and so on. Often right-holders have direct interest in that to which they have derivative rights. But those do not always ground their rights. A right is based on the interest which figures essentially in the justification of the statement that the right exists. The interest relates directly to the core right and indirectly to its derivatives. The relation of core and derivative rights is not that of entailment, but of the order of justification. The fact that a statement that everyone has a right to freedom of expression appears to entail the statement that everyone has a right to free political expression does not establish that the first is the core right and the second its derivative. It may well be that freedom of political speech is justified by considerations which do not apply to other kinds of speech. If it is also the case that, while separate independent considerations justify freedom of commercial speech and others still freedom of artistic expression, scientific and academic communications, etc., there are no general considerations which apply to all of the protected areas of speech, then the general right to freedom of expression is a derivative right. It is a mere generalization from the existence of several independent core rights.

Furthermore, a general right statement does not entail those statements of particular rights which are instances of it. I may have a right to free speech without having a right to libel people. In matters of libel, the right to free expression may be completely defeated by the interests of people in their reputation. I will return to this point later.

3. The Correlativity of Rights and Duties

It is sometimes argued that to every duty there is a corresponding right. It is evident from the proposed definition that there are no conceptual reasons for upholding such a view. Some moral theories may yield such a correlativity thesis as a result of their moral principles, but this possibility cannot be explored here. A more popular thesis maintains that to every right there is a correlative duty. Since a right is a ground for duties there is a good deal of truth in this kind of correlativity thesis. Yet most of its common formulations are very misleading. R. Brandt's definition can serve as an example of many: "x has an absolute right to enjoy, have or be secured in y" means the same as "It is someone's objective overall obligation to secure x in, or in the possession of, or in the enjoyment of y, if y wishes it."[7] He proceeds to define *prima facie* rights in terms of *prima facie* obligations. First, note that Brandt misleadingly suggests that to every right there corresponds one duty, that that duty is to guarantee the enjoyment or possession of the object of the right, and that it is conditional on the desire of the right-holder. All three points are mistaken. A right to education grounds a duty to provide educational opportunities to each individual, whether he wishes it or not. Many rights ground duties which fall short of securing their object, and they may ground many duties not one. A right to personal security does not require others to protect a person from all accidents or injury. The right is, however, the foundation of several duties, such as the duty not to assault, rape or imprison the right-holder.

Secondly, and more importantly, Brandt fails to notice that the right is the ground of the duty. It is wrong to translate statements of rights into statements of "the corresponding" duties. A right of one person is not a duty on another. It is the ground

---

7. Richard Brandt, *Ethical Theory.* (Englewood Cliffs, NJ: Prentice Hall, 1959), p. 438.

of a duty, a ground which, if not counteracted by conflicting considerations, justifies holding that other person to have the duty.

Thirdly, there is no closed list of duties which correspond to the right. The existence of a right often leads to holding another to have a duty because of the existence of certain facts peculiar to the parties or general to the society in which they live. A change of circumstances may lead to the creation of new duties based on the old right. The right to political participation is not new, but only in modern states with their enormously complex bureaucracies does this right justify, as I think it does, a duty on the government to make public its plans and proposals before a decision on them is reached, as well as a duty to publish its reasons for a decision once reached (except in special categories of cases such as those involving defence secrets). This dynamic aspect of rights, their ability to create new duties, is fundamental to any understanding of their nature and function in practical thought. Unfortunately, most if not all formulations of the correlativity thesis disregard the dynamic aspects of rights. They all assume that a right can be exhaustively stated by stating those duties which it has already established.[8] This objection to the reduction of rights to duties does not rule out the possibility of holding that "A has a right to x" is reducible to "There is a duty to secure A in x." But since this duty can be based on grounds other than A's interest, the two statements are not equivalent.

4. Holding Individuals to Be Under a Duty

The proposed definition states that if an individual has a right then a certain aspect of his well-being is a reason for holding others to be under a duty. I used this phrase advisedly to preserve the ambiguity between saying that rights are a reason for judging a person to have a duty and saying that they are reasons for imposing duties on him. They are in fact reasons of both kinds, but primarily of the first. Let me explain. Rights are (part of) the justification of many duties. They justify the view that people have those duties. But, as has already been noted, they justify such a view only to the extent that there are no conflicting considerations of greater weight. Within certain institutional settings, there are weighty reasons not so much against allowing rights to generate new duties as against allowing official action on the basis of new duties unless they are recognised by the appropriate institutions. Institutions such as universities, states, trade unions, and football clubs are based on a concentration of power in certain bodies and a division of labour between officials whose duties are the execution of the institutions' policies and rules and those who make and change those policies and rules. In such an institution it may be proper to say that rights are grounds not so much for judging that certain duties exist as for imposing them.

---

8. Needless to say core rights can lead also to new derivative rights.

The right to political participation is a legal right in English law. But though in contemporary societies this right justifies holding the government to be under a duty to publicize its plans and the reasons for its decisions, there is no such legal duty on the government in English law. The duty is a purely moral duty. But the existence of the legal right to political participation, i.e., the fact that this right is given legal recognition and is already defended by some legal duties, is a ground for the authorized institutions (Parliament or the courts) to impose such a duty on government officials. If and when they do so, they will be making new law. But they will do so on the ground that this is justified and required by existing law. By the same token the legal right to political participation is a reason for investing people with a legal right to free information. It cannot be used to establish that they already have such a right.

5. Promises and Agreements

Some of the points made in the previous sections can be illustrated and clarified by using them to explain the rights involved in promises and agreements. These are two. There is the right to promise which a promisor must have if his promise is to be binding. And there is the right conferred on the promisee by the promise. I will examine them in that order.

The right to promise is based on the promisor's interest to be able to forge special bonds with other people.[9] The right is qualified. Not every person has it. Small children and some mentally deranged people lack it. Furthermore, if it is not permissible to have bonds based on immorality, one's right to promise does not include the right to promise to perform immoral acts. The right to promise is no doubt further qualified. Since we are not here concerned with any of these qualifications I will from now on disregard them.

Those who assign sufficient importance to the interest people have in being able to impose on themselves obligations to other people as a means of creating special bonds with other people believe in a right to promise. But why is it a right? The interest on which it is based validates the promising principle, namely:

If a person communicates an intention to undertake by that very act of communication a certain obligation then he has that obligation.

The promising principle establishes that if we promise we are obligated to act as we promised. It also establishes a present obligation to keep our promises, i.e., we are obligated to perform action x, if we promise to perform x. This is a conditional obligation. The condition is an action of the promisor, and his obligation is conditioned on his action because it is desirable that he should be able to bind himself if

9. I am here summarizing some of the points made in my "Promises and Obligations," in P. M. S. Hacker and J. Raz (Eds.), *Law, Morality and Society*; and in "Promises in Morality and Law," *Harvard Law Rev.*, Vol. 95 (February 1982), p. 916.

he so wishes. It follows that people's interest in being able to bind themselves is the basis of a power to promise which they possess and of an obligation to keep promises imposed on them. But neither the power nor the obligation point to a right to promise. The right exists because the very same interest on which the power to promise and the duty to keep promises are based is also the ground to hold others to be subject to a duty not to interfere with one's promising. The duty requires one not to prevent a person from promising (e.g., by denying him the means of communicating an intention to undertake by that very communication an obligation, or by stopping others from receiving such communications). It also requires one not to force people to promise nor to induce them improperly to promise or not to promise. (Again I avoid examining the way these duties are qualified.) Violation of the duty not to interfere with a person's promising will frustrate his right to promise and the interest on which it is based either by preventing the person from exercising his rights or by perverting the considerations on which he decides whether to promise or not. The fact that such interferences with the right are infrequent is reflected by the fact that the right to promise is rarely invoked in ordinary practical discourse. To conclude, the power to promise and the right to promise are distinct notions. But both stem from a common core, i.e., the interest of persons to be able to forge normative bonds with others. That is why they co-exist, and one has the power to promise if and only if one has a right to do so.

The right to make a particular promise (e.g., to visit my aunt next weekend) is a derivative of the general right to promise. One such derivative right is the right to make a conditional promise. Two kinds of conditional promises are of interest here: First a promise made conditional on an action by the promisee (e.g., "I will give you 10 pounds if you give me the books"). Second (which is in fact a special case of the above), a promise made conditional on a promise to be given by the promisee (e.g., "I will give you 10 pounds if you promise to give me the book").

Whenever such a promise is made and the condition is fulfilled, there is an agreement between the promisor and the promisee. The right to make such promises is therefore a right to enter into agreements. There are other ways of making agreements but their analysis does not matter to our purpose.

So far we have discussed the right to promise. The right which the promise creates in *the promisee* does not derive from the right to promise which is a right of *the promisor*. Many writers on promises insist that the promised act must be or at least must be thought to be in the interest of the promisee. Elsewhere I have challenged the view and I will not return to this controversy here.[10] But it is interesting to relate this issue to the question of the promisee's right created by the promise.

One view regards the promisee's right under any particular promise as a core-right based on his interest in the promised act (and the intention of the promisor to be obligated to perform the act). On this view if there could be binding promises which do not benefit the promisee (and are not intended to do so) then there are promises which do not create rights in the promisee.

---

10. See "Promises and Obligations," *ibid.*

Such a consequence seems at odds with the conventions of discourse concerning promises. I therefore favour a second view (which complements the first) according to which each person has an interest that promises made to him will be kept. Of course, he might lose interest in the specific content of some promises and keeping some of them may even work against his overall interest. But invariably he has a *pro tanto* interest that promises given to him be kept. This interest is the very one which is reflected in his right to promise. Namely, it is the interest to have voluntary special bonds with other people. We should remind ourselves that while the promisee may not be the initiator of the bond of which the promise is the whole or a part, he is not entirely passive either. It is always up to him to waive his right under the promise and thus terminate the binding force of the promise. It is this general interest which explains why every promise, and not only those performance of which are to the specific advantage of the promisee, creates a right in the promisee.

6. Capacity for Rights

The definition of rights itself does not settle the issue of who is capable of having rights beyond requiring that right-holders are creatures who have interests. What other features qualify a creature to be a potential right-holder is a question bound up with substantive moral issues. It cannot by fully debated here. But the special role of statements of rights in practical thought cannot be elucidated and the significance of the definition cannot be evaluated without a brief explanation of the conditions for the capacity for having rights.

There is little that needs to be said here of the capacity of corporations and other "artificial persons" to have rights. Whatever explains and accounts for the existence of such persons, who can act, be subject to duties, etc. also accounts for their capacity to have rights. Whether certain groups, such as families or nations, are artificial or natural persons is important for determining the conditions under which they may have rights. But we need not settle such matters here.

There is a view, which I shall call the reciprocity thesis, that only members of "the same moral community" can have rights. This is narrowly interpreted when the same moral community is a community of interacting individuals whose obligations to each other are thought to derive from a social contract or to represent the outcome of a fair bargaining process or if morality is conceived of in some other way to be a system for the mutual advantage of all members of the community. Wider conceptions of the moral community extend it to all moral agents and regard anyone who is subject to duties as being capable of rights.

The principle of capacity for rights stated above is not committed to the reciprocity thesis but is consistent with it. Since by definition rights are nothing but grounds of duties, if duties observe a reciprocity condition and can be had only toward members of the (same) moral community then the same is true of rights. Alternatively, the reciprocity thesis obtains even if one can have duties toward non-members of the (same) moral community provided those are not based on the interests of the beneficiaries of those duties. For example, if my duties to animals are based on considerations of my own character (I should not be a person who can tolerate causing pain, etc.) and not on the interests of animals, then animals do not have rights despite the fact that I have duties regarding them.

The merits of the reciprocity thesis will not be examined here. The problem to which the principle of capacity for rights is addressed is different. Often we ought or even have duties to act in ways that benefit certain things, and often we ought so to act because of the benefit our action will bring those things. For example, I have a duty to preserve certain plants because I promised their owners to do so while they are away on holiday. My gardener has a duty to look after my garden because his contract of employment says so. Some scientists have a duty to preserve certain rare species of plants because they are the only source of a medicine for a rare and fatal disease. In all these cases the people who have duties to act in certain ways have them because [to have them] benefits plants. Yet in none of these cases is it true that the plants have a right to the benefits. The reason is that in all these cases the benefit is to be conferred on a thing whose existence and prosperity are not of ultimate value.

Being of ultimate, i.e., non-derivative[11] value is being intrinsically valuable, i.e., being valuable independently of one's instrumental value. Something is instrumentally valuable to the extent that it derives its value from the value of its consequences, or from the value of the consequences it is likely to have, or from the value of the consequences it can be used to produce. Being of ultimate value is being valuable even apart from one's instrumental value. But not everything which is intrinsically valuable is also of ultimate value. Consider a person who has a deep attachment to his dog. I share many people's feeling in thinking of the relationship as valuable and of the man's life as richer and better because of it. Many feel that the relationship is intrinsically valuable. Its value is not just that of a cause of a feeling of security and comfort in the man. Such feelings may be produced by some tranquillizers. The relationship is not valued just as a tranquillizer. Its value is in its being a constitutive part of a valuable form of life. For all who share these views the existence of the dog is intrinsically valuable. It is a logically necessary condition of the relationship and one which contributes to its value (it is the more valuable for being a relationship to a living—rather than a dead—dog). But so far as the story goes the intrinsic value of the dog is not ultimate for it derives from the dog's contribution to the well-being of the man. The man's well-being is here taken as the ultimate value. The dog non-instrumentally contributes to it. Hence his existence is intrinsically but derivatively valuable.

Some people are willing to go further and to hold that the value of the relationship between the man and the dog derives equally from its contribution to the well-being

---

11. To say that something is of ultimate value is not to claim that one cannot justify the statement that that thing is valuable. It merely indicates that its value does not derive from its contribution to the value of something else.

of the dog and that the dog's well-being is not merely derivatively important because of its contribution to the man's well-being. They hold it to be ultimately valuable. They regard the relationship between man and dog in the same way as they and most others regard a relationship between two persons.

My proposed principle of capacity for rights entails that those who regard the existence and well-being of (some) dogs as derivatively valuable (even if they believe them to be intrinsically valuable) are committed to the view that dogs can have no rights though we may well have duties to protect or promote their well-being. For such people dogs have the same moral standing that many ascribe to works of art. Their existence is intrinsically valuable in as much as the appreciation of art is intrinsically valuable. But their value is derivative and not ultimate. It derives from its contribution to the well-being of persons.

It seems plausible to suppose[12] that just as only those whose well-being is of ultimate value can have rights so only interests which are considered of ultimate value can be the basis of rights. But there are plenty of counter-examples demonstrating that some rights protect interests which are considered as of merely instrumental value. All the rights of corporations are justified by the need to protect the interests of these corporations but these are merely of instrumental value. But the counter-instances are not confined to the rights of "artificial persons." Consider the rights (however qualified) of journalists to protect their sources (i.e., not to disclose their sources). Those who believe that journalists have such a right base it on the interest of journalists in being able to collect information which is valued because it enables them to inform the public. That is, the journalists' interest is valued because of its usefulness to members of the public at large. The rights of priests, doctors, and lawyers to preserve the confidentiality of their professional contacts are likewise justified ultimately by their value to members of the community at large.

Furthermore, some people, and this seems to be the general view of the English Common Law, regard the interests on which a right as fundamental as freedom of speech is based as instrumentally valuable. Scanlon[13] distinguishes between three kinds of interest on which the right of free speech is based: (1) speaker's interest, (2) audience interest, and (3) third party interest. Only the first is the interest of the right-holder, the interest of a person to be able to communicate with others. The second (the interest of persons that others will be free to communicate with them) and third (the interest of people to live in a society in which communication is free— even if they personally do not wish to communicate with others) are interests of people other than the right-holder in his right. In the Common Law freedom of expression is regularly defended, where it is defended, on grounds of the public interest, that is on the interest of third parties. The right-holder's interest itself conceived independently of its contribution to the public interest is deemed insuffi-

---

12. Something like this supposition is made by K. Campbell, *ibid.*
13. See T. M. Scanlon, Jr., "Freedom of Expression and Categories of Freedom," *U. of Pittsburgh L.R.* (1979), p. 519.

cient to justify holding others to be subject to the extensive duties and disabilities commonly derived from the right to free speech.[14]

We must conclude that (apart from artificial persons) only those whose well-being is intrinsically valuable can have rights. But that rights can be based on the instrumental value of the interests of such people.

7. Rights and Interests

According to the definition, rights-discourse indicates a kind of ground for a requirement of action. To say that a person ought to behave in a certain way is to assert a requirement for action without indicating its ground. To assert that an individual has a right is to indicate a ground for a requirement for action of a certain kind, i.e., that an aspect of his well-being is a ground for a duty on another person. The specific role of rights in practical thinking is, therefore, the grounding of duties in the interests of other beings.

Rights ground requirements for action in the interest of other beings. They therefore assume special importance in individualistic moral thinking. But belief in the existence of rights does not commit one to individualism. States, corporations, and groups may be right-holders. Banks have legal and moral rights. Nations are commonly believed to have a right of self-determination and so on.

Though rights are based on the interests of the right-holders, an individual may have rights which it is against his interest to have. A person may have property which is more trouble than it is worth. It may be in a person's interest to be imprisoned, even while he has a right to freedom. The explanation of this puzzle is that rights are vested in right-holders because they possess certain general characteristics: They are the beneficiaries of a promise, nationals of a certain state, etc. Their rights serve their interests as individuals with those characteristics, but they may be against their interests overall.

Some rights are held by persons as the agents, or organs, of others. Thus company directors have rights as directors of the company. In such cases it is the interest of the principal which the right reflects. The same applies to rights held by persons *qua* guardians, trustees, and the like.

The proposed definition of rights identified the interest on which the right is based as the reason for holding that some persons have certain duties. Later on I referred to the rights themselves as being the grounds for those duties. The explanation is simple: The interests are part of the justification of the rights which are part of the justification of the duties. Rights are intermediate conclusions in arguments from ultimate values to duties. They are, so to speak, points in the argument where many considerations intersect and where their results are summarized to be used with additional premises when need be. Such intermediate conclusions are used and referred to as if they are

14. Two typical English cases are: A. G. v. Jonathan Cape Ltd. (1976) *Q.B.* 752; Home Office v. Harman (1982) 1 *All E.R.* 532.

themselves complete reasons. The fact that practical arguments proceed through the mediation of intermediate stages so that not every time a practical question arises does one refer to ultimate values for an answer is of crucial importance in making social life possible, not only because they save time and tediousness, but primarily because they enable a common culture to be formed round shared intermediate conclusions, in spite of a great degree of haziness and disagreement concerning ultimate values. For example, many who agree that people have a right to promise will disagree with my view, expressed above, of the interest on which it is based and will justify it only by reference to some other interests of the right-holders. The impor-tance of intermediate steps like rights, duties, rules of conduct and the like to a common culture explains and justifies the practice of referring to them as reasons in their own right, albeit not ultimate reasons.

An interest is sufficient to base a right on if and only if there is a sound argument of which the conclusion is that a certain right exists and among its non-redundant premises is a statement of some interest of the right-holder, the other premises supplying grounds for attributing to it the required importance, or for holding it to be relevant to a particular person or class of persons so that they rather than others are obligated to the right-holder. These premises must be sufficient by themselves to entail that if there are no contrary considerations then the individuals concerned have the right. To these premises one needs to add others stating or establishing that these grounds are not altogether outweighed by conflicting reasons.[15] Together they estab-lish the existence of the right.

One result of the fact that a right exists where the interests of the right-holders are sufficient to hold another to be obligated should be noted. Sometimes the fact that an action will serve someone's interest, while being a reason for doing it, is not sufficient to establish a duty to do it. Different moral theories differ on this point. Some utilitarian theories deny that there is a useful difference between moral reasons for action and duties. Some moral views confine duties to matters affecting human needs, or human dignity, etc. Be that as it may, it is in principle possible that a person should not have a right that others shall behave to promote a certain interest of his simply on account of the fact that while they should do so, while it is praiseworthy or virtuous of them if they do, they have no obligation so to act.

These considerations help to explain how it is that even if a person has a right, not everyone is necessarily under an obligation to do whatever will promote the interest on which it is based. Rights are held against certain persons. Some rights are held against the world at large, i.e., against all persons or against all with certain specified exceptions. Thus the right to personal security is the ground of a duty on everyone not to assault, imprison, or rape a person. Other rights are held against certain persons in

---

15. One case deserves special attention: If B's interest does not justify holding A to be under a duty to ø then B has no right that A shall ø even if A has a duty to ø based on the fact that ø-ing will serve the interest of a class of individuals of whom B is one. Thus a government may have a duty to try to improve the standard of living of all the inhabitants of the country even though no single inhabitant has a right that the government shall try to improve his standard of living.

virtue of a special relation they have to the right-holder. Thus children have a right to be maintained by their parents. The reasons many rights are against some definite people are varied. Sometimes the interests on which they are based can be satisfied only by some people and not by others. For example, since contractual rights are based on an interest in being able to create special relations, they give rise to rights against other parties to the agreement as they are the only ones who can satisfy that interest on that occasion. In other cases, even though many can satisfy the interests of the right-holder, these interests may be sufficient to establish a duty on some people and not on others.[16]

Just as rights may impose duties on some person and not on others, so they can impose a duty to do certain things but not others. The right to live may impose a duty not to kill or endanger the life of another without imposing a duty to take whatever action is necessary to keep him alive. Which duties a right gives rise to depends partly on the basis of that right, on the considerations justifying its existence. It also depends on the absence of conflicting considerations. If conflicting considerations show that the basis of the would-be right is not enough to justify holding anyone subject to any duty, then the right does not exist. But often such conflicting considerations, while sufficient to show that some actions cannot be required as a duty on the basis of the would-be right, do not affect the case for requiring other actions as a matter of duty. In such cases, the right exists, but it successfully grounds duties only for some of the actions which could promote the interest on which it is based.

8. Rights and Duties

Rights are the grounds of duties in the sense that one way of justifying holding a person to be subject to a duty is that this serves the interest on which another's right is based. Naturally there may be other grounds for not holding a person to be subject to such a duty. The definition requires that the right is a sufficient reason for a duty. Hence, as we saw, where the conflicting considerations altogether outweigh the interests of the would-be right-holder, and no one could justifiably be held to be obligated on account of those interests, then there is no right. Where the conflicting considerations override those on which the right is based on some but not on all occasions, the general core right exists, but the conflicting considerations may show that some of its possible derivations do not. There is a necessary conflict between free speech on the one hand and the protection of one's reputation or the need to suppress criticism of the authorities in time of a major national emergency on the other. (I assume that in both cases the reasons for suppressing libellous or critical expression are also reasons for not holding individuals to have a duty to protect the

---

16. The fact that rights may hold against some persons only is compatible with the principle that everyone ought to respect everyone's rights. That principle asserts that all persons have a reason (not necessarily a conclusive one) to avoid action which will make it more difficult for those subject to duties toward right-holders to fulfil their obligations.

freedom to express such views.) If in these circumstances the reasons against free expression by their nature override those in favour of free expression, then while it is true that one has a right to free expression, one does not have a right to libel or to criticize the government in an emergency. A general right is, therefore, only a *prima facie* ground for the existence of a particular right in circumstances to which it applies. Rights can conflict with other rights or with other duties, but if the conflicting considerations defeat the right they cannot be necessarily coextensive in their scope.[17]

These remarks help explain one sense in which rights ground duties. Two further points are, however, crucial to the understanding of the priority of rights to the duties which are based on them (and not all duties are based on rights). First, one may know of the existence of a right without knowing who is bound by duties based on it or what precisely are these duties. A person may know that every child has a right to education. He will, therefore, know that there are duties, conditional or unconditional, to provide children with education. But he may have no view who has the duty. This question involves principles of responsibility. It is part of the function of such principles to determine the order of responsibility of different persons to the right-holder. Does the primary responsibility rest with the parents, with the community stepping in only if they can't or won't meet their obligations? Or does the primary responsibility rest with the community? The issue is of great importance. If it is the parents' duty then there is no duty on the community to provide free education to all. And yet one may be in a position to assert that there is a right to education without knowing the answer to such a problem, or to whether the communal responsibility is local or national, whether it extends only to primary education or beyond and so on and so forth.

In a sense such ignorance shows that the person's knowledge of the precise content of the right to education is incomplete. But this merely means that he does not know all the implications of the right to education (given other true premises). It does not mean that he does not understand the statement that every child has a right to education. Furthermore it is reflection on the right to education, its point and the reasons for it, which helps, together with other premises, to establish such implications.

The second point to bear in mind is that the implications of a right, such as the right to education, and the duties it grounds, depend on additional premises, and these cannot in principle be wholly determined in advance. At least if it is true in principle that the future cannot be entirely known in advance then there may be future circumstances which were not predicted and which, given the right to education, give rise to a new duty which was not predicted in advance. Even if no such duty is unpredictable, the total implications of the right to education are in principle unpredictable.

---

17. Conflicts of rights are possible if conflicts of duties are. If the considerations against requiring an action defeat the right-based reasons for requiring it on all the occasions to which they apply, then the right does not create a duty for that action. If, however, they defend the right-based reasons on some occasions only, then the right-based reasons create a duty which is sometimes defeated.

Because of this rights can be ascribed a dynamic character. They are not merely the grounds of existing duties. With changing circumstances they can generate new duties.

9. The Importance of Rights

The main purpose of this article was to state and explain a coherent account of rights which is within a recognisable philosophical tradition while hoping to improve on previous definitions in the details of the account. The argument for my account is in its use in moral, political, and legal thought and in its success in avoiding the shortcomings of its alternatives. These are matters for other occasions. I will conclude by commenting briefly on the main feature of my account, its view of rights as intermediate between individual interests and people's duties.

Rights ground duties. To say this is not to endorse the thesis that all duties derive from rights or that morality is right-based. It merely highlights the precedence of rights over some duties and the dynamic aspect of rights, their capacity to generate new duties with changing circumstances. Notice that precisely because duties can be based on considerations other than someone's rights the statement (1) "Children have a right to education" does not mean the same as the statement (2) "There is a duty to provide education for children." (1) entails (2) but not the other way round. (1) informs us that the duty stated in (2) is based on the interests of the children. This information is not included in (2) by itself.

It may be claimed that by defining rights as based on the well-being of individuals I have ruled out of court the view that morality is right-based. By definition rights are not fundamental but derive from interests. If true this is a damaging criticism. As explained in the first section the account of rights aims to make sense rather than nonsense of rival theories about the role of rights in morality. I think, however, that the view that rights are fundamental can be explained in terms of the proposed account.

All rights are based on interests. Some rights may be based on an interest in having those same rights.[18] No vicious circularity is involved in the claim that x has a certain right because it is in his interest to have it. It is no more circular than the statement that Jack loves Jill because she needs his love. In many cases an individual's interest in a right does not justify holding him to have it unless it serves some other worth-while interest of his (or of others). My son's interest in a right to education justifies holding him to have it only because the right will serve his interest in education.

---

18. One may think that one's right to x always derives from one's interests in x. If so then one's interest in having a right to x yields at best a right to have a right to x. It does not yield the right to x itself. This objection is based on a misunderstanding. While rights are based on the interests of the right-holder, these need not be his interests in the object of the right. They can be any interests which can be served by the possession of the right. Since an interest in having a right can be served by having it, it can be the foundation of such a right.

If school places were saleable I would have had an interest in having a right to education even if further education is not in my interest, because such a right would serve my interest in my economic welfare since it would add to my disposable assets. Such an interest would not, of course, justify holding me to have the right.

A right is a morally fundamental right if it is justified on the ground that it serves the right-holder's interest in having that right inasmuch as that interest is considered to be of ultimate value, i.e., inasmuch as the value of that interest does not derive from some other interests of the right-holder or of other persons.

Thus the proposed account of rights allows for the existence of fundamental moral rights. It has to be admitted that this account makes it highly unlikely that morality is right-based. If morality is right-based then all rights have to be either fundamental rights or be derivable from fundamental rights. It is highly unlikely that no one has any right which does not derive from the ultimate value of his interest in having that right. It seems plausible to suppose that people have rights which derive from other interests. The right to education seems, e.g., to derive from the interest in education. The fact that my account of rights makes the view that morality is right-based improbable is not, however, an argument against it. As mentioned at the beginning of the article it is part of the function of a philosophical account of a concept to use it to advance some controversial thesis. There are in any case independent arguments against the view that morality is right-based.[19]

Balliol College
Oxford, Ox1 3BJ

19. See my "Right-Based Moralities," in *Theories of Rights,* Jeremy Waldron (Ed.). (Oxford: Oxford University Press, 1984), pp. 182–200. I am grateful to K. Campbell, Wayne Summer, and to Jeremy Waldron for helpful criticism of an earlier draft of this article.

The Nature and Value of Rights

JOEL FEINBERG

1

I would like to begin by conducting a thought experiment. Try to imagine Nowheres-ville—a world very much like our own except that no one, or hardly any one (the qualification is not important), has *rights*. If this flaw makes Nowheresville too ugly to hold very long in contemplation, we can make it as pretty as we wish in other moral respects. We can, for example, make the human beings in it as attractive and virtuous as possible without taxing our conceptions of the limits of human nature. In particu-lar, let the virtues of moral sensibility flourish. Fill this imagined world with as much benevolence, compassion, sympathy, and pity as it will conveniently hold without strain. Now we can imagine men helping one another from compassionate motives merely, quite as much or even more than they do in our actual world from a variety of more complicated motives.

This picture, pleasant as it is in some respects, would hardly have satisfied Immanuel Kant. Benevolently motivated actions do good, Kant admitted, and there-fore are better, *ceteris paribus,* than malevolently motivated actions; but no action can have supreme kind of worth—what Kant called "moral worth"—unless its whole motivating power derives from the thought that it is *required by duty.* Accordingly, let us try to make Nowheresville more appealing to Kant by introducing the idea of duty into it and letting the sense of duty be a sufficient motive for many beneficent and honorable actions. But doesn't this bring our original thought experiment to an abortive conclusion? If duties are permitted entry into Nowheresville, are not rights necessarily smuggled in along with them?

Joel Feinberg, "The Nature and Value of Rights," from *The Journal of Value Inquiry,* 4 (1970), pp. 243–251. Reprinted by permission of *The Journal of Value Inquiry.*

The question is well-asked and requires here a brief digression so that we might consider the so-called "doctrine of the logical correlativity of rights and duties." This is the doctrine that (1) all duties entail other people's rights and (2) all rights entail other people's duties. Only the first part of the doctrine, the alleged entailment from duties to rights, need concern us here. Is this part of the doctrine correct? It should not be surprising that my answer is: "In a sense yes and in a sense no." Etymologically, the word "duty" is associated with actions that are *due* someone else, the payments of debts *to* creditors, the keeping of agreements with promises, the payment of club dues, or legal fees, or tariff levies to appropriate authorities or their representatives. In this original sense of "duty," all duties are correlated with the rights of those *to* whom the duty is owed. On the other hand, there seem to be numerous classes of duties, both of a legal and non-legal kind, that are *not* logically correlated with the rights of other persons. This seems to be a consequence of the fact that the word "duty" has come to be used for *any* action understood to be *required,* whether by the rights of others, or by law, or by higher authority, or by conscience, or whatever. When the notion of requirement is in clear focus it is likely to seem the only element in the idea of duty that is essential, and the other component notion—that a duty is something *due* someone else—drops off. Thus, in this widespread but derivative usage, "duty" tends to be used for any action we feel we *must* (for whatever reason) do. It comes, in short, to be a term of moral modality merely; and it is no wonder that the first thesis of the logical correlativity doctrine often fails.

Let us then introduce duties into Nowheresville, but only in the sense of actions that are, or believed to be, morally mandatory, but not in the older sense of actions that are due others and can be claimed by others as their right. Nowheresville now can have duties of the sort imposed by positive law. A legal duty is not something we are implored or advised to do merely; it is something the law, or an authority under the law, *requires* us to do whether we want to or not, under pain of penalty. When traffic lights turn red, however, there is no determinate person who can plausibly be said to claim our stopping as his due, so that the motorist owes it to *him* to stop, in the way a debtor owes it to his creditor to pay. In our own actual world, of course, we some-times owe it to our *fellow motorists* to stop; but that kind of right-correlated duty does not exist in Nowheresville. There, motorists "owe" obedience to the Law, but they owe nothing to one another. When they collide, no matter who is at fault, no one is accountable to anyone else, and no one has any sound grievance or "right to complain."

When we leave legal contexts to consider moral obligations and other extra-legal duties, a greater variety of duties-without-correlative-rights present themselves. Duties of charity, for example, require us to contribute to one or another of a large number of eligible recipients, no one of whom can claim our contribution from us as his due. Charitable contributions are more like gratuitous services, favours, and gifts than like repayments of debts or reparations; and yet we do have duties to be charitable. Many persons, moreover, in our actual world believe that they are required by their own consciences to do more than that "duty" that *can* be demanded of them by their prospective beneficiaries. I have quoted elsewhere the citation from H. B.

Acton of a character in a Malraux novel who "gave all his supply of poison to his fellow prisoners to enable them by suicide to escape the burning alive which was to be their fate and his." This man, Acton adds, "probably did not think that [the others] had more of a right to the poison than he had, though he thought it his duty to give it to them."[1] I am sure that there are many actual examples, less dramatically heroic than this fictitious one, of persons who believe, rightly or wrongly, that they *must do* something (hence the word "duty") for another person in excess of what that person can appropriately demand of him (hence the absence of "right").

Now the digression is over and we can return to Nowheresville and summarize what we have put in it thus far. We now find spontaneous benevolence in somewhat larger degree than in our actual world, and also the acknowledged existence of duties of obedience, duties of charity, and duties imposed by exacting private consciences, and also, let us suppose, a degree of conscientiousness in respect to those duties somewhat in excess of what is to be found in our actual world. I doubt that Kant would be fully satisfied with Nowheresville even now that duty and respect for law and authority have been added to it; but I feel certain that he would regard their addition at least as an improvement. I will now introduce two further moral practices into Nowheresville that will make the world very little more appealing to Kant, but will make it appear more familiar to us. These are the practices connected with the notions of *personal desert* and what I call a *sovereign monopoly of rights.*

When a person is said to deserve something good from us what is meant in part is that there would be a certain propriety in our giving that good thing to him in virtue of the kind of person he is, perhaps, or more likely, in virtue of some specific thing he has done. The propriety involved here is a much weaker kind than that which derives from our having promised him the good thing or from his having qualified for it by satisfying the well-advertised conditions of some public rule. In the latter case he could be said not merely to deserve the good thing but also to have a *right* to it, that is to be in a position to demand it as his due; and of course we will not have that sort of thing in Nowheresville. That weaker kind of propriety which is mere desert is simply a kind of *fittingness* between one party's character or action and another party's favorable response, much like that between humor and laughter, or good performance and applause.

The following seems to be the origin of the idea of deserving good or bad treatment from others: A master or lord was under no obligation to reward his servant for especially good service; still a master might naturally feel that there would be a special fittingness in giving a gratuitous reward as a grateful response to the good service (or conversely imposing a penalty for bad service). Such an act while surely fitting and proper was entirely supererogatory. The fitting response in turn from the rewarded servant should be gratitude. If the deserved reward had not been given him he should have had no complaint, since he only *deserved* the reward, as opposed to having a *right* to it, or a ground for claiming it as his due.

1. H. B. Acton, "Symposium of 'Rights,'" *Proceedings of the Aristotelian Society,* Supplementary Volume 24 (1950), pp. 107–108.

The idea of desert has evolved a good bit away from its beginnings by now, but nevertheless, it seems clearly to be one of those words J. L. Austin said "never entirely forget their pasts."[2] Today servants qualify for their wages by doing their agreed upon chores, no more and no less. If their wages are not forthcoming, their contractual rights have been violated and they can make legal claim to the money that is their due. If they do less than they agreed to do, however, their employers may "dock" them, by paying them proportionately less than the agreed upon fee. This is all a matter of right. But if the servant does a splendid job, above and beyond his minimal contractual duties, the employer is under no further obligation to reward him, for this was not agreed upon, even tacitly, in advance. The additional service was all the servant's idea and done entirely on his own. Nevertheless, the morally sensitive employer may feel that it would be exceptionally appropriate for him to respond, freely on *his* own, to the servant's meritorious service, with a reward. The employee cannot demand it as his due, but he will happily accept it, with gratitude, as a fitting response to his desert.

In our age of organized labor, even this picture is now archaic; for almost every kind of exchange of service is governed by hard-bargained contracts so that even bonuses can sometimes be demanded as a matter of right, and nothing is given for nothing on either side of the bargaining table. And perhaps that is a good thing; for consider an anachronistic instance of the earlier kind of practice that survives, at least as a matter of form, in the quaint old practice of "tipping." The tip was originally conceived as a reward that has to be earned by "zealous service." It is not something to be taken for granted as a standard response to *any* service. That is to say that its payment is a *"gratuity,"* not a discharge of obligation, but something given apart from, or in addition to, anything the recipient can expect as a matter of right. That is what tipping originally meant at any rate, and tips are still referred to as "gratuities" in the tax forms. But try to explain all that to a New York cab driver! If he has *earned* his gratuity, by God, he has it coming, and there had better be sufficient acknowledgment of his desert or he'll give you a piece of his mind! I'm not generally prone to defend New York cab drivers, but they do have a point here. There is the making of a paradox in the queerly unstable concept of an "earned gratuity." One can understand how "desert" in the weak sense of "propriety" or "mere fittingness" tends to generate a stronger sense in which desert is itself the ground for a claim of right.

In Nowheresville, nevertheless, we will have only the original weak kind of desert. Indeed, it will be impossible to keep this idea out if we allow such practices as teachers grading students, judges awarding prizes, and servants serving benevolent but class-conscious masters. Nowheresville is a reasonably good world in many ways, and its teachers, judges, and masters will generally try to give students, contestants, and servants the grades, prizes, and rewards they deserve. For this the recipients will be grateful; but they will never think to complain, or even feel aggrieved, when expected responses to desert fail. The masters, judges, and teachers don't *have* to do good things, after all, for *anyone*. One should be happy that they *ever* treat us well, and

---

2. J. L. Austin, "A Plea for Excuses," *Proceedings of the Aristotelian Society,* Vol. 57 (1956–57).

not grumble over their occasional lapses. Their hopes for responses, after all, are *gratuities,* and there is no wrong in the omission of what is merely gratuitious. Such is the response of persons who have no concept of *rights,* even persons who are proud of their own deserts.[3]

Surely, one might ask, rights have to come in somewhere, if we are to have even moderately complex forms of social organization. Without rules that confer rights and impose obligations, how can we have ownership of property, bargains, and deals, promises and contracts, appointments and loans, marriages and partnerships? Very well, let us introduce all of these social and economic practices into Nowheresville, but *with one big twist.* With them I should like to introduce the curious notion of a "sovereign right-monopoly." You will recall that the subjects in Hobbes's *Leviathan* had no rights whatever against their sovereign. He could do as he liked with them, even gratuitously harm them, but this gave them no valid grievance against him. The sovereign, to be sure, had a certain duty to treat his subjects well, but this duty was owed not to the subjects directly, but to God, just as we might have a duty to a person to treat his property well, but of course no duty to the property itself but only to its owner. Thus, while the sovereign was quite capable of *harming* his subjects, he could commit no wrong against them that they could complain about, since they had no prior claims against his conduct. The only party *wronged* by the sovereign's mistreatment of his subject was God, the supreme lawmaker. Thus, in repenting cruelty to his subjects, the sovereign might say to God, as David did after killing Uriah, "to Thee only have I sinned."[4]

Even in the *Leviathan,* however, ordinary people had ordinary rights *against one another.* They played roles, occupied offices, made agreements, and signed contracts. In a genuine "sovereign right-monopoly," as I shall be using that phrase, they will do all those things too, and thus incur genuine obligations toward one another; but the obligations (here is the twist) will not be owed directly *to* promisees, creditors, parents, and the like, but rather to God alone, or to the members of some elite, or to a single sovereign under God. Hence, the rights correlative to the obligations that derive from these transactions are all owned by some "outside" authority.

As far as I know, no philosopher has ever suggested that even our role and contract obligations (in this, our actual world) are all owed directly to a divine intermediary, but some theologians have approached such extreme moral occasionalism. I have in mind the familiar phrase in certain widely distributed religious tracts that "it takes three to marry," which suggests that marital vows are not made between bride and groom directly but between each spouse and God, so that if one breaks his vow, the other cannot rightly complain of being wronged, since only God could have claimed performance of the marital duties as his *own* due; and hence God alone had a claim-right violated by nonperformance. If John breaks his vow to God, he might then properly repent in the words of David: "To Thee only have I sinned."

---

3. For a fuller discussion of the concept of personal desert see my "Justice and Personal Desert," *Nomos VI, Justice,* C. J. Chapman (Ed.). (New York: Atherton Press, 1963), pp. 69–97.
4. II Sam. 11. Cited with approval by Thomas Hobbes in *The Leviathan,* Part II, Chap. 21.

In our actual world, very few spouses conceive of their mutual obligations in this way; but their small children, at a certain stage in their moral upbringing, are likely to feel precisely this way toward *their* mutual obligations. If Billy kicks Bobby and is punished by Daddy, he may come to feel contrition for his naughtiness induced by his painful estrangement from the loved parent. He may then be happy to make amends and sincere apology to *Daddy*; but when Daddy insists that he apologize to his wronged brother, that is another story. A direct apology to Billy would be a tacit recognition of Billy's status as a right-holder against him, someone he can wrong as well as harm, and someone to whom he is directly accountable for his wrongs. This is a status Bobby will happily accord Daddy; but it would imply a respect for Billy that he does not presently feel, so he bitterly resents according it to him. On the "three-to-marry" model, the relations between each spouse and God would be like those between Bobby and Daddy; respect for the other spouse as an independent claimant would not even be necessary; and where present, of course, never sufficient.

The advocates of the "three-to-marry" model who conceive it either as a description of our actual institution of marriage or a recommendation of what marriage ought to be, may wish to escape this embarrassment by granting rights to spouses in capacities other than as promisees. They may wish to say, for example, that when John promises God that he will be faithful to Mary, a right is thus conferred not only on God as promisee but also on Mary herself as third-party beneficiary, just as when John contracts with an insurance company and names Mary as his intended beneficiary, she has a right to the accumulated funds after John's death, even though the insurance company made no promise to her. But this seems to be an unnecessarily cumbersome complication contributing nothing to our understanding of the marriage bond. The life insurance transaction is necessarily a three party relation, involving occupants of three distinct offices, no two of whom alone could do the whole job. The transaction, after all, is defined as the purchase by the customer (first office) from the vendor (second office) of protection for a beneficiary (third office) against the customer's untimely death. Marriage, on the other hand, in this our actual world, appears to be a binary relation between a husband and wife, and even though third parties such as children, neighbors, psychiatrists, and priests may sometimes be helpful and even causally necessary for the survival of the relation, they are not logically necessary to our *conception* of the relation, and indeed many married couples do quite well without them. Still I am not now purporting to describe our actual world, but rather trying to contrast it with a counterpart world of the imagination. In *that* world, it takes three to make almost *any* moral relation and all rights are owned by God or some sovereign under God.

There will, of course, be delegated authorities in the imaginary world, empowered to give commands to their underlings and to punish them for their disobedience. But the commands are all given in the name of the right-monopoly who in turn are the only persons to whom obligations are owed. Hence, even intermediate superiors do not have claim-rights against their subordinates but only legal *powers* to create obligations in the subordinates *to* the monopolistic right-holders, and also the legal *privilege* to impose penalties in the name of that monopoly.

2

So much for the imaginary "world without rights." If some of the moral concepts and practices I have allowed into that world do not sit well with one another, no matter. Imagine Nowheresville with all of these practices if you can, or with any harmonious subset of them, if you prefer. The important thing is not what I've let into it, but what I have kept out. The remainder of this paper will be devoted to an analysis of what precisely a world is missing when it does not contain rights and why that absence is morally important.

The most conspicuous difference, I think, between the Nowheresvillians and ourselves has something to do with the activity of *claiming*. Nowheresvillians, even when they are discriminated against invidiously, or left without the things they need, or otherwise badly treated, do not think to leap to their feet and make righteous demands against one another though they may not hesitate to resort to force and trickery to get what they want. They have no notion of rights, so they do not have a notion of what is their due; hence they do not claim before they take. The conceptual linkage between personal rights and claiming has long been noticed by legal writers and is reflected in the standard usage in which "claim-rights" are distinguished from other mere liberties, immunities, and powers, also sometimes called "rights," with which they are easily confused. When a person has a legal claim-right to X, it must be the case (1) that he is at liberty in respect to X, i.e., that he has no duty to refrain from or relinquish X, and also (2) that his liberty is the ground of other people's *duties* to grant him X or not to interfere with him in respect to X. Thus, in the sense of claim-rights, it is true by definition that rights logically entail other people's duties. The paradigmatic examples of such rights are the creditor's right to be paid a debt by his debtor, and the landowners' right not to be interfered with by anyone in the exclusive occupancy of his land. The creditor's right against his debtor, for example, and the debtor's duty to his creditor, are precisely the same relation seen from two different vantage points, as inextricably linked as the two sides of the same coin.

And yet, this is not quite an accurate account of the matter, for it fails to do justice to the way claim-rights are somehow prior to, or more basic than, the duties with which they are necessarily correlated. If Nip has a claim-right against Tuck, it is because of this fact that Tuck has a duty to Nip. It is only because something from Tuck is *due* Nip (directional element) that there is something Tuck *must do* (modal element). This is a relation, moreover, in which Tuck is bound and Nip is free. Nip not only *has* a right, but he can choose whether or not to exercise it, whether to claim it, whether to register complaints upon its infringement, even whether to release Tuck from his duty, and forget the whole thing. If the personal claim-right is also backed up by criminal sanctions, however, Tuck may yet have a duty of obedience to the law from which no one, not even Nip, may release him. He would even have such duties if he lived in Nowheresville; but duties subject to acts of claiming, duties derivative from the contingent upon the personal rights of others, are unknown and undreamed of in Nowheresville.

Many philosophical writers have simply identified rights with claims. The diction-aries tend to define "claims," in turn as "assertions of right," a dizzying piece of circularity that led one philosopher to complain—"We go in search of rights and are directed to claims, and then back again to rights in bureaucratic futility."[5] What then is the relation between a claim and a right?

As we shall see, a right *is* a kind of claim, and a claim is "an assertion of right," so that a formal definition of either notion in terms of the other will not get us very far. Thus if a "formal definition" of the usual philosophical sort is what we are after, the game is over before it has begun, and we can say that the concept of a right is a "simple, undefinable, unanalysable primitive." Here as elsewhere in philosophy this will have the effect of making the commonplace seem unnecessarily mysterious. We would be better advised, I think, not to attempt definition of either "right" or "claim," but rather to use the idea of a claim in informal elucidation of the idea of a right. This is made possible by the fact that *claiming* is an elaborate sort of rule-governed *activity*. A claim is that which is claimed, the object of the act of claiming. . . . If we concentrate on the whole activity of claiming, which is public, familiar, and open to our observation, rather than on its upshot alone, we may learn more about the generic nature of rights than we could ever hope to learn from a formal definition, even if one were possible. Moreover, certain facts about rights more easily, if not solely, expressible in the language of claims and claiming are essential to a full understanding not only of what rights are, but also why they are so vitally important.

Let us begin then by distinguishing between: (1) making claim to . . . , (2) claiming that . . . , and (3) having a claim. One sort of thing we may be doing when we claim is to *make claim to something*. This is "to petition or seek by virtue of supposed right; to demand as due." Sometimes this is done by an acknowledged right-holder when he serves notice that he now wants turned over to him that which has already been acknowledged to be his, something borrowed, say, or improperly taken from him. This is often done by turning in a chit, a receipt, an I.O.U., a check, an insurance policy, or a deed, that is, a *title* to something currently in the possession of someone else. On other occasions, making claim is making application for titles or rights themselves, as when a mining prospector stakes a claim to mineral rights, or a householder to a tract of land in the public domain, or an inventor to his patent rights. In the one kind of case, to make claim is to exercise rights one already has by presenting title; in the other kind of case it is to apply for the title itself, by showing that one has satisfied the conditions specified by a rule for the ownership of title and therefore that one can demand it as one's due.

Generally speaking, only the person who has a title or who has qualified for it, or someone speaking in his name, can make claim to something as a matter of right. It is an important fact about rights (or claims), then, that they can be claimed only by those who have them. Anyone can claim, of course, *that* this umbrella is yours, but only you or your representative can actually claim the umbrella. If Smith owes Jones five dollars, only Jones can claim the five dollars as his own, though any bystander can

---

5. H. B. Acton, *op. cit.*

claim that it belongs to Jones. One important difference then between *making legal claim to* and *claiming that* is that the former is a legal performance with direct legal consequences whereas the latter is often a mere piece of descriptive commentary with no legal force. Legally speaking, *making claim to* can itself make things happen. This sense of "claiming," then, might well be called "the performative sense." The legal power to claim (performatively) one's right or the things to which one has a right seems to be essential to the very notion of a right. A right to which one could not make claim (i.e., not even for recognition) would be a very "imperfect" right indeed!

Claiming that one has a right (what we can call "propositional claiming" as opposed to "performative claiming") is another sort of thing one can do with language, but it is not the sort of doing that characteristically has legal consequences. To claim that one has rights is to make an assertion that one has them, and to make it in such a manner as to demand or insist that they be recognized. In this sense of "claim" many things in addition to rights can be claimed; that is, many other kinds of proposition can be asserted in the claiming way. I can claim, for example, that you, he, or she has certain rights, or that Julius Caesar once had certain rights; or I can claim that certain statements are true, or that I have certain skills, or accomplishments, or virtually anything at all. I can claim that the earth is flat. What is essential to *claiming that* is the manner of assertion. One can assert without even caring very much whether anyone is listening, but part of the point of propositional claiming is to *make sure* people listen. When I claim to others that I know something, for example, I am not merely asserting it, but rather "obtruding my putative knowledge upon their attention, demanding that it be recognized, that appropriate notice be taken of it by those concerned. . . ."[6] Not every truth is properly assertable, much less claimable, in every context. To claim that something is the case in circumstances that justify no more than calm assertion is to behave like a boor. (This kind of boorishness, I might add, is probably less common in Nowheresville.) But not to claim in the appropriate circumstances that one has a right is to be spiritless or foolish. A list of "appropriate circumstances" would include occasions when one is challenged, when one's possession is denied, or seems insufficiently acknowledged or appreciated; and of course even in these circumstances, the claiming should be done only with an appropriate degree of vehemence.

Even if there are conceivable circumstances in which one would admit rights diffidently, there is no doubt that their characteristic use and that for which they are distinctively well suited, is to be claimed, demanded, affirmed, insisted upon. They are especially sturdy objects to "stand upon," a most useful sort of moral furniture. Having rights, of course, makes claiming possible; but it is claiming that gives rights their special moral significance. This feature of rights is connected in a way with the customary rhetoric about what it is to be a human being. Having rights enables us to "stand up like men," to look others in the eye, and to feel in some fundamental way the equal of anyone. To think of oneself as the holder of rights is not to be unduly but properly proud, to have that minimal self-respect that is necessary to be worthy of the

6. G. J. Warnock, "Claims to Knowledge," *Proceedings of the Aristotelian Society,* Supplementary Volume 36 (1962), p. 21.

love and esteem of others. Indeed, respect for persons (this is an intriguing idea) may simply be respect for their rights, so that there cannot be the one without the other; and what is called "human dignity" may simply be the recognizable capacity to assert claims. To respect a person then, or to think of him as possessed of human dignity, simply *is* to think of him as a potential maker of claims. Not all of this can be packed into a definition of "rights"; but these are *facts* about the possession of rights that argue well their supreme moral importance. More than anything else I am going to say, these facts explain what is wrong with Nowheresville.

We come now to the third interesting employment of the claiming vocabulary, that involving not the verb "to claim" but the substantive "a claim." What is to *have a claim* and how is this related to rights? I would like to suggest that *having a claim consists in being in a position to claim, that is, to make claim to* or *claim that.* If this suggestion is correct it shows the primacy of the verbal over the nominative forms. It links claims to a kind of activity and obviates the temptation to think of claims as *things,* on the model of coins, pencils, and other material possessions which we can carry in our hip pockets. To be sure, we often make or establish our claims by presenting titles, and these typically have the form of receipts, tickets, certificates, and other pieces of paper or parchment. The title, however, is not the same thing as the claim; rather it is the evidence that establishes the claim as valid. On this analysis, one might have a claim without ever claiming that to which one is entitled, or without even knowing that one has the claim; for one might simply be ignorant of the fact that one is in a position to claim; or one might be unwilling to exploit that position for one reason or another, including fear that the legal machinery is broken down or corrupt and will not enforce one's claim despite its validity.

Nearly all writers maintain that there is some intimate connection between having a claim and having a right. Some identify right and claim without qualification; some define "right" as justified or justifiable claim, others as recognized claim, still others as valid claim. My own preference is for the latter definition. Some writers, however, reject the identification of rights with valid claims on the ground that all claims as such are valid, so that the expression "valid claim" is redundant. These writers, therefore, would identify rights with claims *simpliciter.* But this is a very simple confusion. All claims, to be sure, are *put forward* as justified, whether they are justified in fact or not. A claim conceded even by its maker to have no validity is not a claim at all, but a mere demand. The highwayman, for example, *demands* his victim's money; but he hardly makes claim to it as rightfully his own.

But it does not follow from this sound point that it is redundant to qualify claims as justified (or as I prefer, valid) in the definition of a right; for it remains true that not all claims put forward as valid really are valid; and only the valid ones can be acknowledged as rights.

If having a valid claim is not redundant, i.e., if it is not redundant to pronounce *another's* claim valid, there must be such a thing as having a claim that is not valid. What would this be like? One might accumulate just enough evidence to argue with relevance and cogency that one has a right (or ought to be granted a right), although one's case might not be overwhelmingly conclusive. In such a case, one might have strong enough argument to be entitled to a hearing and given fair consideration.

When one is in this position, it might be said that one "has a claim" that deserves to be weighed carefully. Nevertheless, the balance of reasons may turn out to militate against recognition of the claim, so that the claim, which one admittedly had, and perhaps still does, is not a valid claim or right. "Having a claim" in this sense is an expression very much like the legal phrase "having a *prima facie* case." A plaintiff establishes a *prima facie* case for the defendant's liability when he establishes grounds that will be sufficient for liability unless outweighed by reasons of a different sort that may be offered by the defendant. Similarly, in the criminal law, a grand jury returns an indictment when it thinks that the prosecution has sufficient evidence to be taken seriously and given a fair hearing, whatever countervailing reasons may eventually be offered on the other side. That initial evidence, serious but not conclusive, is also sometimes called a *prima facie* case. In a parallel *"prima facie* sense" of "claim," having a claim to X is not (yet) the same as having a right to X, but is rather having a case of at least minimal plausibility that one has a right to X, a case that does establish a right, not to X, but to a fair hearing and consideration. Claims, so conceived, differ in degree: some are stronger than others. Rights, on the other hand, do not differ in degree; no one right is more of a right than another.[7]

Another reason for not identifying rights with claims *simply* is that there is a well-established usage in international law that makes a theoretically interesting distinction between claims and rights. Statesmen are sometimes led to speak of "claims" when they are concerned with the natural needs of deprived human beings in conditions of scarcity. Young orphans *need* good upbringings, balanced diets, education, and technical training everywhere in the world; but unfortunately there are many places where these goods are in such short supply that it is impossible to provision all who need them. If we persist, nevertheless, in speaking of these needs as constituting rights and not merely claims, we are committed to the conception of a right which is an entitlement *to* some good, but not a valid claim *against* any particular individual; for in conditions of scarcity there may be no determinate individuals who can plausibly be said to have a duty to provide the missing goods to those in need. J. E. S. Fawcett therefore prefers to keep the distinction between claims and rights firmly in mind. "Claims," he writes, "are needs and demands in movement, and there is a continuous transformation, as a society advances [toward greater abundance] of economic and social claims into civil and political rights . . . and not all countries or all claims are by any means at the same stage in the process."[8] The manifesto writers on the other side who seem to identify needs, or at least basic needs, with what they call "human rights," are more properly described, I think, as urging upon the world

7. This is the important difference between rights and mere claims. It is analogous to the difference between *evidence* of guilt (subject to degrees of cogency) and conviction of guilt (which is all or nothing). One can "have evidence" that is not conclusive just as one can "have a claim" that is not valid. "Prima-facieness" is built into the sense of "claim," but the notion of a "prima-facie right" makes little sense. On the latter point see A. I. Melden, *Rights and Right Conduct.* (Oxford: Basil Blackwell, 1959), pp. 18–20, and Herbert Morris, "Persons and Punishment," *The Monist,* Vol. 52 (1968), pp. 498–9.
8. J. E. S. Fawcett, "The International Protection of Human Rights," in *Political Theory and the Rights of Man.* D. D. Raphael (Ed.). (Bloomington: Indiana University Press, 1967), pp. 125 and 128.

community the moral principle that *all* basic human needs ought to be recognized as *claims* (in the customary *prima facie* sense) worthy of sympathy and serious consideration right now, even though, in many cases, they cannot yet plausibly be treated as *valid* claims, that is, as grounds of any other people's duties. This way of talking avoids the anomaly of ascribing to all human beings now, even those in pre-industrial societies, such "economic and social rights" as "periodic holidays with pay."[9]

Still for all of that, I have a certain sympathy with the manifesto writers, and I am even willing to speak of a special "manifesto sense" of "right," in which a right need not be correlated with another's duty. Natural needs are real claims if only upon hypothetical future beings not yet in existence. I accept the moral principle that to have an unfulfilled need is to have a kind of claim against the world, even if against no one in particular. A natural need for some good as such, like a natural desert, is always a reason in support of a claim to that good. A person in need, then, is always "in a position" to make a claim, even when there is no one in the corresponding position to do anything about it. Such claims, based on need alone, are "permanent possibilities of rights," the natural seed from which rights grow. When manifesto writers speak of them as if already actual rights, they are easily forgiven, for this is but a powerful way of expressing the conviction that they ought to be recognized by states here and now as potential rights and consequently as determinants of *present* aspirations and guides to *present* policies. That usage, I think, is a valid exercise of rhetorical license.

I prefer to characterize rights as valid claims rather than justified ones, because I suspect that justification is rather too broad a qualification. "Validity," as I understand it, is justification of a peculiar and narrow kind, namely justification within a system of rules. A man has a legal right when the official recognition of his claim (as valid) is called for by the governing rules. This definition, of course, hardly applies to moral rights, but that is not because the genus of which moral rights are a species is something other than *claims*. A man has a moral right when he has a claim the recognition of which is called for—not (necessarily) by legal rules—but by moral principles, or the principles of an enlightened conscience.

There is one final kind of attack on the generic identification of rights with claims, and it has been launched with great spirit in a recent article by H. J. McCloskey, who holds that rights are not essentially claims at all, but rather entitlements. The springboard of his argument is his insistence that rights in their essential character are always *rights to,* not *rights against:*

> My right to life is not a right against anyone. It is my right and by virtue of it, it is normally permissible for me to sustain my life in the face of obstacles. It does give rise to rights against others *in the sense* that others have or may come to have duties to refrain from killing me, but it is essentially a right of mine, not an infinite list of claims, hypothetical and actual, against an infinite number of actual, potential, and

9. As declared in Article 24 of *The Universal Declaration of Human Rights* adopted on December 10, 1948, by the General Assembly of the United Nations.

as yet nonexistent human beings. . . . Similarly, the right of the tennis club member to play on the club courts is a right to play, not a right against some vague group of potential or possible obstructors.[10]

The argument seems to be that since rights are essentially rights *to,* whereas claims are essentially claims *against,* rights cannot be claims, though they can be grounds for claims. The argument is doubly defective though. First of all, contrary to McCloskey, rights (at least legal claim-rights) *are* held *against* others. McCloskey admits this in the case of *in personam* rights (what he calls "special rights") but denies it in the case of *in rem* rights (which he calls "general rights"):

> Special rights are sometimes against specific individuals or institutions—e.g., rights created by promises, contracts, etc. . . . but these differ from . . . characteristic . . . general rights where the right is simply a right to. . . . [11]

As far as I can tell, the only reason McCloskey gives for denying that *in rem* rights are against others is that those against whom they would have to hold make up an enormously multitudinous and "vague" group, including hypothetical people not yet even in existence. Many others have found this a paradoxical consequence of the notion of *in rem* rights, but I see nothing troublesome in it. If a general rule gives me a right of noninterference in a certain respect against everybody, then there are literally hundreds of millions of people who have a duty toward me in that respect; and if the same general rule gives the same right to everyone else, then it imposes on me literally hundreds of millions of duties—or duties towards hundreds of millions of people. I see nothing paradoxical about this, however. The duties, after all, are negative; and I can discharge all of them at a stroke simply by minding my own business. And if all human beings make up one moral community and there are hundreds of millions of human beings, we should expect there to be hundreds of millions of moral relations holding between them.

McCloskey's other premise is even more obviously defective. There is no good reason to think that all *claims* are "essentially" *against,* rather than *to.* Indeed most of the discussion of claims above has been of claims *to,* and we have seen, the law finds it useful to recognize claims *to* (or "mere claims") that are not yet qualified to be claims *against,* or rights (except in a "manifesto sense" of "rights").

Whether we are speaking of claims or rights, however, we must notice that they seem to have two dimensions, as indicated by the prepositions "to" and "against," and it is quite natural to wonder whether either of these dimensions is somehow more fundamental or essential than the other. All rights seem to merge *entitlements to* do, have, omit, or be something with *claims against* others to act or refrain from acting in certain ways. In some statements of rights the entitlement is perfectly determinate

---

10. H. J. McCloskey, "Rights," *Philosophical Quarterly,* Vol. 15 (1965), p. 118.
11. *Loc. cit.*

(e.g., *to* play tennis) and the claim vague (e.g., *against* "some vague group of potential or possible obstructors"); but in other cases the object of the claim is clear and determinate (e.g., *against* one's parents) and the entitlement general and indeterminate (e.g., to be given a proper upbringing). If we mean by "entitlement" that *to* which one has a right and by "claim" something directed at those against whom the right holds (as McCloskey apparently does), then we can say that all claim-rights necessarily involve both, though in individual cases the one element or the other may be in sharper focus.

In brief conclusion: To have a right is to have a claim against someone whose recognition as valid is called for by some set of governing rules or moral principles. To have a *claim* in turn, is to have a case meriting consideration, that is, to have reasons or grounds that put one in a position to engage in performative and propositional claiming. The activity of claiming, finally, as much as any other thing, makes for self-respect and respect for others, gives a sense to the notion of personal dignity, and distinguishes this otherwise morally flawed world from the even worse world of Nowheresville.

Human Rights
and Civil Rights

REX MARTIN

It is striking the degree to which our ordinary day-to-day discussion of politics is permeated with talk of rights. We hear of women's right to control their own bodies set off against the rights of the unborn, of the right of privacy, of the rights of future generations, of the rights of persons versus the rights of property. Surely part of what is problematic in all these assertions and counterassertions is that the notion of a right is not itself clear. This difficulty is heightened when one feels that a different sense of "right" is being employed for different cases. Indeed, no point has given more trouble than the apparent different sense in which the term "right" is used in *human* right and in *legal* right.

I want to begin my paper with a consideration of what is probably the most influential of the current analytical theories of rights. In this theory a core sense of "right" (that of claim or valid claim) is identified and the sense of "right" is said to be the same between *human* rights and *legal* rights. The difference between them is accounted for, then, within a single generic theory of rights (of rights treated as claims).

In Feinberg's analysis, perhaps the best worked out of these accounts, rights as valid claims have two distinct dimensions: they are claims *to* something and, as claims on the specific duties of assignable people, they are claims *against* someone. A right in the full or proper sense is both these things; it is a merger of the two dimensions. Thus whatever is to be counted a human right, in the proper sense, must hold in both these dimensions.[1]

Rex Martin, "Human Rights and Civil Rights," *Philosophical Studies,* 37, No. 4, (1980), pp. 391–403. Copyright © 1980 by D. Reidel Publishing Co. Reprinted by permission of Kluwer Academic Publishers.

When it is said that a human right is a valid claim one means at a minimum that the thing claimed is endorsed by moral considerations. For this reason human rights are often regarded as a class of moral rights. But any such claim to a service (or a freedom from injury or a liberty) must hold good on other important counts in order to qualify as relevantly valid: The thing claimed must be morally endorsed for *all* persons; and that thing must be practicable and, hence, able to serve as a justifiable basis for calling on duties (of other people) in the fulfilling of that which is claimed. Only such claims-to as are fully valid in the way just described can properly figure in a human right. And, if we turn to the other main dimension of what can be called valid claims, that of claims *against,* it is clear such claims require that there be specific duties which fall on determinate individuals. Lacking these, claims-against could not take hold and would thereby be defective. The filling in of the requisite background need not, however, involve creating new duties; it may involve simply hooking on to existing ones. In both cases, though, a fully valid moral claim, hence a human right, will combine a valid claim *to* with a valid claim on or *against.*[2]

The important thing to note here is that in this account a moral claim can be valid even though it has not been "answered," so to speak, by governmental or by individual action; for the validity of the claim is in no way infirmed by the fact that the called for responses have not been forthcoming. A morally valid claim can be purely a claim, for it is possible to conceive any such claim as one which holds in the absence of practices of acknowledgment and promotion, and yet is fully valid as a claim.

Thus in assessing the thesis that human rights are valid claims we must test it by considering valid claims as claims, whether responded to or not. For the proposed thesis stands or falls on the point that morally valid claims, just in virtue of being morally valid, are rights and that human rights owe their status as rights solely to the element of valid claim. Hence the thesis analyzes human rights as morally valid claims (insofar as universal): Such rights can be conceived, without loss, as valid claims and nothing more.

A valid claim can exist solely in the domain of moral argument but that which satisfies the claim cannot. It cannot because what satisfies the claim is the maintenance of a course of action and such maintenance is not confined to the realm of argument. Simply because human rights (as valid claims) have the capacity to be theoretical entities, in the moral domain, which are then responded to (for example, in the law), a certain instability has crept into our conception of them. We should, if possible, attempt to fix the notion more firmly through analysis. I want to do so by canvassing the issue of what counts as an exemplification of a human right.

Let us imagine the case of travel. Suppose we were able to formulate matters fairly precisely here: We could distinguish travel from emigration; we could exclude some obvious cases of unlawful travel; we were able to add in a reasonably good exceptions clause (allowing for restrictions for reasons of public health or to avoid the dangers of a war zone—or of a bridge out). Not only this; we could show also a decisive moral endorsement of travel so conceived: At least up to the point that no morally good reasons could be advanced to prevent travel, as we have been conceiving it; whereas morally good reasons could be put forward that a practice of innocent travel, of the sort of specified, should be maintained. The idea of a liberty to travel enters the reflective consciousness of mankind as something morally endorsed and well grounded; the claim is valid: The liberty in question has an impeccable moral title, is widely practicable, the relevant duties are in place, etc.

It would seem then that there is a human right to travel. But the guard at the border or the agent at the passport office says no.

Now, clearly, what the balky official was doing did not satisfy the claim. But that wouldn't detract from the integrity of the claim; it would still be a valid one. Even if everyone acted as he did, the claim would still stand; there would be no defect in the claim, as a claim, on that account. (Though we would begin to suspect that the widespread assent to the claim was merely rhetorical.)

But the matter stands differently with a right: The right to travel would be vitiated *as a right* if it were not enforced or promoted at all. In such a case the right is a merely nominal one, a right that existed in name only but not in fact. A nominal right is in principle never an enforceable one; enforcement simply does not belong to its nature. Its permanent "recognition" could be assured (the liberty put in writing, enshrined in a Declaration or Bill of Rights, honored by lip service), but its perpetual nonenforcement would be equally assured. Such rights do not, as some have suggested, constitute a special class of rights.[3] Rather, they constitute a degenerate and limiting case; they are, properly speaking, rights only on paper and nowhere else.

Hence we regard total nonenforcement as infirming the right, as rendering it defective. Let us take a further step. It was recognition, of some appropriate sort, that allowed us to describe the right in question as even a nominal one. Were a morally valid claim to lose that too—the recognition itself—we would have to say that it had ceased to be a right altogether. And if we supposed that it never had been recognized at all, we would have to say simply that it never was a right. We do not, then, regard a right simply as a morally valid claim; rather it is more like a combination of claim with what it takes to satisfy the claim.

The defender of the view I am criticizing might have here a ready reply. He could say that what my argument licensed was merely the conclusion that there is not, or never had been, a legal right in such cases of non-recognition. But the matter is different, he could say, with a human right.

This would be a damaging rejoinder for him to make; it supposes that legal rights differ significantly from human rights on the point at issue: the existence of appropriate mechanisms of recognition and promotion. Thus, whatever a legal right as valid claim might be, it does appear to include those very things which are (in this rejoinder) specifically excluded from moral rights as valid claims. This suggests, in turn, that "claim" does not have the same sense in the one case that it has in the other. Such a rejoinder, then, would diminish appreciably the attraction of one of the contentions put forward originally on behalf of the theory of rights as valid claims, where it was alleged that this theory gave us a univocal sense of "rights," one moreover that was capable of capturing both legal and human rights under a single generic heading.

More important, the rejoinder is beside the point. For it was not said in the discussion of the example cited, the liberty to travel, that this right was to be regarded as a legal one: The suggestion, rather, was that it was a moral or human right. And the argument there was perfectly general, covering without distinction moral as well as legal rights.

To sharpen the argument, however, let us direct it specifically to moral rights. (a) Moral rights which are more than merely nominal are appropriately promoted, as maintained ways of acting, etc., and appropriately enforced. Correspondingly, non-promotion or non-enforcement infirms such a right *as a right*. For a moral right would be a merely nominal right if it were not promoted or maintained at all. (b) Take away that thing which gives the nominal (moral) right the little status it has, that qualifies it as a right, though only a nominal one, and you have no right left. (c) And were the thing in question never even recognized as a morally accredited way of acting it would have failed to be a right at all.

This argument suggests that the concept of a human right includes within it practices of recognition and promotion of some appropriate sort: These things are internal to the concept in that they are necessarily considered in determining whether any such right has been instantiated. And since a morally valid claim would fail to instantiate a human right at precisely the point where that claim is just a claim, it follows, contrary to the analysis we have been examining, that a human right is not simply a morally valid claim.

A morally valid claim, when effectively recognized and maintained, is a claim *plus* something else (the "something else" being precisely what is lacking in the claim considered simply as a claim). A claim is not defective in the absence of these things, but a right is. A human right is defective, not as a claim but as a right, in the absence of appropriate practices of recognition and maintenance. The absolute difference between morally valid claims and human rights, then, is that rights do, and claims do not, include such practices within their concept.

Of course, it is not implausible to say that a morally valid claim could appropriately secure a way of acting simply by qualities it has, by elements in the claim: by the fact of endorsement in accordance with moral principles or the fact of widescale practicability, or what have you. I grant this, but these elements would do no securing if they weren't recognized (or if they didn't help to maintain the way of acting in question). The point is that if we focus just on the claim, and on the elements that make for its validity, then we leave out features that would qualify such a claim as a right.

It is possible, though, to restate the thesis that human rights are morally valid claims so as to make it effective against this particular line of attack. If a proper claim with some sort of appropriate recognition, etc., can be a right, then there could be rights which are peculiarly moral in character. Some rights are secured by law, some by social convention or arrangement, some by moral recognition and the practices of maintenance appropriate to moral life (education, the development of character, reproof, encouragement, putting oneself imaginatively in the place of others, etc.). Here the notion of what is to count as morally valid is "thickened" so as to include those very points (acceptance, promotion and maintenance) which had earlier been urged against the valid claims thesis. Still, a distinction would remain between ways of action secured by moral considerations alone and those that involved recognition in law and maintenance by governmental action as well. So the crucial sense in which human rights are morally valid claims is that they are the securing of ways of acting by normative measures but not necessarily by legal ones.

Now, clearly, this restatement amounts to a rejection of the thesis from which we started (in that human rights are no longer being regarded merely as valid claims, whether responded to or not). We cannot, therefore, regard it as an acceptable restatement of that thesis: for the hallmark of the approach there was that recognition and maintenance, under which heading we also would put enforcement, were specifically excluded from any part in the characterization of "a right" in the full or proper sense. It was precisely this exclusion that made talk of valid claims distinctive and gave the thesis philosophical bite. Even so, the position as restated does seem to capture what is intended by many of those who characterize human rights as morally valid claims. And this seems justification enough to consider it.

I do not think, however, that the thesis even when restated is adequate. My reason can best be brought out by considering an important feature which it shares with the argument I have been advancing. In both cases it is accepted that appropriate practices of recognition and maintenance are intrinsic to human rights. Hence I would want to argue that, insofar as human rights claims are addressed principally to governments, we have to regard practices of governmental recognition and promotion as included within the notion of human rights. They are (or have become) a part of the concept in question. On this view, the right is not just the claim, to which there are added the "called for" protective devices; instead, the right is the claim *as* recognized in law and maintained by governmental action. And the issue whether something is a human right, or whether such rights "exist" or whether people "have" them, cannot be decided without consideration of the whole range of relevant practices, which include recognition in law and governmental maintenance of the claimed way of acting. Such practices are ingredient in the very notion of what it is for something to be a human right, or so my argument is meant to show.

Many people are not prepared to accept this. They will balk at the contention that human rights require governmental practices of recognition and maintenance. But this point about government was not inserted capriciously or casually into the human rights picture. It is there as the result of an argument.

Specifically, I argued that the notion of a right (hence a human right) contains the element of appropriate practices of recognition and maintenance within it. The determination of what is appropriate for each kind of right then becomes the exact point at issue. Here I argued that since human rights are conventionally asserted as claims against governments, governmental practices of recognition and promotion are necessarily included within the range of relevant practices.[4] It follows, then, that this kind of practice is specifically to be considered, as one of those appropriate to human rights, and it can be said to that degree to belong to the very notion of such a right. A human rights claim which lacks such recognition is still a claim, and may even be a morally valid one; but it cannot qualify as a human right.

I see no way of effectively turning this argument short of denying that human rights are addressed to governments in particular. Thus Cranston does not mention governments at all in his characterization of human rights. On his view human rights are rights of all individuals *against all individuals*: "To say that all men have a right to life is to impose on all men the duty of respecting human life."[5] A similar position is taken by Raphael, who distinguishes two senses of "universal moral right." "In the stronger sense it means a right of all men against all men; in the weaker sense it means simply a right of all men, but not necessarily against all men."[6] The latter rights involve the responsibilities of states and are viewed as "rights of the citizen." Universal moral rights in the stronger sense are viewed as "rights of the citizen." Universal moral rights in the stronger sense are viewed as genuine "rights of man" (p. 66)—although Raphael thinks it appropriate to include rights of the citizen in international declarations of rights.

Cranston's view ignores history. The great human rights manifestoes were intended to impose restraints upon governments. Individuals were involved as beneficiaries of these restraints but, for the most part, were not the parties to whom the manifestoes were addressed. Cranston's view also has the implausible consequence that the right to a fair trial, which he gives as an example of a human right (in Raphael PTRM, 43, and again in WHR?, 65), is a right which one has against all people rather than against governments in particular, especially one's own.

The example is by no means atypical; others are ready to hand. The right to travel (Universal Declaration, article 13) certainly contemplates the absence of restraints imposed by governments; indeed insofar as the issue is the liberty to travel, as distinct from the wherewithal to do so, it is primarily government that is addressed. And the right to freedom from the injury of torture is peculiarly held against governments; this is clear from the context—court proceedings and, in particular, punishment—in which the right is set (article 5). The same pattern holds with rights to the provision of a service. The duty of providing social security is explicitly enjoined on governments (articles 22, 25), and the duty to provide for elementary education, which "shall be compulsory" (article 26), is clearly addressed, in this crucial detail at least, to states in particular. (On the right to an education see also article 13 of the UN's International Covenant on Economic, Social and Cultural Rights—found in WHR?, 101–102.)

It seems, then, that government's being an intended addressee of human rights claims is too deeply imbedded to be erased. Whether we look at details of specific rights, as we've just done, or at the theory of human rights (including its actual history),[7] we find that government is in fact the principal addressee. So a consideration of the relevant governmental practices is never a dispensable or even a negligible matter as regards the human rights status of these moral claims.

It is, of course, true that some human rights claims are "*double-barreled*" (the term is Feinberg's, PPA, 96); thus the right to life (as a freedom from injury) is addressed both to the "world at large" as a demand that individuals respect life and to the state as a demand for its respect—in the form of legal security and enforcement for protection of life (see PPA, 96, 103–104). It would be a serious mistake, then, to leave the individual out completely as an addressee of human rights.

Among the "*double-barreled*" human rights, the right to freedom from the injury of torture is probably properly placed. In the UN's International Covenant on Civil and Political Rights (in article 7, found in WHR?, 111) the only point added to the original language, of 1948, respecting the right not to be tortured is that "no one shall be subjected without his free consent to medical or scientific experimentation." Even here, though, where the norm is addressed to individual persons (as well as to governments), there is a claim against governments to see that this particular way of acting, on the part of individual persons toward others, is effectively maintained. Thus, the right to life or the right to be free from torture is, insofar as it is claimed against individual persons, ultimately also a claim against government, for backup promotion and maintenance.

Now, it may even be that for some universal moral rights the role of government is incidental or even non-existent. The moral right to be told the truth (or at least not lied to) or the moral right to gratitude for benefits provided or, perhaps, the moral right to have promises kept are examples. Such rights differ from, say, the right not to be killed—even when we're talking about the latter right as held against individuals— in being rights maintained by "conscience." They are moral rights merely and in no way claims against government. Interestingly, though, it is often in these very cases that, while we are willing to call such rights moral rights, we would tend to withhold the name of human (or natural) right.[8]

There is sound basis for saying, then, that human rights norms (i.e., claims) are addressed to governments in particular, most of them to governments primarily. And human rights can be distinguished from other universal moral rights in this very circumstance.

It is not clear, however, that from the point just made about addressees it follows that governmental practices are *necessarily* relevant let alone that they are properly regarded as included within the *concept* of human rights. Thus Bernard Mayo, though he stresses that human rights are principally claimed of governments and not of men in general (pp. 227, 231, 234–235), alleges this is so for "historical" rather than "conceptual" reasons (p. 233, and also 235).[9] I cannot follow him on this point. It may be that our conception of human rights might have been different from what it is. In any event, it is admittedly a conception that came into being at a certain time (somewhere between Ockham and Hobbes) and has had a definite history (natural rights theory, the eighteenth-century declarations, nineteenth-century criticisms, human rights theory and practice today). It is even true that what Hobbes intended by his talk of natural rights (and presumably meant by "a right") is quite different from what we mean and intend today with roughly the same language. But none of this justifies saying that governments and public law are subject to rights claims for reasons that are not contained in the notion of human rights.

How is the matter to be decided? We could begin by recalling that human rights typically are not claims made on men in general. There is, we also should note, an important asymmetry between the claims-to part and the claims-against part of a complete (or full) valid moral claim. It may be that a valid moral claim-to will have an unrestricted universality (in that it holds good for everyone—for the ground of the claim is simply a title to something or other given to all persons in accordance with moral principles), yet it does not follow automatically here that the claim-against element will be similarly universal. For example, all human beings are, or were at one time, children and all have (or had) the appropriate claims to care and concern: to nourishment, upbringing, and so on. But these claims on the part of each child are principally addressed, not to anyone and everyone, but to that child's parents in particular. Rights so restricted are called special (rather than general) rights.[10] I want to suggest that something like this functions in the case of human rights; they too are special rights. The claim-to element is unrestricted: It holds of every person. But the claim-against element is typically restricted: Not all persons, but only some, are addressed as having the moral duty in question.

There is an important reason, which needs bringing out, for precisely this restriction. It is assumed in talk of human rights that men live in societies. Many of the goods identified in claims-to are goods obtained and enjoyed in a social setting. Here claims against others are for the most part addressed not to individuals as such but, rather, to individuals insofar as they exercise the powers of some assigned agency in that particular social setting. Such claims-against hold not against everyone individually but against an organized society; and it is of the institutions—or agencies—of that society that satisfaction is expected.

In cases of this sort, individual persons play only a secondary and sometimes incidental role. And since individuals *per se* are not addressed here in claims-against, it follows that the class of all persons—the class of all individuals considered simply as individuals—is not the primary addressee either. Hence there is a definite sense in which the universality of human rights is not defined by the (universal) class of all persons: It is not when we have regard to the class of those addressed in such claims. Moreover, the group of claimants, though anyone possibly could be included in it, is actually—for any given society—those who live in that society or who are significantly involved with it. Even if some other person actually did the claiming, it would be done on their behalf; for they are the specific group to whom is due that which was claimed of the society in question. These important points, though little noted, set a powerful constraint on the sense in which human rights can be regarded as universal.

The role and character of government in human rights claims follows from these facts. Admittedly, it is not so much governments as it is organized societies that are selected out by claims-against. The point, though, is that such societies are correctly regarded as *politically* organized; and it is governments that typically play, and have played, a major role in such organization. Thus government enters the human rights picture as the organizer, and as one of the major agencies, of the kind of organized society against which a human rights claim is characteristically lodged.

Even if an organized society happened to be big enough and complex enough and overarching enough to be so addressed, but did not have over it a government in the conventional sense (lacking certain coercive mechanisms or, perhaps, a territory of operation), it would still in some sense be a politically organized society. And there would still be significant analogues to government as we understand it. Thus the addressing of claims would not be markedly different from the way I've been describing even in an anarchist society (so long, that is, as it is—relatively speaking—an organized society and not a disorganized one).

What I have argued, then, is that those institutions and agencies which are central to organized society are necessarily relevant to the status of human rights claims in all societies. In any given society it is these institutions that count.

If my analysis is correct, or even plausible, we have a reason for the central place occupied by government in our concept of human rights; given this reason, we find it natural that recognition and maintenance by governmental action—the satisfaction principally sought in human rights claims—should be relativized to particular societies. For these claims, insofar as we have regard to their primary addressee, are satisfied by laws having an appropriately universal scope within a particular society. Such a law would exist when, for example, a freedom to travel on the part of every citizen (or preferably, every person) was recognized in the law of that society and scrupulously enforced. We can call any such operative and universal legal right (that is, universal within a given society) a civil right.[11]

Civil rights fit the picture here simply because there is a significant restriction on universality inherent in the concept of a human right. Civil rights reflect the fact that human rights typically are special rights and are claimed, on moral grounds which hold good for all persons, against particular politically organized societies—specifically, against governments. And the question whether a particular valid and universal moral claim has been appropriately responded to in law is answered by considering the class of civil rights. Such rights, when molded and subsequently shaped under the influence of these claims, are the kind of right involved. Their existence is a necessary element in a morally valid claim's being (or becoming) a human right.

In a society which has no civil rights (e.g., a caste society, in particular one with a slave caste) there are no human rights. They are not observed there. If a particular civil right is missing in a given country, then lacking this necessary ingredient, the human right fails to jell or it dissolves, for that country or for that time and place, and we are at best left with a moral claim (presumably valid) that something should be a civil right.

There is, we see upon reflection, an irreducible duality to human rights. On the one side they are morally validated claims to some benefit or other. Each claim is an endorsement of a way of acting: as morally worthwhile, as practicable, as supportable by existing duties. Each is, in effect, a set of good moral reasons why a way of acting open to all ought to be recognized, of reasons why it ought not be prevented and ought, indeed, be maintained. Such a moral claim can be wholly sufficient as a claim and fully valid without entailing that it is recognized or maintained by those against whom the claim is made; this feature preserves the integrity of the moral element in the case of any human right. On the other side such rights require recognition in law and promotion by government of the way of acting claimed; the addition of these features, which serves to constitute the claim a right, also serves to maintain the integrity of the political-legal element. Neither side is dispensable in a human right.

On its legal side a human right would have the form of a civil right. If there are any human rights at all, it follows that there are civil rights in at least some countries.[12]

University of Kansas

Notes

1. For his discussion of rights as valid claims, see Joel Feinberg, *Social Philosophy,* Foundations of Philosophy Series (Prentice-Hall, Englewood Cliffs, NJ, 1973), pp. 64–67 (hereafter: SP, 64–67). Roughly the same discussion is found in Feinberg's paper, "The Nature and Value of Rights,"

Journal of Value Inquiry, 4 (1970), pp. 253–255 (hereafter: JVI, 253–255). For the "merger" thesis in particular, see JVI, 256–257, and also Joel Feinberg, "The Rights of Animals and Unborn Generations," in W. Blackstone (Ed.), *Philosophy and Environmental Crisis* (University of Georgia Press, Athens, 1974). pp. 43–44 (hereafter: in Blackstone PEC, 43–44).

2. Feinberg *defines* "human rights" as "generically moral rights of a fundamentally important kind held equally by all human beings, unconditionally and unalterably" (SP, 85). For his discussion of human rights as morally valid claims, see SP, Ch. 6 (esp. pp. 84–85), the argument of his paper in Blackstone PEC, and also Joel Feinberg, "Voluntary Euthanasia and the Inalienable Right to Life," *Philosophy and Public Affairs* 7 (1978), pp. 96–97 (hereafter: PPA, 96–97).

   In Feinberg's view some of the rights listed in the UN's Universal Declaration of Human Rights (of 1948) are full-fledged moral rights; others—the ones he calls "manifesto" rights—lay claims to things which are not fully practicable at present; hence these claims are at best only emerging or proto-rights. Chief among these truncated or "manifesto" rights are most of those listed among the "social and economic rights" (in articles 22–27) of the UN Declaration (see JVI, 255; SP, 67, 94–95).

3. For one example see Maurice Cranston, "Human Rights, Real and Supposed," in D. D. Raphael (Ed.), *Political Theory and the Rights of Man,* pp.47–48, esp. p. 48 (hereafter Raphael PTRM, 47–48).

4. "[A]s a matter of fact men speak of their moral rights mainly when advocating their incorporation into a legal system. . . ." (H. L. A. Hart, "Are There Any Natural Rights?," *Philosophical Review* 64 (1955), p. 177 [hereafter: PR, 177]). Human rights are explicitly represented, in the preamble to the UN *Declaration,* as rights to be secured "among the peoples of Member States"; they are enjoined on governments, in particular, as rights that "should be protected by the rule of law." In the two United Nations Covenants (1966, entered into force 1976), one on "economic and social rights" and the other on "civil and political rights," it is the "States Parties," as they are called, that expressly undertake to do these things, as specified in the earlier Universal Declaration (1948).

5. Maurice Cranston, *What Are Human Rights?,* 2d ed. (Bodley Head, London, 1973), p. 69 (hereafter: WHR?, 69). For Cranston's view here see also pp. 6–7, 21, 67, 69 (in WHR?), and his "Human Rights: A Reply to Professor Raphael" (in Raphael PTRM, 95–100).

6. D. D. Raphael, "Human Rights, Old and New," in Raphael PTRM, 65. See also his "The Rights of Man and the Rights of the Citizen," in Raphael PTRM, esp. 108–110, 112–113. A view similar to that of Raphael and Cranston is also found in Richard Wasserstrom, "Rights, Human Rights, and Racial Discrimination," *Journal of Philosophy* 61 (1964), p. 632.

7. See Mordecai Roshwald, "The Concept of Human Rights," *Philosophy and Phenomenological Research* 19 (1958–1959), pp.354–379, esp. pp. 370–371, 379.

8. "Declarations of the Rights of Man did not include his right to be told the truth, to have promises kept which had been made to him, to receive gratitude from those he had benefited, etc. The common thread among the variety of natural rights is their political character" (Margaret Macdonald, "Natural Rights," in A. I. Melden (Ed.), *Human Rights* (Belmont, CA: Wadsworth, 1970, p. 52).

9. The citations here are to B. Mayo, Symposium on "Human Rights" II, *Proceedings of the Aristotelian Society,* Supplementary Volume 39 (1965), pp. 219–236. This paper is reprinted in shortened form as "What are human rights?," in Raphael PTRM, 68–80 (see esp. pp. 73, 75, 77–78; also 78–80).

10. The distinction of special/general rights is drawn from Hart (PR, esp. 187–188). My discussion here is also indebted to William Nelson's analysis (in his "Special Rights, General Rights, and Social Justice," *Philosophy and Public Affairs* 3 (1974), pp.410–430).

11. I am following T. H. Green in using the term "civil rights" to designate those legal rights which attach to *all* persons within a society. See, for example, his Lectures on the Principles of Political Obligation (Longmans, London, impression of 1960). Sections 24–25, pp.43–44.

12. For an extended discussion of Feinberg's views see my "The Nature of Human Rights," in *Proceedings of the 1979 IVR World Congress* (forthcoming). The present paper draws on R. Martin and I. W. Nickel, "Recent Work on the Concept of Rights," *American Philosophical Quarterly* 17 (1980); see esp. Section 3.

An earlier version of the first part of "Human Rights and Civil Rights" was presented at the meeting of the American Philosophical Association, Western Division, in Denver, CO, in April 1979; earlier versions of the paper were also read to colleagues at several universities. I appreciate the comments provided on those occasions. And I am especially indebted, for helpful written criticisms, to Richard DeGeorge, Gerry MacCallum, Jim Nickel, Janet Sisson, Carl Wellman, and Mike Young.

A New
Conception
of
Human Rights

CARL WELLMAN

The demand that individual privacy be respected is becoming more common and more insistent in our age. This probably reflects a rapidly increasing need for privacy arising from converging ecological, cultural, technical and social changes. The population explosion together with modern urbanization have made it much more difficult for the individual to get away, physically and psychologically, from the crowd of strangers around him. The growing allegiance to political individualism and moral autonomy have caused the individual to resent and resist legal regulation and social interference more intensely. At a time when bugging and other techniques of surveillance have been perfected to an alarming degree, the development of computers enables us to store and retrieve vastly increased amounts of information about any specified individual in even very large populations. Finally, as organizations have grown larger in size and more bureaucratic in structure, their tendency to invade the life of the individual has grown apace.

In the United States, whatever may be the case in other societies, the legal system has responded to these changes by relying more and more heavily upon the constitutional right to privacy. Only recently has the student's right to privacy been protected by legal restrictions upon the kinds of information that may be put into his academic file, the length of time potentially adverse material may be kept in his file, and the conditions under which it may be released without his written consent. The bugging of one's premises or telephone is now recognized as a violation of the prohibition in the Fourth Amendment against unreasonable searches and seizures. And in the landmark decision of *Roe v. Wade* (410 US 113), the Supreme Court found state laws prohibiting abortion during the first six months of pregnancy a violation of the pregnant woman's constitutional right to privacy.

Since the constitution does not explicitly mention any right to privacy, one may wonder why the Supreme Court has repeatedly recognized it as a fundamental legal right. In the earlier case of *Griswold v. Connecticut* (381 US 479), it had been successfully argued that the right to privacy is one of the unenumerated rights retained by the people and guaranteed to them by the Ninth Amendment. Since these rights are said to be "retained by" the people, they are taken to be rights prior to and independent of the constitution and to any laws made pursuant thereto. In short, the legal right to privacy is legally and morally grounded in the human right to privacy.

Unfortunately, any such appeal to human rights, whether made within a legal system or in the arena of political debate, raises at least three awkward philosophical questions. First, how do we know that there really is any human right to privacy? It is not just that there is widespread disagreement about the assertion, "there is a human right to privacy"; philosophers and jurists have not given us any convincing account of the kind of evidence that could establish rationally the truth or falsehood of this statement. Second, assuming that there is a human right to privacy, what duties or obligations does it imply? It might imply that the state ought to establish and enforce a legal right to privacy or merely that it ought to refrain from invading the privacy of those subject to its jurisdiction. It might or might not imply that one state has an obligation to put economic or political pressure upon another state to cause that state to respect the privacy of the citizens of that second state. The legal philosopher has provided no helpful principles or method for determining just what the practical implications of any human right are. Third, precisely how is the content of the human right to privacy to be defined? Not only is the concept of privacy obscure and unexplained, it is far from clear what it means to say that someone has a *right to* privacy. Does this mean that second parties ought not to invade one's privacy or that it is never wrong to resist such invasions or both or neither of these things?

In this chapter, I propose to focus my attention on the third problem: How is the content of the human right to privacy to be defined? What concerns me is not so much the correct definition of this particular human right as the understanding of the way in which the content of any human right may best be conceived. For only if we can achieve a clear conception of the content of any specified human right can we fully understand what it means to assert or deny the existence of that right. And understanding what assertions of human rights mean is an essential preliminary to understanding what sort of evidence is required to establish their truth and what they logically imply.

The problem of defining the precise content of a mentioned right occurs in the law much as it does in the appeal to human rights. Just as we speak glibly of the human rights to privacy, security of person and an adequate standard of living, so we speak of the legal rights to life, free speech, and the equal protection of the laws. How, then, does the practising lawyer or presiding judge know precisely what in every detail is meant by such mere names and catch phrases? Often he does not; that is what lawsuits are all about. Nevertheless, this problem is much less serious in the law than in the sphere of human rights. Why?

The law provides two reasonably effective solutions to this problem of defining the content of any legal right, one practical and the other theoretical. Legal rights are institutional; they are created, defined and maintained by the legal system in some society. Hence, whenever their content proves to be insufficiently defined to cope with some new situation or case, they can be *re*defined by the legal institutions, particularly the legislature and the courts, that originally created them and continue to sustain them. Thus through a growing body of statutes and precedents, legal rights gradually achieve a precision and specificity sadly lacking in human rights. This sort of practical solution is not possible in the case of human rights. Since these rights, if they exist at all, exist prior to and independently of society and its institutions, they cannot be rendered determinate by the vote of any philosophical congress or the definition of any jurist. Fortunately, jurisprudence also offers a more theoretical solution to this problem. Wesley Hohfeld has identified certain legal conceptions that can be used to define, precisely and unambiguously, the content of any legal right.

Hohfeld identified and illustrated, but refused to define, eight fundamental legal conceptions—four conceptions of legal advantages and four of legal disadvantages. Since possessing a legal right is obviously having some sort of advantage in the law, it is the first four that primarily concern us here. Let us review them briefly. Our review is at one and the same time an articulation of four legal concepts and a characterization of four legal realities. They are:

1. *A legal liberty.* One party x has a legal liberty in face of some second party y to perform some action A if and only if x has no legal duty to y to refrain from doing A. I have, for example, the legal liberty in face of Professor Tay to use her name in this example; I do not, however, have the legal liberty of referring to her in any libelous manner. Let us suppose that I have secretly, and profitably, contracted with Professor Kamenka to mention him rather than Professor Tay at this point. I would still have the legal liberty in face of Professor Tay to use her name here, for I have no legal duty *to her* to refrain from doing so. But I would not have the legal liberty vis-à-vis Professor Kamenka to mention Professor Tay here, for under our contract I have a legal duty to him not to do so.

2. *A legal claim.* One party x has a legal claim against some second party y that y do some action A if and only if y has a legal duty to x to do A. Thus, I have a legal claim against Jones, to whom I loaned ten dollars on the understanding that he repay me today; similarly, I have a legal claim against Smith, whoever Smith may be, that he not strike me.

3. *A legal power.* One party x has a legal power over some second party y to bring about some specific legal consequence C for y if and only if some voluntary action of x would be legally recognized as having this consequence for y. For example, a policeman has the legal power over a fleeing suspect to place him under arrest, and

the owner of a car has the legal power over someone offering to buy his car of making him the new owner of the car.

4. *A legal immunity.* One party x has a legal immunity against some second party y from some specified legal consequence C if and only if y lacks the legal power to do any action whatsoever that would be recognized by the law as having the consequence C for x. Thus, I have a legal immunity against my wife's renouncing my United States citizenship, but I lack a legal immunity against her spending the monies in our joint bank account.

These, roughly indicated and briefly illustrated, are the four legal advantages Hohfeld takes to be fundamental in the law.[1] (The four corresponding legal disadvantages are a legal no-claim, a legal duty, a legal liability and a legal disability.)

Hohfeld shows us in quotation after quotation how the expression "a right" is used almost indiscriminately to refer to any one of these four legal advantages. No one who has studied Hohfeld can imagine for a moment that the content of the right to life is simply life. He forces us to ask whether the right to life is essentially the liberty to defend one's life when under attack or the claim against being killed by another or the power to sue in the courts for legal protection of one's life or all of these or none of them. His conceptual analysis does not, of course, tell us precisely what the content of this or any other legal right is; only a detailed study of the law of the land can tell us that. What his fundamental legal conceptions do for us is to show us what questions we must ask in order to arrive at a clear understanding of the content of any legal right and to provide us with a terminology in which we can formulate our answers in the most helpful way. There are two very important reasons why it is particularly helpful to define the content of any legal right in Hohfeld's terms. First, such a formulation renders the modality or modalities of any right unambiguous. There is a very real legal difference between a liberty and a claim, or a liberty and a power, or a claim and an immunity. Any vocabulary that does not distinguish between liberty-rights and claim-rights, power-rights and immunity-rights, describes the legal realities inadequately and invites conceptual confusion. Secondly, such a formulation translates the content of any right into practical terms. Each of Hohfeld's fundamental legal conceptions refers to some action. For instance, a legal liberty is a liberty to do some action A and a legal power is the power to perform some action with the legal consequence C. Because Hohfeld's conceptions focus upon actions, they are especially appropriate to the law, which regulates and facilitates human actions.

Reflection upon considerations like these has led me to formulate two heuristic principles to guide my investigation of human rights. Since the law has solved the problem of defining the content of its rights better than ethics has, I will take legal rights as my model of human rights. And since Hohfeld provides a terminology for defining legal rights in unambiguous and practical terms, the most theoretically precise and practically fruitful conception of legal rights will be articulated in terms of his fundamental legal conceptions.

1. W. N. Hohfeld, *Fundamental Legal Conceptions As Applied in Judicial Reasoning, and Other Legal Essays,* W. W. Cook (Ed.). (New Haven, 1919, reprinted 1923), pp. 35–64.

Precisely how one can best translate the language of legal rights into Hohfeld's legal advantages is a matter for much debate. Presumably we would like our philosophical analysis of the concept of a legal right to preserve all or most of those features of legal rights we presuppose in our pre-philosophical thinking about them. For one thing, a legal right seems to be permissive for its possessor. In contract with my legal duty to pay my taxes whether I wish to do so or not, my right to free speech permits, but does not require, me to speak out on controversial political issues. It is this feature that Thomas Hobbes tries to capture by defining a right as a liberty. Again, a legal right of one party imposes one or more duties upon some second party. Thus, the creditor's right to be repaid imposes a duty upon the debtor to repay him. On this model, Wesley Hohfeld identifies a legal right with a legal claim of x against y, the correlative of a corresponding legal duty of y to x. Third, the possessor of any legal right can typically choose to have his right enforced by society. Thomas Holland accordingly defines a legal right as the power of influencing the acts of another by the force of society, specifically through its legal system. The most obvious instance is the legal power of the possessor to sue in the courts for remedy in the event that his right is threatened or violated. Fourth, a legal right is usually secured to its possessor by society. At the very least, the possessor must be legally immune to the annihilation of his right at the mere whim of any second party. Jurists have tended to fasten on one of these features of our thinking about legal rights and build it into their definitions of "a right," thereby ignoring or rejecting the other aspects of our pre-philosophical thinking. Debate then centres on the issue of which one of these features is most important, even essential, to legal rights. I propose to preserve all four of these features, if I can, because all four are normally taken for granted in our thinking about rights and all four are important in the legal reality to which "a right" refers. Rather than cut our conception of a legal right down to a single fundamental legal conception, I conceive of a legal right as a cluster of legal liberties, claims, powers, and immunities.

But how can anything as complex as this constitute *a* legal right? What unifies any right is its core. At the centre of any legal right stand one or more legal advantages that define the essential content of the right. Change the core and any remaining right would no longer be this same right. At the core of my right to be repaid is my legal claim to repayment. At the core of my right to free speech is my legal liberty of speaking out on controversial issues. At the core of my right to sell my car is my legal power of transferring ownership in my car to the second party of my choice. When we classify rights as claim-, power- or immunity-rights, it is to their defining cores that we refer. Whatever other legal elements may be contained in any right, they belong to this right because of their relation to its core. Thus, a legal right is not a mere aggregate or collection of disparate legal liberties, claims, powers and immunities; it is a system of legal advantages tied to its defining core.

What are the strings that tie some legal advantage to the core of a right? Upon reflection, it seems to be that every associated liberty, claim, power or immunity contributes some measure of freedom or control over the core to the possessor of the right. Thus, my legal liberty of accepting repayment from the debtor gives me the freedom to cooperate with my debtor should he choose to fulfil my core claim against him. My immunity from having my core claim terminated at the whim of my debtor and my power to sue him should he refuse to repay me both give me control over my legal claim against him, but in different ways. How many such associated elements there are and of what sorts is not a matter to be decided by philosophical analysis; that all depends on the detailed facts of the legal system. Clustered around the core of any legal right, then, are a number of associated legal advantages that give various sorts of freedom and control with respect to that core to the possessor of the right.

Freedom and control are not unrelated; they are two aspects of a single phenomenon. There can be no genuine freedom without control and no real control without freedom. It is not just that I am not free to do or refrain from doing something as long as my action is under the control of others; it is also that my freedom to do or refrain from doing requires that I have some measure of control over their attempts to prevent me from acting or to force me to act against my will. Again, I cannot have control over some part of my life without the freedom to choose and act in this area. Perhaps the most apt label for this totality of freedom and control is "autonomy" in the sense of self-government. Accordingly, I conceive of a legal right as a system of legal autonomy, a cluster of legal elements that together give its possessor legal freedom with respect to and control over its defining core.

Taking legal rights, thus conceived, as my model, my plan is to develop an analogous conception of human rights. My first step must be to identify and define ethical analogues of Hohfeld's fundamental legal conceptions. Just as he distinguished between legal liberties, claims, powers and immunities, so I hope to define ethical liberties, claims, powers and immunities.

1. *An ethical liberty.* A party has an ethical liberty to perform some action *A* if and only if he does not have any duty not to do *A*. I shall not attempt to define the word "duty" here, but I do wish to point out that a duty, in the strict sense, must be grounded in specifically moral reasons and that it need not be a duty *to* any assignable second party. I have the ethical liberties of dressing as I please, within the bounds of decency, of spending my spare cash as I wish, and of attending the church of my choice.

2. *An ethical claim.* One party *x* has an ethical claim against some second party *y* that *y* perform some action A if and only if *y* has a duty to *x* to do *A*. Again, I shall leave the word "duty" undefined, but I must say a word about what makes a duty a duty *to* some second party. A duty is a duty to whoever would be seriously injured by its non-performance. Thus my duty to refrain from striking you is a duty to you because you are the party who would be seriously injured were I to punch you in the nose or kick you in the stomach. Again, my ethical duty to support my child financially is primarily a duty to my child, for it is he who would in the first instance be harmed were I to fail to support him; it may secondarily be a duty to my wife, for she would also suffer seriously were she forced to become both breadwinner and housemother by my failure to perform my duty. Accordingly, you have an ethical claim against me that I not strike you, and my child has an ethical claim against me that I support him.

3. *An ethical power.* A party has the ethical power to bring about some ethical consequence *C* if and only if that party possesses the competence required for performing some act with this ethical consequence. For example, I have the ethical power of making a promise, an act that brings into existence an obligation to do what I have promised, and the promisee has the ethical power to release me from my promise if he so chooses. Notice that not everyone is competent to make promises or release promisees. Children too young to understand what it is to commit themselves to future undertakings cannot promise, even if they have learned to parrot the words "I promise" in the appropriate linguistic context; similarly, the mentally deranged husband who says to his wife "I release you from your marriage vows" does not thereby release her from her promise to him. By "competence" I refer to the qualifications or characteristics one must possess in order that one's action can actually bring about some sort of ethical consequence. What, then, do I mean by "bringing about an ethical consequence?" To say that some act *A* brings about some ethical consequence *C* is to say that the statement "act *A* has been done" implies as a consequence that the ethical statement "*C* is the case" is true. Thus, my act of promising to submit this paper before 1 June brought about my obligation to do so just because "Carl Wellman promised to submit this paper before 1 June" implies "Carl Wellman had an obligation to submit this paper before 1 June." Precisely what kinds of sentences are ethical sentences is a question best left for discussion on another occasion.

4. *An ethical immunity.* A party is immune from some specified ethical consequence *C* if and only if there is no other party who is competent to perform any action with this ethical consequence. For example, I am immune from the loss through any act of another of my ethical claim against second parties that they refrain from striking me and equally immune from being morally bound by promises made by others on my behalf—unless, of course, I have authorized some second party to act for me in such ways.

My next step is to articulate a conception of ethical rights analogous to my conception of legal rights. Just as a legal right is a complex system of legal advantages, so an ethical right is a complex system of ethical advantages, a cluster of ethical liberties, claims, powers and immunities. At the centre of every ethical right stands some unifying core, one or more ethical advantages that define the essential content of the right. Thus, at the centre of my ethical right to dress as I please is my ethical liberty of wearing in public any decent clothing I wish, and the core of my ethical right to equal protection of the laws is my ethical claim against the state that its legal system afford me just as much protection as it affords any other individual subject to it. Around the core of any ethical right cluster an assortment of associated ethical liberties, claims, powers and immunities. What ties these ethical elements together into a single right is the way in which each associated element contributes some sort of freedom or control with respect to the defining core to the possessor of the right. Because freedom and control are two aspects of autonomy, any ethical right can accurately be thought of as a system of ethical autonomy.

My third and last step is to distinguish human rights from other species of ethical rights. It would be at least confusing, and probably an abuse of language, to describe as "human rights" the ethical rights that any individual human being has by virtue of being a promisee, a wife, or a citizen, for these are not rights one has simply by virtue of being human. Traditionally, human rights have been thought of as those ethical rights that every human being must possess simply because he or she is human. Thus, human rights are the rights any individual possesses *as* a human being. Although this seems to capture current usage pretty well, I propose a more narrow conception of human rights. I define a human right as an ethical right of the individual as human being vis-à-vis the state. Excluded by this definition are the ethical rights one has as a human being that hold against other individuals or against organizations other than the state. I propose this restriction for two reasons. For one thing, all the important human rights documents, and the declarations of natural rights that preceded them, have been essentially political documents; their primary and definitive purpose has traditionally been to proclaim the rights of the individual human being in face of the state. For another thing, the fundamental ethical relations of any individual human being to the state must surely be very different from his or her ethical relations to other individuals just because the state is a special sort of organization with a distinctive role to play in human affairs. Therefore, the ethical rights of an individual against the state will be rather different from his or her rights against other individuals or organizations. To mark this difference I propose to reserve the expression "a human right" to refer to a right any individual has *as* a human being *in face of* the state.

In three swift steps we have moved from an intepretation of legal rights in terms of Hohfeld's fundamental legal conceptions to a new conception of human rights. A human right is a cluster of ethical liberties, claims, powers and immunities that together constitute a system of ethical autonomy possessed by an individual as a human being vis-à-vis the state. Let me illustrate this new conception by showing how one might use it to interpret the human right to privacy. I shall not pretend to give any complete or precise analysis of this sample right, but my partial description will serve to illustrate a new and helpful way of thinking about human rights.

As the United Nations Declaration of Human Rights recognizes, the core of the human right to privacy is complex. It contains both a claim to freedom from invasions of one's privacy and a claim to legal protection from invasions of one's privacy by the state or other individuals. Both of these are ethical claims of the individual as human being against the state, primarily against his or her own state, but secondarily against other politically organized societies. I would add a third core claim, the ethical claim of the individual against the state that it sustain the conditions necessary for the existence of privacy for the individual.

To define these core claims more fully, it is necessary to say something about the nature of privacy and the areas within which one has justified ethical claims to privacy. Privacy is the state of being unobserved or unknown, confidential, undisturbed or secluded. It is the opposite of being public, and hence the condition of not being open to or shared with the public. One's privacy is invaded when peeping Tom watches one undress, when an entire family must live in a single crowded room, when one's personal letters are published, and when one receives a threatening or obscene telephone call.

Areas within which the claim to privacy are justified include the home, the family, personal correspondence, and certain relationships such as that of husband and wife or doctor and patient. What is it about these areas that singles them out as areas where privacy ought to be respected and protected? In areas such as these, privacy is essential for the preservation of one's sense of security, the development of one's individual personality, and the maintenance of extremely important human relationships. The privacy of the home, for example, is clearly of tremendous value in all three ways: It provides a haven from the dangers, the crowds, and simply the confusions of the public world; it gives one an area where one can be oneself more fully and freely than when subject to alien scrutiny, criticism and even punishment; and it affords an environment in which the intimate relations of husband and wife or parent and child can flourish. The three core claims to privacy are limited to areas where privacy is important in these ways.

Around this complex core cluster a number of associated ethical elements, including at least the following:

1. The ethical liberty of the state to perform its duties corresponding with the three core claims of the individual human being. If the state had any genuine duty not to do these things, then the defining core of the human right to privacy would be vacuous or illusory.

2. The ethical claim of the possessor of the human right to privacy against other individuals that they take political action to ensure that the state perform its duties to meet his core claims. The same considerations that justify the ethical claims of the individual human being concerning privacy against the state justify his claim against other human beings that they intervene on his behalf should the state fail or refuse to perform its core duties to him.

3. The ethical power of the individual to waive his core claims to privacy against the state. For example, it is no longer wrong for a policeman to search a house without a warrant if the owner has freely given his permission to enter and search; and when one marries, one is normally relieving the state of any ethical duty to protect one from invasions of one's privacy by one's spouse.

4. The ethical liberty of the possessor of the right to exercise his ethical power of waiving his core claims to privacy. Although there probably are instances in which one can, but has a duty not to, waive some core claim to privacy, there are many instances in which the exercise of this ethical power is ethically permitted.

5. The ethical immunity of the individual human being against having his core claims to privacy extinguished, suspended or reduced by any action of the state. For example, the state cannot diminish in the least its duty to refrain from invading my privacy by proclaiming a public breakdown of law and order and announcing its intention to search my house or person at any time it sees fit. Each of these associated ethical elements belongs to the human right to privacy because each of

them contributes some sort of ethical freedom or control over the core claims to the possessor of that right. Therefore, the core claims together with these, and other, associated elements constitute a system of ethical autonomy with respect to privacy.

I do not insist that my analysis of the human right to privacy is correct in every detail. I do suggest that it illustrates the fruitfulness of a new conception of human rights simply because it is detailed. We tend to speak and think of human rights in terms of mere names or noun phrases that obscure their full and precise content by their very brevity. It is a considerable merit in this conception of a human right that it provides the vocabulary in which one can spell out, explicitly and in detail, the exact content of any right. Another advantage of this conception is that it renders the modality or modalities of any right unambiguous. In this case, it shows us that the core of the human right to privacy is a triple claim and that some associated elements are liberties, others powers and so on. Finally, it translates the content of any human right into practical terms. Since the description of any ethical liberty, claim, power or immunity includes the specification of some sort of action, to think of human rights as clusters of ethical advantages is to think of them in terms of human actions. This is a theoretical virtue for those who believe that the theory of human rights ought to be relevant to moral choice and a practical asset for those who wish to appeal to human rights in taking political action to reform the law to fit a changing society.

Taking Rights Seriously

RONALD DWORKIN

I. The Rights of Citizens

The language of rights now dominates political debate in the United States. Does the Government respect the moral and political rights of its citizens? Or does the Government's foreign policy, or its race policy, fly in the face of these rights? Do the minorities whose rights have been violated have the right to violate the law in return? Or does the silent majority itself have rights, including the right that those who break the law be punished? It is not surprising that these questions are now prominent. The concept of rights, and particularly the concept of rights against the Government, has its most natural use when a political society is divided, and appeals to cooperation or a common goal are pointless.

The debate does not include the issue of whether citizens have *some* moral rights against their Government. It seems accepted on all sides that they do. Conventional lawyers and politicians take it as a point of pride that our legal system recognizes, for example, individual rights of free speech, equality, and due process. They base their claim that our law deserves respect, at least in part, on that fact, for they would not claim that totalitarian systems deserve the same loyalty.

Some philosophers, of course, reject the idea that citizens have rights apart from what the law happens to give them. Bentham thought that the idea of moral rights was "nonsense on stilts." But that view has never been part of our orthodox political theory, and politicians of both parties appeal to the rights of the people to justify a great part of what they want to do. I shall not be concerned, in this essay, to defend the thesis that citizens have moral rights against their governments; I want instead to explore the implications of that thesis for those, including the present United States Government, who profess to accept it.

It is much in dispute, of course, what *particular* rights citizens have. Does the acknowledged right to free speech, for example, include the right to participate in nuisance demonstrations? In practice the Government will have the last word on what an individual's rights are, because its police will do what its officials and courts say. But that does not mean that the Government's view is necessarily the correct view; anyone who thinks it does must believe that men and women have only such moral rights as Government chooses to grant, which means that they have no moral rights at all.

All this is sometimes obscured in the United States by the constitutional system. The American Constitution provides a set of individual *legal* rights in the First Amendment, and in the due process, equal protection, and similar clauses. Under present legal practice the Supreme Court has the power to declare an act of Congress or of a state legislature void if the Court finds that the act offends these provisions. This practice has led some commentators to suppose that individual moral rights are fully protected by this system, but that is hardly so, nor could it be so.

The Constitution fuses legal and moral issues, by making the validity of a law depend on the answer to complex moral problems, like the problem of whether a particular statute respects the inherent equality of all men. This fusion has important consequences for the debates about civil disobedience; I have described these elsewhere[1] and I shall refer to them later. But it leaves open two prominent questions. It does not tell us whether the Constitution, even properly interpreted, recognizes all the moral rights that citizens have, and it does not tell us whether, as many suppose, citizens would have a duty to obey the law even if it did invade their moral rights.

Both questions become crucial when some minority claims moral rights which the law denies, like the right to run its local school system, and which lawyers agree are not protected by the Constitution. The second question becomes crucial when, as now, the majority is sufficiently aroused so that Constitutional amendments to elimi-nate rights, like the right against self-incrimination, are seriously proposed. It is also crucial in nations, like the United Kingdom, that have no constitution of a compar-able nature.

Even if the Constitution were perfect, of course, and the majority left it alone, it would not follow that the Supreme Court could guarantee the individual rights of citizens. A Supreme Court decision is still a legal decision, and it must take into account precedent and institutional considerations like relations between the Court and Congress, as well as morality. And no judicial decision is necessarily the right decision. Judges stand for different positions on controversial issues of law and morals and, as the fights over Nixon's Supreme Court nominations showed, a Presi-dent is entitled to appoint judges of his own persuasion, provided that they are honest and capable.

---

1. See Chapter 8, [*Taking Rights Seriously* (Cambridge, MA: Harvard University Press, 1977)].

So, though the constitutional system adds something to the protection of moral rights against the Government, it falls far short of guaranteeing these rights, or even establishing what they are. It means that, on some occasions, a department other than the legislature has the last word on these issues, which can hardly satisfy someone who thinks such a department profoundly wrong.

It is of course inevitable that some department of government will have the final say on what law will be enforced. When men disagree about moral rights, there will be no way for either side to prove its case, and some decision must stand if there is not to be anarchy. But that piece of orthodox wisdom must be the beginning and not the end of a philosophy of legislation and enforcement. If we cannot insist that the Government reach the right answers about the rights of its citizens, we can insist at least that it try. We can insist that it take rights seriously, follow a coherent theory of what these rights are, and act consistently with its own professions. I shall try to show what that means, and how it bears on the present political debates.

2. Rights and the Right to Break the Law

I shall start with the most violently argued issue. Does an American ever have the moral right to break a law? Suppose someone admits a law is valid; does he therefore have a duty to obey it? Those who try to give an answer seem to fall into two camps. The conservatives, as I shall call them, seem to disapprove of any act of disobedience; they appear satisfied when such acts are prosecuted, and disappointed when convictions are reversed. The other group, the liberals, are much more sympathetic to at least some cases of disobedience; they sometimes disapprove of prosecutions and celebrate acquittals. If we look beyond these emotional reactions, however, and pay attention to the arguments the two parties use, we discover an astounding fact. Both groups give essentially the same answer to the question of principle that supposedly divides them.

The answer that both parties give is this. In a democracy, or at least a democracy that in principle respects individual rights, each citizen has a general moral duty to obey all the laws, even though he would like some of them changed. He owes that duty to his fellow citizens, who obey laws that they do not like, to his benefit. But this general duty cannot be an absolute duty, because even a society that is in principle just may produce unjust laws and policies, and a man has duties other than his duties to the State. A man must honour his duties to his God and to his conscience, and if these conflict with his duty to the State, then he is entitled, in the end, to do what he judges to be right. If he decides that he must break the law, however, then he must submit to the judgment and punishment that the State imposes, in recognition of the fact that his duty to his fellow citizens was overwhelmed but not extinguished by his religious or moral obligation.

Of course this common answer can be elaborated in very different ways. Some would describe the duty to the State as fundamental, and picture the dissenter as a religious or moral fanatic. Others would describe the duty to the State in grudging terms, and picture those who oppose it as moral heroes. But these are differences in tone, and the position I described represents, I think, the view of most of those who find themselves arguing either for or against civil disobedience in particular cases.

I do not claim that it is everyone's view. There must be some who put the duty to the State so high that they do not grant that it can ever be overcome. There are certainly some who would deny that a man ever has a moral duty to obey the law, at least in the United States today. But these two extreme positions are the slender tails of a bell curve, and all those who fall in between hold the orthodox position I described—that men have a duty to obey the law but have the right to follow their consciences when it conflicts with that duty.

But if that is so, then we have a paradox in the fact that men who give the same answer to a question of principle should seem to disagree so much, and to divide so fiercely, in particular cases. The paradox goes even deeper, for each party, in at least some cases, takes a position that seems flatly inconsistent with the theoretical position they both accept. This position was tested, for example, when someone evaded the draft on grounds of conscience, or encouraged others to commit this crime. Conservatives argued that such men must be prosecuted, even though they are sincere. Why must they be prosecuted? Because society cannot tolerate the decline in respect for the law that their act constitutes and encourages. They must be prosecuted, in short, to discourage them and others like them from doing what they have done.

But there seems to be a monstrous contradiction here. If a man has a right to do what his conscience tells him he must, then how can the State be justified in discouraging him from doing it? Is it not wicked for a state to forbid and punish what it acknowledges that men have a right to do?

Moreover, it is not just conservatives who argue that those who break the law out of moral conviction should be prosecuted. The liberal is notoriously opposed to allowing racist school officials to go slow on desegregation, even though he acknowledges that these school officials think they have a moral right to do what the law forbids. The liberal does not often argue, it is true, that the desegregation laws must be enforced to encourage general respect for law. He argues instead that the desegregation laws must be enforced because they are right. But his position also seems inconsistent: Can it be right to prosecute men for doing what their conscience requires, when we acknowledge their right to follow their conscience?

We are therefore left with two puzzles. How can two parties to an issue of principle, each of which thinks it is in profound disagreement with the other, embrace the same position on that issue? How can it be that each side urges solutions to particular problems which seem flatly to contradict the position of principle that both accept? One possible answer is that some or all of those who accept the common position are hypocrites, paying lip service to rights of conscience which in fact they do not grant.

There is some plausibility in this charge. A sort of hypocrisy must have been involved when public officials who claim to respect conscience denied Muhammed Ali the right to box in their states. If Ali, in spite of his religious scruples, had joined the Army, he would have been allowed to box even though, on the principles these officials say they honour, he would have been a worse human being for having done so. But there are few cases that seem so straightforward as this one, and even here the officials did not seem to recognize the contradiction between their acts and their principles. So we must search for some explanation beyond the truth that men often do not mean what they say.

The deeper explanation lies in a set of confusions that often embarrass arguments about rights. These confusions have clouded all the issues I mentioned at the outset and have crippled attempts to develop a coherent theory of how a government that respects rights must behave.

In order to explain this, I must call attention to the fact, familiar to philosophers, but often ignored in political debate, that the word "right" has different force in different contexts. In most cases when we say that someone has "right" to do something, we imply that it would be wrong to interfere with his doing it, or at least that some special grounds are needed for justifying any interference. I use this strong sense of right when I say that you have the right to spend your money gambling, if you wish, though you ought to spend it in a more worthwhile way. I mean that it would be wrong for anyone to interfere with you even though you propose to spend your money in a way that I think is wrong.

There is a clear difference between saying that someone has a right to do something in this sense and saying that it is the "right" thing for him to do, or that he does no "wrong" in doing it. Someone may have the right to do something that is the wrong thing for him to do, as might be the case with gambling. Conversely, something may be the right thing for him to do and yet he may have no right to do it, in the sense that it would not be wrong for someone to interfere with his trying. If our army captures an enemy soldier, we might say that the right thing for him to do is to try to escape, but it would not follow that it is wrong for us to try to stop him. We might admire him for trying to escape, and perhaps even think less of him if he did not. But there is no suggestion here that it is wrong of us to stand in his way; on the contrary, if we think our cause is just, we think it right for us to do all we can to stop him.

Ordinarily this distinction, between the issues of whether a man has a right to do something and whether it is the right thing for him to do, causes no trouble. But sometimes it does, because sometimes we say that a man has a right to do something when we mean only to deny that it is the wrong thing for him to do. Thus we say that the captured soldier as a "right" to try to escape when we mean, not that we do wrong to stop him, but that he has no duty not to make the attempt. We use "right" this way when we speak of someone having the "right" to act on his own principles, or the "right" to follow his own conscience. We mean that he does no wrong to proceed on his honest convictions, even though we disagree with these convictions, and even though, for policy or other reasons, we must force him to act contrary to them.

Suppose a man believes that welfare payments to the poor are profoundly wrong, because they sap enterprise, and so declares his full income-tax each year but declines to pay half of it. We might say that he has a right to refuse to pay, if he wishes, but that the Government has a right to proceed against him for the full tax, and to fine or jail him for late payment if that is necessary to keep the collection system working efficiently. We do not take this line in most cases; we do not say that the ordinary thief has a right to steal, if he wishes, so long as he pays the penalty. We say a man has the right to break the law, even though the State has a right to punish him, only when we think that, because of his convictions, he does no wrong in doing so.[2]

These distinctions enable us to see an ambiguity in the orthodox question: Does a man ever have a right to break the law? Does that question mean to ask whether he ever has a right to break the law in the strong sense, so that the Government would do wrong to stop him, by arresting and prosecuting him? Or does it mean to ask whether he ever does the right thing to break the law, so that we should all respect him even though the Government should jail him?

If we take the orthodox position to be an answer to the first—and most important—question, then the paradoxes I described arise. But if we take it as an answer to the second, they do not. Conservatives and liberals do agree that sometimes a man does not do the wrong thing to break a law, when his conscience so requires. They disagree, when they do, over the different issue of what the State's response should be. Both parties do think that sometimes the State should prosecute. But this is not inconsistent with the proposition that the man prosecuted did the right thing in breaking the law.

The paradoxes seem genuine because the two questions are not usually distinguished, and the orthodox position is presented as a general solution to the problem of civil disobedience. But once the distinction is made, it is apparent that the position has been so widely accepted only because, when it is applied, it is treated as an answer to the second question but not the first. The crucial distinction is obscured by the troublesome idea of a right to conscience; this idea has been at the centre of most recent discussions of political obligation, but it is a red herring drawing us away from the crucial political questions. The state of a man's conscience may be decisive, or central, when the issue is whether he does something morally wrong in breaking the law; but it need not be decisive or even central when the issue is whether he has a right, in the strong sense of that term, to do so. A man does not have the right, in that sense, to do whatever his conscience demands, but he may have the right, in that sense, to do something even though his conscience does not demand it.

If that is true, then there has been almost no serious attempt to answer the questions that almost everyone means to ask. We can make a fresh start by stating these questions more clearly. Does an American ever have the right, in a strong sense, to do something which is against the law? If so, when? In order to answer these questions put in that way, we must try to become clearer about the implications of the idea, mentioned earlier, that citizens have at least some rights against their government.

I said that in the United States citizens are supposed to have certain fundamental rights against their Government, certain moral rights made into legal rights by the

---

2. It is not surprising that we sometimes use the concept of having a right to say that others must not interfere with an act and sometimes to say that the act is not the wrong thing to do. Often, when someone has *no* right to do something, like attacking another man physically, it is true *both* that it is the wrong thing to do and that others are entitled to stop it, by demand, if not by force. It is therefore natural to say that someone has a right when we mean to deny *either* of these consequences, as well as when we mean to deny both.

Constitution. If this idea is significant, and worth bragging about, then these rights must be rights in the strong sense I just described. The claim that citizens have a right to free speech must imply that it would be wrong for the Government to stop them from speaking, even when the Government believes that what they will say will cause more harm than good. The claim cannot mean, on the prisoner-of-war analogy, only that citizens do no wrong in speaking their minds, though the Government reserves the right to prevent them from doing so.

This is a crucial point, and I want to labour it. Of course a responsible government must be ready to justify anything it does, particularly when it limits the liberty of its citizens. But normally it is a sufficient justification, even for an act that limits liberty, that the act is calculated to increase what the philosophers call general utility—that it is calculated to produce more over-all benefit than harm. So, though the New York City government needs a justification for forbidding motorists to drive up Lexington Avenue, it is sufficient justification if the proper officials believe, on sound evidence, that the gain to the many will outweigh the inconvenience to the few. When individual citizens are said to have rights against the Government, however, like the right of free speech, that must mean that this sort of justification is not enough. Otherwise the claim would not argue that individuals have special protection against the law when their rights are in play, and that is just the point of the claim.

Not all legal rights, or even Constitutional rights, represent moral rights against the Government. I now have the legal right to drive either way on Fifty-seventh Street, but the Government would do no wrong to make that street one-way if it thought it in the general interest to do so. I have a Constitutional right to vote for a congressman every two years, but the national and state governments would do no wrong if, following the amendment procedure, they made a congressman's term four years instead of two, again on the basis of a judgment that this would be for the general good.

But those Constitutional rights that we call fundamental like the right of free speech, are supposed to represent rights against the Government in the strong sense; that is the point of the boast that our legal system respects the fundamental rights of the citizen. If citizens have a moral right of free speech, then governments would do wrong to repeal the First Amendment that guarantees it, even if they were persuaded that the majority would be better off if speech were curtailed.

I must not overstate the point. Someone who claims that citizens have a right against the Government need not go so far as to say that the State is *never* justified in overriding that right. He might say, for example, that although citizens have a right to free speech, the Government may override that right when necessary to protect the rights of others, or to prevent a catastrophe, or even to obtain a clear and major public benefit (though if he acknowledged this last as a possible justification he would be treating the right in question as not among the most important or fundamental). What he cannot do is to say that the Government is justified in overriding a right on the minimal grounds that would be sufficient if no such right existed. He cannot say that the Government is entitled to act on no more than a judgment that its act is likely to produce, overall, a benefit to the community. That admission would make his claim of a right pointless, and would show him to be using some sense of "right" other than the strong sense necessary to give his claim the political importance it is normally taken to have.

But then the answers to our two questions about disobedience seem plain, if unorthodox. In our society a man does sometimes have the right, in the strong sense, to disobey a law. He has that right whenever that law wrongly invades his rights against the Government. If he has a moral right to free speech, that is, then he has a moral right to break any law that the Government, by virtue of his right, had no right to adopt. The right to disobey the law is not a separate right, having something to do with conscience, additional to other rights against the Government. It is simply a feature of these rights against the Government, and it cannot be denied in principle without denying that any such rights exist.

These answers seem obvious once we take rights against the Government to be rights in the strong sense I described. If I have a right to speak my mind on political issues, then the Government does wrong to make it illegal for me to do so, even if it thinks this is in the general interest. If, nevertheless, the Government does make my act illegal, then it does a further wrong to enforce that law against me. My right against the Government means that it is wrong for the Government to stop me from speaking; the Government cannot make it right to stop me just by taking the first step.

This does not, of course, tell us exactly what rights men do have against the Government. It does not tell us whether the right of free speech includes the right of demonstration. But it does mean that passing a law cannot affect such rights as men do have, and that is of crucial importance, because it dictates the attitude that an individual is entitled to take toward his personal decision when civil disobedience is in question.

Both conservatives and liberals suppose that in a society which is generally decent everyone has a duty to obey the law, whatever it is. That is the source of the "general duty" clause in the orthodox position, and though liberals believe that this duty can sometimes be "overridden," even they suppose, as the orthodox position maintains, that the duty of obedience remains in some submerged form, so that a man does well to accept punishment in recognition of that duty. But this general duty is almost incoherent in a society that recognizes rights. If a man believes he has a right to demonstrate, then he must believe that it would be wrong for the Government to stop him, with or without benefit of a law. If he is entitled to believe that, then it is silly to speak of a duty to obey the law as such, or of a duty to accept the punishment that the State has no right to give.

Conservatives will object to the short work I have made of their point. They will argue that even if the Government was wrong to adopt some law, like a law limiting speech, there are independent reasons why the Government is justified in enforcing the law once adopted. When the law forbids demonstration, then, so they argue, some principle more important than the individual's right to speak is brought into play, namely the principle of respect for law. If a law, even a bad law, is left unenforced, then respect for law is weakened, and society as a whole suffers. So an individual loses his moral right to speak when speech is made criminal, and the Government must, for the common good and for the general benefit, enforce the law against him.

But this argument, though popular, is plausible only if we forget what it means to say that an individual has a right against the State. It is far from plain that civil disobedience lowers respect for law, but even if we suppose that it does, this fact is irrelevant. The prospect of utilitarian gains cannot justify preventing a man from doing what he has a right to do, and the supposed gains in respect for law are simply utilitarian gains. There would be no point in the boast that we respect individual rights unless that involved some sacrifice, and the sacrifice in question must be that we give up whatever marginal benefits our country would receive from overriding these rights when they prove inconvenient. So the general benefit cannot be a good ground for abridging rights, even when the benefit in question is a heightened respect for law.

But perhaps I do wrong to assume that the argument about respect for law is only an appeal to general utility. I said that a state may be justified in overriding or limiting rights on other grounds, and we must ask, before rejecting the conservative position, whether any of these apply. The most important—and least well understood—of these other grounds invokes the notion of *competing rights* that would be jeopardized if the right in question were not limited. Citizens have personal rights to the State's protection as well as personal rights to be free from the State's interference, and it may be necessary for the Government to choose between these two sorts of rights. The law of defamation, for example, limits the personal right of any man to say what he thinks, because it requires him to have good grounds for what he says. But this law is justified, even for those who think that it does invade a personal right, by the fact that it protects the right of others not to have their reputations ruined by a careless statement.

The individual rights that our society acknowledges often conflict in this way, and when they do it is the job of government to discriminate. If the Government makes the right choice, and protects the more important at the cost of the less, then it has not weakened or cheapened the notion of a right; on the contrary it would have done so had it failed to protect the more important of the two. So we must acknowledge that the Government has a reason for limiting rights if it plausibly believes that a competing right is more important.

May the conservative seize on this fact? He might argue that I did wrong to characterize his argument as one that appeals to the general benefit, because it appeals instead to competing rights, namely the moral right of the majority to have its laws enforced, or the right of society to maintain the degree of order and security it wishes. These are the rights, he would say, that must be weighed against the individual's right to do what the wrongful law prohibits.

But this new argument is confused, because it depends on yet another ambiguity in the language of rights. It is true that we speak of the "right" of society to do what it wants, but this cannot be a "competing right" of the sort that may justify the invasion of a right against the Government. The existence of rights against the Government would be jeopardized if the Government were able to defeat such a right by appealing to the right of a democractic majority to work its will. A right against the Government must be a right to do something even when the majority thinks it would be wrong to do it, and even when the majority would be worse off for having it done. If we now say that society has a right to do whatever is in the general benefit, or the right to preserve whatever sort of environment the majority wishes to live in, and we mean that these are the sort of rights that provide justification for overruling any rights against the Government that may conflict, then we have annihilated the latter rights.

In order to save them, we must recognize as competing rights only the rights of other members of the society as individuals. We must distinguish the "rights" of the majority as such, which cannot count as a justification for overruling individual rights, and the personal rights of members of a majority, which might well count. The test we must use is this. Someone has a competing right to protection, which must be weighed against an individual right to act, if that person would be entitled to demand that protection from his government on his own title, as an individual, without regard to whether a majority of his fellow citizens joined in the demand.

It cannot be true, on this test, that anyone has a right to have all the laws of the nation enforced. He has a right to have enforced only those criminal laws, for example, that he would have a right to have enacted if they were not already law. The laws against personal assault may well fall into that class. If the physically vulnerable members of the community—those who need police protection against personal violence—were only a small minority, it would still seem plausible to say that they were entitled to that protection. But the laws that provide a certain level of quiet in public places, or that authorize and finance a foreign war, cannot be thought to rest on individual rights. The timid lady on the streets of Chicago is not entitled to just the degree of quiet that now obtains, nor is she entitled to have boys drafted to fight in wars she approves. There are laws—perhaps desirable laws—that provide these advantages for her, but the justification for these laws, if they can be justified at all, is the common desire of a large majority, not her personal right. If, therefore, these laws do abridge someone else's moral right to protest, or his right to personal security, she cannot urge a competing right to justify the abridgement. She has no personal right to have such laws passed, and she has no competing right to have them enforced either.

So the conservative cannot advance his argument much on the ground of competing rights, but he may want to use another ground. A government, he may argue, may be justified in abridging the personal rights of its citizens in an emergency, or when a very great loss may be prevented, or perhaps, when some major benefit can clearly be secured. If the nation is at war, a policy of censorship may be justified even though it invades the right to say what one thinks on matters of political controversy. But the emergency must be genuine. There must be what Oliver Wendell Holmes described as a clear and present danger, and the danger must be one of magnitude.

Can the conservative argue that when any law is passed, even a wrongful law, this sort of justification is available for enforcing it? His argument might be something of this sort. If the Government once acknowledges that it may be wrong—that the legislature might have adopted, the executive approved, and the courts left standing, a law that in fact abridges important rights—then this admission will lead not simply to a marginal decline in respect for law, but to a crisis of order. Citizens may decide to obey only those laws they personally approve, and that is anarchy. So the Government must insist that whatever a citizen's rights may be before a law is passed and upheld by the courts, his rights thereafter are determined by that law.

But this argument ignores the primitive distinction between what may happen and what will happen. If we allow speculation to support the justification of emergency or decisive benefit, then, again, we have annihilated rights. We must, as Learned Hand said, discount the gravity of the evil threatened by the likelihood of reaching that evil. I know of no genuine evidence to the effect that tolerating some civil disobedience, out of respect for the moral position of its authors, will increase such disobedience, let alone crime in general. The case that it will must be based on vague assumptions about the contagion of ordinary crimes, assumptions that are themselves unproved, and that are in any event largely irrelevant. It seems at least as plausible to argue that tolerance will increase respect for officials and for the bulk of the laws they promulgate, or at least retard the rate of growing disrespect.

If the issue were simply the question whether the community would be marginally better off under strict law enforcement, then the Government would have to decide on the evidence we have, and it might not be unreasonable to decide, on balance, that it would. But since rights are at stake, the issue is the very different one of whether tolerance would destroy the community or threaten it with great harm, and it seems to me simply mindless to suppose that the evidence makes that probable or even conceivable.

The argument from emergency is confused in another way as well. It assumes that the Government must take the position either that a man never has the right to break the law, or that he always does. I said that any society that claims to recognize rights at all must abandon the notion of a general duty to obey the law that holds in all cases. This is important, because it shows that there are no short cuts to meeting a citizen's claim to right. If a citizen argues that he has a moral right not to serve in the Army, or to protest in a way he finds effective, then an official who wants to answer him, and not simply bludgeon him into obedience, must respond to the particular point he makes, and cannot point to the draft law or a Supreme Court decision as having even special, let alone decisive, weight. Sometimes an official who considers the citizen's moral arguments in good faith will be persuaded that the citizen's claim is plausible, or even right. It does not follow, however, that he will always be persuaded or that he always should be.

I must emphasize that all these propositions concern the strong sense of right, and they therefore leave open important questions about the right thing to do. If a man believes he has the right to break the law, he must then ask whether he does the right thing to exercise that right. He must remember that reasonable men can differ about whether he has a right against the Government, and therefore the right to break the law, that he thinks he has; and therefore that reasonable men can oppose him in good faith. He must take into account the various consequences his acts will have, whether they involve violence, and such other considerations as the context makes relevant; he must not go beyond the rights he can in good faith claim, to acts that violate the rights of others. . . .

3. Controversial Rights

The argument so far has been hypothetical: If a man has a particular moral right against the Government, that right survives contrary legislation or adjudication. But this does not tell us what rights he has, and it is notorious that reasonable men disagree about that. There is wide agreement on certain clearcut cases; almost everyone who believes in rights at all would admit, for example, that a man has a moral right to speak his mind in a non-provocative way on matters of political concern and that this is an important right that the State must go to great pains to protect. But there is great controversy as to the limits of such paradigm rights, and the so-called "anti-riot" law involved in the famous Chicago Seven trial of the last decade is a case in point.

The defendants were accused of conspiring to cross state lines with the intention of causing a riot. This charge is vague—perhaps unconstitutionally vague—but the law apparently defines as criminal emotional speeches which argue that violence is justified in order to secure political equality. Does the right of free speech protect this sort of speech? That, of course, is a legal issue, because it invokes the free-speech clause of the First Amendment of the Constitution. But it is also a moral issue, because, as I said, we must treat the First Amendmenet as an attempt to protect a moral right. It is part of the job of governing to 'define' moral rights through statutes and judicial decisions, that is, to declare officially the extent that moral rights will be taken to have in law. Congress faced this task in voting on the anti-riot bill, and the Supreme Court has faced it in countless cases. How should the different departments of government go about defining moral rights?

They should begin with a sense that whatever they decide might be wrong. History and their descendants may judge that they acted unjustly when they thought they were right. If they take their duty seriously, they must try to limit their mistakes, and they must therefore try to discover where the dangers of mistake lie.

They might choose one of two very different models for this purpose. The first model recommends striking a balance between the rights of the individual and the demands of society at large. If the Government *infringes* on a moral right (for example, by defining the right of free speech more narrowly than justice requires), then it has done the individual a wrong. On the other hand, if the Government *inflates* a right (by defining it more broadly than justice requires) then it cheats society of some general benefit, like safe streets, that there is no reason it should not have. So a mistake on one side is as serious as a mistake on the other. The course of government is to steer to the middle, to balance the general good and personal rights, giving to each its due.

When the Government, or any of its branches, defines a right, it must bear in mind, according to the first model, the social cost of different proposals and make the necessary adjustments. It must not grant the same freedom to noisy demonstrations as it grants to calm political discussion, for example, because the former causes much more trouble than the latter. Once it decides how much of a right to recognize, it must enforce its decision to the full. That means permitting an individual to act within his rights, as the Government has defined them, but not beyond, so that if anyone breaks the law, even on grounds of conscience, he must be punished. No doubt any government will make mistakes, and will regret decisions once taken. That is inevitable. But this middle policy will ensure that errors on one side will balance out errors on the other over the long run.

The first model, described in this way, has great plausibility, and most laymen and lawyers, I think, would respond to it warmly. The metaphor of balancing the public interest against personal claims is established in our political and judicial rhetoric, and this metaphor gives the model both familiarity and appeal. Nevertheless, the first model is a false one, certainly in the case of rights generally regarded as important, and the metaphor is the heart of its error.

The institution of rights against the Government is not a gift of God, or an ancient ritual, or a national sport. It is a complex and troublesome practice that makes the Government's job of securing the general benefit more difficult and more expensive, and it would be a frivolous and wrongful practice unless it served some point. Anyone who professes to take rights seriously, and who praises our Government for respecting them, must have some sense of what that point is. He must accept, at the minimum, one or both of two important ideas. The first is the vague but powerful idea of human dignity. This idea, associated with Kant, but defended by philosophers of different schools, supposes that there are ways of treating a man that are inconsistent with recognizing him as a full member of the human community, and holds that such treatment is profoundly unjust.

The second is the more familiar idea of political equality. This supposes that the weaker members of a political community are entitled to the same concern and respect of their government as the more powerful members have secured for themselves, so that if some men have freedom of decision whatever the effect on the general good, then all men must have the same freedom. I do not want to defend or elaborate these ideas here, but only to insist that anyone who claims that citizens have rights must accept ideas very close to these.[3]

It makes sense to say that a man has a fundamental right against the Government, in the strong sense, like free speech, if that right is necessary to protect his dignity, or his standing as equally entitled to concern and respect, or some other personal value of like consequence. It does not make sense otherwise.

So if rights make sense at all, then the invasion of a relatively important right must be a very serious matter. It means treating a man as less than a man, or as less worthy of concern than other men. The institution of rights rests on the conviction that this is a grave injustice, and that it is worth paying the incremental cost in social policy or efficiency that is necessary to prevent it. But then it must be wrong to say that inflating rights is as serious as invading them. If the Government errs on the side of the individual, then it simply pays a little more in social efficiency than it has to pay; it pays a little more, that is, of the same coin that it has already decided must be spent. But if it errs against the individual it inflicts an insult upon him that, on its own reckoning, it is worth a great deal of that coin to avoid.

So the first model is indefensible. It rests, in fact, on a mistake I discussed earlier, namely the confusion of society's rights with the rights of members of society. "Balancing" is appropriate when the Government must choose between competing

---

3. He need not consider these ideas to be axiomatic. He may, that is, have reasons for insisting that dignity or equality are important values, and these reasons may be utilitarian. He may believe, for example, that the general good will be advanced, *in the long run,* only if we treat indignity or inequality as very great injustices, and never allow our *opinions* about the general good to justify them. I do not know of any good arguments for or against this sort of "institutional" utilitarianism, but it is consistent with my point, because it argues that we must treat violations of dignity and equality as special moral crimes, beyond the reach of ordinary utilitarian justification.

claims of right—between the Southerner's claim to freedom of association, for example, and the black man's claim to an equal education. Then the Government can do nothing but estimate the merits of the competing claims, and act on its estimate. The first model assumes that the "right" of the majority is a competing right that must be balanced in this way; but that, as I argued before, is a confusion that threatens to destroy the concept of individual rights. It is worth noticing that the community rejects the first model in that area where the stakes for the individual are highest, the criminal process. We say that it is better that a great many guilty men go free than that one innocent man be punished, and that homily rests on the choice of the second model for government.

The second model treats abridging a right as much more serious than inflating one, and its recommendations follow from that judgment. It stipulates that once a right is recognized in clear-cut cases, then the Government should act to cut off that right only when some compelling reason is presented, some reason that is consistent with the suppositions on which the original right must be based. It cannot be an argument for curtailing a right, once granted, simply that society would pay a further price for extending it. There must be something special about that further cost, or there must be some other feature of the case, that makes it sensible to say that although great social cost is warranted to protect the original right, this particular cost is not necessary. Otherwise, the Government's failure to extend the right will show that its recognition of the right in the original case is a sham, a promise that it intends to keep only until that becomes inconvenient.

How can we show that a particular cost is not worth paying without taking back the initial recognition of a right? I can think of only three sorts of grounds that can consistently be used to limit the definition of a particular right. First, the Government might show that the values protected by the original right are not really at stake in the marginal case, or are at stake only in some attenuated form. Second, it might show that if the right is defined to include the marginal case, then some competing right, in the strong sense I described earlier, would be abridged. Third, it might show that if the right were so defined, then the cost to society would not be simply incremental, but would be of a degree far beyond the cost paid to grant the original right, a degree great enough to justify whatever assault on dignity or equality might be involved.

It is fairly easy to apply these grounds to one group of problems the Supreme Court faced, imbedded in constitutional issues. The draft law provided an exemption for conscientious objectors, but this exemption, as interpreted by the draft boards, has been limited to those who object to *all* wars on *religious* grounds. If we suppose that the exemption is justified on the ground that an individual has a moral right not to kill in violation of his own principles, then the question is raised whether it is proper to exclude those whose morality is not based on religion, or whose morality is sufficiently complex to distinguish among wars. The Court held, as a matter of Constitutional law, that the draft boards were wrong to exclude the former, but competent to exclude the latter.

None of the three grounds I listed can justify either of these exclusions as a matter of political morality. The invasion of personality in forcing men to kill when they believe killing immoral is just as great when these beliefs are based on secular grounds, or take account of the fact that wars differ in morally relevant ways, and there is no pertinent difference in competing rights or in national emergency. There are differences among the cases, of course, but they are insufficient to justify the distinction. A government that is secular on principle cannot prefer a religious to a non-religious morality as such. There are utilitarian arguments in favour of limiting the exception to religious or universal grounds—an exemption so limited may be less expensive to administer, and may allow easier discrimination between sincere and insincere applicants. But these utilitarian reasons are irrelevant, because they cannot count as grounds for limiting a right.

What about the anti-riot law, as applied in the Chicago trial? Does the law represent an improper limitation of the right to free speech, supposedly protected by the First Amendment? If we were to apply the first model for government to this issue, the argument for the anti-riot law would look strong. But if we set aside talk of balancing as inappropriate, and turn to the proper grounds for limiting a right, then the argument becomes a great deal weaker. The original right of free speech must suppose that it is an assault on human personality to stop a man from expressing what he honestly believes, particularly on issues affecting how he is governed. Surely the assault is greater, and not less, when he is stopped from expressing those principles of political morality that he holds most passionately, in the face of what he takes to be outrageous violations of these principles.

It may be said that the anti-riot law leaves him free to express these principles in a non-provocative way. But that misses the point of the connection between expression and dignity. A man cannot express himself freely when he cannot match his rhetoric to his outrage, or when he must trim his sails to protect values he counts as nothing next to those he is trying to vindicate. It is true that some political dissenters speak in ways that shock the majority, but it is arrogant for the majority to suppose that the orthodox methods of expression are the proper ways to speak, for this is a denial of equal concern and respect. If the point of the right is to protect the dignity of dissenters, then we must make judgments about appropriate speech with the personalities of the dissenters in mind, not the personality of the "silent" majority for whom the anti-riot law is no restraint at all.

So the argument fails, that the personal values protected by the original right are less at stake in this marginal case. We must consider whether competing rights, or some grave threat to society, nevertheless justify the anti-riot law. We can consider these two grounds together, because the only plausible competing rights are rights to be free from violence, and violence is the only plausible threat to society that the context provides.

I have no right to burn your house, or stone you or your car, or swing a bicycle chain against your skull, even if I find these to be natural means of expression. But the defendants in the Chicago trial were not accused of direct violence; the argument runs that the acts of speech they planned made it likely that others would do acts of violence, either in support of or out of hostility to what they said. Does this provide a justification?

The question would be different if we could say with any confidence how much and what sort of violence the anti-riot law might be expected to prevent. Will it save two lives a year, or two hundred, or two thousand? Two thousand dollars of property, or two hundred thousand, or two million? No one can say, not simply because prediction is next to impossible, but because we have no firm understanding of the process by which demonstration disintegrates into riot, and in particular of the part played by inflammatory speech, as distinct from poverty, police brutality, blood lust, and all the rest of human and economic failure. The Government must try, of course, to reduce the violent waste of lives and property, but it must recognize that any attempt to locate and remove a cause of riot, short of a reorganization of society, must be an exercise in speculation, trial, and error. It must make its decisions under conditions of high uncertainty, and the institution of rights, taken seriously, limits its freedom to experiment under such conditions.

It forces the Government to bear in mind that preventing a man from speaking or demonstrating offers him a certain and profound insult, in return for a speculative benefit that may in any event be achieved in other if more expensive ways. When lawyers say that rights may be limited to protect other rights, or to prevent catastrophe, they have in mind cases in which cause and effect are relatively clear, like the familiar example of a man falsely crying "Fire!" in a crowded theater.

But the Chicago story shows how obscure the causal connections can become. Were the speeches of Hoffman and Rubin necessary conditions of the riot? Or had thousands of people come to Chicago for the purposes of rioting anyway, as the Government also argues? Were they in any case sufficient conditions? Or could the police have contained the violence if they had not been so busy contributing to it, as the staff of the President's Commission on Violence said they were?

These are not easy questions, but if rights mean anything, then the Government cannot simply assume answers that justify its conduct. If a man has a right to speak, if the reasons that support that right extend to provocative political speech, and if the effects of such speech on violence are unclear, then the Government is not entitled to make its first attack on that problem by denying that right. It may be that abridging the right to speak is the least expensive course, or the least damaging to police morale, or the most popular politically. But these are utilitarian arguments in favor of starting one place rather than another, and such arguments are ruled out by the concept of rights.

This point may be obscured by the popular belief that political activists look forward to violence and "ask for trouble" in what they say. They can hardly complain, in the general view, if they are taken to be the authors of the violence they expect, and treated accordingly. But this repeats the confusion I tried to explain earlier between having a right and doing the right thing. The speaker's motives may be relevant in deciding whether he does the right thing in speaking passionately about issues that may inflame or enrage the audience. But if he has a right to speak, because the danger in allowing him to speak is speculative, his motives cannot count as independent evidence in the argument that justifies stopping him.

But what of the individual rights of those who will be destroyed by a riot, of the passer-by who will be killed by a sniper's bullet or the shopkeeper who will be ruined by looting? To put the issue in this way, as a question of competing rights, suggests a principle that would undercut the effect of uncertainty. Shall we say that some rights to protection are so important that the Government is justified in doing all it can to maintain them? Shall we therefore say that the Government may abridge the rights of others to act when their acts might simply increase the risk, by however slight or speculative a margin, that some person's right to life or property will be violated?

Some such principle is relied on by those who oppose the Supreme Court's recent liberal rulings on police procedure. These rulings increase the chance that a guilty man will go free, and therefore marginally increase the risk that any particular member of the community will be murdered, raped, or robbed. Some critics believe that the Court's decisions must therefore be wrong.

But no society that purports to recognize a variety of rights, on the ground that a man's dignity or equality may be invaded in a variety of ways, can accept such a principle. If forcing a man to testify against himself, or forbidding him to speak, does the damage that the rights against self-incrimination and the right of free speech assume, then it would be contemptuous for the State to tell a man that he must suffer this damage against the possibility that other men's risk of loss may be marginally reduced. If rights make sense, then the degrees of their importance cannot be so different that some count not at all when others are mentioned.

Of course the Government may discriminate and may stop a man from exercising his right to speak when there is a clear and substantial risk that his speech will do great damage to the person or property of others, and no other means of preventing this are at hand, as in the case of the man shouting "Fire!" in a theater. But we must reject the suggested principle that the Government can simply ignore rights to speak when life and property are in question. So long as the impact of speech on these other rights remains speculative and marginal, it must look elsewhere for levers to pull.

4. Why Take Rights Seriously?

I said at the beginning of this essay that I wanted to show what a government must do that professes to recognize individual rights. It must dispense with the claim that citizens never have a right to break its law, and it must not define citizens' rights so that these are cut off for supposed reasons of the general good. Any Government's harsh treatment of civil disobedience, or campaign against vocal protest, may therefore be thought to count against its sincerity.

One might well ask, however, whether it is wise to take rights all that seriously after all. America's genius, at least in her own legend, lies in not taking any abstract doctrine to its logical extreme. It may be time to ignore abstractions and concentrate instead on giving the majority of our citizens a new sense of their Government's concern for their welfare, and of their title to rule.

That, in any event, is what former Vice-President Agnew seemed to believe. In a policy statement on the issue of "weirdos" and social misfits, he said that the liberals' concern for individual rights was a headwind blowing in the face of the ship of state. That is a poor metaphor, but the philosophical point it expresses is very well taken. He recognized, as many liberals do not, that the majority cannot travel as fast or as far as it would like if it recognizes the rights of individuals to do what, in the majority's terms, is the wrong thing to do.

Spiro Agnew supposed that rights are divisive and that national unity and a new respect for law may be developed by taking them more skeptically. But he is wrong. America will continue to be divided by its social and foreign policy, and if the economy grows weaker again the divisions will become more bitter. If we want our laws and our legal institutions to provide the ground rules within which these issues will be contested then these ground rules must not be the conqueror's law that the dominant class imposes on the weaker, as Marx supposed the law of a capitalist society must be. The bulk of the law—that part which defines and implements social, economic, and foreign policy—cannot be neutral. It must state, in its greatest part, the majority's view of the common good. The institution of rights is therefore crucial, because it represents the majority's promise to the minorities that their dignity and equality will be respected. When the divisions among the groups are most violent, then this gesture, if law is to work, must be most sincere.

The institution requires an act of faith on the part of the minorities, because the scope of their rights will be controversial whenever they are important, and because the officers of the majority will act on their own notions of what these rights really are. Of course these officials will disagree with many of the claims that a minority makes. That makes it all the more important that they take their decisions gravely. They must show that they understand what rights are, and they must not cheat on the full implications of the doctrine. The Government will not re-establish respect for law without giving the law some claim to respect. It cannot do that if it neglects the one feature that distinguishes law from ordered brutality. If the Government does not take rights seriously, then it does not take law seriously either.

■■□□

Part II

The Content
of
Human Rights

Statement on Human Rights

AMERICAN ANTHROPOLOGICAL ASSOCIATION

Submitted to the Commission on Human Rights, United Nations, by the Executive Board, American Anthropological Association

The problem faced by the Commission on Human Rights of the United Nations in preparing its Declaration on the Rights of Man must be approached from two points of view. The first, in terms of which the Declaration is ordinarily conceived, concerns the respect for the personality of the individual as such and his right to its fullest development as a member of his society. In a world order, however, respect for the cultures of differing human groups is equally important.

These are two facets of the same problem, since it is a truism that groups are composed of individuals, and human beings do not function outside the societies of which they form a part. The problem is thus to formulate a statement of human rights that will do more than just phrase respect for the individual as an individual. It must also take into full account the individual as a member of the social group of which he is a part, whose sanctioned modes of life shape his behavior, and with whose fate his own is thus inextricably bound.

Because of the great numbers of societies that are in intimate contact in the modern world, and because of the diversity of their ways of life, the primary task confronting those who would draw up a Declaration on the Rights of Man is thus, in essence, to resolve the following problem: How can the proposed Declaration be applicable to all human beings and not be a statement of rights conceived only in terms of the values prevalent in the countries of Western Europe and America?

American Anthropological Association, "Statement on Human Rights," *American Anthropologist,* 49, No. 4 (1947), pp. 539–543. Reprinted with permission of The American Anthropological Association.

Before we can cope with this problem, it will be necessary for us to outline some of the findings of the sciences that deal with the study of human culture that must be taken into account if the Declaration is to be in accord with the present state of knowledge about man and his modes of life.

If we begin, as we must, with the individual, we find that from the moment of his birth not only his behavior, but his very thought, his hopes, aspirations, the moral values which direct his action and justify and give meaning to his life in his own eyes and those of his fellows, are shaped by the body of custom of the group of which he becomes a member. The process by means of which this is accomplished is so subtle, and its effects are so far-reaching, that only after considerable training are we conscious of it. Yet if the essence of the Declaration is to be, as it must, a statement in which the right of the individual to develop his personality to the fullest is to be stressed, then this must be based on a recognition of the fact that the personality of the individual can develop only in terms of the culture of his society.

Over the past fifty years, the many ways in which man resolves the problems of subsistence, of social living, of political regulation of group life, of reaching accord with the Universe and satisfying his aesthetic drives has been widely documented by the researches of anthropologists among peoples living in all parts of the world. All peoples do achieve these ends. No two of them, however, do so in exactly the same way, and some of them employ means that differ, often strikingly, from one another.

Yet here a dilemma arises. Because of the social setting of the learning process, the individual cannot but be convinced that his own way of life is the most desirable one. Conversely, and despite changes originating from within and without his culture that he recognizes as worthy of adoption, it becomes equally patent to him that, in the main, other ways than his own, to the degree they differ from it, are less desirable than those to which he is accustomed. Hence valuations arise, that in themselves receive the sanction of accepted belief.

The degree to which such evaluations eventuate in action depends on the basic sanctions in the thought of a people. In the main, people are willing to live and let live, exhibiting a tolerance for behavior of another group different than their own, especially where there is no conflict in the subsistence field. In the history of Western Europe and America, however, economic expansion, control of armaments, and an evangelical religious tradition have translated the recognition of cultural differences into a summons to action. This has been emphasized by philosophical systems that have stressed absolutes in the realm of values and ends. Definitions of freedom, concepts of the nature of human rights, and the like, have thus been narrowly drawn. Alternatives have been decried, and suppressed where controls have been established over non-European peoples. The hard core of *similarities* between cultures has consistently been overlooked.

The consequences of this point of view have been disastrous for mankind. Doctrines of the "white man's burden" have been employed to implement economic exploitation and to deny the right to control their own affairs to millions of peoples over the world, where the expansion of Europe and America has not meant the literal extermination of whole populations. Rationalized in terms of ascribing cultural inferiority to these peoples, or in conceptions of their backwardness in development of their "primitive mentality," that justified their being held in the tutelage of their superiors, the history of the expansion of the western world has been marked by demoralization of human personality and the disintegration of human rights among the peoples over whom hegemony has been established.

The values of the ways of life of these peoples have been consistently misunderstood and decried. Religious beliefs that for untold ages have carried conviction and permitted adjustment to the Universe have been attacked as superstitious, immoral, untrue. And, since power carries its own conviction, this has furthered the process of demoralization begun by economic exploitation and the loss of political autonomy. The white man's burden, the civilizing mission, has been heavy indeed. But its weight has not been borne by those who, frequently in all honesty, have journeyed to the far places of the world to uplift those regarded by them as inferior.

We thus come to the first proposition that the study of human psychology and culture dictates as essential in drawing up a Bill of Human Rights in terms of existing knowledge:

1. *The individual realizes his personality through his culture, hence respect for individual differences entails a respect for cultural differences.*

There can be no individual freedom, that is, when the group with which the individual identifies himself is not free. There can be no full development of the individual personality as long as the individual is told, by men who have the power to enforce their commands, that the way of life of his group is inferior to that of those who wield the power.

This is more than an academic question, as becomes evident if one looks about oneself at the world as it exists today. Peoples who on first contact with European and American might were awed and partially convinced of the superior ways of their rulers have, through two wars and a depression, come to re-examine the new and the old. Professions of love of democracy, of devotion to freedom have come with something less than conviction to those who are themselves denied the right to lead their lives as seems proper to them. The religious dogmas of those who profess equality and practice discrimination, who stress the virtue of humility and are themselves arrogant in insistence on their beliefs, have little meaning for peoples whose devotion to other faiths makes these inconsistencies as clear as the desert landscape at high noon. Small wonder that these peoples, denied the right to live in terms of their own cultures, are discovering new values in old beliefs they had been led to question.

No consideration of human rights can be adequate without taking into account the related problem of human capacity. Man, biologically, is one. *Homo sapiens* is a single species, no matter how individuals may differ in their aptitudes, their abilities, their interests. It is established that any normal individual can learn any part of any culture other than his own, provided only he is afforded the opportunity to do so. That cultures differ in degree of complexity, of richness of content, is due to historic forces, not biological ones. All existing ways of life meet the test of survival. Of those cultures that have disappeared, it must be remembered that their number includes some that were great, powerful, and complex as well as others that were modest, content with the *status quo,* and simple. Thus we reach a second principle:

2. *Respect for differences between cultures is validated by the scientific fact that no technique of qualitatively evaluating cultures has been discovered.*

This principle leads us to a further one, namely that the aims that guide the life of every people are self-evident in their significance to that people. It is the principle that emphasizes the universals in human conduct rather than the absolutes that the culture of Western Europe and America stresses. It recognizes that the eternal verities only seem so because we have been taught to regard them as such; that every people, whether it expresses them or not, lives in devotion to verities whose eternal nature is as real to them as are those of Euroamerican culture to Euroamericans. Briefly stated, this third principle that must be introduced into our consideration is the following:

3. *Standards and values are relative to the culture from which they derive so that any attempt to formulate postulates that grow out of the beliefs or moral codes of one culture must to that extent detract from the applicability of any Declaration of Human Rights to mankind as a whole.*

Ideas of right and wrong, good and evil, are found in all societies, though they differ in their expression among different peoples. What is held to be a human right in one society may be regarded as anti-social by another people, or by the same people in a different period of their history. The saint of one epoch would at a later time be confined as a man not fitted to cope with reality. Even the nature of the physical world, the colors we see, the sounds we hear, are conditioned by the language we speak, which is part of the culture into which we are born.

The problem of drawing up a Declaration of Human Rights was relatively simple in the eighteenth century, because it was not a matter of *human* rights, but of the rights of men within the framework of the sanctions laid by a single society. Even then, so noble a document as the American Declaration of Independence, or the American Bill of Rights, could be written by men who themselves were slave-owners, in a country where chattel slavery was a part of the recognized social order. The revolutionary character of the slogan "Liberty, Equality, Fraternity" was never more apparent than in the struggles to implement it by extending it to the French slave-owning colonies.

Today the problem is complicated by the fact that the Declaration must be of world-wide applicability. It must embrace and recognize the validity of many different ways of life. It will not be convincing to the Indonesian, the African, the Indian, the Chinese, if it lies on the same plane as like documents of an earlier period. The rights of Man in the twentieth century cannot be circumscribed by the standards of any single culture or be dictated by the aspirations of any single people. Such a document will lead to frustration, not realization of the personalities of vast numbers of human beings.

Such persons, living in terms of values not envisaged by a limited Declaration, will thus be excluded from the freedom of full participaton in the only right and proper way of life that can be known to them, the institutions, sanctions and goals that make up the culture of their particular society.

Even where political systems exist that deny citizens the right of participation in their government, or seek to conquer weaker peoples, underlying cultural values may be called on to bring the peoples of such states to a realization of the consequences of the acts of their governments, and thus enforce a brake upon discrimination and conquest. For the political system of a people is only a small part of their total culture.

World-wide standards of freedom and justice, based on the principle that man is free only when he lives as his society defines freedom, that his rights are those he recognizes as a member of his society, must be basic. Conversely, an effective world-order cannot be devised except insofar as it permits the free play of personality of the members of its constituent social units, and draws strength from the enrichment to be derived from the interplay of varying personalities.

The world-wide acclaim accorded the Atlantic Charter, before its restricted applicability was announced, is evidence of the fact that freedom is understood and sought after by peoples having the most diverse cultures. Only when a statement of the right of men to live in terms of their own traditions is incorporated into the proposed Declaration, then, can the next step of defining the rights and duties of human groups as regards each other be set upon the firm foundation of the present-day scientific knowledge of Man.

June 24, 1947

Human Rights, Real and Supposed

MAURICE CRANSTON

It is said that when that remarkable American jurist Wesley Newcomb Hohfield tried to make the students at Yale Law School discriminate carefully between different uses of the term "right" in Anglo-American law, he earned himself considerable unpopularity; his pupils even got up a petition to have him removed from his Chair.[1] If the analysis of positive rights is thus resisted by law students we should not be surprised if the analysis of human rights is ill-regarded by many politicians, publicists, and even political theorists. Some politicians, indeed, have a vested interest in keeping talk about human rights as meaningless as possible. For there are those who do not want to see human rights become positive rights by genuine enactments; hence the more nebulous, unrealistic, or absurd the concept of human rights is made out to be, the better such men are pleased.

I shall argue in this paper that a philosophically respectable concept of human rights has been muddied, obscured, and debilitated in recent years by an attempt to incorporate into it specific rights of a different logical category. The traditional human rights are political and civil rights such as the right to life, liberty, and a fair trial. What are now being put forward as universal human rights are social and economic rights, such as the right to unemployment insurance, old-age pensions, medical services, and holidays with pay. I have both a philosophical and a political objection to this. The philosophical objection is that the new theory of human rights does not make sense. The political objection is that the circulation of a confused notion of human rights hinders the effective protection of what are correctly seen as human rights.

One distinction which seems now well established in people's minds is that between human rights or the Rights of Man or natural rights (I take these expressions

Maurice Cranston, "Human Rights, Real and Supposed," in *Political Theory and the Rights of Man,* D. D. Raphael (Ed.). (Bloomington, IN: Indiana University Press, 1967), pp. 43–53. © Maurice Cranston 1988.

to mean the same thing) and positive rights, a distinction which corresponds to the distinction between natural law (or justice, or the moral law) and positive law. The distinction has been made better understood by the critics of natural rights, by men like Edmund Burke, who could understand what was meant by the rights of Englishmen but not by the Rights of Man, and Jeremy Bentham, who said "Right is the child of law; from real laws come real rights, but from imaginary law, from "laws of nature," come imaginary rights. . . . Natural rights is simply nonsense, natural and imprescriptible rights [an American phrase] rhetorical nonsense, nonsense upon stilts."[2]

I do not think Bentham's remark is true, but it was worth saying, because it obliges those of us who think natural rights is *not* nonsense to explain what sort of sense it is. For Bentham—and for Burke—the only test of a right was "Is it actually enjoyed?," "Is it really enforced?" In other words, "Is it a positive right?" On this analysis, any right which is not a positive right is not granted the name of a right at all. For Burke the Rights of Man were mere abstractions: The rights of Englishmen were realities—a "positive recorded hereditary title to all that can be dear to the man and the citizen."[3] Real rights, again, were positive rights.

Both Burke and Bentham had a political as well as a philosophical interest in this question. Both regarded talk about the Rights of Man as mischievous as well as meaningless. Burke, the conservative, objected to such talk because it stimulated revolutionary sentiments, it injected "false ideas and vain expectations into men destined to travel the obscure walk of laborious life." Bentham, the radical, objected to talk about the Rights of Man because it produced declarations and manifestos that had no real significance in positive law, declarations which took the place of effective legislation for the public welfare. Burke disliked the rhetoric that led to public unrest and Bentham disliked the rhetoric that enabled politicians to fob off the public with words instead of deeds. Being thus attacked from Right and Left, it is no wonder that the idea of the Rights of Man, and of Natural Law, became unfashionable in the nineteenth century.

The present century has seen a marked revival of consciousness of what is now generally known as human rights—a term which has the advantage over the older expression "natural rights" of not committing one too ostentatiously to any traditional doctrine of Natural Law. The reason for this revival is perhaps to be sought in history, first, in the great twentieth-century evils, Nazism, fascism, total war, and racialism, which have all presented a fierce challenge to human rights; and secondly, in an increased belief in, or demand for, equality among men. When the United Nations was set up by the victorious powers in the Second World War, one of the first and most important tasks assigned to it was what Winston Churchill called "the enthronement of human rights." The efforts that have been made at the United Nations to fulfil this promise have much to teach a political theorist.

At the inaugural meeting of the Economic and Social Council of the U.N. in May 1946, a Commission on Human Rights was appointed to submit to the General Assembly recommendations and reports regarding an "International Bill of Rights." English-speaking delegates on this Commission promptly put forward a draft "Bill of Rights" in the form of a draft convention or treaty which both named the specific rights to be recognized and provided for the setting up of international institutions to deal with any alleged breach of those rights. The English-speaking delegations not unnaturally interpreted the expression "Bill of Rights" as meaning an instrument of positive law, and therefore understood the duty of the Commission to be that of finding a formula for making human rights positive rights by making them enforceable. The Russian representative objected to these proposals. He said that it was premature to discuss any measure of a binding or judicial nature; the Soviet Union was willing to support a "Bill of Rights" only if it was understood as a manifesto or declaration of rights. Some years afterwards the United States followed the Russian example, and announced that it, too, would not commit itself to any legally binding convention for the international protection of human rights.

In the U.N. Commission on Human Rights a compromise was settled on. The Commission agreed first to produce a manifesto or declaration of human rights, and then afterwards begin to work out "something more legally binding" which it was decided to call a Covenant. The manifesto did not take long to produce. It was given the name of Universal Declaration of Human Rights and proclaimed by the General Assembly of the United Nations in December 1948. . . .

One of the difficulties of translating the Universal Declaration of Human Rights into any kind of positive law is that the Declaration contains so much. It has no fewer than thirty articles. The first twenty spell out in detail the sort of rights that were named in the various classical statements of the Rights of Man: the rights to life, liberty, property, equality, justice, and the pursuit of happiness are articulated as, among other things, the right to freedom of movement; the right to own property alone as well as in association with others; the right to marry; the right to equality before the law and to a fair trial if accused of any crime; the right to privacy; the right to religious freedom; the right to free speech and peaceful assembly; the right to asylum. Among the institutions outlawed are slavery, torture, and arbitrary detention.

The Universal Declaration of 1948 did not, however, limit itself to this restatement of the familiar Rights of Man; it includes a further ten articles which name rights of a new and different kind.[4] Article 21 states that everyone has the right to take part in the government of his country, and further articles affirm the right to education; the right to work and to form trade unions; the right to equal pay for equal work; the right of everyone to a standard of living adequate to the health and well-being of himself and his family; the right to security in the event of unemployment, sickness, disability, widowhood, old age, or other lack of livelihood; the right to enjoy the arts and to share in scientific advancement and its benefits; and, what is even more novel, the right to rest, leisure, and "periodic holidays with pay."

The difference between these new rights and the traditional natural rights was not unnoticed by those responsible for drafting the Declaration. In the records of the Commission, the first twenty articles are called "political and civil rights" and the further rights "economic and social rights." These later rights appear to have been included under pressure from the Left; but there are many humanitarian people, apart from those on the Left, who (in my belief, unwisely) agree with their inclusion.[5]

So far as the United Nations is concerned, the Commission on Human Rights soon discovered, when it came to draft the "more legally binding" Covenant, that the two kinds of rights did not mix together well; and the Commission was therefore obliged to draft *two* covenants, one concerning the political and civil rights, the other the social and economic rights. Neither draft has so far proved acceptable to the General

Assembly. In the meantime altogether more progress has been made in the field of human rights by another international organization, the Council of Europe. In 1950 a European Convention for the Protection of Human Rights was signed by the member States of the Council of Europe at Strasbourg. This time the so-called "social and economic rights" were omitted; the rights that were named were the traditional "political and civil rights." Moreover, in this case, a European Commission and a European Court of Human Rights were set up with full judicial powers to investigate and remedy any alleged breach of the rights named in the Convention. Here, clearly, is a tangible attempt to translate the human rights into positive rights on an international scale. The only weakness of the European Convention is that some leading European powers, France, Italy, Greece, and Turkey, have refused to recognize the jurisdiction of the European Court or to grant the right to individual petition to the Commission or the Court. Nevertheless a dozen other nations *do* recognize these institutions; so that changes in positive law have helped in those places to make men's "human rights" positive rights.[6]

One of the objections to regarding the "social and economic" rights as authentic human rights is that it would be totally impossible to translate them in the same way into positive rights by analogous political and legal action. There are other objections: But the time has now come to consider more carefully what is meant by a right, and then what kind of right a human right is. We have already noted the distinction between human rights and positive rights; I propose now to rearrange rights into two other categories; the one I shall call legal rights, the other moral rights.

(1) **Legal Rights** may be distinguished as follows:

a. *General positive rights:* The rights that are enjoyed and fully assured to everyone living under a given jurisdiction or constitution.

b. *Traditional rights and liberties:* Burke said that the English people had risen against James II because he had taken away their traditional rights and liberties as Englishmen. The Vichy government took away many of the traditional rights and liberties of Frenchmen. This class of rights includes lost positive rights as well as existing positive rights.

c. *Nominal "legal" rights:* Even the least liberal nations tend to have "façade" constitutions[7] which "guarantee" freedom of speech, movement, assembly, and other such rights to their inhabitants. But where these nominal rights are not enforced, they cannot, of course, be classed as positive rights. We nevertheless see the demand in some such places for the nominal "legal" rights being made positive rights. One example is the demand of certain Polish intellectuals for that freedom of expression which their constitution assures them. An even more publicized example is the demand of the Negroes in the United States for the nominal legal right to vote, enter State schools, and so forth, to be translated into positive rights.

d. *Positive rights, liberties, privileges, and immunities of a limited class of persons:* Under this category we should have to include all rights which are attached to membership of a given category, e.g., the rights of clergymen, of peers, of doctors, of graduates of the University of Oxford, and of freemen of the City of London. The twentieth century has become impatient of privileges, and rights which were once enjoyed by a limited class of persons are often now claimed by all the inhabitants of a country. For example, the privileges of citizenship, the rights of ratepayers, as they were known in nineteenth-century England, are now enjoyed by all adult British subjects. A demand for the extension of rights within a political society is often confused with the demand for human rights. But the two are quite distinct.

e. *The positive rights, liberties, privileges, and immunities of a single person:* Here the examples are few, because the cases are few: the rights of the President of the United States, of the Chairman of the Senate; the rights of the King, or the Lord Chancellor, or the Archbishop of Canterbury, are examples. Since the decay of the doctrine of the Divine Right of Kings, this class of rights does not present much of a problem.

The foregoing classes cover the category of legal rights. Next in turn is the category of moral rights. In this case it will be convenient to reverse the order of generality.

(2) **Moral Rights**

a. *Moral rights of one person only:* We remember Bradley's famous phrase "my station and its duties": we can equally speak of "my station and its rights." I, and I alone, have a network of rights which arise from the fact that I have done certain deeds, paid certain monies, been elected to certain places, and so forth. Some of these rights are legal rights as well as moral rights. But in considering them as moral rights the question is not "Does the law uphold them?" but "Have I just claim to them?" Not all my moral rights may in fact be enjoyed. Often we become most conscious of our moral rights precisely when they are *not* upheld. I am inclined to say "I have a moral right to be told what is going on in my own house" when I realize I am not being told. So just as the crucial question with legal rights is "Are they secured and enjoyed?," the crucial question in a moral right is "Is there a just title?" Is there a sound moral claim? *Justification* is the central question.

b. *The moral rights of anyone in a particular situation:* This is the class of moral rights which belongs to everyone who comes into a certain specific category, e.g., that of a parent, or a tutor, or an *au pair* girl. So we can say of a person, if he is a member of this class, he is entitled to so and so. Claims to have such moral rights are pressed by proving that one does belong to the appropriate category.

c. *The moral rights of all people in all situations:* Because these rights are universal we should naturally expect them to be few in number; and we should expect them to be highly generalized in their formulation. It is easier to agree, for example, about the kind of deed which violates the right to life than it is to agree about any philosophical expression of the right to life. Moreover, it is inevitable that such a right as that to liberty will be somewhat differently understood in different societies, where the boundary between liberty and licence will be differently drawn. Again, our understanding of the right to property will differ according to the meaning we give to that richly ambiguous word.

The place which human rights occupy in my classification is readily understood. Human rights are a form of moral right, and they differ from other moral rights in being the rights of all people at all times and in all situations. This characteristic of human rights is recognized in the first paragraph of the preamble to the Universal Declaration of 1948, which says: "Whereas recognition of the inherent dignity and of the equal and inalienable rights of all members of the human family is the foundation of freedom, justice and peace in the world. . . ."

Part of the difficulty of justifying human rights is their very universality. Moral rights of classes (2a.) and (2b.) above are justified by reference to the definite station or situation of the claimants. I claim a right to be told about the health of Nicholas Cranston by showing that I am his father. I do not think anyone else (except his mother) has the same right. But human rights do not depend in any way on the station or the situation of the individual. This is part of what is meant by saying they are "rights that pertain to a human being merely because he is a human being." If the validity of a moral right is commonly established by reference to the station or situation of the claimant, it is not altogether easy to see by what tests one could validate the rights which are *not* considered in relation to any definite situation.

Nevertheless there are some tests for the authenticity of a human right or universal moral right. Rights bear a clear relationship to duties. And the first test of both is that of practicability. It is not my duty to do what it is physically impossible for me to do. You cannot reasonably say it was my duty to have jumped into the Thames at Richmond to rescue a drowning child if I was nowhere near Richmond at the time the child was drowning. What is true of duties is equally true of rights. If it is impossible for a thing to be done, it is absurd to claim it as a right. At present it is utterly impossible, and will be for a long time yet, to provide "holidays with pay" for everybody in the world. For millions of people who live in those parts of Asia, Africa, and South America where industrialization has hardly begun, such claims are vain and idle.

The traditional "political and civil rights" can (as I have said) be readily secured by legislation; and generally they can be secured by fairly simple legislation. Since those rights are for the most part rights against government interference with a man's activities, a large part of the legislation needed has to do no more than restrain the government's own executive arm. This is no longer the case when we turn to "the right to work," "the right to social security," and so forth. For a government to provide social security it needs to do more than make laws; it has to have access to great capital wealth, and many governments in the world today are still poor. The government of India, for example, simply cannot command the resources that would guarantee each one of the 480 million inhabitants of India "a standard of living adequate for the health and well-being of himself and his family," let alone "holidays with pay."

Another test of a human right is that it shall be a genuinely universal moral right. This the so-called human right to holidays with pay plainly cannot pass. For it is a right that is necessarily limited to those persons who are *paid* in any case, that is to say, to the *employé* class. Since not everyone belongs to this class, the right cannot be a universal right, a right which, in the terminology of the Universal Declaration, "everyone" has. That the right to a holiday with pay is for many people a real moral right, I would not for one moment deny. But it is a right which falls into section (2b.)

of the classification of rights which I have set out above; that is, a right which can be claimed by members of a specific class of persons *because* they are members of that class.

A further test of a human right, or universal moral right, is the test of *paramount importance*. Here the distinction is less definite, but no less crucial. And here again there is a parallel between rights and duties. It is a paramount duty to relieve great distress, as it is not a paramount duty to give pleasure. It would have been my duty to rescue the drowning child at Richmond if I had been there at the time; but it is not, in the same sense, my duty to give Christmas presents to the children of my neighbours. This difference is obscured in the crude utilitarian philosophy which analyses moral goodness in terms of the greatest happiness of the greatest number: But common sense does not ignore it. Common sense knows that fire engines and ambulances are essential services, whereas fun fairs and holiday camps are not. Liberality and kindness are reckoned moral virtues; but they are not moral duties in the sense that the obligation to rescue a drowning child is a moral duty.

It is worth considering the circumstances in which ordinary people find themselves invoking the language of human rights. I suggest they are situations like these:

A black student in South Africa is awarded a scholarship to Oxford and then refused a passport by the South African government simply because he is black. We feel this is clear invasion of the human right to freedom of movement.

Jews are annihilated by the Nazi government, simply because they are Jews. We feel this is a manifest abuse (an atrocious abuse) of the human right to life.

In several countries men are held in prison indefinitely without trial. We feel this a gross invasion of the human right to liberty and to a fair trial on any criminal charge.

In considering cases of this kind, we are confronted by matters which belong to a totally different moral dimension from questions of social security and holidays with pay. A human right is something of which no one may be deprived without a grave affront to justice. There are certain deeds which should never be done, certain freedoms which should never be invaded, some things which are supremely sacred. If a Declaration of Human Rights is what it purports to be, a declaration of universal moral rights, it should be confined to this sphere of discourse. If rights of another class are introduced, the effect may even be to bring the whole concept of human rights into disrepute. "It would be a splendid thing," people might say, "for everyone to have holidays with pay, a splendid thing for everyone to have social security, a splendid thing to have equality before the law, and freedom of speech, and the right to life. One day, perhaps, this beautiful ideal may be realized. . . ."

Thus the effect of a Universal Declaration which is overloaded with affirmations of so-called human rights which are not human rights at all is to push *all* talk of human rights out of the clear realm of the morally compelling into the twilight world of utopian aspiration. In the Universal Declaration of 1948 there indeed occurs the phrase a "common standard of achievement" which brands that Declaration as an attempt to translate rights into ideals. And however else one might choose to define moral rights, they are plainly *not* ideals or aspirations.

Rights have been variously defined by jurists and philosophers. Some have spoken of them in terms of "justifiable claims" or "moral titles"; others have analysed rights in terms of duty ("what we have an overwhelming duty to respect"); others again have preferred to speak of right conduct or obligation or of ought ("a man has a right whenever other men ought not to prevent his doing what he wants or refuse him some service he asks for or needs"). All these words—"right," "justice," "duty," "ought," "obligation"—are the key terms of what Kant called the "categorical imperative." What ought to be done, what is obligatory, what is right, what is duty, what is just, is not what it would be nice to see done one day; it is what is demanded by the basic norms of morality or justice.

An ideal is something one can aim at, but cannot by definition immediately realize. A right, on the contrary, is something that can, and from the moral point of view *must,* be respected here and now. If this were not so, we should have to agree with Bentham; if the Rights of Man were ideals, to talk of them as rights at all would indeed be rhetorical nonsense. We can give sense to human rights only because we can reasonably claim that men have moral rights and that among the moral rights which each man has are some that he shares with all other men.

To deny that the "economic and social rights" are the universal moral rights of all men is not to deny that they may be the moral rights of some men. In the moral criticism of legal rights, it is certainly arguable that the privileges of some members of a certain community ought to be extended to other members (and perhaps all members) of that community. But this matter is correctly seen as a problem of *socialization* or *democratization*—that is, the extension of privileges and immunities—rather than as a problem about the universal rights of all men: And the case for any such specific claims to an extension of legal rights must be argued on other grounds.

Notes

1. Arthur L. Corbin in his Introduction to Hohfield's *Fundamental Legal Conceptions.* (Yale University Press: New Haven, 1964).

2. *Anarchical Fallacies.*

3. *The Philosophy of Edmund Burke,* Bredvold and Ross (Eds.). (Michigan University Press: Ann Arbor, 1960), p. 205.

4. C. J. Friedrich, in "Rights, Liberties, Freedoms: A Reappraisal," *American Political Science Review,* LVII, 4, (Dec. 1963), shows that some "social and economic rights" were known to the Age of Reason. He quotes the "right to work" being named by Turgot and Robespierre and gives references to eighteenth-century claims to the right to education.

5. E.g., Professor C. J. Friedrich (cf. previous note). Another champion of the view that social and economic rights should be interpreted as human rights is the late Pope, John XXIII. I have discussed his views in an article, "Pope John XXIII on Peace and the Rights of Man," *Political Quarterly,* Oct. 1963.

6. See A. H. Robertson, *Human Rights in Europe.* (Manchester University Press: 1964).

7. See G. Sartori, "Constitutionalism," *American Political Science Review,* Vol. LVI (Dec. 1962), pp. 853–65.

International
Human Rights
As "Rights"

LOUIS HENKIN[1]

"International human rights" is now a common subject for intellectual as well as popular discourse, but few have written about it in relation to the massive literature on "rights." Are "international human rights" "rights," and what is the source and basis of their authority? Are they moral rights? Are they legal rights and, if so, in what legal universe? Whose rights are they? Are there correlative duties and if so upon whom? What remedies are there when the rights are violated? Are the remedies necessary and adequate to support their quality as rights?

The International Human
Rights Movement

"International human rights" is a term used with varying degrees of precision (or imprecision) and with different connotation in different context. In wide usage it corresponds to the "international human rights movement," born during World War II out of a spreading conviction that how human beings are treated anywhere concerns everyone, everywhere. That attitude itself perhaps blended several different "statements": an assertion of fact about human psychology and emotion, that human beings cannot close their minds and hearts to mistreatment or suffering of other human beings; a moral statement, that mistreatment or suffering of human beings violates a common morality (perhaps also natural law, or God's law) and that all human beings

Louis Henkin, "International Rights as 'Rights,'" in *Nomos XXIII: Human Rights,* J. Roland Pennock and John W. Chapman (Eds.), (New York: New York University Press, 1981), pp. 257–280. Reprinted with permission of the publisher.

are morally obligated to do something about such mistreatment or suffering, individually and through their political and social institutions; an international political statement, that governments will attend to such mistreatment or suffering in other countries through international institutions and will take account of them also in their relations with other states. These three kinds of statement combined to support a concept of "human rights" and a program to promote their enjoyment, as implied in declarations like President Franklin Roosevelt's "Four Freedoms" message, in various articulations of the war aims of the Allies in World War II and in their plans for the postwar world.

The end of the war saw wide acceptance of "human rights" reflected in two forms. Human rights appeared in the constitutions and laws of virtually all states. Conquerors wrote them into law for occupied countries; for example, Germany and Japan. Departing colonial powers sometimes required them of newborn states as part of the price of "liberation," and many new states wrote them into their constitutions as their own commitment. Older states, responding to the *Zeitgeist,* also emphasized human rights in new national documents.

The human rights movement also took a second, transnational form. Human rights were prominent in the new postwar international order: in treaties imposed upon vanquished nations (e.g., Italy, Rumania); in the UN Charter and the Nuremberg Charter; in numerous resolutions and declarations of the new international institutions, notably, the United Nations and regional institutions in Latin America and Europe. In the United Nations "human rights" was on every agenda, and the dedicated efforts of individuals and some governments resulted in important international political and legal instruments, beginning with the Universal Declaration on Human Rights and the Convention on the Prevention and Punishment of the Crime of Genocide, both adopted without dissent in 1948.[2] There has followed a series of other resolutions and declarations and an impressive array of other international covenants and conventions, principally the International Covenant on Civil and Political Rights and the International Covenant on Economic, Social, and Cultural Rights, both completed in 1966 and both in force since 1976. Europe and Latin America also developed important human rights laws and institutions.

I stress—and distinguish—those two different manifestations of general, worldwide concern with human rights. "Universalization" has brought acceptance, at least in principle and rhetoric, of the concept of individual human rights by all societies and governments and its reflection in national constitutions and laws. "Internationalization" has brought agreement, at least in political-legal principle and in rhetoric, that individual human rights are of "international concern" and a proper subject for diplomacy, international law, and international institutions.

My subject is "international human rights," that is, human rights as a subject of international law and politics, not individual rights in national societies under national legal systems. But the two are not unrelated in law or in politics. The international movement sees human rights as rights that, under accepted moral principle, the individual should enjoy under the constitutional-legal system of his society. To induce states to arrange their constitutional-legal systems to achieve that result, and to supply any failures to do so, the international system has, *inter alia,* promulgated an international law of human rights. International human rights, then, were born because national protections for accepted human rights were deemed deficient and can be seen as merely additional international protections for rights under national law. The international law of human rights is implemented largely by national laws and institutions; it is satisfied when national laws and institutions are sufficient. Ambiguities in the content or scope of international rights are resolved (at least in the first instance) by national governments in the light of national standards. The international law of human rights differs little from many national human rights laws. Where there are differences, international rights supplement national rights; in the United States, for example, the two sets of rights would be cumulated and both given effect by courts and other national institutions. In peripheral respects there may be conflict between the conceptions of rights or between particular rights in the two systems, and in most countries national institutions will give effect to the national requirement, placing the country in violation of the international obligation.

The International Law of Human Rights

The international law of human rights derives principally from contemporary international agreements in which states undertake to recognize, respect, and promote specific rights for the inhabitants of their own countries.[3] There are also older obligations in international law that today fit in the human rights category. Traditional international law imposed on states a responsibility not to "deny justice" to nationals of other states in regard to their persons, probably also to their property.[4] Although that law is now highly uncertain as regards some forms of alien property, it remains otherwise effective and is supplemented, not superseded, by the new human rights law that applies to nationals and aliens alike. There are also old and less old treaties containing undertakings to treat individuals in ways corresponding to respect for some of their human rights; for example, to accord nationals of another state certain rights and freedoms under domestic law (freedom of religion, the right to work) or to provide status and rights for members of friendly foreign forces. Some agreements—for example, those providing protection for minorities, or the many conventions promoted by the International Labor Organization which set minimum labor and social standards—apply to nationals as well as to aliens.

Content.   The international law of human rights is contained principally in the International Covenant on Civil and Political Rights and the International Covenant on Economic, Social, and Cultural Rights, which together legislate essentially what the Universal Declaration had declared.[5] In the Covenant on Civil and Political Rights, states undertake to respect and insure rights to life and personal integrity; to due process of law and a humane penal system; freedom to travel within as well as outside one's country; freedom of expression, religion, and conscience; cultural and linguistic rights for minority groups; the right to participate in government (including free elections); the right to marry and found a family; and the right to equality and freedom from discrimination—a dominant theme in international human rights.[6] Most (but not all) rights are subject to derogation or limitation "to the extent strictly required," in "time of public emergency which threatens the life of the nation and the existence of which is officially proclaimed."[7] Some rights—freedom of movement, assembly, association—may be curtailed by law as necessary to protect national security, public order, health or morals, or the rights and freedoms of others.[8]

In the Covenant on Economic, Social, and Cultural Rights, states undertake to "take steps" "to the maximum of available resources," "with a view to achieving progressively the full realization" of designated rights.[9] These include the right to work, to enjoy just and favorable conditions of work, and to join trade unions; the right to social security, to protection for the family, for mothers and children; the right to be "free from hunger," to have an adequate standard of living, including adequate food, clothing and housing, and the continuous improvement of living conditions; the right to the highest attainable standards of physical and mental health; to education; the right to take part in cultural life. In this covenant, too, equality and nondiscrimination are a pervasive theme. Derogations and limitations by law are permitted if they are compatible with the nature of these rights and are solely for the purpose of promoting the general welfare in a democratic society.[10] Some rights—for example, trade union freedom—are subject only to limitations "necessary in a democratic society in the interests of national security or public order or for the protection of the rights and freedoms of others."[11]

Remedies.   The remedies for violation of international obligations to respect human rights are in principle the same as for other violations of international obligation. A "promisee," a state to which the obligation runs, can make claim and seek redress through diplomatic channels or by agreed-upon international "machinery" or, in some limited respects, by self-help. In human rights agreements the promisee is a state, and the true beneficiary is an individual (and usually a national of the violating state), but that does not detract from the right of any state party to an agreement to seek its observance by others.[12] Particular conventions provide additional "enforcement machinery." Under the Covenant on Civil and Political Rights, states are required to report on their compliance to a Human Rights Committee.[13] As regards states that agree to optional provisions, the committee may also receive complaints of violation from other states or from individuals.[14] The committee's powers are essentially to inquire, intercede, quietly seek redress, later expose unrepaired violations to publicity. Under the Covenant on Economic, Social, and Cultural Rights, states are required to report on their compliance to the UN Economic and Social Council,[15] which may transmit reports to the UN Commission on Human Rights "for study and general recommendation" and "may submit from time to time to the General Assembly reports with recommendations of a general nature."[16] The European human rights system has a more complex and more effective system of remedies, combining an active European Commission on Human Rights (which receives petitions also from individuals and nongovernmental organizations), a Council of Ministers, and a Court of Human Rights to which cases may be brought by the Commission or by states. The

Organization of American States also has an active commission; the American Convention on Human Rights has just come into force and the Inter-American Court of Human Rights has been established.

Philosophical Inquiries

The framers of international human rights were not philosophers, but politicians, citizens. The international instruments do not articulate any philosophical foundations or reflect any clear philosophical assumptions, either for the "human rights" they were recognizing or the international human rights "system" they were establishing. We can only attempt to characterize what we find, deriving—perhaps imposing—a philosophical perspective and answers to a philosopher's questions. In passing to exploration of international human rights as "rights" I nod to other, related philosophical issues.

Philosophical inquiry about international human rights must distinguish and proceed on two different levels. The international law of human rights creates legal rights and obligations that invite examination in the light of "rights theory." But international discourse, including international law, refers repeatedly to "human rights" aparently as preexisting in some other universe. The individual had human rights before the international system took notice of them and would continue to have them if the international law of human rights were repealed and the international system turned its back on them. Are these human rights "rights," and how do they relate to the legal rights created by the international law of human rights?

Human Rights in International Perspective. Philosophers properly inquire how seriously the word "rights" is to be taken in the frequent reference to "human rights" in international discourse. Some will argue that it carries no philosophical "rights" implications at all but is essentially rhetorical. It suggests an affirmative value, a "good," that is universal, fundamental, overriding. Particular reference, too—say, to a "right to education"—means only that it is desirable and important, indeed very highly desirable and important, that every human being be educated.

International reference to human rights commonly indicates also, however, a positive attitude to the concept of individual rights vis-à-vis national societies and largely also to the content of such rights, generally as set forth in international documents. Nominally, at least, this positive attitude is now common to all states, governments, and societies, even those that proclaim allegiance to collectivism and sometimes decry individualism. Indeed, international discourse insists that these human rights exist and that they are rights, although it is not clear what kind of rights they are and in what universe. Most plausibly they appear to be moral rights in an accepted moral order, or even legal rights under some modern version of natural law. Perhaps every human being is "entitled" to essential freedom and basic needs and has valid "claims" to them against the moral order, or the universe or God; at least, the individual in society has valid claim to them against his society and it is obligated to respect and insure them.[17] In the good society, such rights are also legal rights in the domestic legal order and valid legal claims, supported by effective remedies, against the society. These rights are human in that they are universal, for all persons in all societies. Some rights—to form a trade union or to enjoy vacation with pay—of course apply only to workers in industrialized societies, but these too are universal in that they apply to all to whom they are relevant. Perhaps they are human rights, too, in the sense that they are particular expressions of an overall, *a priori,* universal moral principle, that a human being is entitled to what he requires for his "human dignity."

International human rights derive of course from national rights theories and systems, harking back through English, American, and French constitutionalism to John Locke et al. and earlier natural rights and natural law theory. In its American version that constitutionalism included concepts of original individual autonomy translated into popular sovereignty; social compact providing for continued self-government through chosen, accountable representatives; limited government for limited purposes; and retained, inalienable, individual rights.[18] But the profound influence of that constitutionalism on international acceptance of human rights did not depend on, or take with it, commitment to all the underlying theory. International adoption of human rights reflects no comprehensive political theory of the relation of individual to society, only what is implied in the idea of individual rights against society. Human rights are "inherent" but not necessarily "retained" from any hypothetical state of nature anteceding government. There is a nod to popular sovereignty but nothing of social compact or of continuing consent of the governed. Retained rights are not the condition of government, and violating them does not necessarily give rise to a right to undo government by revolution. Inevitably, international human rights also implicate the purposes for which governments are created, but they surely do not imply a commitment to government for limited purposes only. Born after various socialisms were established and spreading, and commitment to welfare economics and the welfare state was nearly universal, international human rights implied rather a conception of government as designed for all purposes and seasons. The rights deemed to be fundamental include not only limitations precluding government from invading civil and political rights but positive obligations for government to promote economic and social well-being, implying government that is activist, intervening, planning, committed to economic-social programs for the society that would redound as economic-social rights for the individual.

That there are "fundamental human rights" was a declared article of faith, "reaffirmed" by "the peoples of the United Nations" in the UN Charter. The Universal Declaration of Human Rights, striving for a pronouncement that would appeal to diverse political systems governing diverse peoples, built on that faith and eschewed philosophical exploration. Because of that faith—and of political and ideological forces—governments accepted the concept of human rights, agreed that they were appropriate for international concern, cooperated to define them, assumed international obligations to respect them, and submitted to some international scrutiny as regards compliance with these obligations. Tacitly, those who built international human rights accepted individual rights as "natural," in a contemporary sense: They correspond to the nature of man and of society, his psychology and its sociology. Rights "derive from the inherent dignity of the human person."[19] Rights are instrumental, leading to conditions whose value is axiomatic for individuals, societies, and the international system: "Recognition of the inherent dignity and of the equal and inalienable rights of all members of the human family is the foundation of freedom, justice and peace in the world."[20] Respect for and observance of human rights will help create "conditions of stability and well-being which are necessary for peaceful and friendly relations among nations."[21] There is no agreed theory justifying "human dignity" as the source of rights, and we are not told how the needs of human dignity are determined. We are not told what was the conception of justice which human rights would support and whence it came, nor are we given the evidence that, or the theory on which, preserving human rights will promote peace in the world.

Human Rights As Positive International Law.   I have suggested that, independently of any international law on human rights, international discourse sees human rights as either:

a. "goods," desiderata, that are not rights but that might be translated into legal rights in domestic or international law;
b. moral rights in an accepted moral order (or under some natural law), the individual having "claims" to freedoms and basic needs, seen perhaps as claims upon the moral order, or the universe, or God;
c. moral (or natural law) claims by every individual upon his society; or
d. legal claims upon his society under its constitutional system and law.

The purpose of international political and legal preoccupation with human rights, and of recognizing their quality as rights of some order, is to help obtain for them the quality of legal rights in domestic societies and to enhance the likelihood that they will be enjoyed in fact.

The international law of human rights builds on faith in the validity and desirability of human rights, but it largely avoids the philosophical uncertainties that trouble human rights discourse generally. Whatever the status and character of human rights in the moral order or in some other legal order, for international law human rights are a subject of positive law, conventional or customary.[22]

The positive character of international legal human rights disposes of one part of the debate about economic and social rights. Maurice Cranston can properly ask whether one can have a right to two weeks' vacation with pay, and whether that is a human right, and he and others (including the governments of the West) argued against treating social and economic aspirations as rights and giving them status as law.[23] But the majority of states did not heed those admonitions, and the Covenant on Economic, Social and Cultural Rights is now in force.

There are, of course, important differences between that covenant and the Covenant on Civil and Political Rights. The latter is designed for full and immediate realization; the former requires steps only "to the maximum of [a state's] available resources" and with a view to achieving the full realization of rights "progressively." There is even a subtle but conscious and pervasive difference in tone and in the terms of legal prescription. The Covenant on Civil and Political Rights speaks throughout in terms of the rights which the individual has: "Every human being has the inherent right to life"; "No one shall be held in slavery"; "Everyone shall be free to leave any country, including his own"; "Everyone shall have the right to hold opinions without interference." The Covenant on Economic, Social, and Cultural Rights, on the other hand, is couched in terms of the state's action (or obligation), not the individual's right: "The states-parties to the present covenant recognize the right to work"; "the states . . . undertake to ensure . . . the right of everyone to form trade unions"; "the states . . . recognize the right of everyone to social security," "to adequate standard of living," "to education." There are also important political and practical differences between the two sets of rights, especially in that the economic-social rights tend to be collective and to depend on national planning and policies and on their success. As a matter of law, however, I do not think any of these differences critical. The Convention on Economic, Social, and Cultural Rights uses language of obligation, not merely of aspiration or hope. An undertaking to do something "to the maximum of its available resources" and to achieve "progressively" creates a clear and firm legal obligation, subject to those limitations. That a state "recognizes the right to an education" is not different, legally, from "everyone shall have a right to an education." Both create a legal claim against the state for failure to provide what was promised or for not insuring it against interruption ("to the maximum of its available resources").[24] A state's failure to perform its undertakings gives rise to the same kind of remedies as do other international agreements.[25]

Rights Under the International Law of Human Rights

What has this international law done to human rights qua rights? What new legal rights have the international legal instruments created?

I can only allude lightly to the literature on "rights." In a word, according to the common view one has a legal right only against some other; to say one has a legal right against another is to say that one has a valid legal claim upon him and that the addressee has a corresponding legal obligation in the relevant legal system. Commonly, it is deemed to imply also that the system provides a recognized and institutionalized legal remedy to the right-holder to compel the performance of the obligation or otherwise vindicate the right. It may imply also that the right claimed is, in fact, commonly enjoyed (and "as of right," not by grace), and the corresponding duty is, in fact, generally carried out (and from a sense of legal obligation).

To examine the international law of human rights from the perspective of "rights" theory, it helps to keep in mind special characteristics of international law and of the international legal system. Because international law is made by states assuming legal obligations, the states-parties to international human rights instruments might be seen in two different roles. Acting together, the states-parties are legislators, making law. As a result of that legislation every state-party is an "obligor," having obligations, duties, to respect and insure what are designated as the "human rights" of their inhabitants. After the agreement comes into force, the state as legislator largely disappears (except in the sense that lawmaking continues by interpretation and application); only the state as obligor remains.

Because the international law of human rights is made by states assuming obligations (the state as legislator), the international instruments focus at first on the state's obligations: It is the state's undertaking that creates the law. But under that law after it is in effect, the focus shifts sharply. The instruments are designated as dealing with the "rights" of individuals, and there is reference to individual "rights" in every article.[26] But the state's obligation and the individual's right are not necessarily correlative, or even in the same legal order. There are different possible perspectives on the relation between them:

1. The simple, undaring view sees international human rights agreements essentially, if not exclusively, in interstate terms. The agreements constitute undertakings by each state-party to every other state-party, creating rights and obligations between them. For violations of the agreement, as for other international agreements, there are "horizontal" inter-state remedies: The victim state can make diplomatic claims upon the violator, request redress and reparation, sometimes may (lawfully) resort to "self-help." Insofar as the victim state has a legal right and pursues legal remedies, the violating state has correlative duties, including the duty, after violation, to provide redress and reparation, and even to accept the victim state's self-help where it is appropriate. The human rights agreements contemplate also special remedies, and a victim state—or the agreed international body—has the right to invoke those remedies, and the violating state has a duty to submit to them.[27]

In this perspective, the only rights and duties created by international human rights are the duty of every state-party to act as it had promised and the right of every other state-party to have that promise to it kept. The individual has no international legal rights; he is only the "incidental beneficiary" of rights and duties between the state-parties. The individual has no international remedies; he is only the incidental beneficiary of the remedies available between states-parties. He stands no better even as regards states that have adhered to the optional protocol to the civil-political rights covenant. A state party to the protocol "recognizes the competence of the [Human Rights] Committee to receive and consider communications from individuals subject to its jurisdiction who claim to be victims of a violation by that State Party of any of the rights set forth in the Covenant."[28] That, it will be argued, does not establish a private remedy for violation of a private right, but only an additional mechanism for enforcing the rights and duties of the states under the covenant, by providing the committee with evidence as to whether those rights and duties have been honored. If a party to the protocol should interfere with an individual's attempt to transmit a communication to the committee, or with the committee's action upon that communication, the state is violating its duty to other parties to the protocol, not any right of the individual, and the only remedies for that violation, too, are interstate remedies.

A fortiori, there are no individual legal rights under the Covenant on Economic, Social, and Cultural Rights. The obligations assumed are by states to other states and

even these are collective, long-term; the individual is not only an incidental beneficiary but a contingent and remote one and has no remedies whatever.

From this perspective, I stress, there are no international legal rights for the
individual. When international law speaks of "human rights," it does not refer to,
establish, or recognize them as international legal rights in the international legal
system. By establishing interstate rights and duties in regard to "human rights,"
international law indicates its adherence to the morality and moral values that under-
lie them and strengthens the consensus in regard to that morality; it encourages
societies to convert those moral principles into legal rights in their domestic legal
order; it creates international legal remedies and promotes other forces to induce
states to make such "rights" effective in the domestic legal system; it does not, however, make them international legal rights for individuals in the international legal order.

2. A second perspective would see the international agreements, while creating
rights and duties for the states-parties, as also giving the individual rights against his
state under international law (in addition to any rights he has under his national
constitutional-legal system).[29] The language of the agreements clearly declares these
individual rights in every clause: "Every human being has the inherent right to life";
"No one shall be held in slavery"; "Everyone shall be free to leave any country,
including his own." The individual has these international legal rights even though
they are enforceable only by inter-state remedies, by governments or international
bodies acting in his behalf. Under the optional protocol to the Covenant on Civil and
Political Rights providing for consideration by the Human Rights Committee of
individual complaints, or under the provision in the European Convention that the
European Commission "may receive petitions" from any person claiming to be the
victim of a violation, the individual enforces his own right by his own remedy.

The same argument might apply even to economic and social rights. In the
Covenant on Economic, Social, and Cultural Rights, the covenant speaks of rights for
the individual in every article. In principle, surely, one can have a legal right to an education, or even to a vacation with pay, and the states assumed obligations to accord
these, thereby giving the individual a right—a valid, legal claim—to them. That there
are no individual remedies provided, that even the international remedies hardly
guarantee that the individual will enjoy the indicated rights presently, may weaken the
real enjoyment of these rights but does not derogate from their quality as rights. Every
individual has a legal right under international law to have his society "take steps . . .
to the maximum of its available resources with a view to achieving" all the enumer-
ated rights.

3. A third perspective, which is independent of but might be combined with either
of the two set forth, would suggest that the states-parties, as legislators, have legislated
"human rights" into international law giving them status as affirmative independent
values. That status is supported and furthered by the rights and duties that were established, whether the rights be those of states or of individuals. Although directly
creating status of values, independent of rights and duties, is an unusual conception in
international law,[30] since law is made wholly by way of states assuming obligations, one
can say, perhaps, that every state-party assumes two different kinds of obligations corresponding to the two roles I have described. Acting with other states (the state as

legislator), each state agrees to recognize and give legal status in the international system to "human rights" as claims that every individual has—or should have—upon his own society. In addition, each state (the state as obligor) undertakes to respect and ensure these values for its own citizens, thereby also creating rights in other states, and perhaps in individuals.

Rights, Remedies, and Enjoyment.   The different perspectives I have suggested depend, of course, on different conceptions of rights. Immediately, whether the individual can be said to have legal rights in the international legal system depends in large part on the subtleties of "third-party beneficiary." At common law a third-party beneficiary generally had no remedy and had to depend on the remedy of the promisee.[31] The third party was the "true beneficiary" of a binding legal promise; the promise was likely to be kept, and the threat of a remedy by the promisee helped make it even more likely. Did the third party nonetheless have no "right" because he himself had no remedy that he could initiate in his own name?[32] Later, American states began to give the third-party beneficiary a remedy; did that convert a nonright into a right?

International law has moved to recognize a *ius tertii* for another state when the parties intend to accord it.[33] In our context the beneficiary is not a third state, but a mass of individuals. The individual's relation to the promise is not the same as that of third-party beneficiaries generally. The law declares that there is an individual "right." The individual is the true beneficiary, perhaps even the exclusive beneficiary (although one can find indirect "benefits" to the states impelling them to adhere to these agreements). Although the remedies are state to state and international, individuals or nongovernmental organizations and other forces in their behalf often activate those remedies in fact. Under the optional protocol—even more so under the European Convention—the individual himself can formally activate the principal international machinery. As a matter of fact, and as regards some rights also as a matter of law, the individual can waive the obligations and rights created by the international agreements. Can that add up to an individual "right" under international law?

To me, these questions about the rights of individual third-party beneficiaries are aspects of larger issues about rights. What do we achieve by characterizing some claims as "legal rights"? What determines our definition of rights and the elements we require to satisfy it? Why do we ordinarily insist that a legal right must have a formal, institutional, legal remedy and that the remedy must be in the "right-holder"?

Of course, one can define a legal right *a priori* as a valid legal claim supported by a formal remedy that lies with the right-holder. I would suggest, however, that the concept and definition of "right" are not arbitrary but serve a social purpose. In part, the concept of right is descriptive: Jurisprudence (and language) developed it to describe legal relations, implying special entitlement, respected by the society with a sense of obligation, and generally enjoyed by the right-holder in fact. In large part, the concept of right is normative: a society develops the notion that someone has a legal right to something in order to assure, or at least enhance the likelihood, that he will enjoy it in fact. Recognizing that a claim is valid, giving it legal status as a right, itself contributes to the likelihood that it will be enjoyed in fact. Usually, however, it is not sufficient. An institutionalized remedy not only enhances the legal quality of the right and its contribution to the likelihood of enjoyment but creates practical "machinery" to help bring about enjoyment. The remedy is more likely to be used, and therefore to bring about enjoyment, if it is controlled by the right-holder.

If the definition of "right" has a purpose, if it is intimately related to probability of enjoyment, one must ask how the requirement of remedy fits that purpose. Even in domestic law, the relation of right to remedy to enjoyment is not simple or perfect. We do not insist that a remedy for violation of a right assure its prompt and full enjoyment. A promise by A to sell B a book is often said to give B the legal right to have that promise performed, but for breach of the correlative obligation the available legal remedy does not assure enjoyment of the book, but only compensation for its value, and only much later. Even when domestic law gives B the remedy of "specific performance," he obtains the object only much later, often after a long proceeding. The remedy for vindicating other legal rights is not necessarily more prompt, adequate, and effective; even when B takes a book A owns and possesses, the remedy will bring prompt and effective enjoyment of it only in rare cases where a policeman is present or A can exercise "self-help." As a practical matter, of course, the real purpose of an available remedy is to deter violation of the right, and often it will be not the right-holder's remedy but the state's penal "remedy" that will serve as the effective deterrent and make enjoyment of the right highly probable.

Some rights in domestic law are even further removed from remedy. Except perhaps for some strict Austinians, constitutional rights in the United States are surely legal rights, yet the principal remedy for violations is judicial review, a limited remedy at best: It may prevent future violations but does not undo the past; for many violations there is not even compensation to the victim.[34] Some constitutional rights moreover have no judicial remedy at all: They are "political questions," not justiciable ones.[35] Judicial review is accepted as an adequate remedy, moreover, although it has unarmed judges dictating to powerful executives, because "it works": Rights are in fact vindicated. If so, why not other remedies, other institutions, other forces, which enhance the likelihood that rights will be enjoyed, bringing about some repair or compensation and deterring violators?

A legal right, I suggest, is a claim that the law recognizes as valid, as to which it recognizes a legal obligation on the addressee, and whose benefit the legal system renders likely to be enjoyed. Ordinarily that likelihood depends on the availability of legal remedies in the hands of the right-holder. But in special contexts and circumstances it can be supplied as well by other remedies or other forces—criminal penalties, advisory opinion by judges, an ombudsman, even effective public accountability, and other societal deterrents.

Again, except to the eye of some strict Austinians, the international legal system creates legal rights and duties, generally between states. The right-holding state has valid legal claims, but the remedy for its violation often consists only of the right to make the claim, infrequently also to assert it in some judicial or arbitral forum. Yet the remedy "works" to achieve probability of enjoyment because it is supported by political-systemic forces, the general desire to keep the system going, and the particular "right" and power of the victim state to respond in ways the violator would not like.[36] In a word, the sense of legal obligation exists, and although institutional remedies are few and infrequent, there are inducements to comply, creating a likelihood of enjoyment and warranting the character of legal rights and duties.

As regards the international law of human rights too, even the rights and duties of states under the conventions depend on institutional "remedies" that are at best no stronger than those operating in international law generally. But there are, ever waiting in the wings, other forces inducing compliance—political criticism by other states and international bodies (and sometimes stronger reaction, sanctions as in regard to *apartheid*); criticism by nongovernmental organizations including various activist organizations, and world-press available to mobilize hostile opinion. Might these qualify as well, or in addition, as "remedies" that support the quality of international legal rights because they enhance the likelihood that the rights will be enjoyed in fact?

From this perspective, it may not matter whether one sees the rights created by international human rights law as rights of states or rights of individuals. But seeing them as individual rights may in fact help make it more likely that they will be enjoyed in fact. And especially if the states do not act to vindicate their rights, so that their rights lack effective "remedies" (i.e., effective inducements to comply), it becomes desirable to see the rights as those of the individual so he can mobilize whatever remedies (inducements to comply) are available to him or to nongovernmental organizations in his behalf.

Rights in Theory and in Fact. The relation of rights to remedies to enjoyment raises other questions for the international law of human rights. In principle, whether the human rights agreements are being honored, whether the individuals are in fact enjoying the human rights promised, is not immediately relevant legally (or philo-sophically). For the short term, at least, failure of one or more states to carry out their international human rights undertakings does not vitiate the character of the under-takings as legal obligations, or the rights and duties they create. But if international human rights obligations fail to make any difference in fact over an extended time; if the states that undertook these obligations act continuously and consistently as though they had not, or as if they were not legal obligations; if the promisee states do not seek to have the undertakings enforced and otherwise acquiesce in violations and act as though no obligations exist—then one would have to consider whether there are legal obligations and consequent rights and duties. One might then ask whether, despite the legal forms followed and the legal words used, legal obligations were intended and were consummated; or, perhaps, whether despite original intentions to make law, the obligations were ended by implied mutual agreement or acquiescence, or lapsed from "desuetude." (In regard to economic-social rights, in particular, the future may provide evidence belying the assumption that legal obligations were intended.)

A different question is whether the derogations and limitations permitted by the agreements are so large as to render the undertakings illusory, especially since they are, in the first instance at least, interpreted and applied by every acting state for itself, and—to date—no other state (or international body) scrutinizes that interpretation and application in fact. Those are subjects for fuller exposition another day, but, in a preliminary word, I do not think these and other "loopholes" render the undertakings illusory or derogate from the quality of any rights created. In my view the derogation clauses are not destructive of the obligations (or the rights) so long as they are in fact interpreted and applied as written and intended, and the other states and the international bodies scrutinize their interpretation and application. Similarly I do not consider undertakings to realize economic, social, and cultural rights "progressively" as essentially illusory. The economic-social undertakings were made legal obligations in order to establish the idea of economic-social benefits as rights and to increase the likelihood of their enjoyment; it was not clear what else was expected to flow from making them legal obligations. Even those purposes may be sufficient to support law and rights; the future may show whether there are in fact other purposes and consequences for seeing, and continuing to see, the covenant as law and as creating rights.

I have written about rights and duties and remedies, formally conceived, but have felt impelled to allude to a prevalent skepticism about their reality and effectiveness. If questions of reality are philosophically relevant, they cut both ways. The formal edifice of rights, duties, and remedies is not wholly realistic; in particular, to date the "state promisees" do not commonly assert their rights or invoke their remedies; these may not therefore meaningfully contribute to the probability of enjoyment. On the other hand, there is a network of other forces, including some formal machinery, notably the international committees, and some domestic machinery, whether courts, ombudsmen or something else; and there are informal influences, both international and domestic—the influence of norms themselves, intergovernmental intercessions, "activist" nongovernmental organizations, the effects of publicity by media of information—which combine to achieve substantial respect for the international obligations to different extents in different countries. Some students of law and of politics have learned to ask not only what are the formal rights and remedies and who enforces legal rights but what are the inducements to comply with them and are they respected in fact.[37] If judicial remedies make rights, why not ombudsmen, whether initiated by the individual or self-initiated? And internationally, why not a Human Rights Committee, or—some day—a UN human rights commissioner, especially if they "work" and induce compliance? Does not philosophy have place for these "realities" in its conception of remedies for rights?

Notes

1. In this paper I draw on previous writings: "The Internationalization of Human Rights," in *Human Rights: A Symposium,* in *Columbia University Proceedings of the General Education Seminar,* Vol. 6, No. 1, Part I: (Fall 1977); *The Rights of Man Today.* (Boulder, CO: Westview Press, 1978); "Constitutional Rights and Human Rights," *Harvard Civil Rights—Civil Liberties Law Review,* 13 (1978), 593, and a revision, "Rights: American and Human, *Columbia Law Review* 79 (1979), 405.

2. When the Universal Declaration was adopted, "the communist bloc" (then including Yugoslavia, but not China) abstained, as did Saudi Arabia and South Africa. The European communist states have since accepted the Declaration in various ways, formally by explicit reference in the Final Act

of the Conference on Security and Cooperation in Europe, Helsinki 1975. Spokesmen for The People's Republic of China have also invoked the Declaration in the United Nations.

3. It has been suggested that states may have undertaken also to help other states insure the economic-social rights of their inhabitants. See Article 2 or the Covenant on Economic, Social, and Cultural Rights, discussed below. That apart, the international acceptance of human rights is seen in the context of the state system, with obligations only upon an individual's own society.

4. The older law had inspiration different from that for the contemporary international law of human rights. State responsibility in respect of aliens probably did not stem primarily from concern for the individual alien, although the term "denial of justice" might suggest that; it was designed to protect friendly relations between states. The obligation ran to the state of which the alien was a national, violation was an offense against the state, and in principle the remedy also ran to the state. (Denying justice to a stateless person, therefore, was probably not a violation of law; surely there was no international remedy for it.) Contemporary human rights law, on the other hand, is idealistic, not merely political, in motivation, although in legal principle the obligations and the principal remedies run to other states, not the victim.

5. There may also be some customary law of human rights, as a result of continued general practice of states with a sense of legal obligation. Thus, it is widely accepted that slavery and slave trade are now prohibited by customary international law and therefore forbidden even to states that are not party to any formal agreement outlawing them; apartheid may also now be prohibited by customary law and, therefore, binding on the Republic of South Africa, although it is not party to any agreement prohibiting it. Similar argument makes a case that customary international law now forbids torture and other "consistent patterns of gross violations"; some believe that, by a combination of words and practice, some—or all—of the provisions of the Universal Declaration have become legally binding.

An alternative formulation finds obligations, not in customary law strictly, but in the UN Charter to which virtually all states (including notably South Africa and the People's Republic of China) are parties. In the Charter all "Members pledge themselves to take joint and separate action in cooperation with the [UN] Organization for the achievement," *inter alia,* of "universal respect for, and observance of, human rights and fundamental freedoms for all without distinction as to race, sex, language, or religion." (I have combined Articles 55 and 56.) Although human rights are not defined and the character of the undertaking may be uncertain, later instruments, resolutions, and practices, in particular the Universal Declaration and its aftermath, have realized and concretized the original, inchoate undertakings in the Charter. While this argument would render all the provisions of the Universal Declaration legally binding on all UN members, which most governments would resist, many of them might accept it as regards selected, widely accepted rights—freedom from slavery, from racial discrimination, from torture.

Human rights might come into international law in yet another way, as "general principles of law recognized by civilized nations." See Article 38, Statute of International Court of Justice. Since national legal systems now generally outlaw slavery, racial discrimination, torture, these may arguably be deemed prohibited by international law.

There are also undertakings which the parties agreed would not have binding legal character but which are important "political obligations," like the Final Act at Helsinki, note 2 above. See generally Thomas Buergenthal (Ed.), *Human Rights, International Law and the Helsinki Accord* (Montclair, NJ: Allanheld, Osum, 1977).

6. Both principal covenants begin with articles declaring that all peoples have the right of self-determination, as well as economic self-determination, "the right to freely dispose of their natural resources." Western states argued in vain that these are not human rights of individuals.

The Covenant on Civil and Political Rights also includes group cultural rights. Article 27.

7. Article 4.

8. Articles 12 (3), 21, 22 (2).

9. Article 2 (1).

10. Article 4.

11. Article 8 (1) (a).

12. I state this with confidence and have argued it in an article, "Human Rights and 'Domestic Jurisdiction,'" in Buergenthal (Ed.), *Human Rights, International Law and the Helsinki Accord,* p. 21. Some others have argued that in human rights agreements that establish special "machinery" and remedies, these are generally intended to be the sole and exclusive remedies and replace the ordinary remedies between parties for violations of international agreements generally. See, e.g., the article by Professor Frohwien in that volume.

13. Article 40.

14. A state may submit to interstate complaints by a declaration under Article 41 and to private complaints by adherence to the optional protocol to the covenant. As of January 1, 1980, 61 states had adhered to the Covenant on Civil and Political Rights; 12 had declared under Article 41; 21 had adhered to the protocol.

15. Through the U.N. secretary general (article 16).

16. Articles 17–23.

17. References to some agreed moral, political, or "natural law" code is implicit in resolutions condemning violations of human rights in circumstances where no international legal undertaking seems in play.

18. I summarize the American conceptions in "Constitutional Fathers, Constitutional Sons," *Minnesota Law Review,* 60 (June 1976): 1113; see also my article, "Privacy and Autonomy," *Columbia Law Review,* 74 (December 1974): 1410. I compare American and international conceptions in my article, "Constitutional Rights and Human Rights."

19. See the Preambles to both the International Covenant on Civil and Political Rights and the International Covenant on Economic, Social, and Cultural Rights.

20. *Ibid.* Also the Preamble to the Universal Declaration.

21. UN Charter, Article 55.

22. The positive law may incorporate some morality or natural law by reference, as in phrases like "cruel, inhuman or degrading treatment or punishment," or "arbitrary arrest or detention," or treatment "with humanity and with respect for the inherent dignity of the human person."

23. The argument for treating economic-social benefits as rights is not countered persuasively by ridiculing "vacation-with-pay" as a human right. That may only suggest that this particular benefit is not "right-worthy." Adequate food and other necessities, however, are surely fundamental, and essential to human dignity. The argument against treating them as rights was that they depended on available resources and large national policies and could not be enforced by the means available for enforcing civil-political rights. Treating them as rights, therefore, would only dilute international efforts to obtain respect for civil and political rights. These fears have been realized to some extent, although perhaps in forms different from those anticipated: Many states have asserted the priority of long-term economic and social development (even as against present economic-social rights) and the need to sacrifice or defer civil and political rights. Compare UNGA Res. 32/130, Dec. 16, 1977; see by book, *The Rights of Man Today,* pp. 111–13.

24. The United States Constitution contains only limitations on government, not positive obligations upon them; and if affirmative obligations were to be constitutionally imposed, the existing legal system does not readily provide for remedies that would mandate affirmative actions by legislatures, say to appropriate adequate funds for education. See my "Constitutional Rights and Human Rights." But there is no inherent reason why such a system could not be, and legislatures (and officials) who obey judicial prohibitions could also learn to obey affirmative mandates. Compare *Griffin v. County School Board,* 337 U.S. 218 (1964).

25. But compare note 12, above; the argument that interstate remedies were not intended is stronger here.

26. Even in the Covenant on Economic, Social, and Cultural Rights, which is written with the state as the subject. See p. 268.

27. The parties have analogous rights and duties also under the Covenant on Economic, Social, and Cultural Rights. Every state-party assumes legal obligations and is also the "addressee" of such

obligations by the others. There are the usual international remedies as well as the additional remedies provided by the Covenant, that is, requirements of reporting to the UN Economic and Social Council, reports and recommendations by the Council.

28. Protocol, Article 1.

29. If international law creates such individual rights against the state some will argue that indirectly the individual acquires rights also against other individuals, since the state is obligated not only to respect these rights but also to "ensure" them, apparently against private interference with their enjoyment. Compare note 34 below. Others will argue that even if an individual is entitled to have the state protect his rights against private interference, the entitlement under international law is against the state only, not against the would-be interferer. Somewhat similarly, the Covenant on Civil and Political Rights provides that any propaganda for war, or advocacy of national, racial, or religious hatred, shall be prohibited. The covenant creates an international legal duty upon the state to prohibit, and a right in other states-parties to the agreement to have the prohibition enacted; there is no international legal duty upon any individual not to publish. Compare American constitutional theory, which also sees constitutional rights as only against the state. The freedom of speech is freedom from official interference. The state is not even constitutionally obligated to protect my freedom from private interference. If it does so, by tort or criminal law, I acquire rights against the interferer and he duties to me, but these are not constitutional rights or duties. See my "Constitutional Rights and Human Rights."

   A different question—a variation on a classic "monist-dualist" debate—is whether the international agreement serves to create (or confirm) legal rights and remedies for the individual under his society's municipal law. Some will say that since international law obligates the state to accord such legal rights, international law effectively puts these rights into domestic law (and domestic courts and other institutions must give them effect). The "preferred view" would have it that whereas the state is obliged by international law to accord such legal rights, it remains master of its domestic legal system, although a state's failure to accord such rights in the domestic legal order would, of course, violate its duties under international law to the other states-parties to the human rights agreements.

30. International agreements have created institutions with international status and character independent of, and going beyond, obligations assumed by states in regard to them. Thus, the UN Organization, created by the UN Charter, is deemed to have status and character in the international system even in relation to states not party to the UN Charter. Compare the Advisory Opinion of the International Court of Justice in "The Bernadotte Case," "Reparation for Injuries Suffered in the Service of the United Nations" [1949] *I.C.J.* 174.

31. In the United States the change came with *Lawrence v. Fox,* 20 N.Y. 268 (1859).

32. Some would also consider relevant whether the beneficiary had the power to cancel the obligation by the promisor.

33. Vienna Convention on the Law of Treaties, Article 36. The consent of the third state is required, but is ordinarily assumed. The treaty does not speak to rights for third "parties" which are not states.

34. See my "Constitutional Rights and Human Rights."

35. See *Baker v. Carr,* 369 U.S. 186 (1962); cf. *United States v. Richardson,* 418 U.S. 166 (1974). See generally, Louis Henkin, "Is There a 'Political Question' Doctrine?," *Yale Law Journal,* 85 (April 1976): 597.

36. Under the traditional view insisting that there can be no right without a formal, institutional remedy, those who claim that the usual interstate remedies are excluded and only those specially provided are available, note 12 above, might even question whether the state promisees have rights under the covenants. The only expressed remedies are reporting to and "follow-up" by the Human Rights Committee (or by the Economic and Social Council). A provision that the committee might consider interstate complaints is optional (Art. 41). Even where it applies, is it a sufficient remedy to support a right?

37. See, for example, my *How Nations Behave: Law and Foreign Policy* (New York: Columbia University Press, 2d ed., 1979), esp. Chaps. 3 and 4.

Part III

The Justification of Human Rights

Moral Relativism
As a
Foundation for
Natural Rights

GILBERT HARMAN

The theory of natural rights is often put forward as competition of moral relativism, most recently in an article in this journal by Loren Lomasky.[1] I want to suggest, on the contrary, that the two positions are compatible and, indeed, that moral relativism provides the only plausible foundation for a theory of natural rights.

Natural rights are rights people have simply by virtue of being people, for example, the right not to be harmed by others; and to say that people have the right not to be harmed is to say more than that it is bad to harm them or that one ought not to harm them. People have the right not to be harmed even if this will prevent more harm to others. A doctor may not kill one patient and distribute his healthy organs among his other patients even if the result is to save five people who would otherwise have died, because that would violate the murdered patient's right not to be killed. Rights are also stronger than oughts. One ought to be charitable, but it is doubtful anyone has a right to one's charity.

A foundation for the theory of natural rights must explain why there should be a strong duty not to harm others but not an equally strong symmetrical duty to help others avoid harm. If there were an equally strong symmetrical duty to help others, people would not have the natural right not to be harmed, since they could be and indeed should be harmed in order to prevent more harm to others. The doctor could kill and cut up one patient and then distribute his organs to the others.

Gilbert Harman, "Moral Relativism As a Foundation for Natural Rights," *Journal of Libertarian Studies,* 4 (1980), pp. 367–371. Reprinted by permission of the publisher.

Why is there a strong duty not to harm others but not an equally strong symmetrical duty to prevent harm to others? The answer, I suggest, is that morality is the result of implicit bargaining and adjustments among people of varying powers and resources and, although it is in everyone's interest that there should be a strong duty not to harm others, it is not in everyone's interest that there should be an equally strong symmetrical duty to help others avoid harm. A duty to prevent harm to others favors the interests of the poorer and weaker members of society over the richer and more powerful members. The richer and more powerful members of society have less need of outside help in order to avoid being harmed than the poorer and would end up doing most of the helping, given a strong symmetrical duty to help people avoid harm. The rich and powerful would do best with a strong duty not to harm others and no duty to help others. The poor and weak would do best with equally strong duties of both sorts. Implicit bargaining should therefore yield as a compromise a strong duty not to harm others and a weaker duty to help others avoid harm; it should in other words yield a natural right not be be harmed, which is what we have.

It might be objected that such a sociological explanation cannot account for the right not to be harmed but can account only for our beliefs that there is such a right. Indeed, it might be thought that such a sociological explanation of our belief in this right casts doubt on the truth of the belief, since the explanation appears to show we would have the belief whether or not it were true. But that would be to assume moral relativism is false. If moral relativism is true and morality has its source in convention, then a sociological account of our moral conventions can explain why we have the rights we have. That is why I suggest moral relativism provides a more adequate foundation for natural rights, such as the right not to be harmed, than moral absolutism does.

Of course, moral relativism needs to be formulated carefully. To say that morality has its source in convention is not to say that what is right is what people say is right or that the moral conventions of a group are beyond criticism. A set of conventions is subject to internal criticism if some of the conventions do not cohere well with others given the facts. And one group's moral conventions might be evaluated in the light of another group's values.[2]

In his article,[3] Lomasky raises several questions about the sociological explanation of the right not to be harmed and then offers a nonrelativistic explanation instead. I will say something about his own account in a moment. First let me take up the objection he raises to the claim that a strong duty not to harm others and a weaker duty to help others arises from a compromise between the richer and stronger on the one hand and the poorer and weaker on the other hand.

He begins by asking why the richer stronger people should agree to any duty to help others at all, given that such a duty is not in their interest. The answer, of course, is that they have to agree for the sake of social stability, so that the poorer and weaker people will accept the duty not to harm others. Otherwise there is the threat of a breakdown in law and order, even revolution.

Next, he commends Christopher New's observation[4] that the sociological explanation talks only about people who are richer and stronger or poorer and weaker, ignoring people who are richer but weaker or stronger but poorer. The reason for this is that the richer tend to be the stronger and the poorer tend to be the weaker. The strong can take from the weak. The rich can afford armies.

Lomasky goes on to note Robert Coburn's suggestion[5] that there might be an evolutionary explanation of why we acknowledge a stronger duty not to harm others and only a weaker duty to help them avoid harm. That would indeed undermine the sociological explanation, but (as Lomasky acknowledges) neither Coburn nor anyone else has offered a plausible evolutionary explanation of this sort.

Lomasky ultimately opts for a different explanation of why the duty to help others is not as strong as the duty not to harm them. His own explanation is that accepting a strong duty to help others would involve taking others' ends as one's own in a way that would actually undermine the distinction between one person's goals and another's. But at best that explains why we do not have a strong duty to help others in the sense of benefiting them, of doing whatever will promote their interests. What has to be explained is why there is not a strong duty to help others in a stricter sense, to help them when they really need help to avoid harm. Such a duty would be symmetrical with the strong duty not to harm others oneself. The duty to avoid harming others is not a duty to refrain from anything that is against another person's interest. If one raises one's prices, that makes things more expensive for others without harming them in the relevant sense. Similarly, a symmetrical duty to help others would not be an all-encompassing duty to do anything and everything that would advance another person's interest. The duty to avoid harming others is a duty to avoid certain specific harms to others (where in my view exactly what counts as such a harm is itself partly determined by convention), so a symmetrical duty to help others avoid harm would be a duty to help them in situations of real need when they are threatened with the sort of harm specified by the duty not to harm others. Lomasky's account does not explain why there is no such symmetrical duty to help others.

It might be suggested that so many people are threatened with harm from disease, famine, ruffians, and bullies that a strong symmetrical duty to help others avoid harm would after all require one to spend almost all one's time helping others, with little time for projects of one's own, so that Lomasky's argument is basically correct even for such a symmetrical duty. And it is true that, as things are now, one could probably help save many people's lives if, instead of pursuing one's own narrow goals, one were to devote one's energies to famine relief or to helping people escape from totalitarian regimes. But things are as they are now because a strong duty to help others avoid harm is not widely accepted. If it were widely accepted, one could rely for the most part on others who were better placed to help out; one would be called upon oneself to help only rarely where one was in the best position to help. It would indeed be foolish or saintly to accept for oneself a strong duty to help others if no one else was going to do so, but that does not show such a duty to be unworkable. It would be similarly foolish or saintly to accept for oneself the strong duty not to harm others if no one else accepted that duty. Either duty is acceptable only if generally accepted. In this respect then there seems no reason to prefer the duty not to harm others to the duty to help them avoid harm, so there is no explanation of the natural right to be free from harm. We are left with moral relativism as the only plausible foundation for that natural right.

I conclude with a remark about "inner judgments." A moral relativist does not suppose that there is a single set of basic moral demands which everyone accepts or has reason to accept, as demands on everyone, from which derive all moral reasons to do things. The moral relativist supposes that different people accept different moralities which can give them different moral reasons. So there can be and no doubt are people who have no reason to act in accordance with the basic principles of one's own morality. If a moral judgment based on one's own principles implies that an agent has reasons deriving from those principles to do something, then that judgment cannot be made truly about "outsiders" who do not accept the relevant principles and therefore do not have those reasons. I call such judgments "inner" since they can be truly made only about insiders who have reasons to follow the relevant principles. Judgments about what someone ought morally to do and judgments about what it would be morally wrong of someone to do are inner judgments in this sense since they imply the agent has certain reasons. Moral relativists will distinguish inner moral judgments ("it was wrong of him to do that") from other moral judgments, not implying the agent had certain moral reasons, which can be made of outsiders ("it was evil of him to do that"). Nonrelativists who think there is a single true morality that gives everyone reasons will not distinguish insiders and outsiders in this way and will not need to distinguish inner moral judgments from others. Lomasky therefore misrepresents the notion of inner judgment in saying that such judgments are "motivating" and are odd if made in certain situations or made to certain people.[6] And the fact (if it is a fact) that *he* takes *his* principles to apply to everyone, including those who do not accept those principles, shows only that *he* is not a moral relativist. Many other people are moral relativists and clearly do restrict their inner judgments in the relevant way. And anyone who believes in natural rights had better be a moral relativist if that belief is to receive an adequate foundation.

Notes

1. Loren E. Lomasky, "Harman's Moral Relativism," *Journal of Libertarian Studies* 3 (1979): 279–91.

2. Gilbert Harman, "Moral Relativism Defended," *Philosophical Review* 84 (1975): 3–22; "Relativistic Ethics: Morality as Politics," *Midwest Studies in Philosophy* 3 (1978): 109–21; "What Is Moral Relativism?" in A. I. Goldman and J. Kim (Eds.), *Values and Morals*. (Dordrechet, Holland: D. Reidel, 1979), pp. 143–61.

3. Lomasky, "Harman's Moral Relativism."

4. Christopher New, "Implicit Bargaining and Moral Beliefs," *Analysis* 37 (1977): 130–33.

5. Robert Coburn, "Relativism and the Basis of Morality," *Philosophical Review* 85 (1976): 87–93.

6. This misrepresentation derives from David Lyons, "Ethical Relativism and the Problem of Incoherence," *Ethics* 86 (1976): 121, cited by Lomasky.

Security
and Subsistence

HENRY SHUE

Rights

A moral right provides (1) the rational basis for a justified demand (2) that the actual enjoyment of a substance be (3) socially guaranteed against standard threats. Since this is a somewhat complicated account of rights, each of its elements deserves a brief introductory explanation.[1] The significance of the general structure of a moral right is, however, best seen in concrete cases of rights, to which we will quickly turn.[2]

A right provides the rational basis for a justified demand. If a person has a particular right, the demand that the enjoyment of the substance of the right be socially guaranteed is justified by good reasons, and the guarantees ought, therefore, to be provided. I do not know how to characterize in general and in the abstract what counts as a rational basis or an adequate justification. I could say that a demand for social guarantees has been justified when good enough reasons have been given for it, but this simply transfers the focus to what count as good enough reasons. This problem pervades philosophy, and I could not say anything very useful about it without saying a lot. But to have a right is to be in a position to make demands of others, and to be in such a position is, among other things, for one's situation to fall under general principles that are good reasons why one's demands ought to be granted. A person who has a right has especially compelling reasons—especially deep principles—on his or her side. People can of course have rights without being able to explain them—without being able to articulate the principles that apply to their cases and serve as the reasons for their demands. This book as a whole is intended to express a set of reasons that are good enough to justify the demands defended here. If the book is adequate, the principles it articulates are at least one specific example of how some particular demands can be justified. For now, I think, an example would be more useful than an abstract characterization.

The significance of being justified is very clear. Because a right is the basis for a justified demand, people not only may, but ought to, insist. Those who deny rights do so at their own peril. This does not mean that efforts to secure the fulfillment of the demand constituting a right ought not to observe certain constraints. It does mean that those who deny rights can have no complaint when their denial, especially if it is part of a systematic pattern of deprivation, is resisted. Exactly which countermeasures are justified by which sorts of deprivations of rights would require a separate discussion.

A right is the rational basis, then, for a justified demand. Rights do not justify merely requests, pleas, petitions. It is only because rights may lead to demands and not something weaker that having rights is tied as closely as it is to human dignity. Joel Feinberg has put this eloquently for the case of legal rights, or, in his Hohfeldian terminology, claim-rights:

> Legal claim-rights are indispensably valuable possessions. A world without claim-rights, no matter how full of benevolence and devotion to duty, would suffer an immense moral impoverishment. Persons would no longer hope for decent treatment from others on the ground of desert or rightful claim. Indeed, they would come to think of themselves as having no special claim to kindness or consideration from others, so that whenever even minimally decent treatment is forthcoming they would think themselves lucky rather than inherently deserving, and their benefactors extraordinarily virtuous and worthy of great gratitude. The harm to individual self-esteem and character development would be incalculable.
>
> A claim-right, on the other hand, can be urged, pressed, or rightly demanded against other persons. In appropriate circumstances the right-holder can "urgently, peremptorily, or insistently" call for his rights, or assert them authoritatively, confidently, unabashedly. Rights are not mere gifts or favors, motivated by love or pity, for which gratitude is the sole fitting response. A right is something that can be demanded or insisted upon without embarrassment or shame. When that to which one has a right is not forthcoming, the appropriate reaction is indignation; when it is duly given there is no reason for gratitude, since it is simply one's own or one's due that one received. A world with claim-rights is one in which all persons, as actual or potential claimants, are dignified objects of respect, both in their own eyes and in the view of others. No amount of love and compassion, or obedience to higher authority, or noblesse oblige, can substitute for those values.[3]

At least as much can be said for basic moral rights, including those that ought to, but do not yet, have legal protection.

That a right provides the rational basis for a justified demand for actual enjoyment is the most neglected element of many rights. A right does not yield a demand that it should be said that people are entitled to enjoy something, or that people should be promised that they will enjoy something. A proclamation of a right is not the fulfillment of a right, any more than an airplane schedule is a flight. A proclamation may or may not be an initial step toward the fulfillment of the rights listed. It is frequently the substitute of the promise in the place of the fulfillment.

The substance of a right is whatever the right is a right to. A right is not a right to enjoy a right—it is a right to enjoy something else, like food or liberty. We do sometimes speak simply of someone's "enjoying a right," but I take this to be an elliptical way of saying that the person is enjoying something or other, which is the substance of a right, and, probably, enjoying it *as* a right. Enjoying a right to, for example, liberty normally means enjoying liberty. It may also mean enjoying liberty in the consciousness that liberty is a right. Being a right is a status that various subjects of enjoyment have. Simply to enjoy the right itself, the status, rather than to enjoy the subject of the right would have to mean something like taking satisfaction that there is such a status and that something has that status. But ordinarily when we say someone is enjoying a right, we mean the person is enjoying the substance of the right.

Being socially guaranteed is probably the single most important aspect of a standard right, because it is the aspect that necessitates correlative duties.[4] A right is ordinarily a justified demand that some other people make some arrangements so that one will still be able to enjoy the substance of the right even if—actually, *especially* if—it is not within one's own power to arrange on one's own to enjoy the substance of the right. Suppose people have a right to physical security. Some of them may nevertheless choose to hire their own private guards, as if they had no right to social guarantees. But they would be justified, and everyone else is justified, in demanding that somebody somewhere make some effective arrangements to establish and maintain security. Whether the arrangements should be governmental or non-governmental; local, national, or international; participatory or non-participatory, are all difficult questions to which I may or may not be able to give definitive or conclusive answers here. But it is essential to a right that it is a demand upon others, however difficult it is to specify exactly which others.

And a right has been guaranteed only when arrangements have been made for people with the right to enjoy it. It is not enough that at the moment it happens that no one is violating the right.[5] Just as a proclamation of a right is not the fulfillment of a right and may in fact be either a step toward or away from actually fulfilling the right, an undertaking to create social guarantees for the enjoyment of various subjects of rights is by no means itself the guaranteeing and may or may not lead to real guarantees. But a right has not been fulfilled until arrangements are in fact in place for people to enjoy whatever it is to which they have the right. Usually, perhaps, the arrangements will take the form of law, making the rights legal as well as moral ones. But in other cases well-entrenched customs, backed by taboos, might serve better than laws—certainly better than unenforced laws.

The vague term "arrangements" is used in order to keep this general introductory explanation neutral on some controversial questions of interpretation. If the "arrangements" for fulfilling, for example, the duty to protect security are to be that every citizen is to be furnished a handgun and local neighborhoods are to elect residents to night patrols, then the right to security has not been socially guaranteed until the handguns have been distributed, the patrols elected, etc. (The right has still not been guaranteed if this arrangement will usually not work, as I would certainly assume would be the case.) On the other hand, if the "arrangements" are to have well-trained, tax-supported, professional police in adequate numbers, then the right has not been socially guaranteed until the police candidates have in fact been well-trained, enough public funds budgeted to hire an adequate force, etc.

I am not suggesting the absurd standard that a right has been fulfilled only if it is impossible for anyone to be deprived of it or only if no one is ever deprived of it. The standard can only be some reasonable level of guarantee. But if people who walk alone after dark are likely to be assaulted, or if infant mortality is 60 per 1000 live births, we would hardly say that enjoyment of, respectively, security or subsistence had yet been socially guaranteed. It is for the more precise specification of the reasonable level of social guarantees that we need the final element in the general structure of moral rights: the notion of a standard threat. This notion can be explained satisfactorily only after we look at some cases in detail, and I will take it up in the final section of his chapter.

That a right involves a rationally justified demand for social guarantees against standard threats means, in effect, that the relevant other people have a duty to create, if they do not exist, or, if they do, to preserve effective institutions for the enjoyment of what people have rights to enjoy.[6] From no theory like the present one is it possible to deduce precisely what sort of institutions are needed, and I have no reason to think that the same institutions would be most effective in all places and at all times. On its face, such universality of social institutions is most improbable, although some threats are indeed standard. What is universal, however, is a duty to make and keep effective arrangements, and my later threefold analysis of correlative duties will suggest that these arrangements must serve at least the functions of avoiding depriving people of the substances of their rights, protecting them against deprivation, and aiding them if they are nevertheless deprived of rights.[7] What I am now calling the duty to develop and preserve effective institutions for the fulfillment of rights is a summary of much of what is involved in performing all three of the duties correlative to typical rights, but to discuss duties now would be to jump ahead of the story.

Basic Rights

Nietzsche, who holds strong title to being the most misunderstood and most under-rated philosopher of the last century, considered much of conventional morality—and not conceptions of rights only—to be an attempt by the powerless to restrain the powerful: an enormous net of fine mesh busily woven around the strong by the masses of the weak.[8] And he was disgusted by it, as if fleas were pestering a magnificent leopard or ordinary ivy were weighing down a soaring oak. In recoiling from Nietzsche's *assessment* of morality, many have dismissed too quickly his insightful *analysis* of morality. Moral systems obviously serve more than one purpose, and different specific systems serve some purposes more fully or better than others, as of course Nietzsche himself also recognized. But one of the chief purposes of morality in general, and certainly of conceptions of rights, and of basic rights above all, is indeed to provide some minimal protection against utter helplessness to those too weak to protect themselves. Basic rights are a shield for the defenseless against at least some of the more devastating and more common of life's threats, which include, as we shall see, loss of security and loss of subsistence. Basic rights are a restraint upon economic and political forces that would otherwise be too strong to be resisted. They are social guarantees against actual and threatened deprivations of at least some basic needs. Basic rights are an attempt to give to the powerless a veto over some of the forces that would otherwise harm them the most.

Basic rights are the morality of the depths. They specify the line beneath which no one is to be allowed to sink. This is part of the reason that basic rights are tied as closely to self-respect as Feinberg indicates legal claim-rights are.[9] And this helps to explain why Nietzsche found moral rights repugnant. His eye was on the heights, and he wanted to talk about how far some might soar, not about how to prevent the rest from sinking lower. It is not clear that we cannot do both.[10]

And it is not surprising that what is in an important respect the essentially negative goal of preventing or alleviating helplessness is a central purpose of something as important as conceptions of basic rights. For everyone healthy adulthood is bordered on each side by helplessness, and it is vulnerable to interruption by helplessness, temporary or permanent, at any time. And many of the people in the world now have very little control over their fates, even over such urgent matters as whether their own children live through infancy.[11] Nor is it surprising that although the goal is negative, the duties correlative to rights will turn out to include positive actions. The infant and the aged do not need to be assaulted in order to be deprived of health, life, or the capacity to enjoy active rights. The classic liberal's main prescription for the good life—do not interfere with thy neighbor—is the only poison they need. To be helpless they need only to be left alone. This is why avoiding the infliction of deprivation will turn out . . . not to be the only kind of duty correlative to basic rights.

Basic rights, then, are everyone's minimum reasonable demands upon the rest of humanity.[12] They are the rational basis for justified demands the denial of which no self-respecting person can reasonably be expected to accept. Why should anything be so important? The reason is that rights are basic in the sense used here only if enjoyment of them is essential to the enjoyment of all other rights. This is what is distinctive about a basic right. When a right is genuinely basic, any attempt to enjoy any other right by sacrificing the basic right would be quite literally self-defeating, cutting the ground from beneath itself. Therefore, if a right is basic, other, non-basic rights may be sacrificed, if necessary, in order to secure the basic right. But the protection of a basic right may not be sacrificed in order to secure the enjoyment of a non-basic right. It may not be sacrificed because it cannot be sacrificed successfully. If the right sacrificed is indeed basic, then no right for which it might be sacrificed can actually be enjoyed in the absence of the basic right. The sacrifice would have proven self-defeating.[13]

In practice, what this priority for basic rights usually means is that basic rights need to be established securely before other rights can be secured. The point is that people should be able to *enjoy,* or *exercise,* their other rights. The point is simple but vital. It is not merely that people should "have" their other rights in some merely legalistic or otherwise abstract sense compatible with being unable to make any use of the substance of the right. For example, if people have rights to free association, they ought not merely to "have" the rights to free association but also to enjoy their free association itself. Their freedom of association ought to be provided for by the relevant social institutions. This distinction between merely having a right and actually enjoying a right may seem a fine point, but it turns out later to be critical.

What is not meant by saying that a right is basic is that the right is more valuable or intrinsically more satisfying to enjoy than some other rights. For example, I shall soon suggest that rights to physical security, such as the right not to be assualted, are basic, and I shall not include the right to publicly supported education as basic. But I do not mean by this to deny that enjoyment of the right to education is much greater and richer—more distinctively human, perhaps—than merely going through life without ever being assaulted. I mean only that, if a choice must be made, the prevention of assault ought to supersede the provision of education. Whether a right is basic is independent of whether its enjoyment is also valuable in itself. Intrinsically valuable rights may or may not also be basic rights, but intrinsically valuable rights can be enjoyed only when basic rights are enjoyed. Clearly few rights could be basic in this precise sense.

Security Rights

Our first project will be to see why people have a basic right to physical security—a right that is basic not to be subjected to murder, torture, mayhem, rape, or assault. The purpose in raising the questions why there are rights to physical security and why they are basic is not that very many people would seriously doubt either that there are rights to physical security or that they are basic. Although it is not unusual in practice for members of at least one ethnic group in a society to be physically insecure—to be, for example, much more likely than other people to be beaten by the police if arrested—few, if any, people would be prepared to defend in principle the contention that anyone lacks a basic right to physical security. Nevertheless, it can be valuable to formulate explicitly the presuppositions of even one's most firmly held beliefs, especially because these presuppositions may turn out to be general principles that will provide guidance in other areas where convictions are less firm. Precisely because we have no real doubt that rights to physical security are basic, it can be useful to see why we may properly think so.[14]

If we had to justify our belief that people have a basic right to physical security to someone who challenged this fundamental conviction, we could in fact give a strong argument that shows that if there are any rights (basic or not basic) at all, there are basic rights to physical security:

No one can fully enjoy any right that is supposedly protected by society if someone can credibly threaten him or her with murder, rape, beating, etc. when he or she tries to enjoy the alleged right. Such threats to physical security are among the most serious and—in much of the world—the most widespread hindrances to the enjoyment of any right. If any right is to be exercised except at great risk, physical security must be protected. In the absence of physical security people are unable to use any other rights that society may be said to be protecting without being liable to encounter many of the worst dangers they would encounter if society were not protecting the rights.

A right to full physical security belongs, then, among the basic rights—not because the enjoyment of it would be more satisfying to someone who was also enjoying a full range of other rights, but because its absence would leave available extremely effective means for others, including the government, to interfere with or prevent the actual exercise of any other rights that were supposedly protected. Regardless of whether the enjoyment of physical security is also desirable for its own sake, it is desirable as part of the enjoyment of every other right. No rights other than a right to physical security can in fact be enjoyed if a right to physical security is not protected. Being physically secure is a necessary condition for the exercise of any other right, and guaranteeing physical security must be part of guaranteeing anything else as a right.

A person could, of course, always try to enjoy some other right even if no social provision were made to protect his or her physical safety during attempts to exercise the right. Suppose there is a right to peaceful assembly but it is not unusual for peaceful assemblies to be broken up and some of the participants beaten. Whether any given assembly is actually broken up depends largely on whether anyone else (in or out of government) is sufficiently opposed to it to bother to arrange an attack. People could still try to assemble, and they might sometimes assemble safely. But it would obviously be misleading to say that they are protected in their right to assemble if they are as vulnerable as ever to one of the most serious and general threats to enjoyment of the right, namely physical violence by other people. If they are as helpless against physical threats with the right "protected" as they would have been without the supposed protection, society is not actually protecting their exercise of the right to assembly.

So anyone who is entitled to anything as a right must be entitled to physical security as a basic right so that threats to his or her physical security cannot be used to thwart the enjoyment of the other right. This argument has two critical premises. The first is that everyone is entitled to enjoy something as a right.[15] The second, which further explains the first, is that everyone is entitled to the removal of the most serious and general conditions that would prevent or severely interfere with the exercise of whatever rights the person has. I take this second premise to be part of what is meant in saying that everyone is entitled to enjoy something as a right, as explained in the opening section of this chapter. Since this argument applies to everyone, it establishes a right that is universal.

Subsistence Rights

The main reason for discussing security rights, which are not very controversial, was to make explicit the basic assumptions that support the usual judgment that security rights are basic rights. Now that we have available an argument that supports them, we are in a position to consider whether matters other than physical security should, according to the same argument, also be basic rights. It will emerge that subsistence, or minimal economic security, which is more controversial than physical security, can also be shown to be as well justified for treatment as a basic right as physical security is—and for the same reasons.

By minimal economic security, or subsistence, I mean unpolluted air, unpolluted water, adequate food, adequate clothing, adequate shelter, and minimal preventive public health care. Many complications about exactly how to specify the boundaries of what is necessary for subsistence would be interesting to explore. But the basic idea is to have available for consumption what is needed for a decent chance at a reasonably healthy and active life of more or less normal length, barring tragic interventions. This central idea is clear enough to work with, even though disputes can occur over exactly where to draw its outer boundaries. A right to subsistence would not mean, at one extreme, that every baby born with a need for open-heart surgery has a right to have it, but it also would not count as adequate food a diet that produces a life expectancy of thirty-five years of fever-laden, parasite-ridden listlessness.

By a "right to subsistence" I shall always mean a right to at least subsistence. People may or may not have economic rights that go beyond subsistence rights, and I do not want to prejudge that question here. But people may have rights to subsistence even if they do not have any strict rights to economic well-being extending beyond subsistence. Subsistence rights and broader economic rights are separate questions, and I want to focus here on subsistence.

I also do not want to prejudge the issue of whether healthy adults are entitled to be provided with subsistence *only* if they cannot provide subsistence for themselves. Most of the world's malnourished, for example, are probably also diseased, since malnutrition lowers resistance to disease, and hunger and infestation normally form a tight vicious circle. Hundreds of millions of the malnourished are very young children. A large percentage of the adults, besides being ill and hungry, are also chronically unemployed, so the issue of policy toward healthy adults who refuse to work is largely irrelevant. By a "right to subsistence," then, I shall mean a right to subsistence that includes the provision of subsistence at least to those who cannot provide for themselves. I do not assume that no one else is also entitled to receive subsistence—I simply do not discuss cases of healthy adults who could support themselves but refuse to do so. If there is a right to subsistence in the sense discussed here, at least the people who cannot provide for themselves, including the children, are entitled to receive at least subsistence. Nothing follows one way or the other about anyone else.

It makes no difference whether the legally enforced system of property where a given person lives is private, state, communal, or one of the many more typical mixtures and variants. Under all systems of property people are prohibited from simply taking even what they need for survival. Whatever the property institutions and the economic system are, the question about rights to subsistence remains: If persons are forbidden by law from taking what they need to survive and they are unable within existing economic institutions and policies to provide for their own survival (and the survival of dependents for whose welfare they are responsible), are they entitled, as a last resort, to receive the essentials for survival from the remainder of humanity whose lives are not threatened?

The same considerations that support the conclusion that physical security is a basic right support the conclusion that subsistence is a basic right. Since the argument is now familiar, it can be given fairly briefly.

It is quite obvious why, if we still assume that there are some rights that society ought to protect and still mean by this the removal of the most serious and general hindrances to the actual enjoyment of the rights, subsistence ought to be protected as a basic right:

> No one can fully, if at all, enjoy any right that is supposedly protected by society if he or she lacks the essentials for a reasonably healthy and active life. Deficiencies in the means of subsistence can be just as fatal, incapacitating, or painful as violations of physical security. The resulting damage or death can at least as decisively prevent the enjoyment of any right as can the effects of security violations. Any form of malnutrition, or fever due to exposure, that causes severe and irreversible brain damage, for example, can effectively prevent the exercise of any right requiring clear thought and may, like brain injuries caused by assault, profoundly disturb personality. And, obviously, any fatal deficiencies end all possibility of the enjoyment of rights as firmly as an arbitrary execution.
>
> Indeed, prevention of deficiencies in the essentials for survival is, if anything, more basic than prevention of violations of physical security. People who lack protection against violations of their physical security can, if they are free, fight back against their attackers or flee, but people who lack essentials, such as food, because of forces beyond their control, often can do nothing and are on their own utterly helpless.[16]

The scope of subsistence rights must not be taken to be broader than it is. In particular, this step of the argument does not make the following absurd claim: Since death and serious illness prevent or interfere with the enjoyment of rights, everyone has a basic right not to be allowed to die or to be seriously ill. Many causes of death and illness are outside the control of society, and many deaths and illnesses are the result of very particular conjunctions of circumstances that general social policies cannot control. But it is not impractical to expect some level of social organization to protect the minimal cleanliness of air and water and to oversee the adequate production, or import, and the proper distribution of minimal food, clothing, shelter, and elementary health care. It is not impractical, in short, to expect effective management, when necessary, of the supplies of the essentials of life. So the argument is: When death and serious illness could be prevented by different social policies regarding the essentials of life, the protection of any human right involves avoidance of fatal or debilitating deficiencies in these essential commodities. And this means fulfilling subsistence rights as basic rights. This is society's business because the problems are serious and general. This is a basic right because failure to deal with it would hinder the enjoyment of all other rights.

Thus, the same considerations that establish that security rights are basic for everyone also support the conclusion that subsistence rights are basic for everyone. It is not being claimed or assumed that security and subsistence are parallel in all, or even very many, respects. The only parallel being relied upon is that guarantees of security and guarantees of subsistence are equally essential to providing for the actual exercise of any other rights. As long as security and subsistence are parallel in this respect, the argument applies equally to both cases, and other respects in which security and subsistence are not parallel are irrelevant.

It is not enough that people merely happen to be secure or happen to be subsisting. They must have a right to security and a right to subsistence—the continued enjoyment of the security and the subsistence must be socially guaranteed. Otherwise a person is readily open to coercion and intimidation through threats of the deprivation of one or the other, and credible threats can paralyze a person and prevent the exercise of any other right as surely as actual beatings and actual protein/calorie deficiencies can.[17] Credible threats can be reduced only by the actual establishment of social arrangements that will bring assistance to those confronted by forces that they themselves cannot handle.

Consequently the guaranteed security and guaranteed subsistence are what we might initially be tempted to call "simultaneous necessities" for the exercise of any other right. They must be present at any time that any other right is to be exercised, or people can be prevented from enjoying the other right by deprivations or threatened deprivations of security or of subsistence. But to think in terms of simultaneity would be largely to miss the point. A better label, if any is needed, would be "inherent necessities." For it is not that security from beatings, for instance, is separate from freedom of peaceful assembly but that it always needs to accompany it. Being secure from beatings if one chooses to hold a meeting is part of being free to assemble. If one cannot safely assemble, one is not free to assemble. One is, on the contrary, being coerced not to assemble by the threat of the beatings.

The same is true if taking part in the meeting would lead to dismissal by the only available employer when employment is the only source of income for the purchase of food. Guarantees of security and subsistence are not added advantages over and above enjoyment of the right to assemble. They are essential parts of it. For this reason it would be misleading to construe security or subsistence—or the substance of any other basic right—merely as "means" to the enjoyment of all other rights. The enjoyment of security and subsistence is an essential part of the enjoyment of all other rights. Part of what it means to enjoy any other right is to be able to exercise that right without, as a consequence, suffering the actual or threatened loss of one's physical security or one's subsistence. And part of what it means to be able to enjoy any other right is not to be prevented from exercising it by lack of security or of subsistence. To claim to guarantee people a right that they are in fact unable to exercise is fraudulent, like furnishing people with meal tickets but providing no food.

What is being described as an "inherent necessity" needs to be distinguished carefully from a mere means to an end. If A is a means to end B and it is impossible to reach the end B without using the means A, it is perfectly correct to say that A is necessary for B. But when I describe the enjoyment of physical security, for example, as necessary for the enjoyment of a right to assemble, I do not intend to say merely that enjoying security is a means to enjoying assembly. I intend to say that part of the meaning of the enjoyment of a right of assembly is that one can assemble in physical security. Being secure is an essential component of enjoying a right of assembly, so that there is no such thing as a situation in which people do have social guarantees for assembly and do not have social guarantees for security. If they do not have guarantees that they can assemble in security, they have not been provided with assembly as a right. They must assemble and merely hope for the best, because a standard threat to assembling securely has not been dealt with. The fundamental argument is that when one fully grasps what an ordinary right is, and especially which duties are correlative to a right, one can see that the guarantee of certain things (as basic rights) is part of—is a constituent of—is an essential component of—the establishment of the conditions in which the right can actually be enjoyed. These conditions include the prevention of the thwarting of the enjoyment of the right by any "standard threat," at the explanation of which we must soon look.

A final observation about the idea of subsistence rights is, however, worth making here: Subsistence rights are in no way an original, new, or advanced idea. If subsistence rights seem strange, this is more than likely because Western liberalism has had a blind spot for severe economic need.[18] Far from being new or advanced, subsistence rights are found in traditional societies that are often treated by modern societies as generally backward or primitive.

James C. Scott has shown that some of the traditional economic arrangements in Southeast Asia that were in other respects highly exploitative nevertheless were understood by both patrons and clients—to use Scott's terminology—to include rights to subsistence on the part of clients and duties on the part of patrons not only to forbear from depriving clients of subsistence but to provide assistance to any clients who were for any reason deprived:

> If the need for a guaranteed minimum is a powerful motive in peasant life, one would expect to find institutionalized patterns in peasant communities which provide for this need. And, in fact, it is above all within the village—in the patterns of social control and reciprocity that structure daily conduct—where the subsistence ethic finds social expression. The principle which appears to unify a wide array of behavior is this: "All village families will be guaranteed a minimal subsistence niche insofar as the resources controlled by villagers make this possible." Village egalitarianism in this sense is conservative not radical; it claims that all should have a place, a living, not that all should be equal. . . . Few village studies of Southeast Asia fail to remark on the informal social controls which act to provide for the minimal needs of the village poor. The position of the better-off appears to be legitimized only to the extent that their resources are employed in ways which meet the broadly defined welfare needs of villagers.[19]

As Benedict J. Kerkvliet, also writing about an Asian society, put it: "A strong patron-client relationship was a kind of all-encompassing insurance policy whose coverage, although not total and infinitely reliable, was as comprehensive as a poor family could get."[20]

Many reasons weigh in favor of the elimination of the kind of patron-client relationships that Scott and Kerkvliet have described—no one is suggesting that they should be, or could be, preserved. The point here is only that the institutionalization of subsistence rights is in no way tied to some utopian future "advanced" society. On the contrary, the real question is whether modern nations can be as humane as, in *this* regard, many traditional villages are. If we manage, we may to a considerable extent merely have restored something of value that has for some time been lost in our theory and our practice.

Standard Threats

Before we turn over the coin of basic rights and consider the side with the duties, we need to establish two interrelated points about the rights side. One point concerns the final element in the account of the general structure of all rights, basic and non-basic, which is the notion of standard threats as the targets of the social guarantees for the enjoyment of the substance of a right. The other point specifically concerns basic rights and the question whether the reasoning in favor of treating security and subsistence as the substances of basic rights does not generate an impractically and implausibly long list of things to which people will be said to have basic rights. The two points are interrelated because the clearest manner by which to establish that the list of basic rights must, on the contrary, be quite short is to invoke the fact that the social guarantees required by the structure of a right are guarantees, not against all possible threats, but only against what I will call standard threats. In the end we will find a supportive coherence between the account of basic rights and the account of the general structure of most moral rights. We may begin by reviewing the reasons for taking security and subsistence to be basic rights and considering whether the same reasons would support treating many other things as basic rights. Answering that question will lead us to see the role and importance of a conception of standard threats.

Why, then, according to the argument so far, are security and subsistence basic rights? Each is essential to a normal healthy life. Because the actual deprivation of either can be so very serious—potentially incapacitating, crippling, or fatal—even the threatened deprivation of either can be a powerful weapon against anyone whose security or subsistence is not in fact socially guaranteed. People who cannot provide for their own security and subsistence and who lack social guarantees for both are very weak, and possibly helpless, against any individual or institution in a position to deprive them of anything else they value by means of threatening their security or subsistence. A fundamental purpose of acknowledging any basic rights at all is to prevent, or to eliminate, insofar as possible the degree of vulnerability that leaves people at the mercy of others. Social guarantees of security and subsistence would go a long way toward accomplishing this purpose.

Security and subsistence are basic rights, then, because of the roles they play in both the enjoyment and the protection of all other rights. Other rights could not be enjoyed in the absence of security or subsistence, even if the other rights were somehow miraculously protected in such a situation. And other rights could in any case not be protected if security or subsistence could credibly be threatened. The enjoyment of the other rights requires a certain degree of physical integrity, which is temporarily undermined, or eliminated, by deprivations of security or of subsistence. Someone who has suffered exposure or a beating is incapable of enjoying the substances of other rights, although only temporarily, provided he or she receives good enough care to recover the use of all essential faculties.

But as our earlier discussion of helplessness made clear, either the actual or the credibly threatened loss of security or subsistence leaves a person vulnerable to any other deprivations the source of the threat has in mind. Without security or subsistence one is helpless, and consequently one may also be helpless to protect whatever can be protected only at the risk of security or subsistence. Therefore, security and subsistence must be socially guaranteed, if any rights are to be enjoyed. This makes them basic rights.

In the construction of any philosophical argument, a principal challenge is to establish what needs to be established without slipping into the assertion of too much. By "too much" I mean a conclusion so inflated that, even if it is not a reduction to absurdity in the strict sense, it nevertheless strains credulity. The argument for security rights and subsistence rights may seem to suffer this malady, which might be called the weakness of too much strength. Specifically, the argument may be feared to have implicit implications that people have rights to an unlimited number of things, in addition to security and subsistence, that it is difficult to believe that people actually could justifiably demand of others.

Now it is true that we have no reason to believe that security and subsistence are the only basic rights, and Chapter 3 [the author refers to Chapter 3 of his book *Basic Rights,* which is not included in this volume. —Ed.] is devoted to the question of whether some kinds of liberties are also basic rights. But as we shall see in that chapter, it is quite difficult to extend the list of basic rights, and we face little danger that the catalogue of basic rights will turn out to be excessively long. Before it becomes perhaps painfully obvious from the case of liberty, it may be helpful to see why in the abstract the list of basic rights is sharply limited even if it may have some members not considered here.

The structure of the argument that a specific right is basic may be outlined as follows, provided we are careful about what is meant by "necessary":

1. Everyone has a right to something.
2. Some other things are ncessary for enjoying the first thing as a right, whatever the first thing is.
3. Therefore, everyone also has rights to the other things that are necessary for enjoying the first as a right.

Since this argument abstracts from the substance of the right assumed in the first premise, it is based upon what it normally means for anything to be a right or, in other words, upon the concept of a right. So, if the argument to establish the substances of basic rights is summarized by saying that these substances are the "other things . . . necessary" for enjoying any other right, it is essential to interpret "necessary" in the restricted sense of "made essential by the very concept of a right." The "other things" include not whatever would be convenient or useful, but only what is indispensable to anything else's being enjoyed as a right. Nothing will turn out to be necessary, in this sense, for the enjoyment of any right unless it is also necessary for the enjoyment of every right and is, for precisely this reason, qualified to be the substance of a basic right.

Since the concept of a right is a profoundly Janus-faced concept, this conceptual necessity can be explained both from the side of the bearer of the right and . . . from the side of the bearers of the correlative duties. The content of the basic rights is such that for the bearer of any right (basic or non-basic) to pursue its fulfillment by means of the trade-off of the fulfillment of a basic right is self-defeating, and such that for the bearer of duties to claim to be fulfilling the duties correlative to any right in spite of not fulfilling the duties correlative to a basic right is fraudulent. But both perspectives can be captured more concretely by the notion of common, or ordinary, and serious but remediable threats or "standard threats," which was introduced earlier as the final element in the explanation of the structure of a right.[21] Certainly from the viewpoint of the bearer of a right it would be false or misleading to assert that a right had been fulfilled unless in the enjoyment of the substance of that right, a person also enjoyed protection against the threats that could ordinarily be expected to prevent, or hinder to a major degree, the enjoyment of the initial right assumed. And certainly from the viewpoint of the bearers of the correlative duties it would be false or misleading to assert that a right had been honored unless social guarantees had been established that would prevent the most common and serious threats from preventing or acutely hindering the enjoyment of the substance of the right. On the side of duties this places especially heavy emphasis upon preventing standard threats, which . . . is the joint function of the fulfillment of duties to avoid depriving and duties to protect against deprivation.

But the measure of successful prevention of thwarting by ordinary and serious but remediable threats is not utopian. People are neither entitled to social guarantees against every conceivable threat nor entitled to guarantees against ineradicable threats like eventual serious illness, accident, or death. Another way to indicate the restricted scope of the argument, then, is as follows. The argument rests upon what might be called a transitivity principle for rights: If everyone has a right to y, and the enjoyment of x is necessary for the enjoyment of y, then everyone also has a right to x. But the necessity in question is analytic. People also have rights—according to this argument—only to the additional substances made necessary by the paired concepts of a right and its correlative duties. It is analytically necessary that if people are to be provided with a right, their enjoyment of the substance of the right must be protected against the typical major threats. If people are as helpless against ordinary threats as they would be on their own, duties correlative to a right are not being performed. Precisely what those threats are, and which it is feasible to counter, are of course largely empirical questions, and the answers to both questions will change as the situation changes.[22] In the argument for acknowledging security and subsistence as basic rights I have taken it to be fairly evident that the erosion of the enjoyment of any assumed right by deficiencies in subsistence is as common, as serious, and as remediable at present as the destruction of the enjoyment of any assumed right by assaults upon security.

What is, for example, eradicable changes, of course, over time. Today, we have very little excuse for allowing so many poor people to die of malaria and more excuse probably for allowing people to die of cancer. Later perhaps we will have equally little excuse to allow deaths by many kinds of cancer, or perhaps not. In any case, the measure is a realistic, not a utopian, one, and what is realistic can change. . . .

We noticed in an earlier section that one fundamental purpose served by acknowledging basic rights at all is, in Camus' phrase, that we "take the victim's side," and the side of the potential victims. The honoring of basic rights is an active alliance with those who would otherwise be helpless against natural and social forces too strong for them. A basic right has, accordingly, not been honored until people have been provided rather firm protection—what I am calling "social guarantees"—for enjoying the substance of their basic rights. What I am now stressing is that this protection need neither be ironclad nor include the prevention of every imaginable threat.

But the opposite extreme is to offer such weak social guarantees that people are virtually as vulnerable with their basic rights "fulfilled" as they are without them. The social guarantees that are part of any typical right need not provide impregnable protection against every imaginable threat, but they must provide effective defenses against predictable remediable threats. To try to count a situation of unrelieved vulnerability to standard threats as the enjoyment of basic rights by their bearers or the fulfillment of these rights by the bearers of the correlative duties is to engage in double-speak, or to try to behave as if concepts have no boundaries at all. To allow such practices to continue is to acquiesce in not only the violation of rights but also the destruction of the concept of rights.

Insofar as it is true that moral rights generally, and not basic rights only, include justified demands for social guarantees against standard threats, we have an interesting theoretical result. The fulfillment of both basic and non-basic moral rights consists of effective, but not infallible, social arrangements to guard against standard threats like threats to physical security and threats to economic security or subsistence. One way to characterize the substances of basic rights, which ties the account of basic rights tightly to the account of the structure of moral rights generally, is this: The substance of a basic right is something the deprivation of which is one standard threat to rights generally. The fulfillment of a basic right is a successful defense against a standard threat to rights generally. This is precisely why basic rights are basic. That to which they are rights is needed for the fulfillment of all other rights. If the substance of a basic right is not socially guaranteed, attempts actually to enjoy the substance of other rights remain open to a standard threat like the deprivation of security or subsistence. The social guarantees against standard threats that are part of moral rights generally *are the same as* the fulfillment of basic rights.[23] This is why giving less priority to any basic right than to normal non-basic rights is literally impossible.

Notes

1. Obviously this is not the usual North Atlantic account of what a right is, although it incorporates, I think, what is correct in the usual accounts. Perhaps the most frequently cited philosophical discussion is the useful one in Joel Feinberg, *Social Philosophy*. (Englewood Cliffs, NJ: Prentice-Hall, 1973), pp.55–97. A more recent and extended account is A. I. Melden, *Rights and Persons*. (Oxford: Basic Blackwell, 1977). The best collection of recent English and American philosophical essays is probably *Rights*, David Lyons (Ed.). (Belmont, CA: Wadsworth, 1979). For a broader range of views, in less rigorous form, see *Human Rights: Cultural and Ideological Perspectives*, Adamantia Pollis and Peter Schwab (Eds.). (New York: Praeger, 1979). For additional references,

mostly to work in English, see Rex Martin and James W. Nickel, "A Bibliography on the Nature and Foundations of Rights, 1947–1977," *Political Theory,* 6:3 (August 1978), pp. 395–413. Some older but more wide-ranging bibliographies are *International Human Rights: A Bibliography 1965– 1969* and *International Human Rights: A Bibliography 1970–1976,* both edited by William Miller (Notre Dame: University of Notre Dame Law School, Center for Civil Rights, 1976).

2. In saying that these three features constitute "the general structure of a moral right" I do not mean that every moral right always has every one of the three. Wittgenstein, for one, has argued persuasively that we have no particular reason to expect all authentic instances of any concept to have all features—indeed, to have any one feature—in common and that what instance A shares with instance B need not be the same as what instance B shares with instance C. See Ludwig Wittgenstein, *Philosophical Investigations,* 3rd ed. (Oxford: Basic Blackwell, 1967), Part I, paragraphs 66–67. What we are left with is the more realistic but more elusive notion of standard, central, or typical cases. The danger then rests in the temptation to dismiss as deviant or degenerate cases that ought to be treated as counter-examples to our general claims. We have no mechanical method for deciding what is standard and what is deviant and so must consider individual cases fairly and thoroughly, as we shall soon be trying to do.

   Two important characteristics of this list of features should be emphasized. First, the list of features is, not the premises for, but the conclusion from, the detailed description of individual rights considered in the body of the book. Thus, the order of presentation is not the order of derivation. These general features were distilled from the cases of security rights, subsistence rights, and liberty rights discussed in the first three chapters. These general conclusions are presented here as a means of quickly sketching the bold outlines of what is still to be justified.

   Second, most of the argument of the book depends only upon its being correct to say that all *basic* rights have these three features. Since the features are derived from the detailed consideration only of basic rights, it would be conceivable that basic rights were peculiar in having all three. Yet, many other rights obviously do have this same structure. So I advance the less fully justified broader claim, not merely the safer, narrower claim.

3. Feinberg, pp. 58–59. The terminology of "claim-rights" is of course from Wesley Hohfeld, *Fundamental Legal Conceptions.* (New Haven: Yale University Press, 1923).

4. Standard moral rights are, in the categories devised by Hohfeld for legal rights, claim-rights, not mere liberties. Certainly all basic rights turn out to be moral claim-rights rather than moral liberties. See Chapter 2. [Such chapter references refer to the author's book *Basic Rights.* —Ed.]

5. This becomes clearest in the discussion of rights to liberty in Chapter 3.

6. Who exactly are the relevant people is an extremely difficult question, to which Chapter 6 is devoted.

7. See Chapter 2.

8. For his clearest single presentation of this analysis, see Friedrich Neitzsche, *On the Genealogy of Morals,* Walter Kaufmann (Ed.) and Walter Kaufmann and R. J. Hollingdale (Trans.). (New York: Vintage Books, 1967). Much, but not all, of what is interesting in Nietzsche's account was put into the mouth of Callicles in Plato's *Gorgias.*

9. Many legal claim-rights make little or no contribution to self-respect, but moral claim-rights (and the legal claim-rights based upon them) surely do.

10. Nietzsche was also conflating a number of different kinds of power/weakness. Many of today's politically powerful, against whom people need protection, totally lack the kind of dignified power Nietzsche most admired and would certainly have incurred his cordial disgust.

11. Anyone not familiar with the real meaning of what gets called "infant mortality rates" might consider the significance of the fact that in nearby Mexico seven out of every 100 babies fail to survive infancy—see United States, Department of State, *Background Notes: Mexico,* revised February 1979 (Washington: Government Printing Office, 1979), p. 1. For far worse current children's death rates still, see below, Chapter 4, note 13.

12. It is controversial whether rights are claims only upon members of one's own society or upon other persons generally. For some support for the conclusion assumed here, see Chapter 6.

13. Since the enjoyment of a basic right is necessary for the enjoyment of all other rights, it is basic not only to non-basic rights but to other basic rights as well. Thus the enjoyment of the basic rights is an all-or-nothing matter. Each is necessary to the other basic ones as well as to all non-basic ones. Every right, including every basic right, can be enjoyed only if all basic rights are enjoyed. An extended discussion of a case of this mutual dependence is found in Chapter 3.

At the cost of being somewhat premature it may be useful to comment here on an objection that often strikes readers at this point as being a clear counter-example to the thesis that subsistence rights are basic rights in the sense just explained. Mark Wicclair has put the objection especially forcefully for me. The arguments for the thesis have of course not yet been given and occupy much of the remainder of the chapter and, indeed, of the book.

Suppose that in a certain society people are said to enjoy a certain security right—let us say the right not to be tortured. But they do not in fact enjoy subsistence rights: Food, for example, is not socially guaranteed even to people who find it impossible to nourish themselves. The thesis that subsistence rights are basic means that people cannot enjoy any other right if subsistence rights are not socially guaranteed. It follows that the people in the society in question could not actually be enjoying the right not to be tortured, because their right to adequate food is not guaranteed. But—this is the objection—it would appear that they could enjoy the right not to be tortured even though they were starving to death for lack of food they could do nothing to obtain. The objection grants that starvation is terrible. The theoretical point is, however, said to remain: Starvation without torture is preferable to starvation with torture, and the right not to be tortured is still worth something even in isolation and, in particular, even in the absence of subsistence rights. Subsistence rights are, therefore, not necessary for the enjoyment of all other rights and thus not basic in the relevant sense.

But could there actually be a case of the kind brought forward as a counter-example? Could there actually be a right not to be tortured in the absence of a right to subsistence? The difficulty is that a person who had no social guarantee of, say, food and was in fact deprived of food might, without other recourse, be willing to submit to limited torture in exchange for food. In other words, what is being called a right not to be tortured is open to being undermined by the threat of doing nothing about a shortage of food. If this perverse trade of submission to torture for receipt of food were possible, it would be accurate to say that although the person may *have* a right not to be tortured, he cannot actually *enjoy* the right because he must choose between undergoing torture and undergoing starvation, or malnutrition (to make the alternative involving subsistence more like much torture: painful and damaging but not fatal). Insofar as the person has anything approximating a right not to be tortured, the "right" is a merely conditional one—conditional upon the person's not in fact being without some necessity for subsistence for which the substance of the "right" not to be tortured could, in effect, be sold.

Three ways of trying to save the original objection come to mind. First, it might be suggested that trading the immunity to torture for the means to eat is not an instance of failing to enjoy a right, but an instance of renouncing a right. Only because one has the right not to be tortured does one have something to trade for food.

This response is fairly obviously mistaken. If one's only hope of eating adequately is to submit to torture, one is being coerced into submitting to torture, not renouncing one's right not to be tortured. This is a case of coercion analogous in the relevant respects to the demand, your money or your life. One is not renouncing one's right to the money—one is being forced to surrender one's money in order to stay alive. In prisons, where people are already deprived of the freedom of physical movement ordinarily needed for obtaining their own food, the threat to withhold food as well is in fact a common means of coercion.

Second, it could be noted that the torture-for-food exchange might simply not be available. Certainly in light of the perversity of the bargain, there might be no one in the business of supplying people with food in exchange for the privilege of torturing them. Only some sort of wealthy sadist would engage in this transaction.

Now, of course the exchange described is in fact very unlikely, as is the original situation that constitutes the counter-example. The response to the objection is as fantastical as the objection, but the objector cannot expect otherwise. (In what country are people both provided guarantees against torture and denied guarantees of food for subsistence?) But this second response misses the point. That people were not in fact undergoing torture in order to obtain food (or for any other reason) would not constitute their enjoying a right not to be tortured. Enjoying any right includes, among other things, some social guarantees. It is not merely that one does not undergo objectionable events or that one does undergo desirable events—it includes provisions having been made to see to it that the objectionable does not occur and the desirable does.

Hence, the third way to save the counter-example would be to add to it a prohibition against trading the right not to be tortured for anything else, including what was needed to meet an even more serious threat. The counter-example would have to say: One may not be tortured and one must not surrender, trade, renounce, etc. this right for anything else. This would be a weak version of something roughly like what was traditionally called inalienability, except that as traditionally understood inalienability was essential to or inherent in a right: It was thought to be somehow absolutely impossible to alienate or trade the right. In the objector's counter-example anyone obviously *could* trade the right not to be tortured for something else. The best that could be done would be an exceptionless and enforceable prohibition against trading away this right. The trade would, perhaps, be illegal. We can call this an alienation-prohibition, in order to distinguish it from the traditional notion of intrinsic inalienability.

With the inclusion of the alienation-prohibition the case may be an actual counter example, but it is difficult to tell. Possibly one is enjoying a right not to be tortured when one is not only protected against torture but also prevented from exchanging that protection for protection against other threats. As the argument of the book unfolds, two of the main contentions will be (a) that in order to enjoy any right one must be protected against the standard threats to the right and (b) that the best way to be protected against a standard threat is to have social guarantees for the absence of the threat. Thus, the way to enjoy a right to subsistence is to be guaranteed that no torture, among other things, will be used to implement an economic strategy that produces malnutrition, and the way to enjoy a right not to be tortured is to be guaranteed that no deprivations of subsistence needs like food, among other things, will be used to implement a political strategy that includes torture (not that the latter is a realistic case).

Now instead of protecting the enjoyment of one right against standard threats by also protecting the other rights the enjoyment of which includes social guarantees against the standard threats, one could conceivably "protect" one right in isolation by prohibiting the use of that right to fend off threats against which one has no guarantees because one lacks other rights. This is what is done by the right not to be tortured that includes the alienation-prohibition. But the attempted counter-example has now become quite contorted and exotic. One is being prohibited from saving one's own life (from lack of subsistence) at a cost of pain and damage that one is willing to accept if one must. Is this an example of enjoying one right (not to be tortured) in the absence of the enjoyment of another right (subsistence)? This case is now so different from an ordinary case of enjoying a right (in which, I will contend, part of the right is social guarantees against standard threats) that it is uncertain what to say. Obviously I could not without circularity invoke what I take to be the normal and adequate conception of enjoying a right in order to judge the proffered case not to be a case of enjoying a right and therefore not a counter-example to the thesis that subsistence rights are basic. However, treating this eccentric example as a clear case would be question-begging against my view, I think. So, I leave it to the reader—and to the argument in the text.

14. It is odd that the list of "primary goods" in Rawlsian theory does not mention physical security as such. See John Rawls, *A Theory of Justice.* (Cambridge, MA: The Belknap Press of Harvard University Press, 1971), p. 62 and p. 303. The explanation seems to be that security is lumped in with political participation and a number of civil liberties, including freedom of thought, of speech, of press, et al. To do this is to use "liberty" in a confusingly broad sense. One can speak intelligibly of "freedom from" almost anything bad: The child was free from fear, the cabin was free from snakes, the picnic was free from rain. Similarly, it is natural to speak of being free from assault, free from the threat of rape, etc., but this does not turn all these absences of evils into liberties. Freedom from assault, for example, is a kind of security or safety, not a kind of liberty. It may of course be a necessary condition for the exercise of any liberties, which is exactly what I shall now be arguing, but a necessary condition for the exercise of a liberty may be many things

other than another kind of liberty. The most complete indication of why I believe physical security and liberty—even freedom of physical movement—need to be treated separately is Chapter 3.

15. At considerable risk of encouraging unflattering comparisons I might as well note myself that in its general structure the argument here has the same form as the argument in H. L. A. Hart's classic, "Are There Any Natural Rights?" *Philosophical Review,* 64:2 (April 1955), pp. 175–191; that is, Hart can be summarized as maintaining: If there are any rights, there are rights to liberty. I am saying: If there are any rights, there are rights to security—and to subsistence. The finer structures of the arguments are of course quite different. I find Hart's inference considerably less obvious than he did. So, evidently, do many thoughtful people in the third and fourth worlds, which counts against its obviousness but not necessarily against its validity. My struggle with the place of some kinds of liberty, construed more narrowly than Hart's, constitutes Chapter 3.

16. In originally formulating this argument for treating both security and subsistence as basic rights I was not consciously following any philosopher but attempting instead to distill contemporary common sense. As many people have noted, today's common sense tends to be yesterday's philosophy. I was amused to notice recently the following passage from Mill, who not only gives a similar argument for security but notices and then backs away from the parallel with subsistence: "The interest involved is that of security, to everyone's feelings the most vital of all interests. All other earthly benefits are needed by one person, not needed by another; and many of them can, if necessary, be cheerfully foregone or replaced by something else; but security no human being can possibly do without; on it we depend for all our immunity from evil and for the whole value of all and every good, beyond the passing moment, since nothing but the gratification of the instant could be of any worth to us if we could be deprived of everything the next instant by whoever was momentarily stronger than ourselves. Now this most indispensable of all necessaries, after physical nutriment, cannot be had unless. . . ." John Stuart Mill, *Utilitarianism.* (Indianapolis: Bobbs-Merrill, 1957), p. 67 (Chapter V, 14th paragraph from the end).

17. "Many people, therefore, economically dependent as they are upon their employer, hesitate to speak out not because they are afraid of getting arrested, but because they are afraid of being fired. And they are right." Ira Glasser, "Director's Report: You Can Be Fired for Your Politics," *Civil Liberties,* No. 327 (April 1979), p. 8.

18. Exactly how and why Western liberalism has tended to overlook subsistence is another story, but consider, simply as one symptom, the fact that a standard assumption in liberal theory is that there is only moderate scarcity. This has the effect of assuming that everyone's subsistence is taken care of. You must have your subsistence guaranteed in order to be admitted into the domain of the theory. Today this excludes from the scope of liberal theory no fewer than 1,000,000,000 people.

   The figure of over one billion is generally accepted as the minimum number of desperately poor people. The U.S. government's World Hunger Working Group, for example, gave "1.2 billion" as the number of "persons without access to safe drinking water"—see United States, White House, *World Hunger and Malnutrition: Improving the U.S. Response.* (Washington: Government Printing Office, 1978), p. 9. This is, roughly, 25% of all the people there are—and a much higher percentage of the children, since in many very poor countries most people are young.

   I am not criticizing only people who call themselves "liberals" but also, for example, "neoconservatives." For, as Michael Walzer has perceptively observed, "neoconservatives are nervous liberals, and what they are nervous about is liberalism"—see Michael Walzer, "Nervous Liberals," *New York Review of Books,* 26:15 (October 11, 1979), p. 6.

19. James C. Scott, *The Moral Economy of the Peasant: Rebellion and Subsistence in Southeast Asia.* (New Haven: Yale University Press, 1976), pp. 40–41. Scott analyzes the "normative roots of peasant politics" (4) with subtlety and clarity, displaying a coherent and rational conceptual framework implicit in the moral consensus across several peasant societies. I do not mean to suggest, nor does Scott, that all is well in Southeast Asia. For one thing, many traditional village institutions are being eliminated by "modernizing" regimes. With Scott's theory, compare Joel S. Migdal, *Peasants, Politics, and Revolution: Pressures Toward Political and Social Change in the Third World.* (Princeton: Princeton University Press, 1974); and Samuel L. Popkin, *The Rational Peasant: The Political Economy of Rural Society in Vietnam.* (Berkeley: University of California Press, 1979).

For defenses of the suspension of the fulfillment of subsistence rights during an indefinite development period, see Lt. Gen. Ali Moertopo, "Political and Economic Development in Indonesia in the Context of Regionalism in Southeast Asia," *Indonesian Quarterly,* 6:2 (April 1978), pp. 30–47, esp. pp. 32–38; and O. D. Corpuz, *Liberty and Government in the New Society.* (Quezon City: University of the Philippines, Office of the President, 1975), photocopy. For cautions from a nutritional anthropologist about the effects of U.S. aid programs on traditional societies, see Norge W. Jerome, "Nutritional Dilemmas of Transforming Economies," in *Food Policy: The Responsibility of the United States in the Life and Death Choices,* Peter G. Brown and Henry Shue (Eds.). (New York: Free Press, 1977), pp. 275–304.

20. Benedict J. Kerkvliet, *The Huk Rebellion: A Study of Peasant Revolt in the Philippines.* (Berkeley: University of California Press, 1977), p. 252. On the importance for Philippine peasants of their deep belief in a right to subsistence, see pp. 252–255. The most comprehensive legal and normative analysis of economic rights in developing countries is *The International Dimensions of the Right to Development As a Human Right in Relation with Other Human Rights,* United Nations, Economic and Social Council, Commission on Human Rights, E/CN.4/1334 (35th Sess., Agenda item 8, 2 January 1979). (Geneva: Division of Human Rights, 1978).

21. I am grateful to Douglas MacLean for emphasizing the similarity between the notion toward which I am groping here and the one in Thomas M. Scanlon, "Human Rights As a Neutral Concern," in *Human Rights and U.S. Foreign Policy: Principles and Applications,* Peter G. Brown and Douglas MacLean (Eds.). (Lexington, MA: Lexington Books, 1979), pp. 83–92. The Brown and MacLean volume and this volume are products of the same research effort and are designed to complement each other. On nearly every major issue discussed here, alternative views appear in Brown and MacLean, and I am to some degree indebted to the author of almost every chapter of that companion volume, including those with which I am in sharp disagreement philosophically or politically.

22. Although this admission opens a theoretical door to a certain amount of "relativism," I suspect the actual differences across societies in the standard preventable threats are much less than they conceivably might be. Compare Barrington Moore's thesis that although differences in conceptions of happiness are great and important, virtually everyone agrees upon the "miseries"— Barrington Moore, Jr., *Reflections on the Causes of Human Misery and Upon Certain Proposals to Eliminate Them.* (Boston: Beacon Press, 1972), especially Chapter 1, and *Injustice: The Social Bases of Obedience and Revolt.* (White Plains: M. E. Sharpe, 1978). Here, as in many other places, philosophical analysis and political analysis need each other.

The unavoidable mixture of the analytic and the empirical in an element like standard threats is obviously difficult to characterize with any precision. On the one hand, it is clearly part of the meaning of a right that the right-holder may insist that other people take measures to protect the enjoyment of the substance of the right against ordinary, non-inevitable threats—this much is analytic. But which threats are pervasive, which are serious, and which can feasibly be resisted must be discovered from particular situations. Naturally, what is, for example, feasible is a function of how much of the available resources are devoted to the task, as Chapter 4 will emphasize, and that is a heavily value-laden question, not a mere question of efficiency to be left to the economists. So we can draw no neat line between aspects that require philosophical argument and aspects that require economic and political investigation.

23. The coherence of the account of the general structure of a moral right and the account of a basic right with each other is one consideration in favor of both, although coherence is, needless to say, not enough. I am grateful to Charles R. Beitz for perceptively pressing me to make these underlying connections clearer.

Since fulfilling any one basic right involves creating safeguards for the enjoyment of the substance of that basic right against the other standard threats that are the respective concerns of the other basic rights, no basic right can be completely fulfilled until all basic rights are fulfilled. See note 13 above and, for an extended example, Chapter 3, and especially note 14. It would appear that just as (and, because?) deprivations of rights tend to be systematically interrelated, the fulfillment of at least the basic rights also comes in a single package.

Some Consequences of the Failure of the Enlightenment Project

ALASDAIR MacINTYRE

The problems of modern moral theory emerge clearly as the product of the failure of the Enlightenment project. On the one hand, the individual moral agent, freed from hierarchy and teleology, conceives of himself and is conceived of by moral philosophers as sovereign in his moral authority. On the other hand, the inherited, if partially transformed rules of morality have to be found some new status, deprived as they have been of their older teleological character and their even more ancient categorical character as expressions of an ultimately divine law. If such rules cannot be found, a new status which will make appeal to them rational, appeal to them will indeed appear as a mere instrument of individual desire and will. Hence there is a pressure to vindicate them either by devising some new teleology or by finding some new categorical status for them. The first project is what lends its importance to utilitarianism; the second to all those attempts to follow Kant in presenting the authority of the appeal to moral rules as grounded in the nature of practical reason. Both attempts, so I shall argue, failed and fail; but in the course of the attempt to make them succeed social as well as intellectual transformations were accomplished.

Bentham's original formulations suggest a shrewd perception of the nature and scale of the problems confronting him. His innovative psychology provided a view of human nature in the light of which the problem of assigning a new status to moral

Alasdair MacIntyre, "Some Consequences of the Failure of the Enlightenment Project," from *After Virtue: A Study in Moral Theory* by Alasdair MacIntyre, pp. 61–69. © 1981 by University of Notre Dame Press, Notre Dame, IN, 46556. Reprinted by permission.

rules can be clearly stated; and Bentham did not flinch from the notion that he *was* assigning a new status to moral rules and giving a new meaning to key moral concepts. Traditional morality was on his view pervaded by superstition; it was not until we understood that the only motives for human action are attraction to pleasure and aversion to pain that we can state the principles of an enlightened morality, for which the prospect of the maximum pleasure and absence of pain provides a *telos*. "Pleasure" Bentham took to be the name of a type of sensation, just as "pain" is; and sensations of both types vary only in number, intensity and duration. It is worth taking note of this false view of pleasure if only because Bentham's immediate utilitarian successors were so apt to see this as the major source of the difficulties that arise for utilitarianism. They therefore did not always attend adequately to the way in which he makes the transition from his psychological thesis that mankind has two and only two motives to his moral thesis that out of the alternative actions or policies between which we have to choose at any given moment we ought always to perform that action or implement that policy which will produce as its consequences the greatest happiness—that is, the greatest possible quantity of pleasure with the smallest possible quantity of pain—of the greatest number. It is of course on Bentham's view the enlightened, educated mind and it alone which will recognise that the pursuit of my happiness as dictated by my pleasure-seeking, pain-avoiding psychology and the pursuit of the greatest happiness of the greatest number do in point of fact coincide. But it is the aim of the social reformer to reconstruct the social order so that even the unenlightened pursuit of happiness will produce the greatest possible happiness for the greatest possible number; from this aim spring Bentham's numerous proposed legal and penal reforms. Note that the social reformer could not himself find a motive for setting himself to those particular tasks rather than others, were it not the case that an enlightened regard for one's own happiness here and now even in as unreformed a legal and social order as late-eighteenth- and early-nineteenth-century England will lead inexorably to the pursuit of the greatest happiness. This is an empirical claim. Is it true?

It took a nervous breakdown by John Stuart Mill, at once the first Benthamite child and clearly the most distinguished mind and character ever to embrace Benthamism, to make it clear to Mill himself at least that it is not. Mill concluded that it was Bentham's concept of happiness that needed reforming, but what he had actually succeeded in putting in question was the derivation of the morality from the psychology. Yet this derivation provided the whole of the rational grounding for Bentham's project of a new naturalistic teleology. It is not surprising that as this failure was recognised within Benthamism, its teleological content became more and more meagre.

John Stuart Mill was right of course in his contention that the Benthamite conception of happiness stood in need of enlargement; in *Utilitarianism* he attempted to make a key distinction between "higher" and "lower" pleasures and in *On Liberty* and elsewhere he connects increase in human happiness with the extension of human creative powers. But the effect of these emendations is to suggest—what is correct, but what no Benthamite no matter how far reformed could concede—that the notion of human happiness is *not* a unitary, simple notion and cannot provide us with a criterion for making our key choices. If someone suggests to us, in the spirit of Bentham and Mill, that we should guide our own choices by the prospects of our own future pleasure or happiness, the appropriate retort is to enquire: "But which pleasure, which happiness ought to guide me?" For there are too many different kinds of enjoyable activity, too many different modes in which happiness is achieved. And pleasure or happiness are not states of mind for the production of which these activities and modes are merely alternative means. The pleasure-of-drinking-Guinness is not the pleasure-of-swimming-at-Crane's-Beach, and the swimming and the drinking are not two different means for providing the same end-state. The happiness which belongs peculiarly to the way of life of the cloister is not the same happiness as that which belongs peculiarly to the military life. For different pleasures and different happinesses are to a large degree incommensurable; there are no scales of quality or quantity on which to weigh them. Consequently appeal to the criteria of pleasure will not tell me whether to drink or swim and appeal to those of happiness cannot decide for me between the life of a monk and that of a soldier.

To have understood the polymorphous character of pleasure and happiness is of course to have rendered those concepts useless for utilitarian purposes; if the prospect of his or her own future pleasure or happiness cannot for the reasons which I have suggested provide criteria for solving the problems of action in the case of each individual, it follows that the notion of the greatest happiness of the greatest number is a notion without any clear content at all. It is indeed a pseudo-concept available for a variety of ideological uses, but no more than that. Hence when we encounter its use in practical life, it is always necessary to ask what actual project or purpose is being concealed by its use. To say this is not of course to deny that many of its uses have been in the service of socially beneficial ideals, Chadwick's radical reforms in the provision of public health measures, Mill's own support for the extension of the suffrage and for an end to the subjugation of women and a number of other nineteenth-century ideals and causes all invoked the standard of utility to some good purpose. But the use of a conceptual fiction in a good cause does not make it any less of a fiction. We shall have to notice the presence of some other fictions in modern moral discourse later in the argument; but before we do so it is necessary to consider one more feature of nineteenth-century utilitarianism.

It was a mark of the moral seriousness and strenuousness of the great nineteenth-century utilitarians that they felt a continuing obligation to scrutinise and rescrutinise their own positions, so that they might, if at all possible, not be deceived. The culminating achievement of that scrutiny was the moral philosophy of Sidgwick. And it is with Sidgwick that the failure to restore a teleological framework for ethics finally comes to be accepted. He recognised both that the moral injunctions of utilitarianism could not be derived from any psychological foundations and that the precepts which enjoin us to pursue the general happiness are logically independent of and cannot be derived from any precepts enjoining the pursuit of our own happiness. Our basic moral beliefs have two characteristics, Sidgwick found himself forced to conclude not entirely happily; they do not form any kind of unity, they are irreducibly hetero-geneous; and their acceptance is and must be unargued. At the foundation of moral thinking lie beliefs in statements for the truth of which no further reason can be given.

To such statements Sidgwick, borrowing the word from Whewell, gives the name *intuitions*. Sidgwick's disappointment with the outcome of his own enquiry is evident in his announcement that where he had looked for Cosmos, he had in fact found only Chaos.

It was of course from Sidgwick's final positions that Moore was presently to borrow without acknowledgment, presenting his borrowings with his own penumbra of bad argument in *Principia Ethica*. The important differences between *Principia Ethica* and Sidgwick's later writings are ones of tone rather than of substance. What Sidgwick portrays as failure Moore takes to be an enlightening and liberating discovery. And Moore's readers, for whom, as I noticed earlier, the enlightenment and the liberation were paramount, saw themselves as rescued thereby from Sidgwick and any other utilitarianism as decisively as from Christianity. What they did not see of course was that they had also been deprived of any ground for claims to objectivity and that they had begun in their own lives and judgments to provide the evidence to which emotivism was soon to appeal so cogently.

The history of utilitarianism thus links historically the eighteenth-century project of justifying morality and the twentieth century's decline into emotivism. But the philosophical failure of utilitarianism and its consequences at the level of thought and theory are of course only one part of the relevant history. For utilitarianism appeared in a variety of social embodiments and left its mark upon a variety of social roles and institutions. And these remained as an inheritance long after utilitarianism had lost the philosophical importance which John Stuart Mill's exposition had conferred upon it. But although this social inheritance is far from unimportant to my central thesis, I shall delay remarking upon it until I have considered the failure of a second philosophical attempt to give an account of how the autonomy of the moral agent might be consistently combined with a view of moral rules as having an independent and objective authority.

Utilitarianism advanced its most successful claims in the nineteenth century. Thereafter intuitionism followed by emotivism held sway in British philosophy, while in the United States pragmatism provided the same kind of *praeparatio evangelica* for emotivism that intuitionism provided in Britain. But for reasons that we have already noticed emotivism always seemed implausible to analytical philosophers primarily concerned with questions of *meaning* largely because it is evident that moral reasoning *does* take place, that moral conclusions can often be validly derived from sets of premises. Such analytical philosophers revived the Kantian project of demonstrating that the authority and objectivity of moral rules is precisely that authority and objectivity which belongs to the exercise of reason. Hence their central project was, indeed is, that of showing that any rational agent is logically committed to the rules of morality in virtue of his or her rationality.

I have already suggested that the variety of attempts to carry through this project and their mutual incompatibility casts doubt on their success. But it is clearly necessary to understand not only *that* the project fails, but *why* it fails, and to do this it is necessary to examine one such attempt in a little detail. The example which I have chosen is that made by Alan Gewirth in *Reason and Morality* (1978). I choose Gewirth's book because it is not only one of the most recent of such attempts, but also because it deals carefully and scrupulously with objections and criticisms that have been made of earlier writers. Moreover Gewirth adopts what is at once a clear and a strict view of what reason is: In order to be admitted as a principle of practical reason, a principle must be analytic; and in order for a conclusion to follow from premises of practical reason, it must be demonstrably entailed by those premises. There is none of the looseness and vagueness about what constitutes "a good reason" which had weakened some earlier analytic attempts to exhibit morality as rational.

The key sentence of Gewirth's book is: "Since the agent regards as necessary goods the freedom and well-being that constitute the generic features of his successful action, he logically must also hold that he has rights to these generic features and he implicitly makes a corresponding rights-claim" (p. 63). Gewirth's argument may be spelled out as follows. Every rational agent has to recognise a certain measure of freedom and well-being as prerequisites for his exercise of rational agency. Therefore each rational agent must will, if he is to will at all, that he possess that measure of these goods. This is what Gewirth means when he writes in the sentence quoted of "necessary goods." And there is clearly no reason to quarrel with Gewirth's argument so far. It turns out to be the next step that is at once crucial and questionable.

Gewirth argues that anyone who holds that the prerequisites for his exercise of rational agency are necessary goods is logically committed to holding also that he has a right to these goods. But quite clearly the introduction of the concept of a right needs justification both because it is at this point a concept quite new to Gewirth's argument *and* because of the special character of the concept of a right.

It is first of all clear that the claim that I have a right to do or have something is a quite different type of claim from the claim that I need or want or will be benefited by something. From the first—if it is the only relevant consideration—it follows that others ought not to interfere with my attempts to do or have whatever it is, whether it is for my own good or not. From the second it does not. And it makes no difference what kind of good or benefit is at issue.

Another way of understanding what has gone wrong with Gewirth's argument is to understand why this step is so essential to his argument. It is of course true that if I claim a right in virtue of my possession of certain characteristics, then I am logically committed to holding that anyone else with the same characteristics also possess this right. But it is just this property of necessary universalisability that does not belong to claims about either the possession of or the need or desire for a good, even a universally necessary good.

One reason why claims about goods necessary for rational agency are so different from claims to the possession of rights is that the latter in fact presuppose, as the former do not, the existence of a socially established set of rules. Such sets of rules only come into existence at particular historical periods under particular social circumstances. They are in no way universal features of the human condition. Gewirth readily acknowledges that expressions such as "a right" in English and cognate terms in English and other languages only appeared at a relatively late point in the history of the language toward the close of the middle ages. But he argues that the existence of such expressions is not a necessary condition for the embodiment of the concept of a right in forms of human behaviour; and in this at least he is clearly right. But the objection that Gewirth has to meet is precisely that those forms of human behaviour which presuppose notions of some ground to entitlement, such as the notion of a right, always have a highly specific and socially local character, and that the existence of particular types of social institution or practice is a necessary condition for the notion of a claim to the possession of a right being an intelligible type of human performance. (As a matter of historical fact such types of social institution or practice have not existed universally in human societies.) Lacking any such social form, the making of a claim to a right would be like presenting a check for payment in a social order that lacked the institution of money. Thus Gewirth has illicitly smuggled into his argument a conception which does not in any way belong, as it must do if his case is to succeed, to the minimal characterisation of a rational agent.

I take it then that both the utilitarianism of the middle and late nineteenth century and the analytical moral philosophy of the middle and late twentieth century are alike unsuccessful attempts to rescue the autonomous moral agent from the predicament in which the failure of the Enlightenment project of providing him with a secular, rational justification for his moral allegiances had left him. I have already charac-terised that predicament as one in which the price paid for liberation from what appeared to be the external authority of traditional morality was the loss of any authoritative content from the would-be moral utterances of the newly autonomous agent. Each moral agent now spoke unconstrained by the externalities of divine law, natural teleology or hierarchical authority; but why should anyone else now listen to him? It was and is to this question that both utilitarianism and analytical moral philosophy must be understood as attempting to give cogent answers; and if my argument is correct, it is precisely this question which both fail to answer cogently. None the less almost everyone, philosopher and non-philosopher alike, continues to speak and write as if one of these projects had succeeded. And hence derives one of the features of contemporary moral discourse which I noticed at the outset, the gap between the *meaning* of moral expressions and the ways in which they are put to *use*. For the *meaning* is and remains such as would have been warranted only if at least one of the philosophical projects had been successful; but the use, the emotivist use, is precisely what one would expect if the philosophical projects had all failed.

Contemporary moral experience as a consequence has a paradoxical character. For each of us is taught to see himself or herself as an autonomous moral agent; but each of us also becomes engaged by modes of practice, aesthetic or bureaucratic, which involve us in manipulative relationships with others. Seeking to protect the autonomy that we have learned to prize, we aspire ourselves *not* to be manipulated by others; seeking to incarnate our own principles and stand-point in the world of practice, we find no way open to us to do so except by directing toward others those very manipulative modes of relationship which each of us aspires to resist in our own case. The incoherence of our attitudes and our experience arises from the incoherent conceptual scheme which we have inherited.

Once we have understood this it is possible to understand also the key place that three other concepts have in the distinctively modern moral scheme, that of *rights,* that of *protest,* and that of *unmasking.* By "rights" I do not mean those rights conferred by positive law or custom on specified classes of person; I mean those rights which are alleged to belong to human beings as such and which are cited as a reason for holding that people ought not to be interfered with in their pursuit of life, liberty and happiness. They are the rights which were spoken of in the eighteenth century as natural rights or as the rights of man. Characteristically in that century they were defined negatively, precisely as rights *not* to be interfered with. But sometimes in that century and much more often in our own positive rights—rights to due process, to education or to employment are examples—are added to the list. The expression "human rights" is now commoner than either of the eighteenth-century expressions. But whether negative or positive and however named they are supposed to attach equally to all individuals, whatever their sex, race, religion, talents or deserts, and to provide a ground for a variety of particular moral stances.

It would of course be a little odd that there should be such rights attaching to human beings simply *qua* human beings in light of the fact, which I alluded to in my discussion of Gewirth's argument, that there is no expression in any ancient or medieval language correctly translated by our expression "a right" until near the close of the middle ages: The concept lacks any means of expression in Hebrew, Greek, Latin or Arabic, classical or medieval, before about 1400, let alone in Old English, or in Japanese even as late as the mid-nineteenth century. From this it does not of course follow that there are no natural or human rights; it only follows that no one could have known that there were. And this at least raises certain questions. But we do not need to be distracted into answering them, for the truth is plain: There are no such rights, and belief in them is one with belief in witches and in unicorns.

The best reason for asserting so bluntly that there are no such rights is indeed of precisely the same type as the best reason which we possess for asserting that there are no witches and the best reason which we possess for asserting that there are no unicorns: Every attempt to give good reasons for believing that there *are* such rights has failed. The eighteenth-century philosophical defenders of natural rights some-times suggest that the assertions which state that men possess them are self-evident truths; but we know that there are no self-evident truths. Twentieth-century moral philosophers have sometimes appealed to their and our intuitions; but one of the things that we ought to have learned from the history of moral philosophy is that the introduction of the word "intuition" by a moral philosopher is always a signal that something has gone badly wrong with an argument. In the United Nations declaration on human rights of 1948 what has since become the normal U.N. practice of not giving good reasons for *any* assertions whatsoever is followed with great rigour. And the latest defender of such rights, Ronald Dworkin (*Taking Rights Seriously,* 1976), concedes that the existence of such rights cannot be demonstrated but remarks on this point simply that it does not follow from the fact that a statement cannot be demonstrated that it is not true (p. 81). Which is true, but could equally be used to defend claims about unicorns and witches.

Natural or human rights then are fictions—just as is utility—but fictions with highly specific properties. In order to identify them it is worth noticing briefly once more the other moral fiction which emerges from the eighteenth century's attempts to reconstruct morality, the concept of utility. When Bentham first turned "utility" into a quasi-technical term, he did so, as I have already noticed, in a way that was designed to make plausible the notion of summing individual prospects of pleasure and pain. But, as John Stuart Mill and other utilitarians expanded their notion of the variety of aims which human beings pursue and value, the notion of its being possible to sum all those experiences and activities which give satisfaction became increasingly implausible for reasons which I suggested earlier. The objects of natural and educated human desire are irreducibly heterogeneous and the notion of summing them either for individuals or for some population has no clear sense. But if utility is thus not a clear concept, then to use it as if it is, to employ it as if it could provide us with a rational criterion, is indeed to resort to a fiction.

A central characteristic of moral fictions which comes clearly into view when we juxtapose the concept of utility to that of rights is now identifiable: They purport to provide us with an objective and impersonal criterion, but they do not. And for this reason alone there would have to be a gap between their purported meaning and the uses to which they are actually put. Moreover we can now understand a little better how the phenomenon of incommensurable premises in modern moral debate arises. The concept of rights was generated to serve one set of purposes as part of the social invention of the autonomous moral agent; the concept of utility was devised for quite another set of purposes. And both were elaborated in a situation in which substitute artifacts for the concepts of an older and more traditional morality were required, substitutes that had to have a radically innovative character if they were to give even an appearance of performing their new social functions. Hence when claims invoking rights are matched against claims appealing to utility or when either or both are matched against claims based on some traditional concept of justice, it is not surprising that there is no rational way of deciding which type of claim is to be given priority or how one is to be weighed against the other. Moral incommensurability is itself the product of a particular historical conjunction.

This provides us with an insight important for understanding the politics of modern societies. For what I described earlier as the culture of bureaucratic individualism results in their characteristic overt political debates being between an individualism which makes its claims in terms of rights and forms of bureaucratic organisation which make their claims in terms of utility. But if the concept of rights and that of utility are a matching pair of incommensurable fictions, it will be the case that the moral idiom employed can at best provide a semblance of rationality for the modern political process, but not its reality. The mock rationality of the debate conceals the arbitrariness of the will and power at work in its resolution.

It is easy also to understand why *protest* becomes a distinctive moral feature of the modern age and why *indignation* is a predominant modern emotion. "To protest" and its Latin predecessors and French cognates are originally as often or more often positive as negative; to protest was once to bear witness *to* something and only as a consequence of that allegiance to bear witness *against* something else.

But protest is now almost entirely that negative phenomenon which characteristically occurs as a reaction to the alleged invasion of someone's *rights* in the name of someone else's *utility*. The self-assertive shrillness of protest arises because the facts of incommensurability ensure that protestors can never win an *argument*; the indignant self-righteousness of protest arises because the facts of incommensurability ensure equally that the protestors can never lose an argument either. Hence the *utterance* of protest is characteristically addressed to those who already *share* the protestors' premises. The effects of incommensurability ensure that protestors rarely have anyone else to talk to but themselves. This is not to say that protest cannot be effective; it is to say that it cannot be *rationally* effective and that its dominant modes of expression give evidence of a certain perhaps unconscious awareness of this. . . .

The Basis
and Content
of Human Rights

ALAN GEWIRTH

Despite the great practical importance of the idea of human rights, some of the most basic questions about them have not yet received adequate answers. We may assume, as true by definition, that human rights are rights that all persons have simply insofar as they are human. But are there any such rights? How, if at all, do we know that there are? What is their scope or content, and how are they related to one another? Are any of them absolute, or may each of them be overridden in certain circumstances?

I

These questions are primarily substantive or criterial rather than logical or conceptual. Recent moral philosophers, following on the work of legal thinkers,[1] have done much to clarify the concept of a right, but they have devoted considerably less attention to substantive arguments that try to prove or justify that persons have rights other than those grounded in positive law. Such arguments would indicate the criteria for there being human rights, including their scope or content, and would undertake to show why these criteria are correct or justified.

The conceptual and the substantive questions are, of course, related, but still they are distinct. If, for example, we know that for one person A to have a right to something X is for A to be entitled to X and also for some other person or persons to

Alan Gewirth, "The Basis and Content of Human Rights," in *Nomos XXIII: Human Rights,* J. Roland Pennock and John W. Chapman (Eds.). (New York: New York University Press, 1981), pp. 119–147. Reprinted with permission of the publisher.

have a correlative duty to provide X for A as his due or to assist A's having X or at least to refrain from interfering with A's having X; still this does not tell us whether or why A is entitled to X and hence whether or why the other person or persons have such a correlative duty to A. Appeal to positive recognition is obviously insufficient for answering these substantive questions. The answer is not given, for example, by pointing out that many governments have signed the United Nations Universal Declaration of Human Rights of 1948 as well as later covenants. For if the existence or having of human rights depended on such recognition, it would follow that prior to, or independent of, these positive enactments no human rights existed.

The questions "Are there any human rights?" or "Do persons have any human rights?" may indeed be interpreted as asking whether the rights receive positive recognition and legal enforcement. But in the sense in which it is held that humans have rights (so that such rights exist) even if they are not enforced, the existence in question is normative: It refers to what entitlements legal enactments and social regulations ought to recognize, not or not only to what they in fact recognize. Thus, the criterion for answering the question must not be legal or conventional but moral. For human rights to exist there must be valid moral criteria or principles that justify that all humans, qua humans, have the rights and hence also the correlative duties. Human rights are rights or entitlements that belong to every person; thus, they are universal moral rights. There may of course be other moral rights as well, but only those that morally ought to be universally distributed among all humans are human rights.

This answer, however, seems to get us into more rather than less difficulty. In order to ascertain whether there are legal rights we need only look to the statute books; these, for present purposes, may be held to supply the criteria for the existence of such rights. But if for a moral or human right to exist is for it to satisfy valid moral criteria which justify or ground the right, where do we look for such criteria? What is the moral analogue of the statute books? If there were a single set of universally accepted moral criteria, our task might be somewhat easier, although even in this case we should still have to take account of the distinction indicated above between positive social recognition and moral validity.

In fact, however, the field of moral criteria is full of controversy: Consider the competing substantive views epitomized by such thinkers as Kant, Kierkegaard, Nietzsche, Mill, and Marx, who hold, respectively, that the criteria for having rights consist in or are determined by reason, religion, power, utility, and economic class or history. The disagreements among these thinkers do not represent merely different "second-order" analyses of a commonly accepted body of "first-order" moral judgments, in the way philosophers may differ about the analysis of knowledge while recognizing (except for some borderline cases) a commonly accepted body of knowledge. In contrast to these, the divergences among moral philosophers are disagreements of basic substantive first-order moral principle about what rights persons have, about how persons ought to regard and act toward one another, about what interests of which persons are worth pursuing and supporting, and the like. Considerable evidence also indicates that many contemporaries, both philosophers and nonphilosophers, would share (although perhaps less systematically) one or another of such divergent moral principles.

Nor does the difficulty end there. For in many fields of empirical science and of practice where the "authorities" or ordinary persons disagree, we have some common conception at least of the context or subject matter to which one must look as a kind of independent variable for testing their divergent assertions. Examples of these subject matters are natural or experimental phenomena in the case of natural science, physical health in the case of medicine, rates of inflation or unemployment in the case of economics. But it seems that the very context or subject matter to which one should look to resolve the disagreements of moral principle is itself involved in such disagreements. Obviously, we should already be taking sides on this issue of moral principle if we were to urge that religion or economic history or social utility or aesthetic sensibility be appealed to as the independent variable for this purpose. Although Thomas Jefferson, following a long tradition, wrote that "all men . . . are endowed by their Creator with certain unalienable rights," it does not seem true to say that persons are born having rights in the sense in which they are born having legs. At least their having legs is empirically confirmable, but this is not the case with their having rights. And whereas it is indeed possible to confirm empirically, although in a more complex way, that most persons are born having certain *legal* rights, this, as we have seen, is not sufficient to establish that they have *moral* or *human* rights.

These general difficulties about moral criteria are reinforced when we look at recent attempts of moral philosophers to answer the substantive questions of what are the specific criteria for having moral rights and how it can be known that humans have such rights. For even where the philosophers agree at least in part on the scope or content of the rights, they disagree as to how the existence of these rights can be established or justified. We may distinguish five different recent answers. The intuitionist answer that humans' possession of certain inalienable rights is self-evident, most famously expressed in the Declaration of Independence, is reiterated in Nozick's peremptory assertion that "Individuals have rights, and there are things no person or group may do to them (without violating their rights)."[2] Like other intuitionist positions, this one is impotent in the face of conflicting intuitions. The institutionalist answer that rights arise from transactions grounded in formal or informal rules of institutions, such as promising,[3] incurs the difficulty that some institutions may be morally wrong, so that an independent moral justification must still be given for the institutional or transactional rules that are held to ground the rights. A third answer is that persons have rights because they have interests.[4] This, however, indicates at most a necessary condition for having rights, since there would be an enormous and indeed unmanageable proliferation of rights if the having any interest X were sufficient to generate a right to X. Even if "interests" are restricted to basic or primary interests or needs, there still remain both the logical question of how a normative conclusion about rights can be derived from factual premises about empirically ascertainable characteristics such as having interests, and also the substantive question of why moral rights are generated by characteristics that all humans have in common rather than by more restrictive, inegalitarian characteristics that pertain only to some persons, or to persons in varying degrees, such as expert knowledge or will to power or productive ability.

The fourth answer, that persons have moral rights because they have intrinsic worth or dignity or are ends in themselves or children of God,[5] may be held simply to reduplicate the doctrine to be justified. Such characterizations are directly or ultimately normative, and if one is doubtful about whether persons have moral rights one will be equally doubtful about the characterizations that were invoked to justify it. The fifth answer is Rawls's doctrine that if persons were to choose the constitutional structure of their society from behind a veil of ignorance of all their particular qualities, they would provide that each person must have certain basic rights.[6] Insofar, however, as this doctrine is viewed as giving a justificatory answer to the question whether humans have equal moral rights, it may be convicted of circularity. For the argument attains its egalitarian conclusion only by putting into its premises the egalitarianism of persons' universal equal ignorance of all their particular qualities. This ignorance has no independent rational justification, since humans are not in fact ignorant of all their particular qualities. Hence, apart from an initial egalitarian moral outlook, why should any actual rational informed persons accept the principle about equal moral rights that stems from such ignorance?

It may be objected that all the above difficulties about moral or human rights arise because I have taken too "cognitive" or "ontological" a view of them. Thus, it may be held that moral rights are not something known or existent; the correct analysis of a rights-judgment is not "descriptive" but rather "prescriptive" or of some other noncognitivist sort. Rights-judgments are claims or demands made on other persons; they do not state that certain knowable facts exist; rather, they advocate, urge, or exhort that certain facts be brought into existence. Hence, questions of justification or validity are logically irrelevant to such judgments.

Now the prescriptivist interpretation of rights-judgments is partly true, but this does not remove the point of the justificatory questions I have asked. For one thing, as we have seen, different persons may make conflicting rights-claims, so that the question still remains which of these claims is correct. Moreover, ascriptions of correctness or justification are intrinsic to rights-judgments: These consist not only in certain claims or demands but also in the implicit view, on the part of the persons who make them, that the claims have sound reasons in their support. If this were not so, discussion or debate about rights would consist only in vocal ejaculations or attempts at propagandistic manipulation; it would not have even potentially the aspects of rational argument or reflective appraisal of evidence that it in fact can and does display. In addition, the logical connections that hold among rights-judgments would be obscured or even left unexplained if the ejaculatory or manipulative interpretation were the sole or the main correct analysis of such judgments.

II

Let us now begin to develop answers to these questions about human rights. First, since these rights derive from a valid moral criterion or principle, we must consider what I have referred to as the context or subject matter of morality. We saw that although in many other fields their subject matters serve as independent variables for testing the correctness of conflicting judgments made within them, it was difficult to find such a non-question-begging subject matter for morality. Nevertheless, it does exist and can be found. To see what it is, we must consider the general concept of a morality. I have so far been using the words "moral" and "morality" without defining them. Amid the various divergent moralities with their conflicting substantive and distributive criteria, a certain core meaning may be elicited. According to this, a morality is a set of categorically obligatory requirements for actions that are addressed at least in part to every actual or prospective agent, and that are intended to further the interests, especially the most important interests, of persons or recipients other than or in addition to the agent or the speaker.

As we have seen, moralities differ with regard to what interests of which persons they view as important and deserving of support. But amid these differences, all moralities have it in common that they are concerned with actions. For all moral judgments, including right-claims, consist directly or indirectly in precepts about how persons ought to act toward one another. The specific contents of these judgments, of course, vary widely and often conflict with one another. But despite these variations and conflicts, they have in common the context of the human actions that they variously prescribe or prohibit and hence view as right or wrong. It is thus this context which constitutes the general subject matter of all morality.

How does the consideration of human action serve to ground or justify the ascription and content of human rights? To answer this question, let us return to the connection indicated above between rights and claims. Rights may be had even when they are not claimed, and claims are also not in general sufficient to establish or justify that their objects are rights. As against such an assertoric approach to the connection between claims and rights, I shall follow a dialectically necessary approach. Even if persons' having rights cannot be logically inferred in general from the fact that they make certain claims, it is possible and indeed logically necessary to infer, from the fact that certain objects are the proximate necessary conditions of human action, that all rational agents logically must hold or claim, at least implicitly, that they have rights to such objects. Although what is thus directly inferred is a statement not about persons' rights but about their claiming to have them, this provides a sufficient criterion for the existence of human rights, because the claim must be made or accepted by every rational human agent on his own behalf, so that it holds universally within the context of action, which is the context within which all moral rights ultimately have application. The argument is dialectically necessary in that it proceeds from what all agents logically must claim or accept, on pain of contradiction. To see how this is so, we must briefly consider certain central aspects of action. Since I have presented the argument in some detail elsewhere,[7] I shall here confine myself to outlining the main points.

As we have seen, all moral precepts, regardless of their varying specific contents, are concerned directly or indirectly with how persons ought to act. This is also true of most if not all other practical precepts. Insofar as actions are the possible objects of any such precepts, they are performed by purposive agents. Now, every agent regards his purposes as good according to whatever criteria (not necessarily moral ones) are involved in his acting to fulfill them. This is shown, for example, by the endeavor or at least intention with which each agent approaches the achieving of his purposes. Hence, *a fortiori,* he also, as rational, regards as necessary goods the proximate general necessary conditions of his acting to achieve his purposes. For without these conditions he either would not be able to act for any purposes or goods at all or at least would not be able to act with any chance of succeeding in his purposes. These necessary conditions of his action and successful action are freedom and well-being, where freedom consists in controlling one's behavior by one's unforced choice while having knowledge of relevant circumstances, and well-being consists in having the other general abilities and conditions required for agency. The components of such well-being fall into a hierarchy of three kinds of goods: basic, nonsubtractive, and additive. These will be analyzed more fully below.

In saying that every rational agent regards his freedom and well-being as necessary goods, I am primarily making not a phenomenological descriptive point about the conscious thought processes of agents but rather a dialectically necessary point about what is logically involved in the structure of action. Since agents act for purposes they regard as worth pursuing—for otherwise they would not control their behavior by their unforced choice with a view to achieving their purposes—they must, insofar as they are rational, also regard the necessary conditions of such pursuit as necessary goods. Just as the basic goods are generically the same for all agents, so too are the nonsubtractive and additive goods. I shall call freedom and well-being the *generic features* of action, since they characterize all action or at least all successful action in the respect in which action has been delimited above.

It is from the consideration of freedom and well-being as the necessary goods of action that the ascription and contents of human rights follow. The main point is that with certain qualifications to be indicated below, there is a logical connection between necessary goods and rights. Just as we saw before that from "X is an interest of some person A" it cannot be logically inferred that "A has a right to X," so too this cannot be logically inferred from "X is a good of A" or from "X seems good to A." In all these cases the antecedent is too contingent and variable to ground an ascription of rights. The reason for this is that rights involve *normative necessity.* One way to see this is through the correlativity of rights and strict "oughts" or duties. The judgment "A has a right to X" both entails and is entailed by "All other persons ought at least to refrain from interfering with A's having (or doing) X," where this "ought" includes the idea of something due or owed to A. Under certain circumstances, including those where the subject or right-holder A is unable to have X by his own efforts, the rights-judgment also entails and is entailed by "Other persons ought to assist A to have X," where again the "ought" includes the idea of something due or owed to A. Now, these strict "oughts" involve normative necessity; they state what, as of right, other persons *must* do. Such necessity is also involved in the frequently noted use of "due" and "entitlement" as synonyms or at least as components of the substantive use of "right." A person's rights are what belong to him as his due, what he is entitled to, hence what he can rightly demand of others. In all these expressions the idea of normative necessity is central.

This necessity is an essential component in the ascription of rights, but it is not sufficient to logically ground this ascription. Let us recur to freedom and well-being as the necessary goods of action. From "X is a necessary good for A" does it logically follow that "A has a right to X"? To understand this question correctly, we must keep in mind that "necessary good" is here used in a rational and invariant sense. It does not refer to the possibly idiosyncratic and unfounded desires of different protagonists, as when someone asserts, "I must have a Florida vacation (or a ten-speed bicycle); it is a necessary good for me." Rather, a "necessary good" is here confined to the truly grounded requirements of agency; hence, it correctly characterizes the indispensable conditions that all agents must accept as needed for their actions.

Now, it might be argued that when "necessary good" is understood in this universal and rational way, from "X is a necessary good for A" it does follow that "A has a right to X." For since the idea of a right involves normative necessity, "A has a right to X" is entailed by "It is normatively necessary that A have X," and this seems equivalent to "X is a necessary good for A." There are three interrelated considerations, however, that show that "X is a necessary good for A" is not sufficient to provide the logical ground for "A has a right X" as a matter of logical necessity. First, as we have seen, "A has a right to X" entails that other persons, B, C, and so forth, have correlative duties toward A. But how can these duties of other persons be logically derived from "X is a necessary good for A," which refers only to A, not to other persons?

Second, it must be kept in mind that rights involve not only "oughts" or normative necessity but also the idea of entitlement, of something due to the right-holder. There is logical correlativity between "A has a right to X," on the one hand, and "Other persons ought to refrain from interfering with A's having X and ought also, under certain circumstances, to assist A to have X," on the other, only when these "oughts" are viewed as indicating what A is entitled to or ought to have as his due. But in "X is a necessary good for A" this idea of A's entitlement to X, of its being due or owed to him, is not found. Hence, it cannot serve to generate logically the conclusion, "A has a right to X."

A third consideration that shows this is that, as we saw above, a rights-judgment is prescriptive: It advocates or endorses that the subject or right-holder A have the X that is the object of the right. But such advocacy need not be present in "X is a necessary good for A." For this statement, as such, does not necessarily carry with it any advocacy or endorsement on A's behalf by the person who makes the statement, even while he recognizes its truth. Hence, again, "X is a necessary good for A" is not sufficient to logically generate or entail "A has a right to X."

What these considerations indicate is that for the concept of necessary goods logically to generate the concept of rights, both concepts must figure in judgments made by the agent or right-holder himself in accordance with the dialectically necessary method. It will be recalled that this method begins from statements or judgments that are necessarily made or accepted by protagonists or agents, and the method then traces what these statements or judgments logically imply. Thus, in the present context of action, the method requires that the judgments about necessary goods and rights be viewed as being made by the agent himself from within his own internal, conative standpoint in purposive agency.

When this internal, conative view is taken, the logical gaps indicated above between judgments about necessary goods and ascriptions of rights are closed. The agent is now envisaged as saying, "My freedom and well-being are necessary goods." From this there does logically follow his further judgment, "I have rights to freedom and well-being." For the assertion about necessary goods is now not a mere factual means-end statement; on the contrary, because it is made by the agent himself from within his own conative standpoint in purposive agency, it carries his advocacy or endorsement. In effect, he is saying, "I must have freedom and well-being in order to pursue by my actions any of the purposes I want and intend to pursue." Thus his statement is prescriptive.

By the same token, his statement carries the idea of something that is his due, to which he is entitled. It must be kept in mind that these concepts do not have only moral or legal criteria; they may be used with many different kinds of criteria, including intellectual, aesthetic, and prudential ones. In the present context the agent's criterion is prudential: The entitlement he claims to freedom and well-being is grounded in his own needs as an agent who wants to pursue his purposes. He is saying that he has rights to freedom and well-being because these goods are due to him from within his own standpoint as a prospective purposive agent, since he needs these goods in order to act either at all or with the general possibility of success.

This consideration also shows how, from the agent's judgment "My freedom and well-being are necessary goods," there also logically follows a claim on his part against other persons. For he is saying that because he must have freedom and well-being in order to act, he must have whatever further conditions are required for his fulfilling these needs; and these further conditions include especially that other persons at least refrain from interfering with his having freedom and well-being. Thus, the agent's assertion of his necessary needs of agency entails a claim on his part to the noninterference of other persons and also, in certain circumstances, to their help.

There may be further objections against the derivation of the agent's right-claims from his judgments about necessary goods; I have dealt with these elsewhere.[8] What I have tried to show is that every agent must claim or accept, at least implicitly, that he has rights to freedom and well-being, because of the logical connection between rights and necessary goods as involving normative necessity, prescriptiveness, and entitlements when these are viewed from the internal, conative standpoint of the agent himself who makes or accepts the respective judgments. The argument may be summed up by saying that if any agent denies that he has rights to freedom and well-being, he can be shown to contradict himself. For, as we have seen, he must accept (1) "My freedom and well-being are necessary goods." Hence, the agent must also accept (2) "I, as an actual or prospective agent, must have freedom and well-being," and hence also (3) "All other persons must at least refrain from removing or interfering with my freedom and well-being." For if other persons remove or interfere with these, then he will not have what he has said he must have. Now suppose the agent denies (4) "I have rights to freedom and well-being." Then he must also deny (5) "All other persons ought at least to refrain from removing or interfering with my freedom and well-being." By denying (5) he must accept (6) "It is not the case that all other persons ought at least to refrain from removing or interfering with my freedom and well-being," and hence he must also accept (7) "Other persons may (are permitted to) remove or interfere with my freedom and well-being." But (7) contradicts (3). Since, as we have seen, every agent must accept (3), he cannot consistently accept (7). Since (7) is entailed by the denial of (4), "I have rights to freedom and well-being," it follows that any agent who denies that he has rights to freedom and well-being contradicts himself.

III

Thus far I have shown that rights and right-claims are necessarily connected with action, in that every agent, on pain of self-contradiction, must hold or accept that he has rights to the necessary conditions of action. I shall henceforth call these *generic rights,* since freedom and well-being are the generic features of action. As so far presented, however, they are only prudential rights but not yet moral ones, since their criterion, as we have seen, is the agent's own pursuit of his purposes. In order to establish that they are also moral and human rights, we must show that each agent must admit that all other humans also have these rights. For in this way the agent will be committed to take favorable account of the purposes or interests of other persons besides himself. Let us see why he must take this further step.

This involves the question of the ground or sufficient reason or sufficient condition on the basis of which any agent must hold that he has the generic rights. Now, this ground is not subject to his optional or variable decisions. There is one, and only one, ground that every agent logically must accept as the sufficient justifying condition for his having the generic rights, namely, that he is a prospective agent who has purposes he wants to fulfill. Suppose some agent A were to hold that he has these rights only for some more restrictive necessary and sufficient reason R. This would entail that in lacking R he would lack the generic rights. But if A were to accept this conclusion, that he may not have the generic rights, he would contradict himself. For we saw above that it is necessarily true of every agent that he must hold or accept at least implicitly that he has rights to freedom and well-being. Hence, A would be in the position of both affirming and denying that he has the generic rights: Affirming it because he is an agent, denying it because he lacks R. To avoid this contradiction, every agent must hold that being a prospective purposive agent is a sufficient reason or condition for having the generic rights.

Because of this sufficient reason, every agent, on pain of self-contradiction, must also accept the generalization that all prospective purposive agents have the generic rights. This generalization is an application of the logical principle of universalizability: If some predicate P belongs to some subject S because S has the quality Q (where the "because" is that of sufficient reason or condition), then it logically follows that every subject that has Q has P. If any agent A were to deny or refuse to accept this generalization in the case of any other prospective purposive agent, A would contradict himself. For he would be in the position of saying that being a prospective purposive agent both is and is not a sufficient justifying condition for having the generic rights. Hence, on pain of self-contradiction, every agent must accept the generalization that all prospective purposive agents have the generic rights.

Thus, we have now arrived at the basis of human rights. For the generic rights to freedom and well-being are moral rights, since they require of every agent that he take favorable account of the most important interests of all other prospective agents, namely, the interests grounded in their needs for the necessary conditions of agency. And these generic rights are also human rights, since every human being is an actual, prospective, or potential agent. I shall discuss the distribution of these rights among humans more fully below. But first I must also establish that the generic rights are human rights in the further respect indicated above, namely, that they are grounded in or justified by a valid moral criterion or principle.

The above argument for the generic rights as moral rights had already provided the full basis for deriving a supreme moral principle. We have seen that every agent, on pain of self-contradiction, must accept the generalization that all prospective purposive agents have the generic rights to freedom and well-being. From this generalization, because of the correlativity of rights and strict "oughts," it logically follows that every person ought to refrain from interfering with the freedom and well-being of all other persons insofar as they are prospective purposive agents. It also follows that under certain circumstances every person ought to assist other persons to have freedom and well-being, when they cannot have these by their own efforts and he can give them such assistance without comparable cost to himself, although more usually such assistance must operate through appropriate institutions. Since to refrain and to assist in these ways is to act in such a way that one's actions are in accord with the generic rights of one's recipients, every agent is logically committed, on pain of self-contradiction, to accept the following precept: *Act in accord with the generic rights of your recipients as well as of yourself.* I shall call this the *Principle of Generic Consistency (PGC),* since it combines the formal consideration of consistency with the material consideration of the generic features and rights of agency. To act in accord with someone's right to freedom is, in part, to refrain from coercing him; to act in accord with someone's right to well-being is, in part, to refrain from harming him by adversely affecting his basic, nonsubtractive, or additive goods. In addition, to act in accord with these rights may also require positive assistance. These rights, as thus upheld, are now moral ones because they are concerned to further the interests or goods of persons other than or in addition to the agent. The *PGC*'s central moral requirement is the *equality of generic rights,* since it requires of every agent that he accord to his recipients the same rights to freedom and well-being that he necessarily claims for himself.

The above argument has provided the outline of a rational justification of the Principle of Generic Consistency as the supreme principle of morality, both for the formal reason that if any agent denies or violates the principle he contradicts himself and for the material reason that its content, the generic features of action, necessarily imposes itself on every agent. For it is necessarily true of every agent that he at least implicitly attributes to himself the generic rights and that he acts in accord with his own generic rights; hence, he cannot rationally evade the extension of these rights to his recipients. This material necessity stands in contrast to principles centered in the purposes, inclinations, or ideals for which some agent may contingently act and whose requirements he may hence evade by shifting his desires or opinions. The *PGC* is the supreme principle of morality because its interpersonal requirements, derived from the generic features of action, cannot rationally be evaded by any agent. (It must be kept in mind that action is the universal context of morality.) The main point may be put succinctly as follows: What for any agent are necessarily goods of action, namely, freedom and well-being, are equally necessary goods for his recipients, and he logically must admit that they have as much right to these goods as he does, since the ground or reason for which he rationally claims them for himself also pertains to his recipients.

We have now seen that every agent must hold, on pain of self-contradiction, that all other persons as well as himself have moral rights grounded in the *PGC* as the principle of morality. It follows from the argument to the *PGC* that the primary criterion for having moral rights is that all persons have certain needs relative to their being actual or prospective agents, namely, needs for freedom and well-being as the necessary conditions of action. Simply by virtue of being actual or prospective agents who have certain needs of agency, persons have moral rights to freedom and well-being. Since all humans are such agents having such needs, the generic moral rights to freedom and well-being are human rights.

This argument for human rights has avoided the problem of how rights can be logically derived from facts. For, in proceeding by the dialectically necessary method, it has remained throughout within the facts of agents' necessary judgments about goods and rights. The argument has established not that persons have rights *tout court* but rather that all agents logically must claim or at least accept that they have certain rights. This relativity to agents and their claims does not, however, remove the absoluteness of rights or the categoricalness of the *PGC*. For since agency is the proximate general context of all morality and indeed of all practice, whatever is necessarily justified within the context of agency is also necessary for morality, and what logically must be accepted by every agent is necessarily justified within the context of agency. Thus, the argument has established that since every agent logically must accept that he has rights to freedom and well-being, the having of these rights is morally necessary. Hence, the requirement indicated above is fulfilled: The rights to freedom and well-being exist as human rights because there is a valid moral criterion, the *PGC,* which justifies that all humans have these rights.

Questions may be raised about the extent to which the generic rights as I have defined them are indeed human rights. To be human rights they must be had by every human being simply as such. The generic rights, however, are rights to the necessary conditions of agency. But may not some humans lack these rights because they are incapable of agency in one degree or another? Examples of such humans include children, mentally deficient persons, paraplegics, persons with brain damage, fetuses, and so forth. From these examples it might seem to follow that the generic rights to the necessary conditions of action are not truly human rights in the sense in which such rights were initially defined.

This question rests in part on a variant of the dictum that "ought" implies "can," for it assumes that for some person A to have a right to something $X,$ A must be capable of having or doing X. Now this assumption is correct, but only if the capability in question is correctly interpreted. All normal adult humans are fully capable of action as this has been interpreted here, as voluntary and purposive behavior, for all such persons have the proximate ability to control their behavior by their unforced choice with a view to attaining their goals while having knowledge of relevant circumstances. This description applies even to paraplegics, despite the lesser range of the control of which they are proximately capable, for they can think, choose (although within narrower limits), and plan.

In the other cases mentioned, the capabilities for action are less, and hence their rights too are proportionately less. Children are potential agents in that, with normal maturation, they will develop the full abilities of agency. In their case, as well as in that of mentally deficient persons and persons with brain damage, their possession of the generic rights must be proportional to the degree to which they have the abilities of agency, and this must be with a view to taking on the fullest degree of the generic rights of which they are capable so long as this does not result in harm to themselves or others. All other adult humans have the generic rights in full. In the case of the human fetus, this raises problems of the justification of abortion because of possible conflicts with the rights of the mother; I have considered this elsewhere.[9]

The equation of the generic rights with human rights thus does not derogate from the universality of the latter. It enables us to understand the varying degrees to which the rights are had by certain humans, as well as the connection of human rights with action and practice. The derivation of these rights from the argument for the *PCG* also enables us to understand the traditional view that human rights are grounded in reason so that they have a normative necessity or categorical obligatoriness that goes beyond the variable contents of social customs or positive laws.

IV

There remain two broad questions about human rights as so far delineated. First, the rights to freedom and well-being are very general. What more specific contents do they have, and how are these contents related to one another? Second, human rights are often thought of in terms of political effectuation and legal enforcement. How does this relation operate in the case of the generic rights? Should all of them be legally enforced or only some, and how is this to be determined?

To answer the first question we must analyze the components of well-being and of freedom. It was noted above that well-being, viewed as the abilities and conditions required for agency, comprises three kinds of goods: basic, nonsubtractive, and additive. Basic goods are the essential preconditions of action, such as life, physical integrity, and mental equilibrium. Thus, a person's basic rights—his rights to basic goods—are violated when he is killed, starved, physically incapacitated, terrorized, or subjected to mentally deranging drugs. The basic rights are also violated in such cases as where a person is drowning or starving and another person who, at no comparable cost to himself, could rescue him or give him food knowingly fails to do so.

Nonsubtractive goods are the abilities and conditions required for maintaining undiminished one's level of purpose-fulfillment and one's capabilities for particular actions. A person's nonsubtractive rights are violated when he is adversely affected in his abilities to plan for the future, to have knowledge of facts relevant to his projected actions, to utilize his resources to fulfill his wants, and so forth. Ways of undergoing such adversities include being lied to, cheated, stolen from, or defamed; suffering broken promises; or being subjected to dangerous, degrading, or excessively debilitating conditions of physical labor or housing or other strategic situations of life when resources are available for improvement.

Additive goods are the abilities and conditions required for increasing one's level of purpose-fulfillment and one's capabilities for particular actions. A person's additive rights are violated when his self-esteem is attacked, when he is denied education to the limits of his capacities, or when he is discriminated against on grounds of race, religion, or nationality. This right is also violated when a person's development of the self-regarding virtues of courage, temperance, and prudence is hindered by actions that promote a climate of fear and oppression, or that encourage the spread of physically or mentally harmful practices such as excessive use of drugs, or that contribute to misinformation, ignorance, and superstition, especially as these bear on persons' ability to act effectively in pursuit of their purposes. When a person's right to basic well-being is violated, I shall say that he undergoes basic harm; when his rights to nonsubtractive or additive well-being are violated, I shall say that he undergoes specific harm.

Besides these three components of the right to well-being, the human rights also include the right to freedom. This consists in a person's controlling his actions and his participation in transactions by his own unforced choice or consent and with knowledge of relevant circumstances, so that his behavior is neither compelled nor prevented by the actions of other persons. Hence, a person's right to freedom is violated if he is subjected to violence, coercion, deception, or any other procedures that attack or remove his informed control of his behavior by his own unforced choice. This right includes having a sphere of personal autonomy and privacy whereby one is let alone by others unless and until he unforcedly consents to undergo their action.

In general, whenever a person violates any of these rights to well-being or freedom, his action is morally wrong and he contradicts himself. For he is in the position of saying or holding that a right he necessarily claims for himself insofar as he is a prospective purposive agent is not had by some other person, even though the latter, too, is a prospective purposive agent. Hence, all such morally wrong actions are rationally unjustifiable.

It must also be noted, however, that these rights to freedom and well-being may conflict with one another. For example, the right to freedom of one person A may conflict with the right to well-being of another person B when A uses his freedom to kill, rob, or insult B. Here the duty of other persons to refrain from interfering with A's control of his behavior by his unforced choice may conflict with their duty to prevent B from suffering basic or specific harm when they can do so at no comparable cost to themselves. In addition, different persons' rights to well-being may conflict with one another, as when C must lie to D in order to prevent E from being murdered, or when F must break his promise to G in order to save H from drowning. Moreover, a person's right to freedom may conflict with his own right to well-being, as when he commits suicide or ingests harmful drugs. Here the duty of other persons not to interfere with his control of his behavior by his unforced choice may conflict with their duty to prevent his losing basic goods when they can do so at no comparable cost to themselves.

These conflicts show that human rights are only *prima facie,* not absolute, in that under certain circumstances they may justifiably be overridden. Nothing is gained by saying that what is justifiably overridden is not the right but only its exercise. For since a person's having some right has a justificatory basis, when this basis is removed he no longer has the right. In such a case it is his right itself and not only its exercise that is justifiably removed or overridden.

Another argument for the absoluteness of human rights is that their alleged *prima facie* character stems from their being incompletely described. Thus, it is held that the right to life or the right not to be killed, for example, must be specified more fully as the right not to be killed unless one has committed a murder, or as the right of innocent persons not to be killed. Such devices, however, either include in the description of the right the very overriding conditions that are in question, or else they restrict the distribution of the right so that it is not a right of all humans.

But although human rights may be overridden, this still leaves the Principle of Generic Consistency as an absolute or categorically obligatory moral principle. For the *PGC* sets the criteria for the justifiable overriding of one moral right by another and hence for the resolution of conflicts among rights. The basis of these criteria is that the *PGC* is both a formal and a material principle concerned with transactional consistency regarding the possession and use of the necessary conditions of action. The criteria stem from the *PGC*'s central requirement that there must be mutual respect for freedom and well-being among all prospective purposive agents. Departures from this mutual respect are justified only where they are required either to prevent or rectify antecedent departures, or to avoid greater departures, or to comply with social rules that themselves reflect such respect in the ways indicated in the procedural and instrumental applications of the *PGC.* Thus the criteria for resolving conflicts of rights or duties fall under three headings of progressively lesser importance.

The first criterion for resolving the conflicts of rights is the prevention or removal of transactional inconsistency. If one person or group violates or is about to violate the generic rights of another and thereby incurs transactional inconsistency, action to prevent or remove the inconsistency may be justified. Whether the action should always be undertaken depends on such circumstances as the feasibility and importance for subsequent action of removing the inconsistency: This may be very slight in the case of some lies and very great in the case of basic harms. Thus, although the *PGC* in general prohibits coercion and basic harm, it authorizes and even requires these as punishment and for prevention and correction of antecedent basic harm.

This criterion of the prevention of transactional inconsistency sets a limitation on the right to freedom. This right is overridden when a person intends to use his freedom in order to infringe the freedom or well-being of other persons. Such overriding stems from the *PGC*'s general requirement that each person must act in accord with the generic rights of his recipients, since this requirement sets limits on each person's freedom of action. The prohibition against coercion or harm is itself overridden, however, by two considerations, each of which also stems from the *PGC*. First, one person A may coerce or harm another person B in order to prevent B from coercing or harming either A himself or some other person C. Thus if B physically assaults A or C, A may physically assault B in order to resist or prevent the assault. Second, coercion or harm may be justified if it is inflicted in accordance with social rules or institutions that are themselves justified by the *PGC*. I shall discuss this latter justification below.

A second criterion for resolving conflicts of rights is the degree of their necessity for action. Since every person has rights to the necessary conditions of action, one right takes precedence over another if the good that is the object of the former right is more necessary for the possibility of action, and if that right cannot be protected without violating the latter right. For example, A's right not to be lied to is overridden by B's right not to be murdered or enslaved, where B or C has to lie to A in order to prevent him from committing these crimes against B. A person's right to freedom is also overridden in such ways. It will have been noted that whereas the first criterion for resolving conflicts among rights deals mainly with rights to goods of the same degree of importance, the second criterion deals with goods of different degrees, but within the same general context of preventing transactional inconsistency.

This criterion of degrees of necessity for action also applies to such limiting cases as where a person intends to use his freedom in order to attack his own well-being. As we have seen, there are levels of well-being, such that basic well-being is more necessary for action than nonsubtractive well-being, while the latter in turn is usually more necessary for action than additive well-being. Hence, in general, force may be used at least temporarily to prevent a person from killing or maiming himself, especially so long as there is doubt whether he fulfills the emotional and cognitive conditions of freedom or voluntariness. But such interference with someone's freedom is not justified to prevent him from diminishing his nonsubtractive or additive well-being, because his freedom is itself more necessary for his actions than are these levels of his well-being. The remaining complexities of this issue cannot be dealt with here.[10]

V

The conflicts among rights require further criteria besides the two given so far. To deal with these, we must move from the individual, transactional applications of the *PGC* so far considered to its institutional applications. The latter applications will also bring us to the second general question presented above, concerning the legal enforcement and political effectuation of human rights.

Although this legal, institutional context is perhaps the most familiar area of discussion of human rights, it must be emphasized that these rights also figure centrally in individual interpersonal transactions. A person's human rights to freedom and well-being are violated just as surely, although perhaps less powerfully and irrevocably, if he is kidnapped and held for ransom as if he is subjected to unjust imprisonment; and torture by a private person is just as much an infringement of one's human rights as torture by an agent of the state. So, too, although in lesser degrees, a person's human rights are violated when he is lied to, discriminated against, or made to work for starvation wages when better conditions could be made available. Moreover, a large part, although not the whole, of the human rights that should be legally enforced consist in the legal protection of individuals from suffering violations of their most important human rights to just treatment on the part of individuals or groups other than those representing the state.

To deal with the legal context of the protection of human rights, we must turn to another kind of application of the *PGC* besides the one so far considered. The *PGC* has two different kinds of applications: direct and indirect. In the direct applications, the *PGC*'s requirements are imposed on the actions of individual agents; the actions are morally right and the agents fulfill their moral duties when they act in accord with the generic rights of their recipients as well as of themselves. In the indirect aplications, on the other hand, the *PGC*'s requirements are imposed in the first instance on social rules and institutions. These are morally right, and persons acting in accordance with them fulfill their moral duties, when the rules and institutions express or serve to protect or foster the equal freedom and well-being of the persons subject to them. Thus, by the indirect applications recipients may even be coerced or harmed, yet this does not violate their human rights to freedom and well-being, because the rules or institutions that require such coercion or harm are themselves justified by the *PGC*. For example, when the umpire in a baseball game calls three strikes, the batter is out and must leave the batter's box even if he does not consent to this. This calling him out operates to coerce the batter so that he is forced to leave the batter's box. Nevertheless, the umpire's action is morally justified and the batter's right to freedom is not violated insofar as he has freely accepted the rules of the game. Or again, a judge who sentences a criminal to prison operates to coerce and harm him, yet this is morally justified and the criminal's rights to freedom and well-being are not violated insofar as the rules of the criminal law serve to protect and restore the mutuality of occurrent nonharm prescribed by the *PGC*.

As these examples may suggest, the indirect, institutional applications of the *PGC* are of two kinds. The *procedural* applications derive from the *PGC*'s freedom component: They provide that social rules and institutions are morally right insofar as the persons subject to them have freely consented to accept them or have certain consensual procedures freely available to them. The *instrumental* applications derive from the *PGC*'s well-being component: They provide that social rules and institutions are morally right insofar as they operate to protect and support the well-being of all persons.

Each of these applications, in turn, is of two sorts. The procedural applications may be either *optional* or *necessary*. They are optional according as persons consent to form or to participate in voluntary associations. The procedural applications are necessary according as the consent they require operates as a general decision procedure using the civil liberties to provide the authoritative basis, through elections and other consensual methods, of specific laws or governmental officials.

The *PGC*'s instrumental applications may be either *static* or *dynamic*. The static applications, embodied in the minimal state with its criminal law, serve to protect persons from occurrent violations of their rights to basic and other important goods and to punish such violations. The dynamic applications, embodied in the supportive state, serve to provide longer-range protections of basic and other rights where these cannot be obtained by persons through their own efforts.

In the remainder of this chapter I want to indicate how these distinctions of the *PGC*'s indirect applications help to clarify the question of the legal enforcement of human rights. As we have noted, the institutions of law and government are instrumentally justified by the *PGC* as means for enforcing its most important requirements. Not all the human rights upheld by the *PGC* should receive legal enforcement. The specific harms done by violations of a person's nonsubtractive rights, such as when he is lied to or when a promise made to him is broken, are ordinarily less important in their impact on their recipient's well-being than are the harms done by violations of basic rights and hence do not justify the state's coercive legal resources to combat or correct them.

The human rights that should receive legal enforcement are those comprised in the last three of the indirect applications of the *PGC* distinguished above. Each of these applications reflects a certain justification of social rules that set requirements for persons and for the state. First, there is what I have called the static-instrumental justification of social rules, consisting in the criminal law. This serves to protect basic and other important rights from occurrent attack by other persons, including the rights to life, physical integrity, and reputation. But the *PGC* also sets standards or limits as to how this protection is to operate: Only persons who have violated these rights of others are to be punished; all persons must be equal before the law; trials must be fair; *habeas corpus* must be guaranteed; punishment must not be cruel, vindictive, or inhuman.

Second, there is the dynamic-instrumental justification of social rules. This recognizes that persons are dispositionally unequal in their actual ability to attain and protect their generic rights, especially their rights to basic well-being, and it provides for social rules that serve to remove this inequality. Thus, where the static phase (the criminal law) tries to restore an occurrent antecedent status quo of mutual nonharm, the dynamic phase tries to move toward a new situation in which a previously nonexistent dispositional equality is attained or more closely approximated. Social rules supporting the various components of well-being, but especially basic well-being, are justified in this dynamic way.

These supportive rules must have several kinds of contents. First, they must provide for supplying basic goods, such as food and housing, to those persons who cannot obtain them by their own efforts. Second, they must try to rectify inequalities of additive well-being by improving the capabilities for productive work of persons who are deficient in this respect. Education is a prime means of such improvement, but also important is whatever strengthens family life and enables parents to give constructive, intelligent, loving nurture to their children. The wider diffusion of such means is a prime component of increasing equality of opportunity. Third, the rules must provide for various public goods that, while helping all the members of the society, serve to increase the opportunities for productive employment. Fourth, the rules must regulate certain important conditions of well-being by removing dangerous or degrading conditions of work and housing.

A third area of legal enforcement of human rights is found in what I have called the necessary-procedural justification of social rules. This justification is an application of the *PGC*'s freedom component to the constitutional structure of the state. It provides that laws and state officials must be designated by procedures that use the *method of consent*. This method consists in the availability and use of the civil liberties in the political process. The objects of these liberties include the actions of speaking, publishing, and associating with others, so that, as a matter of constitutional requirement, each person is able, if he chooses, to discuss, criticize, and vote for or against the government and to work actively with other persons or groups of various sizes to further his political objectives, including the redress of his socially based grievances. In this way each person has the right to participate actively in the political process.

The civil liberties also extend to contexts of individual and social activity other than the political process. The *PGC*'s protection of the right to freedom requires that each person be left to engage in any action or transaction according to his unforced choice so long as he does not coerce or harm other persons. This requirement sets an important limit on the legitimate powers of the state: It must not interfere with the freedom of the individual except to prevent his coercing or harming others in ways that adversely affect their basic or other important well-being. The criteria of this importance are found in what affects persons' having the abilities and conditions required for purposive action. Thus, an immense array of kinds of action must be exempted from governmental control, while at the same time the freedom to perform these actions must be protected by the state.

These freedoms are hence called "civil liberties" for three interconnected reasons, bearing on three different relations the freedoms must have to the state. First, they are passive and negative in that they must not be restricted or interfered with by the state. Second, they are passive and positive in that they must be protected by the state as rights of persons. Third, they are active in that the actions that are their objects function in the political process to help determine who shall govern in the state. In all relations, the *PGC* requires that the civil liberties pertain equally to each prospective purposive agent (except criminals): Each person has an equal right to use his freedom noncoercively and nonharmfully (according to the criteria of harm specified above), to participate freely and actively in the political process, and to be protected by the state in that participation and in his other actions using his freedom in the way just indicated. Insofar as there are diverse states, this equal right pertains to each citizen, and each person has a right to be a citizen of a state having the civil liberties.

We have now seen that the *PGC*'s indirect aplications require that three kinds of rights receive legal enforcement and protection: the personal-security rights protected by the criminal law, the social and economic rights protected by the supportive state, and the political and civil rights and liberties protected by the Constitution with its method of consent.

The second of these kinds comprises important phases of the right to well-being, the third encompasses a large part of the right to freedom. I wish to conclude by considering two opposite extreme views about how the social and economic rights figure in the legal enforcement and protection of human rights.

One view is that these rights, including the right to be given food and the other goods needed for alleviating severe economic handicaps and insecurities, cannot be "human" rights because they do not meet two tests: universality and practicability.[11] According to the test of universality, for a moral right to be a human one it must be a right of all persons against all persons: All persons must have the strict duty of acting in accord with the right, and all persons must have the strict right to be treated in the appropriate way. Thus, all persons must be both the agents and the recipients of the modes of action required by the right. This test is passed by the rights to life and to freedom of movement: Everyone has the duty to refrain from killing other persons and from interfering with their movements, and everyone has the right to have his life and his freedom of movement respected by other persons. But in the case of the right to be relieved from starvation or severe economic deprivation, it is objected that only some persons have the right: Those who are threatened by starvation or deprivation; and only some persons have the duty: Those who are able to prevent or relieve this starvation by giving aid.

The answer to this objection need not concede that this right, like other economic and social rights, is universal only in a "weaker" sense in that whereas all persons have the right to be rescued from starvation or deprivation, only some persons have the correlative duty. Within the limits of practicability, all persons have the right and all have the duty. For all persons come under the protection and the requirements of the *PGC* insofar as they are prospective purposive agents. Hence, all the generic rights upheld by the *PGC* have the universality required for being human rights.

It is, indeed, logically impossible that each person be at the same time both the rescuer and the rescued, both the affluent provider and the deprived pauper. Nevertheless, the fact that some prospective purposive agent may not at some time need to be rescued from deprivation or be able to rescue others from deprivation does not remove the facts that he has the right to be rescued when he has the need and that he has the duty to rescue when he has the ability and when other relevant conditions are met. This duty stems, in the way indicated earlier, from the claim he necessarily makes or accepts that he has the generic rights by virtue of being a prospective purposive agent. The universality of a right is not a matter of everyone's actually having the related need, nor is it a matter of everyone's actually fulfilling the correlative duty, let alone of his doing so at all times. Nor is it even a matter of everyone's always being able to fulfill the duty. It is rather a matter of everyone's always having, as a matter of principle, the right to be treated in the appropriate way when he has the need, and the duty to act in accord with the right when the circumstances arise that require such action and when he then has the ability to do so, this ability including consideration of cost to himself.

When it is said that the right to be relieved from economic deprivation and the correlative duty pertain to all persons insofar as they are prospective purposive agents, this does not violate the condition that for human rights to be had one must only be human, as against fulfilling some more restrictive description. As was indicated earlier, all normal humans are prospective purposive agents; the point of introducing this description is only to call attention to the aspect of being human that most directly generates the rights to freedom and well-being. In this regard, the right in question differs from rights that pertain to persons not simply by virtue of being prospective purposive agents but only in some more restricted capacity, such as being teachers as against students, umpires as against batters, or judges as against defendants. The universality of human rights derives from their direct connection with the necessary conditions of action, as against the more restrictive objects with which nongeneric rights are connected. And since both the affluent and the economically deprived are prospective purposive agents, the latter's right to be helped by the former is a human right.

These considerations also apply to the contention that the social and economic rights are not human rights because they do not pass the test of practicability, in that many nations lack the economic means to fulfill these rights. Now, it is indeed the case that whereas the political and civil rights may require nonaction or noninterference rather than positive action on the part of governments, the economic rights require the positive use of economic resources for their effective implementation. This does not, however, militate against governments' taking steps to provide support, to the extent of their available resources, to persons who cannot attain basic economic goods by their own efforts. There is a considerable distance between the position that the same high levels of economic well-being are not attainable in all countries and the position that a more equitable distribution of goods and of means of producing goods is not feasible for countries at the lower end of the scale.

This point is also relevant to a view that stands at the opposite extreme from the one just considered: that for most persons in many parts of the world the social and economic rights are the only human rights that should be legally implemented. According to this view, the political and civil rights, by contrast, are of little importance for persons in the third world with its predominant illiteracy, traditionalism, poverty, nonindividualist ethos, and lack of regard for the rule of law. This position is epitomized in the dictum "Food first, freedom later," where the "freedom" in question consists especially in the political and civil liberties. The contention is that until the economic rights to subsistence, housing, and employment are effectively implemented, persons who lack these have little interest in or opportunity or need for the political and civil rights and that fulfillment of the former rights is a necessary prerequisite for fulfilling the latter.

A distinction may be drawn between such personal-security rights as *habeas corpus* and noninfliction of torture or cruel punishment, and the political rights of the method of consent with its civil liberties of speech, press, and association. Nevertheless, the latter provide important safeguards for the former. Both these kinds of rights, in turn, are far from being antithetical to, or needless for, the economic and social rights. Indeed, the order of priority may be the reverse of that upheld in the view under consideration. The effective distribution of the civil liberties, far from being a passive effect of the proper distribution of food, housing, and health care, can strongly facilitate the latter distribution. When governments are not subject to the political process of the method of consent, there is to that extent less assurance that the authorities will be responsive to the material needs of all their citizens. As is shown by sad experience in many of the underdeveloped countries, the lack of effective political participation by the masses of the poor permits a drastic unconcern with their needs for food even when it is locally available.[12]

What I have tried to show in this essay is that all the human rights have a rational foundation in the necessary conditions or needs of human action, so that no human agent can deny or violate them except on pain of self-contradiction. Thus, the demands the human rights make on persons are justified by the *PGC* as the supreme principle of morality. It is also through the moral requirements set by this principle that the political and legal order receives its central justification as providing for the protection of human rights. In addition to this instrumental function, possession of the civil liberties together with the effective capacity for participating in the method of consent is required for the dignity and rational autonomy of every prospective purposive agent. Thus, the rationally grounded requirements of human action provide the basis and content of all human rights, both those that apply in individual transactions and those that must be protected by social rules and institutions.

Notes

1. See W. N. Hohfeld, *Fundamental Legal Conceptions.* (New Haven: Yale University Press, 1919); John Salmond, *Jurisprudence,* 10th ed. (London: Sweet and Maxwell, 1947), pp. 229 ff.

2. Robert Nozick, *Anarchy, State and Utopia.* (New York: Basic Books, 1974), p. ix.

3. See H. L. A. Hart, "Are There Any Natural Rights?" *Philosophical Review,* 64 (1955): 175 ff.

4. See H. J. McCloskey, "Rights," *Philosophical Quarterly,* 15 (1965): 124. Elsewhere, McCloskey holds that persons have a *prima facie* right to the satisfaction of needs: "Human Needs, Rights and Political Values," *American Philosophical Quarterly,* 13 (1976): 9–10.

5. See Jacques Maritain, *The Rights of Man and Natural Law.* (London: Geoffrey Bles, 1944).

6. John Rawls, *A Theory of Justice.* (Cambridge, MA: Harvard University Press, 1971), Chaps. 2, 3.

7. See Alan Gewirth, *Reason and Morality.* (Chicago: The University of Chicago Press, 1978), Chap. 2.

8. *Ibid.,* pp. 82–103.

9. *Ibid.,* pp. 142–144.

10. See *ibid.,* pp. 259–267.

11. See Maurice Cranston, *What Are Human Rights?* (London: Bodley Head, 1963), pp. 66 ff. See also his contribution to D. D. Raphael (Ed.), *Political Theory and the Rights of Man.* (London: Macmillan, 1967), pp. 96 ff. For the "weaker" sense of the universality of rights referred to below, see Raphael in *Political Theory and the Rights of Man,* pp. 65 ff., 112.

12. See Thomas T. Poleman, "World Food: A Perspective," *Science,* 188 (1975): 515; Pierre R. Crosson, "Institutional Obstacles to World Food Production," *ibid.,* pp. 522, 523; Harry Walters, "Difficult Issues Underlying Food Problems," *ibid.,* p. 530; Gunnar Myrdal, *Asian Drama: An Inquiry in the Poverty of Nations.* (New York: Twentieth Century Fund, 1969), Vol. II, pp. 895–899; S. Reutlinger and M. Selowsky, *Malnutrition and Poverty.* (Baltimore: The Johns Hopkins University Press, 1976).

Human Rights
and the
General Welfare

DAVID LYONS

Our Constitution tells us that it aims "to form a more perfect union, establish justice, insure domestic tranquility, provide for the common defense, promote the general welfare, and secure the blessings of liberty to ourselves and our posterity." But these grand words must to some extent be discounted. Because of the "three-fifths rule," [1] which tacitly condoned human slavery, for example, the original Constitution fell short of promising liberty and justice for *all.* At best, the document seems to represent a compromise. But with what? Consider the other aims mentioned: a more perfect union, domestic tranquility, the common defense—these might easily be viewed as either means to, or else included under an enlarged conception of, the general welfare, and it might be thought that this last-mentioned standard is what the Constitution was truly designed to serve—the general welfare, at the expense, if necessary, of those "inalienable rights" and that universal equality which the Declaration of Independence had earlier maintained governments are supposed to serve. At least in that early, critical period of the republic, it might have been argued that the interests of the nation as a whole could be served only through sacrificing the interests of some, even if those interests—in life, liberty, and the pursuit of happiness—amount to basic rights. The Bill of Rights, after all, had to be added to the original document to secure

David Lyons, "Human Rights and the General Welfare," *Philosophy & Public Affairs,* 6, No. 2 (Winter 1977). Copyright © 1977 by Princeton University Press. Reprinted with permission of Princeton University Press.

This essay was originally presented as the Special Bicentennial Invited Address to the Pacific Division A.P.A. Meetings in Berkeley, 25 March 1976. I am grateful to Sharon Hill for her comments on that occasion.

1. In Article 1, Section 2—just after the Preamble.

some of the rights of concern to the drafters of the Declaration of Independence. The general idea behind this interpretation cannot lightly be dismissed; at any rate, critics of utilitarianism have often objected that the general welfare standard condones immoral inequalities, injustice and exploitation, because the interests of a community as a whole might sometimes most efficiently be served by benefiting some individuals at the expense of others. One might be tempted, therefore, to identify the Declaration of Independence with the doctrine of human rights and the Constitution with a commitment to the general welfare and then conceive of the differences between these documents as transcending their distinct functions and representing a fundamental conflict between commitment to the general welfare and the principles of rights and justice.

These issues need examination now, not just because this nation's Bicentennial obliges us to acknowledge its original ideologies. Thanks to a convergence of political and philosophical developments—including movements to secure equal rights at home and a less barbaric policy abroad, and the somewhat connected resuscitation of political and legal theory—substantive questions of public policy are being discussed more fully today than they have been for many years. Nevertheless, the philosophical attitudes expressed sometimes threaten to become, in their way, just as trite and unreflective as the average politician's Bicentennial claptrap. It is very widely assumed that the general welfare standard, or more specifically utilitarianism, is essentially defective; but the grounds on which this conclusion is reached are often so slender as to make it seem like dogma, not a proper philosophic judgment. Our professional obligations make it incumbent on us, I believe, to challenge such dogmas.

I wish to explore the connections between human rights and the general welfare (where I assume that commitment to the general welfare standard does not entail commitment to full-blown utilitarianism, which regards all other standards as either derivative or else invalid). These matters were not pursued very deeply in the eighteenth century, so my historical references, indeed the basis for my suggestions on behalf of the general welfare, go back only half way, to John Stuart Mill (who was, fittingly, a champion of rights and liberty as well as of the general welfare). Mill's contributions to this area have been neglected and so, I believe, somewhat misunderstood. I hope to throw some light on Mill while seeking a better grasp upon the principles that our republic in its infancy endorsed.

Rights as well as justice have been problems for utilitarians. Aside from Mill, only Bentham gave much thought to rights, and Bentham thought enforcement was essential. He could conceive of rights within an institution but not of rights one might invoke when designing or criticizing institutions. He thus rejected what we call "moral" rights. Recent views of utilitarianism seem to imply that this neglect of rights is theoretically unavoidable. Critics and partisans alike generally suppose that a commitment to the general welfare means that rights are not to count in our deliberations except as conduct affecting them also affects the general welfare, and critics contend that this fails to take rights seriously.[2] Rights are supposed to make a

2. See, for example, Ronald Dworkin, "Taking Rights Seriously," *New York Review of Books,* 18 December 1970; reprinted in A.W.B. Simpson (Ed.), *Oxford Essays in Jurisprudence, Second Series.* (Oxford: Clarendon Press, 1973).

difference to our calculations, which they fail to do if we hold—as utilitarians are supposed to maintain—that rights may be infringed if that is necessary to bring about the smallest increase in the general welfare. Perhaps there are no rights that may absolutely never be overridden; some rights, at least, may be infringed in order to prevent calamities, for example; but infringement of a right should always count against a policy, a law, or a course of action, even when considerations of the general welfare argue for infringement. And it is not necessarily the case that infringement of a right always detracts significantly from the general welfare. For such reasons, commitment to the general welfare standard seems to conflict with genuine acknowledgment of rights; utilitarianism seems positively to abhor them. In this paper I shall sketch how Mill challenges such a conclusion.

One strategy of response could be built upon the idea of "rule-utilitarianism." In this century, utilitarianism was initially understood, by Moore and others, as requiring one always to promote the general welfare in the most efficient and productive manner possible, any failure to do so being judged as wrong, the breach of one's sole "moral obligation." Faced with objections that this "act-utilitarianism" neglects ordinary moral obligations, which do not require one to "maximize utility" but indeed require contrary conduct, revisionists constructed new kinds of "utilitarian" principles. They required adherence to useful rules and excluded case-by-case appeal to the general welfare, hoping that these requirements would match the assumed obligations while still being based upon the general welfare. In the present context, one might extend this rebuttal by supposing that some useful rules would also confer rights, infringement of which would generally be prohibited, and infringement of which would never be warranted by direct appeal to the general welfare. Something like this is in fact suggested by Mill.

Mill's system does, in part, resemble a kind of rule utilitarianism with the distinct advantage over recent theories that it explicitly acknowledges rights as well as obligations. It has a further, more general advantage. Recent rule-utilitarian theories seem either to have been concocted to avoid objections to act utilitarianism or else to offer an alternative but equally narrow interpretation of the general welfare standard. Both "act" and "rule" versions of utilitarianism seem arbitrarily to restrict the application of the general welfare standard to just one category of things—acts, say, or rules—among the many to which it might reasonably be applied. In contrast, Mill's endorsement of the general welfare standard leaves him free to judge all things by that measure. But he supplements it with analyses of moral judgments which commit him to acknowledging both moral rights and obligations.

For simplicity's sake, let us postpone examination of Mill's theory of rights and consider first his more famous (and initially simpler) principle of personal liberty.[3] Mill says that the only reason we should entertain in support of coercive social

---

3. Mill's essay *On Liberty* appears consistent with his essay on *Utilitarianism* (written soon after) on all points relevant to the interpretation I am offering here. My interpretation of *On Liberty* does not so much ignore as render it unnecessary to hypothesize nonutilitarian tendencies in Mill's argument; for an alternative account, see Gerald Dworkin, "Paternalism," in Richard A. Wasserstrom (Ed.), *Morality and the Law.* (Belmont, CA: Wadsworth, 1971), Section V.

interference is the prevention of harm to people other than the agent whose freedom may be limited. For example, we should not try to force a person to serve his own happiness or prevent a person from harming himself. In effect, Mill says that we should *not* apply the general welfare standard directly to such intervention. But how could Mill say this—without forsaking his commitment to the general welfare standard? Mill recognizes that his principle of liberty is not entailed by his "general happiness principle" taken by itself. The latter commits him in principle to approving paternalistic intervention that would serve the general welfare. And so Mill *argues* for his principle of liberty. But wouldn't such a principle be emptied of all practical significance by the tacit qualifications that are inevitably imposed by Mill's commitment to the general welfare?

These questions arise when we assume that Mill's commitment to the general welfare standard amounts to the idea that one is always morally bound to serve the general welfare in the most efficient and productive manner possible. His principle of liberty is then conceived of as a "summary rule," a rough guide to action that is meant to insure the closest approximation to the requirements laid down by his principle of utility. This is, I think, mistaken on several counts.

Let me suggest, first, that Mill be understood as reasoning along the following lines. The general welfare will best be served in the long run if we restrict social interference, by both legal and informal means, to the prevention of social harm. Experience shows that less limited intervention is very largely, and unavoidably, counterproductive. Even when we try our best to prevent people from harming themselves, for example, we are in all probability bound to fail. Before embarking on such intervention we are unable to distinguish the productive from the counterproductive efforts. We are able to do that later; but later is always too late. Since the stakes are high for those we coerce, and nonexistent for us, we *ought to make it a matter of principle* never to entertain reasons for interfering save the prevention of harm to others. The general welfare would best be served in the long run by our following such an inflexible rule.

Now this seems to me a perfectly intelligible position, and one even an act-utilitarian might consistently adopt. One need not reject the general welfare standard—as a basis, or even the sole basis, for evaluating things—in order to accept such a principle of liberty. Some possible objections ought however to be noted, though they cannot adequately be considered here. First, it may be said that this could not be a complete account of our objections to paternalism and other forms of social interference (so far as we object to them) because our convictions about the sanctity of liberty are much stronger than our warranted confidence in the factual assumptions required by Mill's argument. This seems to me, however, to prove nothing without independent validations of those judgments. Our moral convictions need justification; they are not self-certifying. If we are uncertain about the relevant facts, then we should retain at least an open mind about the relations between liberty and the general welfare.

Second, the argument attributed to Mill suggests that the general welfare will best be served only if we are something other than utilitarians, for it tells us *not* to apply the general welfare standard. The argument thus seems self-defeating for a utilitarian.

But, while this problem might arise for utilitarianism in some other contexts, I do not think it need worry Mill right here. I might make it a matter of principle to avoid certain situations that I know will lead to choices that are self-destructive, though they will not seem such to me at the time. This is compatible with my continuing to appreciate my reasons for that policy. Mill's argument is similar. Indeed, one would expect the Mill of *On Liberty* to insist that we remind ourselves of the rationales for our rules and principles if we do not wish them to become ineffective dogmas. This presumably advises us to keep in mind the utilitarian foundation for the principle of liberty.

Third, it may be said that Mill's principle is too rigid and inflexible, that the general welfare would in fact be served better by a more complex principle, which incorporates some exceptions. It may be argued, for example, that paternalistic legislation within certain clearly defined limits should be tolerated.[4] But this is a point that Mill might easily accept—provided that any proposed qualifications on the principle of liberty would not lead to such abuse as to be counterproductive.

It should be clear, now, that the principle of liberty is no "summary rule," of the sort associated with act-utilitarianism; nor is it one of those ideal rules of obligation obtained by applying some modern rule-utilitarian formula. It results from a direct application of the general welfare standard to the question, What sorts of reasons would it serve the general welfare for us to entertain when framing social rules?

Mill is not obliged to be either a rule utilitarian or an act-utilitarian because he does not conceive of the general welfare standard in so limited a way. His principle concerns ends, specifically happiness, and provides the basis for evaluating other things in relation to that end. It does not concern acts or rules as such. It says nothing about right or wrong, duty or obligation. And it does not require one, in moral terms, to maximize the general welfare.

These points are indicated in Mill's "proof" of the principle of utility (where one would expect him to be careful at least in his formulation of his principle, even if his argument fails). In a typical passage Mill says: "The utilitarian doctrine is that happiness is desirable, and the only thing desirable, as an end; all other things being only desirable as means to that end" (Chap. IV, par. 2)[5] At the end of the main part of his "proof" Mill says: "If so, happiness is the sole end of human action, and the promotion of it the test by which to judge of all human conduct; from whence it necessarily follows that it must be the criterion of morality, since a part is included in the whole" (Chap. IV, par. 8). The relationship between moral judgments and the general welfare standard is then explained more fully by Mill in the next and longest chapter of *Utilitarianism,* which is devoted to the topic of rights and justice.[6]

Mill maintains that judgments about the justice of acts are a specific form of moral appraisal: Acts can be wrong without being unjust. To call an act unjust is to imply that

---

4. For some suggestions along these lines, see Gerald Dworkin, "Paternalism," Section VI; and, on speech, see Joel Feinberg, "Limits to the Free Expression of Opinion," in Joel Feinberg and Hyman Gross (Eds.), *Philosophy of Law.* (Encino, CA: Dickenson, 1975).
5. All references in the text hereafter will cite chapters and paragraphs of *Utilitarianism.*
6. I discuss this matter more fully in "Mill's Theory of Morality," *Nous* 10 (1976):101–120.

it violates another's right, which is not true of all wrong acts. In a perfectly parallel manner, Mill maintains that moral judgments (about right and wrong, duty and obligation) are a proper subclass of act appraisals in general: Acts can be negatively appraised—as inexpedient, undesirable, or regrettable, for example—without being regarded as immoral or wrong. To call an act wrong is to imply that "punishment" for it (loosely speaking) would be justified (Chap. V, paras. 13–15).

Mill's distinction between immorality and mere "inexpediency" indicates that he is no act-utilitarian and also that his general welfare standard does not lay down moral requirements. There must be some basis within Mill's system for appraising acts negatively even when they are not to be counted as wrong. This is either the general welfare standard or some other. But the general welfare standard is quite clearly Mill's basic, most comprehensive criterion. It therefore seems reasonable to infer that Mill would wish to rank acts according to their instrumental value (their promotion of the general welfare), *preferring* those that rank highest in a set of alternatives, without implying that a merely "inexpedient" act is wrong because it falls below the top of such a ranking and thus fails to serve the general welfare in the most productive and efficient manner possible.

According to Mill, to show that an act is wrong, and not merely inexpedient, one must go further and show that sanctions against it would be justified. For Mill says that to judge an act wrong is to judge that "punishment" of it would be fitting or justified.[7] The "punishment" or sanctions Mill has in mind include not just legal penalties but also public condemnation (both can be classified as "external sanctions") as well as guilt feelings or pangs of conscience (the "internal sanction").[8]

Now, Mill presents this as a conceptual point, independent of his commitment to the general welfare; but it has a bearing on our understanding of that standard. Mill distinguishes between general negative appraisals of the "inexpediency" of acts and moral judgments specifically condemning them as wrong. I have suggested that the criterion of "inexpediency" for Mill is an act's failure to promote the general welfare to the maximum degree possible. If so, this cannot be Mill's criterion of wrongness, for from the fact that an act is inexpedient in this sense it does not follow that sanctions against it could be justified. For sanctions have costs of the sort that a utilitarian always counts, and these costs attach to the distinct acts connected with sanctions. The justification of such acts presumably turns somehow upon *their* relation to the general welfare, not upon (or not alone upon) the relation of the act that is to be sanctioned to the general welfare. On Mill's view, therefore, the general welfare standard *can* be applied directly to acts, but then it simply determines their expediency (and enables one to rank them accordingly). However, this is not, according to Mill, a moral judgment, and it has no direct moral implications.[9]

---

7. For simplicity's sake, I shall understand Mill to mean "justified" or "warranted."
8. Mill uses the terminology of "sanctions" in Chapter III of *Utilitarianism*.
9. The act-utilitarian reading of Mill is most strongly suggested in *Utilitarianism,* Chapter II, paragraph 2. But, as D. G. Brown has noted, the passage is ambiguous; see his paper "What is Mill's Principle of Utility?" *Canadian Journal of Philosophy* 3 (1973): 1–12.

Mill also seems to hold that a wrong act is the breach of a moral obligation, at least in the absence of some overriding obligation.[10] But what differentiates morality from mere expediency, as we have seen, is the justification of sanctions. Mill appears to regard the internal sanction as basic. His formulations imply that public disapproval may be justified even when legal sanctions are not, and that pangs of conscience may be warranted when no external sanctions can be justified. Mill suggests that greater costs and risks attach to social sanctions (which is plausible so long as conscience is not excessively demanding). It may also be observed that the justification of external sanctions involves an extra step, since they require distinct acts by other persons, while guilt feelings are triggered more or less automatically. Errors of judgment aside, to justify the operation of self-reproach in particular cases one must justify no more than the internalization of certain values. But to justify external sanctions one must also justify distinct acts by other persons, based on their corresponding values—acts ranging from expressions of disapproval to legal punishment. In Mill's view, then, to argue that an act is wrong is basically to argue that guilt feelings for it would be warranted. Other sanctions may be justified as well, depending on the stakes involved and on the circumstances.

Following Bentham, Mill clearly thinks of sanctions operating not just after an act, as responses to a wrong already done, but also before hand, in order to discourage such conduct.[11] This conception presupposes that sanctions are attached to general rules, which serve as guides to conduct, and has its more natural application to rules of the social variety, to which external sanctions are also attached. We can combine this with the previous point as follows. Internal sanctions require that the corresponding values be "internalized," thoroughly accepted by the individual. For external sanctions to be justified they must work efficiently, and this requires that the corresponding values be shared widely, within, say, a given community; which amounts to the existence of a common moral code. A reconstruction of Mill's account of moral judgments, then, would go something like this. To argue for a moral obligation is to argue for the widespread internalization (within a community) of a value relevant to conduct; to show that an act is wrong is to show that it breaches such a rule, in the absence of an overriding obligation.

Mill thus suggests a fairly sophisticated version of what would now be called "rule-utilitarianism"—except, of course, that he does not limit the general welfare standard to rules of conduct, any more than he limits it to acts. Following Bentham's conception of social rules and his theory of their justification, Mill also takes into account the costs

10. This paragraph has been revised in response to a very helpful comment by a reader for *Philosophy & Public Affairs,* for which I am grateful. Note, now, that Mill does not differentiate in *Utilitarianism* between duties and obligations. He may link both too closely with wrong actions, but he does not hold that an act is wrong if it simply breaches a moral obligation. This is because he recognizes that obligations can conflict. And when they do, rules or obligations are ranked by reference to the general welfare standard. Mill does not indicate that acts are so evaluated directly, even when obligations conflict; see the last paragraph of Chapter II, as well as Chapter V.
11. Since Mill criticized Bentham's views extensively, but had only praise for Bentham's theory of punishment, I assume that Mill follows Bentham on all relevant points except where the evidence and the requirements of a coherent theory indicate the contrary.

of sanctions—the social price of regulating conduct—which most recent rule utilitarians have ignored.[12] Mill departs from Bentham on two important and related points. First, Mill acknowledges the internal sanction, conscience and guilt feelings, which Bentham had neglected but which Mill thinks is fundamental to the idea of morality. Second, while Bentham analyzed the idea of obligation in terms of actual coercion or institutionally authorized coercion—which might not be justified—Mill analyzes obligation in terms of sanctions that could be justified. That is a much more plausible and promising conception than Bentham's.

I do not mean that Mill's account of moral judgments is adequate as it stands. For example, while Mill seems right in emphasizing the connections between judgments of one's own immoral conduct and guilt feelings, he seems to put the cart before the horse. For we usually think of determining whether guilt feelings would be justified by asking, first, whether one has acted immorally, while Mill finds out whether a given act is wrong by first calculating whether internal sanctions for such an act are justified. Perhaps Mill's analysis of moral judgments is misguided. But his general approach to these matters is instructive.

Since Mill's theory of obligation does not seem inconsistent with his general welfare standard, it seems to show that an advocate of the general welfare standard can take moral obligations seriously. For, in Mill's view, obligations alone determine whether an act is wrong; they alone lay down moral requirements. Even if the general welfare would be served by breaching an obligation, it does not follow, on Mill's account, that one would be morally justified in breaching it.

We are now in a position to consider Mill's account of rights. In distinguishing justice from morality in general, Mill says that obligations of justice in particular, but not all moral obligations, correspond with moral rights. An unjust act is the violation of another's right; but an act can be wrong without being unjust—without violating any person's right. Mill believes that we can act wrongly by failing to be generous or charitable or beneficent, and he treats the corresponding "virtues" as imposing "obligations"; but these do not correspond with anyone's rights. "No one has a moral right to our generosity or beneficence because we are not morally bound to practice those virtues towards any given individual" (Chap. V, par. 15).

Though not all obligations involve corresponding rights, Mill seems to hold that rights entail corresponding obligations. Consequently, it seems reasonable to interpret his explicit analysis of moral rights in terms of moral obligations. This analysis is presented as follows:

> When we call anything a person's right, we mean that he has a valid claim upon society to protect him in the possession of it, either by the force of law or by that of education and opinion. If he has what we consider a sufficient claim, on whatever account, to have something guaranteed him by society, we say he has a right to it [Chap. V, par. 24].

12. An exception is Richard Brandt, see especially his "A Utilitarian Theory of Excuses," *Philosophical Review* 68 (1969): 337–361.

After some elaboration Mill restates the point, and then goes one step further:

> To have a right, then, is, I conceive, to have something that society ought to defend me in the possession of. If the objector goes on to ask why it ought, I can give him no other reason than general utility [Chap. V. par. 25].

Mill first analyzes ascriptions of rights; his analysis refers to arguments with conclusions of a certain type. After completing this account, Mill resumes his advocacy of utilitarianism; he indicates that on his view, such arguments are sound if, and only if, they turn entirely upon the general welfare.

Mill holds that someone has a right when he ought to be treated in a certain way, which serves (or refrains from undermining) some interest of his. Combining this with Mill's theory of obligation, we get the view that someone has a moral right when another person or persons are under a beneficial moral obligation towards him;[13] or in other words, when there are sufficient grounds for the widespread internalization of a value that requires corresponding ways of acting towards him.

Mill's approach seems to me significant. Someone who rejected the general welfare standard could consistently accept Mill's analysis of rights (or something like it) and use a different basis for validating the relevant claims. This is because his analysis of rights, like his analysis of moral obligations, is independent of the general welfare standard.

Now, if something like Mill's approach is correct, then we can say the following. If one's principles actually support the relevant sort of claim, then one is committed to the corresponding rights. Mill believes that some such claims are validated by the general welfare standard—that is, that it would serve the general welfare to protect individuals in certain ways—so he believes himself committed to moral rights. Mill's principle of liberty can be construed as a defense of some such rights and its defense as an argument for—among other things—constitutional protections for them. Since Mill's belief is plausible, it is plausible to suppose that a utilitarian such as MIll—indeed, anyone who accepts the general welfare as a standard for evaluation—is committed to certain categories of rights. And it is vital to observe that this conclusion flows, not from a concocted version of "utilitarianism" designed to yield conclusions that external critics demanded, but from a reasonable interpretation of the general welfare standard coupled with a plausible analysis of rights.

Moreover, since Mill is not committed morally to maximizing welfare—to regarding the failure to so act as wrong—he is not committed to infringing rights whenever it would serve the general welfare in the smallest way to do so. Quite the contrary, since such an act would breach a moral obligation that Mill recognizes, and obligations may be breached only when other obligations override them. In this sense, Mill shows that a proponent of the general welfare standard—even a utilitarian—can take rights seriously.

Mill's account of rights is superior to Bentham's in ways that follow from the differences in their conceptions of obligation. Bentham also held that to have a right is

---

13. For a fuller discussion of this sort of theory, see my "Rights, Claimants, and Beneficiaries," *American Philosophical Quarterly* 6 (1969):173–185.

to be someone who is supposed to benefit from another's obligation. But, as I have noted, Bentham analyzed obligation in terms of actual or authorized coercion, which might not be justified. This led to his notorious rejection of unenforced rights, including the rights that we invoke to argue for changes in the social order (as was done most famously in our Declaration of Independence and the French Declaration of the Rights of Man, both of which Bentham consequently criticized). Mill, however, is free to recognize such rights, which would be clearly in the spirit of his discussion.

It may also be noted that defects in Mill's account of obligation do not necessarily transfer to his account of rights. It is possible to understand both Bentham and Mill as embracing the idea that rights are to be understood in terms of beneficial obligations, and to interpret this in terms of an *adequate* account of obligation (whatever that may be). One could, of course, go further and say that the implications of the general welfare standard concerning moral rights cannot be fully understood without applying it to an adequate account of rights. Failing that, Mill has at least given us some reason to believe that utilitarians need not ignore or reject rights.

Let us now look at the specific commitments that Mill thinks utilitarians have toward moral rights. He holds that rules conferring rights take precedence over those that merely impose useful obligations, because they "concern the essentials of human well-being more nearly, and are therefore of more absolute obligation, than any other rules for the guidance of life" (Chap. V, par. 32). In particular:

> The moral rules which forbid mankind to hurt one another (in which we must never forget to include wrongful interference with each other's freedom) are more vital to human well-being than any maxims, however important, which only point out the best mode of managing some department of human affairs [Chap. V, par. 33].

According to Mill, our most important rights are to freedom of action and security of person; these concern our most vital interests, which must be respected or served if a minimally acceptable condition of life, in any setting, is to be possible. That position, I have tried to show, is not inconsistent with utilitarianism, and may in fact be part of a reasonably developed utilitarian theory. (Other rights concern, for example, specific debts or obligations that are due one and matters of desert.)

Mill's underlying reasoning may be understood as follows. An act is not wrong just because it fails to serve the general welfare to the maximum degree possible. This is because an act's being wrong involves the justification of sanctions, and sanctions (including internal sanctions) have unavoidable costs. The stakes must therefore be high enough so that the benefits to be derived from the redirection of behavior resulting from the existence of the sanctions (including the internalization of the corresponding values) exceed the costs entailed. But this applies to all moral obligations, including those "imperfect" obligations of benevolence which merely require generally helpful, charitable, or compassionate patterns of behavior. The obligations of justice are more demanding, and have greater costs attached, because they are "perfect." In the first place this means that they require one to behave toward certain other individuals in more or less determinate ways—that is, to serve or respect certain interests of theirs—on each and every occasion for so acting. In the second place this means that people are entitled to act in ways connected with their having rights: to demand respect for them, to challenge those who threaten to infringe them, to be indignant and perhaps noisy or uncooperative when their rights are violated or threatened, and so on. The obligations of justice are more demanding on the agent, since they do not leave one nearly as much choice as other moral obligations; they also involve greater liability to internal and external sanctions, as well as to demands by other persons upon one's conduct. This means that on a utilitarian reckoning they have special costs, which must be outweighed by the benefits they bring. The stakes must therefore be higher than for other moral obligations. Thus the interests that they are designed to serve must be more important. Rules concerning them will therefore generally take precedence over other moral rules. Such rights are not "inviolable," but their infringement will not easily be justified.

We can now make some further observations about the general nature of the rights that may be endorsed by the general welfare standard. In the first place, they may be characterized as morally fundamental, since they are grounded on a *non*moral standard and are not derived from some more fundamental moral principle.[14] In the second place, if Mill is correct about the importance to anyone of certain interests (such as personal liberty and security), regardless of particular social settings,[15] some of the rights endorsed by the general welfare standard could reasonably be characterized as "universal human" rights. Mill therefore gives us reason to believe, not only that the general welfare standard would not be hostile to such rights, but that it is positively committed to them—that is, to the sorts of rights associated with the Declaration of Independence. If so, the general welfare standard cannot be blamed for any corresponding injustices that are condoned by arguments invoking the general welfare; for such arguments would simply be mistaken.

I do not wish to imply, however, that Mill's suggestions should be accepted without much more severe scrutiny. I merely wish to emphasize that the matter seems far from settled against the general welfare standard.

One final comment in defense of arguments for rights from the general welfare standard. These rights are grounded upon nonmoral values. This will seem unsatisfactory to someone who thinks that some basic rights, or the principles that proclaim them, are "self-evident," as the Declaration of Independence declares. Now, I am not sure what "self-evidence" amounts to, but I know of no account that makes it plausible to suppose that moral principles can somehow stand on their own feet, without any need for, or even possibility of supporting argument. So I cannot see this as a serious objection to Mill.

A somewhat related and more familiar objection to Mill's manner of defending rights is to note that it relies upon the facts—not just too heavily, but at all. It is sometimes suggested, for example, that the general welfare standard must be rejected

14. In this respect they are just like the basic rights endorsed by John Rawls in *A Theory of Justice.* (Cambridge, MA: Harvard University Press, 1971). Rawls' argument invokes self-interest, not the general interest, but on the view we have been considering the latter is no more a "moral" standard than the former.

15. It is interesting to note that Rawls endorses such a notion with his use of "primary goods."

or severely limited because it is *logically* compatible with unjust arrangements. From any reasonable definition of human slavery, for example, it would not follow that such an institution could never satisfy the general welfare standard. It is therefore *logically possible* that enslaving some would sometimes serve the general welfare better than would any of the available alternatives. This objection does not rest on factual assumptions, and a utilitarian who tried to answer it by citing the *actual* disutility of human slavery would be accused of missing its point. Facts are simply irrelevant, for "basic" moral principles are involved.

A utilitarian might answer as follows. If moral principles independent of utilitarianism are assumed, the idea that the general welfare standard is valid is tacitly rejected at the outset; but that simply begs the question. At this point, any friend of the general welfare standard (even one who accepts other basic principles as well) might join in the rebuttal: Why should we assume that the principles of rights and justice are independent of the general welfare standard? Let us see the arguments for them, so that we can determine whether they are not actually grounded on and limited by considerations of utility.

Moreover, if facts cannot be called upon to help us interpret the general welfare standard, they must not be assumed by any objections to it. But it is difficult to see how facts can be excluded both from arguments for moral principles and from their applications. If moral principles are not regarded as self-evident, then they must be defended in some manner. The only plausible arguments that I know of in defense of moral principles—such as Rawls'—make extensive use of facts.[16] Moreover, most general principles require considerable information for their application to the varied circumstances of human life.[17] Someone who believes that facts are thus relevant to morality cannot reasonably object to the general welfare standard on the grounds of its unavoidable consideration of the facts. Until we have established principles of rights and justice on nonutilitarian grounds and also have shown that utilitarian arguments for them are ineffective, we must consider what proponents of the general welfare standard might have to say about such matters.

16. A good example is Rawls' argument for his principles, which makes much more extravagant use of facts than Mill's.
17. This is true, not just of Rawls' principles, but, I think, of all principles of similar scope.

■■■■
Part IV

The Holders of Human Rights

Possession of
Inalienable Rights

DIANA T. MEYERS

Human rights, it is often said, are rights all persons have simply by virtue of being human. However, . . . persons have inalienable rights because adequate moral systems must be neither self-defeating nor self-rescinding or, in other words, because adequate moral systems must sustain moral agency. Although there may not be any moral agents who are not humans (exploration of outer space will tell), there certainly are humans who are not yet moral agents and some who have little or no prospect of attaining this status. Thus, mere humanity does not suffice for possession of inalienable rights, and humanity may not prove necessary for possession of them, either. Furthermore, since moral agency is not a single uniform property—different persons exhibit it in different ways—it is possible that the content or moral force of inalienable rights varies collaterally. These reflections raise four central questions regarding possession of inalienable rights:

1. Is this divergence from the tradition that to be human is to have inalienable rights warranted?
2. Does this concentration on moral agency as a qualification for inalienable rights possession render them inegalitarian?
3. Are inalienable rights insensible of the needs and interests of children and morally incompetent adults?
4. Can any protections for animals be derived from inalienable rights doctrine?

To answer these queries is to dispose of doubts about excessive elitism as well as overextended populism within the theory of inalienable rights and to clarify the sense in which inalienable rights comprise an egalitarian position.

1. Species Membership and the Qualifications for Inalienable Rights

Salubrious as the conjunction of basic rights with universality in the domain of the human has been from a practical standpoint, the implication that individuals possess certain rights because they are members of a select species sanctifies a conceptual muddle. Individuals qualify for rights as individuals, not as members of species. It may be the case that all or nearly all of the members of a species have a certain right. But if so, they have this right because of properties that characterize all or most members of the species. In view of the impracticality of ascertaining which individuals meet the criteria for various rights on a case by case basis, it may be advisable to presume that all members of a species have a certain right. Yet, this pragmatic approximation should not seduce us into viewing rights possession as a function of species membership. For the biological definitions of species are too sparse to provide the information needed to establish conclusions about rights possession.

That membership in a species is not by itself relevant to possession of rights becomes clear once attention is diverted from members of the human species and focused on some other species, like gophers and robins, to which we are less emotionally attached. Let us grant for the sake of argument that most gophers have a right to a burrow because digging a burrow is the normal gopher's natural way of providing itself with shelter. Along the same lines, suppose that robins have a right to a nest. Is membership in these species the basis for this attribution of rights? The fatuity of attributing a right to a burrow to a mutant gopher who instinctively climbs a tree and constructs a nest of twigs and leaves reveals that species membership is not the critical factor. If anything, this sport should have a right to a nest despite the fact that it is a gopher. Evidently, the properties that usually characterize gophers, not gopherhood, would constitute the basis of our attribution of rights to gophers.

Whatever our ingrained suppositions about the bearing of biological taxonomy on possession of inalienable rights, it becomes plain on reflection that limiting the protection afforded by inalienable rights to whichever capabilities constitute common denominators for the human species would hardly be desirable. Attributes shared by every human being are apt to characterize most living things or, at any rate, most mammals. Few properties characterize every human being (infants as well as adults, ailing as well as healthy individuals), and those that do turn out to be so basic that they extend to similar forms of life as well. All humans breathe, register signs of neural activity, and need nourishment, but all goldfish do, too. As a result, reliance on capabilities that characterize all human beings as qualifications for inalienable rights severely limits the kinds of goods that can be objects of these rights and precipitously diminishes their impact on moral deliberation.

Supposing for the moment that the abilities to respire, fire neurons, and hunger for nourishment qualify individuals for inalienable rights, it must be asked what rights these individuals might have. Presumably, there must be a rational relationship between the qualifications for a right and possession of it. The need for nourishment could conceivably qualify an individual for a right to suitable comestibles, perhaps to intravenously administered nutriments on occasion, but not for a right to the pursuit of happiness unless the need for nourishment signals a desire for well-being in the broad sense. If an individual cannot enjoy and will forever be unable to enjoy the good conferred by a right, attributing it to him is otiose. Thus, the capabilities of prospective right-holders restrict the content of the rights they may possess, and qualifications for inalienable rights geared to universal human possession of these rights would rule out the right to personal liberty, the right to an education, and all other rights which presuppose right-holders' mobility or intelligence.

Natural rights for which all humans would qualify would entitle right-holders only to the most rudimentary benefits. However, two accounts of the right to life illustrate a more serious problem, that is, the weakening of the protection these rights would bestow on each human. Locke holds that the capacity for rationality and vulnerability are necessary and together sufficient conditions for possession of the right to life.[1] Alternatively, the capacity to register signs of neural activity and mortality could be considered necessary and together sufficient conditions for possession of this right. Compare the role of these two rights in the deliberations of a person who must decide whether to kill an average goldfish or an innocent, normally endowed, adult human being. Locke's version is dispositive, whereas my improvisation leaves the issue unresolved. Admittedly, Locke's account decides matters on the wrong grounds, but, at least, he does not pretend that this choice embroils the chooser in a vexing moral quandary pitting irreconcilable rights against each other.

Consistency obliges us both to limit the protection of rights to those creatures that qualify for them and also to extend this protection to all such creatures. If capabilities common to the human species are sufficient conditions for possession of inalienable rights, these rights must not be used to provide extra security for human capabilities which other right-holders lack, and nonhumans that share these elemental capabilities must fully enjoy their rights. On the face of it, acknowledging natural rights which all humans along with sundry fauna are guaranteed to possess elevates moral drivel to the status of serious moral dilemma. But why should this shift be regarded as generating misguided ethical consternation rather than as revealing genuine moral difficulty where none had been noticed?

The trouble with founding the right to life and other inalienable rights on capabilities common to all the members of the human species is that they will not turn out to be capabilities that anyone has compelling reasons to protect. The ability to register signs of neural activity, for example, may seem consequential in the context of recent euthanasia cases, but this is because this ability is taken as a sign of other potentialities that members of the human species typically have. The triviality of this capacity taken by itself becomes evident once it is noticed that persons share it with goldfish and a host of other creatures. No doubt there is a good deal to be said on behalf of nonhuman animals, but their virtues are quite distinct from any attributes they happen to share with humans. Indeed, what worse sort of speciesism could there be than the attitude that members of other species can only gain rights insofar as they resemble humans?

The upshot of these ruminations on people, goldfish, and rights is that the capacity to benefit from a right does not adequately explain the grounds for possession of it. This is obvious in the case of rights that are generated by transactions. If a person agrees to pay another person $10 for ten bales of hay, the seller gains a right to $10 from the buyer. The seller's neighbor who desperately needs $10 but who has no role in this bargain cannot gain a right to the buyer's payment by virtue of the fact that she would benefit from having the money, whereas the seller is too rich to notice $10 one way or the other. Since the neighbor is not a party to the agreement, she has no claim on the buyer's money unless she can establish such a claim on independent grounds.

Yet, when attention is turned to moral rights that are not created by transactions, it is understandable that the capacity to benefit from these rights would be thought a sufficient condition for possession of them.[2] Accounting for possession of these rights presents obstacles that sometimes look insuperable, and invoking capacities to benefit neatly ties the content of rights to the individuals who possess them. Nevertheless, the capacity to benefit from the protection afforded by such rights is only a threshold issue. Inanimate, mechanical, insensate, and self-sufficient entities could not have rights to life, personal liberty, benign treatment, and satisfaction of basic needs since it would be logically impossible to respect or violate their rights. But being alive, locomotive, sentient, and dependent on the natural environment for the means of survival does not suffice for possession of inalienable rights. If it did, these rights would be equivalent to undifferentiated duties not to kill, coerce, torment, or deprive any individual capable of suffering these types of maltreatment. In that case, the rights to life, liberty, benign treatment, and satisfaction of basic needs would have no supervenient moral force.

The proposition that a particular individual has, for example, a right to life is not just a sonorous way of saying that *ceteris paribus* it would be good if he were allowed to go on living. Attributing a right to life to someone entitles him to demand that he not be disturbed in the enjoyment of his life and secures him in the knowledge that only incontrovertible, rarely apposite reasons could justify anyone else's killing him against his will. In the case of moral dependents—individuals unable to assert their own rights—competent individuals must assume responsibility for assuring their wards' enjoyment of their rights. Thus, if children have rights, benevolent adults must protect them from wicked adults and must also supervise them in order to protect them from one another. Unless these services were provided for the morally helpless, their rights would be reduced to the adult population's duties of respect since rights assertion is not possible for them and rights respect is not possible among them. Accordingly, attributing rights to life, personal liberty, benign treatment, and satisfaction of basic needs to every creature that might enjoy these rights would commit adult humans to such tasks as policing carnivores and supplying them with alternate means of sustenance. Apart from the zoological questionability of this intervention in nature, the project of paternal enforcement of these presumptive natural rights has unacceptable moral consequences.

In the attempt to secure special moral protection for all vulnerabilities, none would be secured. If more individuals have claims to noninterference and aid than can possibly be respected and all of these claims are equally weighty, a lottery is the only solution. In extreme situations, this procedure may be a welcome last resort. But if due to an unmanageable claim load these lotteries were to become commonplace events, rights would be drained of any moral force beyond impartiality. Rights protect vulnerabilities and in so doing benefit right-holders, but vulnerabilities are too widespread to shield routinely with rights. So as not to confound moral judgment, rights possession must be confined to a set of individuals whose claims can ordinarily be honored.

Inalienable rights pose a further obstacle to a benefit-based analysis of rights possession. The capacity to benefit from these rights could not fully account for possession of them unless this capacity explained why right-holders could not renounce them. But since a capacity to benefit from a right does not entail an inability to forgo this benefit, possession of inalienable rights must depend on some additional factor.

The capacity inalienable rights single out for protection supplies a reason over and above compassion for recognizing them. Inalienable rights are rights that moral systems must recognize in order not to be self-defeating and self-rescinding. They are rights that individuals need in order to conduct themselves morally and that secure goods that can only be supererogatorily sacrificed for others' benefit. Along with protecting right-holders from untimely death and unnecessary misery, inalienable rights enable individuals to engage in moral interaction. Since this enabling function distinguishes inalienable rights from other moral rights, inalienable right-holders must be capable of moral agency. Furthermore, the requirement that goods secured by inalienable rights be immune to obligatory sacrifice would be unintelligible unless paradigmatic inalienable right-holders had this capacity. Only moral agents can incur obligations that make supererogatory gestures. Though many individuals lacking the capacity for moral agency are capable of enjoying the incidental protections inalienable rights afford because they are vulnerable to the same harms to which individuals with the capacity for moral agency are subject, only individuals capable of enjoying the guarantees of inalienable rights for the reason moral systems must grant them are inalienable right-holders.

2. The Equality of Inalienable Rights

That inalienable rights must be equal rights, that is, rights that entitle every right-holder to accomplish the same things in the same range of circumstances, is often accepted more or less as an article of faith.[3] But this egalitarianism could be challenged on two grounds. First, since capacities for moral agency vary, it might be urged that inalienable rights should be distributed accordingly. Second, since there are good and bad moral agents, it might be argued that their inalienable rights should reflect their moral merit. Neither of these lines of objection successfully makes the case for elitism, however, because they both overlook the foundational role of inalienable rights with respect to moral agency.

The capacity for moral agency is not an irreducible ability to see what would be right and to do it. Apprehending the right course of action and carrying it through summon a whole panoply of capabilities, and different individuals, each of whom is capable of moral agency, have distinctive configurations of constitutive strengths and weaknesses. To justify his position, an advocate of unequal inalienable rights might advert to these variations in endowment, insisting that some of these complex capacities are better than others.

It is important to notice, however, that the value of a person's idiosyncratic combination of capabilities depends on historical conditions and on the unfolding of his own biography. While physical endurance, intellectual perspicacity, emotional stamina, and subtle sensibility generally contribute to moral agency, there is no single ideal endowment, nor is there any way to assign different endowments to fixed positions on a scale of preferability. Under some circumstances maximal physical endurance or emotional stamina would be preferable to a high degree of development in other faculties. In fact, it is easy to imagine situations in which great intellectual powers or acute sensibility would be handicaps. But there are also circumstances in which physical endurance or emotional stamina would be of minor importance or could prove to be liabilities. Thus, any particular mix of strengths and weaknesses will be appraised as more or less desirable depending on circumstances.

To link the moral force of inalienable rights to these shifts in the value of an individual's distinctive endowment would be to weaken severely the protection afforded by these rights. Suppose that persons have rights weighted according to the adaptation of each right-holder's personality to cope with the circumstances she confronts. Anyone bent on attacking someone else could first manipulate these circumstances so as to reduce the stringency of her chosen enemy's rights, thereby removing the moral obstacles to her plan. Though right-holders might try to resist these machinations, their rights would not bar them. Inalienable rights cannot shelter right-holders from devastating, uncontrollable fortune; still, if they are to protect right-holders at all, they cannot be buffered about by insidious designs.

Paradoxically, humanity must be viewed in the aggregate for inalienable rights to function on behalf of the individual. Having a capacity for moral agency enables a person to interact morally and allows others to rely on his self-control. Under circumstances tolerably conducive to moral interaction, that is, circumstances in which inalienable rights can be respected, exceptional abilities are insignificant in maintaining moral responsibility. They may sharpen moral perspicacity or stiffen moral resolve. But unless persons assume special posts, their extraordinary abilities do not burden them with more moral responsibility than others are expected to bear. Diverse capacities for moral agency, then, do not warrant unequal inalienable rights.

Still, an intransigent elitist can turn from capacities to results. Whatever their innate capabilities, some moral agents turn out to be good while others turn out to be bad. Persons could begin life with maximally stringent inalienable rights and keep these powerful rights long enough to prove their mettle. As the bad and the imperfect revealed themselves, they could be demoted to less stringent inalienable rights. Ultimately, only the supremely good and the innocent young would enjoy the full protection of these rights. Of course, the assumptions that persons do sort themselves into good and bad categories and that their moral deserts can be accurately appraised are highly dubious. Nevertheless, it is critical to see why granting these assumptions would not justify introduction of graduated inalienable rights.

Substantial differences in the moral force of inalienable rights would permit abridgment in different ranges of circumstances. These rights devaluations would ostensibly be predicated on right-holders' reduced qualifications for these rights. Since bad agents act immorally more often than good ones, the argument goes, their capacity for moral agency must be impaired. Consequently, they are less qualified for inalienable rights and do not deserve the full protection of these rights.

Two difficulties immediately tell against this position. First, individuals must meet two qualifications for inalienable rights. Not only must they be capable of moral agency, but they must also be vulnerable to the types of harm which inalienable rights forbid. Evil persons are no less susceptible to being killed, coerced, tormented, and deprived of basic necessities than virtuous persons are. From the standpoint of this vulnerability qualification, then, these kinds of individuals are equally qualified for inalienable rights. Second, being a moral agent should not be conflated with being a virtuous agent. The former characterization informs us that the individual can be held responsible for his conduct; the latter indicates that his conduct is usually praise-worthy. A moral monster may be as responsible for his outrages as a minor transgressor is. Accordingly, the capacity for moral agency, not an admirable character, is the prerequisite for possession of inalienable rights.

Self-defeating and self-rescinding moral systems are unacceptable because they are capable of terminating moral interaction by preventing persons from acting as responsible agents. Adequate moral systems recognize inalienable rights and thereby ensure the basic conditions of autonomy. In sum, these rights secure the moral environment which constitutes the opportunity for persons to be virtuous (or, for that matter, vicious). For this reason, prorating a person's inalienable rights in accordance with diminishing moral merit becomes a self-fulfilling prophecy. Persons who have done badly are encouraged to persist or do worse by the decreased security devaluation of their rights brings. To the extent that acting honorably would interfere with their ability to make up for the inferiority of their rights, these persons might understandably opt for dishonor. After all, their needs are the same as others'.

Weakening the stringency of persons' inalienable rights to match their poor moral performance ignores the needs that partially qualify them for these rights, mistakes the moral agency qualification for a virtue requirement, and tricks the right-holder into further depredations. Only equal inalienable rights mirror the equality of right-holders' qualifications for these rights and ensure that right-holders can be held equally responsible for their conduct.[4] Though inalienable rights cannot prevent the advent of pervasive *in extremis* scarcity or personal tragedy from disrupting this balance of mutual responsibility, equal inalienable rights maintain this equilibrium insofar as morality can.

A graduated schedule of inalienable rights would establish a social order in which some individuals could be treated as persons stigmatized by lower castes have been treated. In the normal course of events, persons ascribed weaker rights could be used by their betters, and, in a catastrophe, these unfortunates would almost certainly be sacrificed before anyone possessing rights ranked higher on the stringency scale. To justify this inequality, we must be convinced that some individuals are capable of moral agency but do not qualify for inalienable rights because, not requiring life, personal liberty, benign treatment, and satisfaction of basic needs to conduct themselves morally, they may be obligated to sacrifice these goods altruistically. In other words, it must be shown that there are moral agents who do not have the four inalienable rights. Because their rights to life, personal liberty, benign treatment, and satisfaction of basic needs could be forfeited or revoked, these individuals could licitly be deprived of part or all of the protection of these rights.

Curiously, not the wicked but the extraordinarily good are most likely to be able to disregard their own most urgent interests in the service of lofty moral principles. Cowards and voluptuaries crumble at the slightest menace or temptation while heroes and saints withstand prodigious threats and enticements. These discrepancies in moral fortitude suggest that equal inalienable rights could prove patently inutile in a crisis involving conflicting rights since they might protect a courageous right-holder who could have endured the hardship while abandoning an ignoble right-holder to founder. To avoid this misallocation of moral resources, it might be urged, the virtuous should be awarded less stringent inalienable rights.

This argument for unequal inalienable rights attends insufficiently to the moral obstacles in the way of detecting superior moral strength and to the singular advantages of the right as a moral instrument. Plainly, character and strength of will are not observable properties, and moral excellence and scurrility are found in all kinds of people. Accordingly, nothing short of a licensing system would enable decision-makers to identify persons with less stringent rights. Such a certification program would involve testing for moral virtue by thrusting candidates into situations contrived to expose their moral strengths or deficiencies. To sort out the population, it would ultimately be necessary to ascertain how each individual would react in the face of moral horror. But to make this determination, it would be necessary to present agents with calamities in which their moral performance could be observed. This enterprise is morally out of the question. It is clearly wrong to precipitate catastrophe, and, even if catastrophes could be convincingly faked, it would remain wrong to subject every person to these horrifying conditions periodically in order to check on moral progress or backsliding. Since there is no morally acceptable way to license moral agents, differentially stringent inalienable rights are impracticable.

More important still, unlike duties of self-preservation which lock agents into giving themselves preference, inalienable rights allow individuals to prefer others. Whereas an exceptionally noble and generous person who is duty-bound to protect his own interests must be convinced that countervailing considerations supersede this duty before he can justifiably come to the aid of his weaker fellows, a similarly disposed right-holder can adopt a self-sacrificial course of action purely out of sympathy for others and regardless of whether it will procure a greater amount of good.[5] Equal inalienable rights do not secure superfluous benefits for extraordinarily virtuous individuals at the expense of ordinary people. Just the contrary, these rights make extraordinary virtue possible while acknowledging the limitations most agents labor under. As a result, it is unnecessary to take draconian steps to identify the morally good, for rights enable them to reveal themselves in the event.

3. The Dispossessed

Any acceptable moral system must confer equal inalienable rights on all individuals who are capable of moral agency. Because abridgment of these rights can never be morally required, though it is sometimes permissible, and because alienable rights do not bar obligatory infliction of comparable misfortunes on their bearers, inalienable right-holders enjoy a moral edge over other individuals. This is not to say that inalienable right-holders are always to be preferred to others but rather that when inalienable rights are at stake, the presumption is that these right-holders' claims take precedence.

The strict criterion for possession of inalienable rights coupled with the moral advantage inalienable right-holders enjoy may seem out of phase with our everyday convictions about our moral relations to those who fail to qualify. In particular, nonhuman animals, children, and morally incompetent humans are not capable of moral agency but cannot be mistreated with moral impunity. We are not free to starve our pets wantonly, to beat our children brutally, or to use incompetent humans for experimental purposes. Yet, none of these kinds of individual seems to be entitled to the protection of inalienable rights.

While it is clear that moral agents may have duties to treat other kinds of individuals humanely though these individuals have no rights to this consideration, the exclusion of nonhuman animals, incompetent humans, and, especially, normal children from the class of inalienable right-holders remains somewhat unpalatable. Our qualms about nonhuman animals are a fitting sympathetic response to publicized abuse of these creatures by scientific investigators and agribusiness. Nevertheless, I shall argue, there is no basis for granting any inalienable right to animals. In contrast, a convincing case can be made for acknowledging a derivative, but inalienable right, held by children.

4. Children

Neither animals nor children are capable of moral agency (we do not hold members of these groups morally responsible). Unlike animals, however, normal children have the potential to become moral agents (this is why we teach them to act responsibly). Children are not able to engage in reciprocal moral interaction, but eventually most of them will be able to do so, provided that their development is not stunted. In order for a child's moral development to proceed apace, she must be treated as if she qualified for the rights to life and satisfaction of basic needs; pain must be administered judiciously and in the service of moral training; and such enforced restraints as are forbidden by the right to personal liberty must be progressively removed as her judgment matures. This care can be summed up as a right to moral education.

The right to moral education should not be collapsed into the right to an education which often appears on lists of human rights. Yet, these rights are closely related. It is necessary to teach a child the language that is spoken in her community, to give her guidance and practice in deliberating about conduct, and in many communities to teach her elementary literary and mathematical skills in order to prepare her to assume the role of a responsible agent. The right to moral education entails a right to training in certain linguistic and reasoning skills; however, it does not entail a right to be familiarized with a humanistic or scientific heritage. The right to an education is both broader and narrower than the right to moral education. The right to moral education incorporates the treatment children ought to be accorded in regard to the four primary inalienable rights, as well as explicitly pedagogical care. But the right to an education entitles persons to more extensive cultural exposure than the right to moral education requires.

I shall take it for granted that no one denies that parents ought to provide their offspring with the minimal nurture sketched above. But questions linger as to whether all adult human beings are obligated to secure a moral education for all children and whether the source of this obligation is an inalienable right possessed by every child. These questions are best understood as opposite sides of the question of whether the criteria of adequacy that imply inalienable rights for adults also imply inalienable rights for children.

Infants are oblivious to morality; very young children comply with moral principles only because they are told to do so; older children take morality into account only erratically. Yet, despite the fact that these classes of individuals uphold moral systems, at best, serendipitously, only a stunningly myopic view of moral intercourse could fail to see that a moral system countenancing obligations to withhold moral education from normal children would be self-defeating. Though this kind of moral system might slowly grind moral interaction to a stand-still rather than bringing it to a precipitous halt, its capacity to suppress moral potential is indistinguishable in ultimate effect from a capacity to order destruction of moral agents. Either way the moral system can enjoin termination of moral interaction.

Likewise, the requirement that adequate moral systems not be self-defeating entails that adults capable of giving birth to normal babies cannot be obligated to refrain from procreating and that women who have conceived normal fetuses cannot be obligated to abort them. However, since moral systems need not be self-perpetuating, it is not incumbent upon them to prescribe the propagation of the species. Accordingly, neither potential fetuses nor potential infants have inalienable rights; there is no inalienable right to be conceived or to be brought to term. Rather, the requirement that moral systems not be self-defeating protects the freedom of prospective parents. Unless their reproductive capacities are so severely impaired that their offspring are bound to be morally ineducable or a fetus they conceive proves too severely compromised to be morally educable, they cannot be obligated not to procreate. Indeed, these misfortunes would not automatically obligate them not to procreate.

Still, it might be objected that an inalienable right to moral education for children is unnecessary. Since parents usually love their children and eagerly care for them, there is no need to encumber others with responsibility for strangers' offspring. And failing parental instincts, the requirement that moral systems not be self-defeating could be met by an injunction to rear that fraction of the baby population sufficient to carry on moral relations.

Callous though this proposal undeniably is, it is not immediately evident why adequate moral systems must reject it. Admittedly, a moral system would be self-defeating if it could prohibit giving moral education to individuals who are capable of learning, but the proposed program for rearing strategic numbers of these individuals relies on a permission to withhold moral education, not an obligation to do so. The contention is merely that there is nothing wrong with excluding some children from the moral community and hence that they have no inalienable right to moral education.

The question of whether children have an inalienable right to moral education must be separated from other questions about how they should be treated. Killing a child destroys a living creature as well as a moral potential; banishing or simply ignoring a child subjects a sentient creature to pain and privation; and enslaving a child warps a creature's development. Since moral considerations independent of inalienable rights undoubtedly militate against such practices, a pure case of moral agency excision must be devised. Robert Nozick's "experience machine" admirably serves this purpose.[6] The experience machine consists of a tank with electrodes programmed to stimulate the subject's brain so as to give her experiences like the ones usually produced by living. Children not elected for moral education could be consigned to these tanks where they would undergo a sequence of engrossing and blissful experiences. This arrangement would neither decrease the world's life total nor increase its sum of misery or perversion, but it would prevent moral agents from maturing. Assuming that enough children were morally educated to keep moral interaction flourishing, why could adequate moral systems not permit a tank program?

An initial objection to tank life, one anticipated by Nozick, is that the child would not actually do the things she experienced doing. She might be given the experience of writing a great novel and believe herself to have written one, but there would be no book to show for it. She would leave no mark on the world. To remedy this problem, Nozick invents the "result machine," which "produces in the world any result you would produce and injects your vector input into any joint activity."[7] It would produce a book corresponding to the experience of writing it.

Still, the result machine's supplementary effects only partially dispel the tank dweller's misapprehension of her existence. When a person has the experience of writing a book, she believes both that a book is being written and also that she is writing it. Likewise, when a person experiences friendship, she believes herself to be participating in a relationship with another person. But, in reality, the result machine would be supplying the book or friend and also carrying out the appropriate actions for the tank dweller. Thus, a tank dweller would believe herself to be a functioning member of society, although the machines would have usurped her capacity to do anything. A person who places a baby in the custody of the tank must choose between condemning the child to a lifelong experience of unrelieved passivity and isolation or to unabated delusion regarding her activities and interaction with others. Since subjecting a child to a life devoid of initiative and fellowship deprives her of much more than moral agency, let us grant that tank programmers would be obliged to include various projects and interpersonal contacts in their charges' programs. Though all of these experiences would be incorrigible delusions, tank dwellers would be saved from the dismal prospect of incessant vacuity.

Notice, now, that the tank dweller would not be the only individual deluded by the machines' operations. The person the tank dweller's result machine befriends, for example, must also believe she is involved in a real friendship. If the real-world friend did not believe this, the result machine could be accused of faking the results. Just as the result machine cannot substitute a sheaf of rave reviews for a great novel, it cannot hire an actor to mimic friendship instead of making a friend for the tank dweller. Thus, persons outside the tanks would undergo real-world experiences intermingled with phantom experiences induced by result machines, and they would be unable to distinguish these two types of experience.

The result machine's ingenious mediation of this interpenetration between the tanks and the world obliges moral agents to treat tank dwellers as if they, too, were moral agents. Vulnerability to murder, subjugation, torment, and deprivation along with a realized capacity for moral agency qualifies individuals for inalienable rights. But in simulating these characteristics in their projections on behalf of their wards, result machines would engender pseudo-inalienable rights for tank dwellers, and they would impose pseudo-obligations to respect these rights on moral agents. Admittedly, the tank dwellers' result machine projections, not the tank dwellers themselves, would be the beneficiaries of this treatment.[8] Nevertheless, from the standpoint of the moral agents who are responding to these figments, the important point is that, contrary to their intent, tanking children relieves them of no moral burdens. Since they cannot discern the difference between a person with an inalienable right and a tank manifestation with a pseudo-right, they must respect all of these claims indiscriminately to avoid violating genuine rights.

Still, an advocate of tanking unwanted and unneeded children could concede that tank dwellers would indirectly elicit moral responses but could insist that this one-sided attentiveness is tolerable provided that the guardian-child stage, and with it the especially onerous duty of moral education, were stricken from the tank repertory. One obstacle to this editing of the experiences available to tank dwellers is that experience machines may not be able to condense moral education, let alone catapult infants immediately into adult experience. Surely, some preparation would be necessary before these machines could impart to tank dwellers such sophisticated experiences as understanding witty conversation and being gratified at the delicacy of a courteous gesture. However, even if we grant experience machines the power to dispense with the experience of growing up, the tank program remains an unacceptable population management scheme.

Whether result machines engage independent moral agents in nurturing the projections of their charges or only in mature interaction with these projections, a moral system permitting tank life compels moral agents to accord tank dwellers the same moral consideration that they owe right-holders. Under normal conditions, this obscuring of the line between moral agency and inveterate moral incompetence would merely lead moral agents to display more concern for some individuals than they deserve. Though foolish in the abstract, this excessive solicitude would usually be harmless, rather like eccentrically intense devotion to a pet. However, in a grave crisis necessitating the sacrifice of some individuals, the consequences of the machines' fabrications could well be dire. Specifically, the claims of result machine projections, having the same apparent force as those of normal children and adults, might be honored instead of those of real inalienable right-holders. In the wake of this debacle, experience machines might proceed through their programs, but no one would remain outside the tanks from whom result machines could elicit a moral response.

Moral systems that permit adults to eschew responsibility for raising children by placing them in tanks have the defect of rescission by design. To permit suppression of moral potential is to authorize creation of an opaque social network which bars moral agents from identifying real claimants and which consequently sabotages rational moral deliberation and responsible conduct. If persons cannot penetrate the result machines' illusions, they cannot separate duties of respect contingent upon genuine rights from ersatz duties. This moral blindness obliges them to squander attention on phantoms and prevents them from making informed choices when apparent rights conflict. Inasmuch as these individuals act in ignorance of the moral import of their conduct, they cannot be held responsible for their misjudgments and cannot be regarded as full moral agents in interpersonal matters. Suppression of some children's moral potential, then, infects the whole moral community, and moral systems that authorize this practice jeopardize moral interaction.

Still, there is an obvious rejoinder to the argument I have presented: Whereas the experience and result machines are counterfactual, the problem before us concerns the morality of conduct in the known or probable world. As things are, the only way to suppress a child's moral potential, apart from killing her, is to handicap her so severely that her impediments are readily apparent. Realistically, withholding moral education from some children would not obfuscate social realtions so as to hamper moral agents' knowledgeable deliberation and conduct.

While it must be admitted that ordinarily the suppression of a child's moral potential is empirically discoverable (albeit her potential for recovery may be in doubt), it does not follow that there is no right to moral education, for it remains to consider the perspective of the right-holder, namely, the child. Inalienable rights, I have contended, cannot be renounced because they entitle right-holders to goods which it is always supererogatory to sacrifice altruistically. But children, since they cannot comprehend the consequences of refusing moral education, are in a position neither to sacrifice this good, whether supererogatorily or obligatorily, nor to renounce their right to it. To cope with this asymmetry, an equivalent of rights renunciation and supererogation must be found. For a child, the only way to lose a right is to have it revoked. Accordingly, the right to moral education is inalienable if it cannot be revoked because it can never be obligatory for an adult to deprive a child of the object of the right. Though it can be permissible to abridge any inalienable right, it can only be obligatory to abridge an alienable right.

To abridge the right to moral education without the mitigating assistance of Nozick's machines is to brutalize a child in the strictest sense of the term. It is both to treat the child brutally and to make her a brute. Because children are helpless and their wounds leave them physically and emotionally scarred, abusing them is unspeakable, the lowest sort of criminality. This extra opprobrium that we reserve for child abuse suggests that no predicament could convert comparable actions into obligations. Surely, if killing, subjugating, torturing, and depriving adults of basic necessities cannot be obligatory, there is no reason to suppose that subjecting children to similarly cruel treatment could be. At most, the bleakest circumstances can render such conduct permissible.

The potential for moral agency is integral to the normal human child. To suppress it, the child must be severely incapacitated and frustrated, if not destroyed. Moreover, the experience and result machines show that, if a child whose moral potential is extinguished could be allowed so much as a simulacrum of normal development and contact with the world, she would extract full moral consideration from others. So inextricable from the child is her moral potential that it is not possible to see normal childish behavior stripped of this dimension, and so firm are our precepts requiring that children be accorded gentle care that they are never nullified. Though it is hoped that parents will raise their own children and that parental affection will obviate assertion of the right to moral education, it is clear that moral education is not the exclusive province of willing parents or a calculating moral community. It is an inalienable right held by every normal child which any adequate moral system must recognize.

5. Animals

A moral community requires continuity over generations of moral agents. It will disintegrate despite the presence of the original members if provisions are not made for the moral education of new members. Thus, a moral system that fails to recognize an inalienable right to moral education is unacceptable. Can the same be said for a moral system that does not grant animals a suitably adjusted inalienable right to care?[9]

The most promising support for such a right stems from the fact that animals occupy ecological niches. If the natural environment inhabited by moral agents is destroyed, they will be destroyed, too. Consequently, it might be urged that moral systems must confer rights to be nurtured and protected on animals in order to ensure the survival of moral agents. One difficulty in this proposal is, of course, that it entails inalienable rights for every entity that has an ecological function—panda bears, mosquitoes, and ferns alike. As noted above, neither individuals nor states could keep track of this vast system of inalienable rights and this burgeoning population of right-holders. Since these rights could only be respected haphazardly, they would trivialize other rights without improving the survival outlook for the creatures said to possess them.

Still, it could be urged that rights to noninterference are easy to respect and would suffice for animals. Animals need no special cultivation to fulfill their ecological roles; they need only be left alone. Appealing as this vision of the world as a wildlife sanctuary may in some respects be, its direct and rigid opposition to industry and recreation, that is, to human liberty, seems exceedingly retrograde. Yet, it must be asked whether an argument paralleling the one for the right to moral education can be made on behalf of animals. For if such an argument can be sustained, the implications for the course of civilization would be momentous.

The defense of an inalienable right to moral education for children proceeded in two main steps. First, it was shown that an obligation to suppress moral potential could prove incompatible with the persistence of moral interaction and, therefore, that a moral system capable of generating such an obligation would be self-defeating. Second, it was shown that a permission to suppress moral potential provided only that the population of the moral community did not sink to a dangerously low level would subject those deprived of moral education to empty or deluded lives and, furthermore, that this practice would prevent otherwise competent moral agents from obtaining information crucial to their deliberations about their conduct. Thus, a moral system issuing this permission would also be flawed by rescission by design.

Though there is overwhelming evidence that civilization has often advanced with woeful indifference to nature and that continuing this destruction unabated could eventually make the earth uninhabitable, it remains undeniable that some kinds of plants and animals are expendable from the standpoint of ongoing moral interaction. As a matter of fact, human molestation has brought about the extinction (or near extinction) of many species, without throwing the natural order into insupportable disarray. That this destruction is compatible with the indefinite survival of moral communities is not surprising inasmuch as animals are not participants in these communities and particular animals are not necessary to the moral agency of the members of these communities. Archetypally, inalienable rights have objects which individuals who are capable of moral agency need in order to exercise this capacity. Consequently, if there are any inalienable environmental rights, they would most likely be persons' rights to a habitable environment, however that may be achieved, not animals' rights to noninterference. Since granting inalienable rights to individual animals is not necessary to maintain an environment that supports moral communities, a moral system that denies these rights would not be self-defeating.

Still, it might be thought that the relations obtaining between animals and the ecosystem are such that moral systems must recognize their rights to noninterference in order not to be self-rescinding. Whereas rights necessary to avert self-defeatism redound to moral agents and proximately secure the viability of moral agency, rights necessary to stave off rescission by design ban permissions that generate moral relations threatening to moral agency. Since rights ordained by this latter criterion of adequacy support moral agency indirectly, animals might conceivably gain such rights in virtue of performing functions essential both to the animals themselves and to the conduct of moral interaction.

It might be tempting to suppose that an animal's performance of its ecological function is indistinguishable from the activities it carries out in order to provide for its own needs. For example, a predator's hunting for food prevents the population of its prey from increasing too much, and in this respect the animal's natural impulses coincide with its helping to stabilize the demographic profile of another animal species. Yet, it is not the case that an animal's pursuit of its ends must contribute to the maintenance of an ecological balance between species.

An animal could be obstructed in its performance of its usual ecological function and yet live an entirely satisfying life. If a huge dome were constructed (assume that it is too large for the animal that has been deposited in the middle to reach its circumference) in which an animal's natural environment was carefully simulated and in which it could hunt, eat, sleep, and roam about, just as it would in the wild, the animal would not be repressed although its opportunity to carry out certain ecological functions would have been eliminated. Since its artifical environment would have to be stocked with prey, its hunting would not help to keep the population of these animals in check. If anything, the overall population of this species of prey would be increased because the animal would not be killing members of this species in the natural environment and meanwhile additional animals would be raised to supply the replicated environment. Yet, despite this scheme to prevent the animal from playing an ecological role, there is no reason to consider the animal frustrated since it is not being hindered in any of its normal activities.

In contrast, the development of a child's potential for moral agency cannot be separated from her accustomed activities in the way I have distinguished an animal's quotidian behavior from our understanding of this behavior as an ecological role. A child who is frustrated in the development of her ability to function as a moral agent cannot be provided with a substitute structure that will allow her to proceed normally except for the imperceptible omission of her assuming the status of a moral agent. Only through the fictional device of tank life could we glimpse the impact of pure moral agency suppression on moral interaction.

A further difference between my domed animal's experience and a tank dweller's experience is that the former is not under any illusion regarding its life nor does its life generate delusions for the members of the moral community. Although my animal performs no ecological function, it does not erroneously believe it is performing such a function, for no animal correctly believes it occupies an ecological niche. A lion dozing on the plains of Kenya cannot espy a herd of antelope and think, "I'm not hungry, but I've got to go perform my ecological function." Animals hunt and have the experience of hunting in my dome. Since they do not also believe that they are helping to maintain an ecological system, they cannot be deluded in this regard, and there is no reason to supply them with result machines to compensate for their disabilities. Furthermore, since their captors have created their artificial environment and service it regularly, neither are they confused about which animals are ecologically active. Indeed, if a moral decision ever turned on the distinction between ecological contribution and ecological superfluity, doming animals would, if anything, help to solve the problem.

Ultimately, it is because animals cannot share in moral interaction—they are limited to profiting from others' adherence to moral principles—that moral systems are not obliged to guarantee their interests through inalienable rights. Since animals are not moral agents, moral systems that prescribe their suffering and destruction are not self-defeating. Also, since preventing animals from fulfilling their ecological destinies need not thwart their natural impulses and would not obfuscate moral relations, moral systems that do not credit animals with inalienable rights are not self-rescinding. In sum, the contribution animals make to moral interaction stands at too great a remove from this nexus to warrant inalienable rights for them. They are collectively instrumental in maintaining an environment hospitable to moral agents, but no individual animal's survival and well-being is indispensable to moral interaction. It follows that animals have no inalienable rights.

6. The Universality of Inalienable Rights

Strictly speaking, only moral agents and normal children meet the qualifications for inalienable rights. No moral system could deny their rights and not prove self-defeating and self-rescinding. Nevertheless, two forms of moral incompetence pose problems for this position.

All moral agents are morally incompetent while they sleep. Since inalienable rights would be nugatory if their protection lapsed with the onset of night, the moral incompetence of an individual who has the potential for moral agency cannot justify denying his inalienable rights. Though a theory of inalienable rights could not be founded solely on a never activated potential for moral agency, recognition of the moral significance of this potential, both in normal children and in adults, is critical to a theory of inalienable rights.

More troubling are cases of abnormal moral incompetence induced by psychological and physiological illness. If the disease is curable, moral agency will return with health, but if the disease is incurable, the individual will become a permanent moral invalid. Sometimes it is possible to determine whether a morally incompetent individual is only temporarily stricken. Frequently, no reliable prognosis can be made. Because diagnostic procedures are notoriously fallible and because mistaken denial of a person's inalienable rights can be catastrophic, it is necessary to adopt a conservative policy requiring irrefragable proof of irremediable moral incompetence before an individual's inalienable rights can be denied. Thus, the protection of inalienable rights extends to many humans who may never engage in moral relations. Though it is only accidental if all humans qualify for inalienable rights, few humans will ever be rightfully deprived of the protection these rights afford.

Notes

1. For the sake of simplicity, I leave aside the theological complications of Locke's view and stress his affirmation of the similarity of human faculties and his concern with the possibility of premature death (*The Second Treatise of Government,* Sections 4 and 6).

2. H. J. McCloskey construes the capacity to benefit in terms of interests ("Rights," pp. 125–126). Also, Robert Nozick's discussion of the treatment of animals implicitly appeals to the ability of animals to benefit from what he calls stringent side constraints which are constitutive of rights (*Anarchy, State, and Utopia,* pp. 35–42). For an illuminating general discussion of the relation between rights and benefits, see David Lyons, "Rights, Claimants, and Beneficiaries," pp. 173–185.

3. The arguments that follow parallel and supplement Rawls' discussion of the capacity for moral personality as a range property (*A Theory of Justice,* pp. 504–512).

4. It could be objected that a system of differential inalienable rights is precisely what any penal institution establishes since judicial sentences authorize abridgment of convicted criminals' rights. Nevertheless, two features of penal institutions distinguish them from the system of graduated inalienable rights contemplated here. First, trials consider allegations regarding particular acts; they do not attempt to decide whether agents are good or bad. Second, punishments corresponding in severity to the crime committed specify definite ways in which the convict's rights can be abridged; they do not simply nullify or downgrade the stringency of his rights. As I shall argue . . . , penal sanctions, when properly administered, respect the inalienable rights of perpetrators and their victims alike.

5. It is worth noting that, according to Locke, we have duties to our divine creator which invariably supersede our natural rights and which bind each of us "to preserve himself and not to quit his station wilfully" (*The Second Treatise of Government,* Section 6). But, as I have urged, it is possible for a person to sacrifice the objects of inalienable rights supererogatorily. . . .

6. *Anarchy, State, and Utopia,* pp. 42–45.

7. *Ibid.,* p. 44.

8. I leave aside the suggestion that the result machines themselves are potential moral agents which are activated by the transferral of the tank dwellers' agency and which then merit moral consideration in their own right. Since creation of a set of mechanical moral agents reveals nothing about the propriety of extinguishing moral potential, I shall assume that result machines merely simulate moral agency.

9. I leave aside two important questions: (1) whether animals have alienable rights, and (2) what arguments independent of rights might be given for protecting wildlife.

Why
There Are
No
Human Rights

DOUGLAS HUSAK

1

There are no *human* rights. The chief difficulty in defending this thesis is not in providing a sound argument in its favor. Such an argument (discussed below) has in fact been familiar to philosophers for some time. Instead, the difficulty is in offering an explanation of why so few theorists have been persuaded by this argument. An attack on human rights is bound to give rise to misunderstandings I am anxious to dispell. My purpose is not to discredit the noble purposes to which human rights have been put, but to suggest that these purposes are better served without the highly problematic contention that all human beings share rights. Thus my central project is to undermine the philosophical motivation for believing that human rights must exist. Once the obstacles to rejecting human rights have been identified and removed, my thesis will be found much more palatable.

A preliminary difficulty is to characterize what human rights *are*. Otherwise it is unclear whether philosophers who debate about the existence of human rights are in genuine agreement or disagreement. Unfortunately, there is no consensus about the definition of human rights. I will borrow from philosophers sympathetic to human

Douglas Husak, "Why There Are No Human Rights," *Social Theory and Practice,* 11, No. 2 (Summer 1984), pp. 125–141. Reprinted with permission of *Social Theory and Practice*.

rights, first, an account of what makes a right a *human* right, and second, a theory of *rights.*

All philosophers agree that a right cannot be a human right unless it is possessed (a) *by all human beings.* But apart from this first condition, there are two others that may or may not be necessary for a right to qualify as a human right. Some philosophers insist that the right must be possessed (b) *only by human beings;* and/or (c) by all *human beings equally.* The doctrine of human rights I will attack includes the first condition but rejects the second; thus, if a given right is shared by nonhumans, it is not thereby disqualified as a human right. The third condition, however, is more problematic, largely because it is unclear what is meant by the claim that a given right is possessed equally or unequally. It is not easy to appreciate how the possession of a given right could admit of degrees. If my right is said to be greater or lesser than your right, why suppose we possess the *same* right to different degrees? There simply is no agreement among philosophers about how rights are to be individuated.[1] Thus it seems sensible to adopt a definition of human rights that is noncommittal about this third condition. Hence my attack upon human rights construes them weakly, including only the first condition. If I can show that there are no rights possessed by all human beings, any stronger doctrine of human rights will have been refuted as well.

Differences among philosophers about what makes a right a *human* right account for only a small part of the controversy about the existence, basis, and content of human rights. Of far greater significance is the fact that philosophers are unclear about what *rights* are. Human rights are, presumably, a kind of right,[2] and any confusion about rights is bound to create uncertainty about human rights. Once again, it is fair to conclude that there is no consensus among philosophers about the role played by rights in moral theory. How, if at all, would a moral theory without a concept of rights differ from one in which rights were included?[3] Though there is much room for controversy here, I will assume the truth of a theory about rights that has gained a substantial following among several of the most distinguished moral and political philosophers to have addressed these questions.

According to this theory, rights function to protect their possessors from being subjected to treatment solely in accordance with the outcomes of utilitarian calculations. In many circumstances, acts are justified—even when coercive and contrary to some person's interests—when they produce a net balance of benefits over harms. But when a *right* of such a person is violated, this utilitarian rationale is insufficient to justify the act in question. Thus it is sometimes said that rights "trump" countervailing utilitarian considerations. Many philosophers contend that the chief difficulty with utilitarianism is that it provides a defective account of rights. Hence a moral theory that did not include rights would be vulnerable to many of the difficulties urged against utilitarianism—it would allow the unjust sacrifice of one person's welfare for the greater good, and thus would exhibit disrespect for persons. Despite widespread differences in their moral and political theories, Rawls, Dworkin, and Nozick each share this basic conception of the nature and value of moral rights.[4]

If the above theory of rights is juxtaposed with the earlier description of what makes a right a human right, the following account results. Human rights are those moral considerations that protect each and every human being from being subjected to treatment solely in accordance with the outcomes of utilitarian calculations. If they did not protect *every* human being, they would not be *human* rights; if they did not afford protection from being subjected to the outcomes of utilitarian calculations, they would not be *rights*.

I will adopt the terminology gaining currency among philosophers primarily concerned with the morality of abortion and distinguish between *human beings* and *persons*. The former designates a biological class; criteria for membership are specified by scientists. Membership in the class of persons, however, is determined by moral criteria. By definition, persons possess a higher moral status (perhaps conferred by the enjoyment of rights) than that of nonpersons.[5] This distinction is useful in allowing the possibility that some persons may not be human beings, or, more importantly for present purposes, that some human beings may not be persons. An argument against the existence of human rights will almost certainly attempt to show that some human beings are not persons.

With this account in mind, we can envisage what a moral theory that did not countenance any human rights would be like. The thesis that there are no human rights denies that there is a single right possessed by all human beings. Some human beings either would possess *no* moral rights whatever, *or* different moral rights from those possessed by persons. Though these disjuncts express distinct theses, the former is almost certain to be affirmed by anyone who denies the existence of human rights. There is little motivation to believe that nonpersons have rights, though their rights are entirely distinct from any enjoyed by persons. Thus I will assume that anyone who denies the existence of human rights believes that some human beings are without moral rights. He would hold that at least some human beings—let us call them nonpersons—would properly be subject to treatment solely in accordance with the outcomes of utilitarian calculations. Whether or not this result is plausible is difficult to assess, for it is notoriously problematic to identify what specific treatment utilitarianism would prescribe in any but a few clear cases. But if my thesis that there are no human rights is to be persuasive, I must attempt to show that this result is not as unacceptable as it may first appear. This endeavor, however, will be postponed until Part 3.

The argument against the existence of human rights is familiar, but only because champions of human rights regard its appeal as a challenge to be overcome rather than as an insight to be accommodated. The key premise in the argument is that no morally relevant characteristic(s) that could provide the basis or ground of such rights is possessed by all human beings. Whatever property (or properties) is adduced as a possible foundation for such rights is defective in one or both of two respects: Either it is not shared by each and every human being, or it provides no reason for believing that its possessor enjoys rights. In other words, each proposed foundation of human rights fails what might be called the *universality* or *relevancy* tests. I would not make an original contribution to the voluminous literature on human rights by showing in detail how each of the several candidates put forth as a basis or ground of human rights—e.g., rationality, the ability to use language, reciprocity, the capacity to conform to moral requirements, self-motivated activity, self-consciousness, etc.—fails either or both of these tests.[6] My central project is not to defend this argument so much as to explain why so many sensible moral and political philosophers have gone to such extraordinary and desperate lengths to resist it.

Which human beings are members of the class of nonpersons? Fortunately, I need not propose a definitive answer to this vexing question and commit myself to criteria of personhood. For *some* human beings fail *any* empirical test used to distinguish persons from nonpersons. Some human beings are neither rational, nor able to communicate, nor capable of reciprocity, nor able to conform to the requirements of morality, nor self-motivated, nor self-conscious, etc. Some philosophers have used this result to argue that abortion is morally permissible.[7] The chief difficulty in drawing this conclusion is that most human fetuses possess the *potential* to satisfy the various criteria of personhood. Here I need not decide whether or to what extent the potential to become a person is morally relevant, for the least controversial examples of human nonpersons *lack* the potential to acquire any of the above characteristics. Karen Quinlan is a familiar example of a human member of the class of nonpersons.

It must be conceded that the above argument does not express a deductive proof that human rights cannot exist. I do not contend that human rights *cannot* exist; there is no contradiction in countenancing human rights. There remains the possibility that some ingenious philosopher will identify one or more characteristics that satisfy the universality and relevancy tests, and thus provide the basis or ground of human rights. I do not rely on an alleged "naturalistic fallacy" or any other general principle for maintaining that no such demonstration could be forthcoming. My only evidence for remaining skeptical that such a defense will be provided is the inductive reason that no such characteristic(s) has yet been identified. There is little reason for optimism that any increased understanding of human beings we might gain will call such a characteristic(s) to our attention.

Some human rights theorists are likely to respond by claiming that I am attacking a straw man. They will admit that some human beings are nonpersons, but will insist that this concession is compatible with their conviction that some rights are human rights. They will deny, in other words, that they employ a purely biological criterion of humanity. The problem with this retort is that it runs squarely into a difficulty human rights theorists had hoped to avoid, and threatens to undermine what is largely believed to be attractive about the concept of human rights. These theorists have aspired to show that *all* human beings possess rights, regardless of whatever contingent properties they might happen to have. If they now admit that some biological human beings *lack* rights *because* of their characteristics, they must abandon their claim that all such contingent properties are irrelevant to ascriptions of human rights. Human rights theorists like to emphasize that there are two fundamentally distinct kinds of ideologies about rights—those that extend rights to all of humanity and those that withhold rights from some subclass of mankind. But on this retort, the human rights movement is exposed as merely another instance of the latter ideology from which it had hoped to differentiate itself. Human rights theorists, like their adversaries, attribute or withhold rights from human beings on the basis of contingent properties some human beings possess and others lack. Thus champions of human rights should be uncomfortable about this response.

2

Now that we have some idea of what human rights are, and in what way they might matter to moral theory, we can profitably inquire whether any exist. Why should we believe (or disbelieve) in them? This question can be answered only by addressing the ground or basis of these alleged rights.

Not all philosophers confront this fundamental problem of specifying the foundation of human rights. Some simply provide a list of what are contended to be human rights. There are heated exchanges about whether, e.g., there is a human right to employment or medical care. Obviously, these debates will not impress one who is skeptical about whether there are any human rights at all. Unless the skeptic is to be dismissed without argument—as is too often the case—he is owed a reply.

Recent technological innovation has increased our need for such a reply. Many human rights theorists conveniently ignore the fact that some human beings lack the characteristic(s) on which they purport to base or ground human rights. But there are at least two reasons why the class of human nonpersons can no longer be safely ignored. First, the class continues to grow in number. Our medical science is now able to sustain the lives of many human beings with serious mental handicaps who would have died only a decade ago. The increasing size of this group indicates that it will continue to place greater demands in the competitive struggle for scarce medical resources. Thus it is crucial to determine how our obligations to this group are similar to or different from those owed to persons. Second and even more importantly, technology now offers the promise that nonpersons will become increasingly useful to us. Until recently, the suggestion that this group could constitute a benefit rather than a burden to mankind was dismissed as science fiction. There is some indication, however, that transplants of healthy brain tissue from nonpersons to persons will soon become a reality. Some groups have already begun to protest the ethics of such proposals, and they too are owed a reply.

Only two kinds of strategies are available to those who seek the basis or ground of human rights. The first is to show that the search for such a foundation is somehow misguided, and the second is to defend some basis or another. Among contemporary theorists, Joel Feinberg pursues the first strategy, while Alan Gewirth pursues the second. Despite their painful familiarity with the argument to the contrary, these philosophers remain staunch defenders of human rights. I critically examine their arguments here because the difficulties they encounter are typical of problems that any theorist who works within their frameworks should anticipate. Of course, particular problems are peculiar to theorists who explicate the details of these strategies differently. I do not propose to address each and every defense of human rights. My main purpose is to substantiate the description of defenses of human rights as implausible and somewhat desperate, so that philosophers will be more inclined to reexamine without prejudice the thesis that no human rights exist.

Joel Feinberg describes the burden to be met by philosophers who seek the foundation of human rights: "If two things or two persons have the same worth, they must have in common some other characteristic—a nonvalue characteristic—that is the basis of their equal worth. But what might this common characteristic be?"[8] He notes that "philosophical champions of human rights have replied to this legitimate query with a bewildering variety of answers, almost all of them inadequate."[9] In the course of rejecting a number of unsatisfactory attempts to ground human rights, Feinberg shrewdly observes that several "'explain' human worth only by renaming that which is to be explained."[10] The claims that all human beings are "ends in themselves," or "sacred," or "of infinite value" are themselves in need of a foundation and thus lead to circularity or regress when employed to base human rights. Feinberg concludes that such reasoning should not convince one who professes skepticism about human rights.

It is unclear, however, why Feinberg believes that his own solution should satisfy the skeptic. He maintains that "universal 'respect' for human beings is, in a sense, 'groundless'—a kind of ultimate attitude not itself justifiable in more ultimate terms."[11] He continues: "'Human worth' itself is best understood to name no property in the way that 'strength' names strength and 'redness' names redness. In attributing human worth to everyone we may be ascribing no property or set of qualities, but rather expressing an attitude—the attitude of respect—toward the humanity in each man's person."[12] Though the search for a foundation of human rights was initially described as "legitimate," the enterprise is ultimately rejected as misguided: "If none of this convinces the skeptic, we should turn our backs on him to examine more important problems."[13]

But the skeptic should not be dismissed as stubborn or unreasonable if he is not persuaded so easily. Among other difficulties, Feinberg's "argument" proves too much. It is equally convincing as a defense of universal *dis*respect. I hope it is not uncharitable to Feinberg to summarize his solution as urging philosophers to embrace human rights as an article of faith. Human rights exist but we cannot understand why. This approach does not even attempt to satisfy the relevancy condition. Silence awaits the skeptic who inquires why we should share the attitude of respect toward the Karen Quinlans of the world.

Alan Gewirth employs the capacity for purposive agency as the ground for countenancing human rights. Agents consider their own purposes as "good" and thus, Gewirth argues, are committed to accepting as good the "necessary conditions" which make both action and the achievement of purposes possible.[14] According to Gewirth, freedom and well-being comprise the necessary conditions for purposive action. A need for freedom and well-being, when expressed by the purposive agent himself, is prescriptive and thus contains the normative element necessary to transform these necessary goods into "prudential rights." These rights become human rights through the principle of universalizability; since purposive agency is a sufficient justification for having a right to freedom and well-being for the agent himself, all other purposive agents are equally deserving of these rights.

Gewirth's strategy is plagued with difficulties. One might well wonder how the alleged human rights of freedom and well-being could be necessary conditions for purposive agency. Presumably a great part of the world's population is without these rights; is it therefore logically impossible for them to act—or to attain any of their purposes?[15] Moreover, the notion of "prudential rights" is curious and requires much more detailed elaboration. But conceding *arguendo* that purposive agency provides an adequate foundation for the moral rights of persons, it is crucial to determine whether such rights could qualify as *human* rights, as Gewirth alleges. Does his proposed foundation satisfy the universality condition?

It is difficult to understand how agency can serve as the basis of human rights when, as Gewirth admits, capacities of agency vary among individuals. Gewirth suggests that agency—although possessed by human beings in varying degrees—nonetheless provides a justification for human rights since those with less capacity for agency are to be granted "proportionately less" rights. He claims: "The degree to which different groups approach having the generic features and abilities of action determines the degree to which they have or approach having the generic rights."[16] Gewirth might have anticipated a number of difficulties had he compared his definition of human rights with his project of grounding such rights in purposive agency. He begins: "We may assume, as true by definition, that human rights are rights that all persons have simply insofar as they are human."[17] But it is evident on his account that we do not possess human rights simply in virtue of our humanity, but rather in virtue of our capacity for purposive agency. This discrepancy should have alerted Gewirth to problems that derive from the unfortunate fact that some creatures possessed of humanity are devoid of any capacity for purposive agency.

Gewirth's argument is defective for two reasons. Since Karen Quinlan is not a purposive agent in any ordinary sense, agency could not provide a foundation for the rights of *all* human beings unless the capacity for purposive agency is given a most peculiar interpretation. Moreover, even if it were the case that all human beings were purposive agents in some limited sense, to grant rights in proportion to agency is not merely to grant varying degrees of the same human right; it is tantamount to countenancing different rights with distinct duties. The conclusion that human beings share a number of given rights, but to different extents, is suspiciously similar to the admission that some of us do not have the same rights after all. Champions of human rights cannot be happy with this result. It allows possessors of "full" human rights to dominate those with "lesser" rights, which is the very sort of exploitation human rights were designed to prevent. If some human beings are to receive proportionately less rights than others, then those genuinely human rights which exist could be no greater than those possessed by the individual with the least capacity for agency. Thus purposive agency, while arguably an adequate foundation for the rights of persons, cannot ground *human* rights.

Suppose, e.g., that both Karen Quinlan and (what I have been calling) a person are in need of a life-saving transfusion and there is only enough blood available to save one. Suppose further that all factors that might influence priority (e.g., ownership of the blood, a first-come, first-served policy, etc.) are equal. Human rights theorists could hardly deny that both human beings possess the right to life. Is it therefore a matter of moral indifference who is saved? This result does not seem compelling. Human rights theorists might therefore "fudge" and claim that the right of the (acknowledged) person is more weighty, or more stringent, or overrides that of the (alleged) nonperson. If so, however, it seems hollow to insist that they both possess the *same* right.

These difficulties are reflected in Gewirth's ambivalence toward those human beings who lack a fully developed capacity for purposive agency. The rights of infants, fetuses, and the mentally defective are "watered down" to the point where it becomes evident that they share little in common with the rights of persons. Finally, Gewirth all but contradicts any promise that his rights apply universally to all human beings: "This absoluteness in having the generic rights applies even to a certain degree of human brain damage, so long as there remains the possibility of recovery."[18] Apparently, then, human beings with no prospects of recovery do not possess human rights.

Difficulties and inconsistencies in the work of contemporary theorists who address the ground or basis of human rights do not provide the only reason for skepticism. Belief in the existence of human rights leads to results that should strike philosophers as highly counterintuitive. Much of the extensive literature on the so-called rights of (nonhuman) animals begins with the unsupported premise that there are human rights. Many defenders of animal rights then point out that whatever characteristic(s) provides the foundation of these rights is shared by some animals, who must therefore enjoy the same human rights as persons. The suggestion that some animals possess the same rights as persons would be treated as an absurdity were it not for the fact that human rights theorists can find little fault with the above reasoning. The rejection of human rights undercuts such arguments in favor of the "equal rights for animals" movement and allows us to escape charges of injustice and arbitrariness in many of our discriminations between persons and animals.

Nonhuman animals do not provide the only source of difficulty for human rights theorists. Suppose that a group of living Neanderthals (or even more primitive evolutionary forerunners of modern *homo sapiens*) were discovered. Would human rights theorists insist that they be afforded full human rights, unless shown to be biologically nonhuman? Neither alternative seems plausible. There must have come a time in our evolutionary development when our ancestors required whatever characteristic(s) grounds our human rights, so there must also have been a time before they possessed such a characteristic(s). This transition into personhood need not have coincided with (and may have been subsequent to) our ascendancy into biological humanity.

3

Finally we come to the crux of the matter. If there is no sound argument establishing the existence of human rights, and numerous difficulties in any attempt to defend them, why have moral philosophers not abandoned them? A mere lapse of critical faculties does not explain why good philosophers are persuaded by bad arguments. More typically they are convinced of a conclusion not because of the arguments they marshall in its support, but for independent reasons not explicitly identified. I conjecture that they countenance human rights because of the allegedly devastating implications of the contrary supposition, and therefore reason that if a belief in human rights must be correct, then there must be some good arguments in favor of so believing. Thus they are less likely to be critical of unsound arguments, convinced as they are that *some* good arguments must be available.

This conjecture explains why virtually all defenses of human rights share a similar tone. Typically philosophers begin with the conviction that there are human rights and define their project as "providing an account" of them. Few philosophers seem to approach this area without prejudice, allowing themselves to be carried wherever their arguments might take them. The ground of their antecedent conviction is rarely identified for critical scrutiny. It is this lacuna I now attempt to fill by speculating about (and then undermining) a number of reasons why so few philosophers exhibit skepticism about the existence of human rights.

What are the allegedly devastating consequences that follow from a repudiation of human rights? In what follows I identify three such fears, and argue either that the consequences, though unacceptable, are not genuine implications of my thesis, or that the consequences, though genuine implications of my thesis, are not unacceptable.

1. A philosopher who abandons human rights places himself squarely within a tradition with highly dubious historical credentials. He is understandably uncomfortable to join company with Nazis, racists, and sexists. This is not simply a "guilt by association" objection. The undeniable fact is that repudiations of human rights have frequently been employed by warped theorists to promote pernicious ideologies. Too much bad political theory has traded upon an "us persons versus those nonpersons" mentality. Much of the resistance to skepticism about human rights is an overreaction to such misguided political theories. The claim that some human beings are nonpersons is certain to earn the scorn of well-intentioned philosophers who will remind me of this disastrous legacy.

But these past exclusions of some human beings from the class of persons were unjust because they were arbitrary—no morally relevant characteristic(s) differentiated these unfortunate victims from the class of persons. But if a morally relevant ground for distinguishing between persons and nonpersons is identified, discriminatory treatment based upon it need not be unjust. Everyone, including human rights theorists, is committed to drawing the boundary between persons and nonpersons *somewhere*. Though admittedly much mischief has been done when this line has been drawn to exclude some human beings, the sad but incontrovertible fact is that some human beings do not (and will not) possess whatever characteristic(s) is used for locating this boundary. We should not overreact to the past tendency to cast the net of personhood too narrowly by casting it too broadly.

2. A study of the primary use to which human rights have been put suggests a second reason why philosophers have been largely uncritical of them. Human rights have been a cornerstone of American foreign policy, and function as an effective tool for denouncing political regimes which show a callous disregard for them. Torture, denials of religious freedoms, and racial discrimination are only a small sample of the widespread atrocities that evoke criticism in the name of human rights. If human rights do not exist, this humanitarian movement might have to be reinterpreted as shallow propaganda. The alternative to human rights might be thought to be a kind of relativism, where the only moral rights possessed by persons are products of their

particular social, political and legal systems. Thus a useful device for comparing and contrasting such systems would be lost.

Such fears, however, are grossly exaggerated. Nearly all the criticisms made about human rights violations throughout the world involve the maltreatment of persons. The victims of torture and religious oppression quite obviously satisfy the criteria of personhood, whatever they might be. Only occasionally do politicians decry the treatment of human beings who fall outside the ambit of personhood—the Karen Quinlans of the Soviet Union or South Africa rarely if ever attract our attention and sympathy. We can and should continue to protest the unjust treatment of persons, and to evaluate various social, political and legal systems to the extent that they exhibit respect for persons. But the existence of *human* rights is not required for this noble purpose. The crucial point is that the vast majority of sensible criticisms of unjust political systems can be preserved as intelligible even if it is conceded that no human rights exist.

3. Perhaps the most compelling reason for countenancing human rights is the fear of how it would be permissible to treat human nonpersons in the event that they are held to be without rights. Though it may be controversial whether human nonpersons are entitled to the same concern and respect as persons, the alternative that would treat them as mere things, to be used for our convenience and amusement, seems even more repellent. Does anyone seriously suggest that it would be permissible to breed and eat human nonpersons, provided that the public should develop a taste for their flesh? If not, how can such creatures be without rights?

There is admittedly something appealing in the conception of the moral universe as neatly divided into persons, who have rights and a high moral status, and nonpersons, who have neither. But this picture is an extreme oversimplification. There are any number of living (or extinct) creatures whose moral status is somewhere between persons and inanimate objects with no moral status whatever. Few philosophers have seriously undertaken to map these unchartered waters. There have been persistent attempts to fit intermediate cases into one or the other familiar category, as though the conclusion that Karen Quinlan is not a *person* with rights somehow entails that it is permissible to treat her in any way we wish. But our unwillingness to allow her to be eaten should not convince us that she must therefore be a person. Though she may lack rights altogether, she nonetheless occupies an intermediate category philosophers have seldom been willing to acknowledge, let alone to describe our obligations toward.

We must only be reminded of the earlier theory of rights to appreciate the moral limitations on the treatment of human nonpersons. Because creatures without rights lack the "trumps" of persons, it does not follow that they may be treated in any way we wish. Utilitarianism may be inadequate to govern our behavior toward persons, but it surely imposes *some* limitations on treatment apart from whether or not rights are violated. The supposition that an act cannot be wrongful unless it violates a right grossly exaggerates the role of rights in moral theory. Rights are multiplied indefinitely by the unwarranted assumption that all wrongful conduct necessarily violates one or more rights. A moral theory without rights may be impoverished, but it would not pronounce all actions permissible.[19]

Is utilitarianism adequate to govern our moral relations with nonpersons, human or otherwise? Insofar as the outcomes of utilitarian calculations can be specified with any confidence, the results do not seem especially counterintuitive. The familiar counterexamples to utilitarianism urged by rights theorists all demonstrate (at most) the injustice of subjecting *persons* to utilitarian treatment. If nonpersons are substituted for persons in these hypotheticals, it is arguable that most or all the injustice vanishes.

Let us examine some of these hypotheticals. One familiar example supposes that an innocent patient, in a hospital for a routine examination, is carved up by well-intentioned surgeons in order to distribute his various organs to five patients who will die unless these transplants are performed. We are supposed to recoil in horror at this disregard for the rights of the single patient, even though a net saving of lives is achieved. Let us alter this scenario so that sheep rather than human beings are involved. To avoid complications, suppose that the sheep are unowned, or that all have the same owner. (If one believes that sheep have rights, the example may be amended so that trees rather than sheep are involved.) Presumably in this case the fact that a net saving of lives is achieved is an excellent reason for killing the single sheep and distributing his organs. My argument is, admittedly, solely on an intuitive level. My point is that utilitarianism seems to provide a plausible account of our considered moral judgments in those cases in which no persons or rights are involved.

In short, numbers are decisive in our considered moral judgments about the proper treatment of nonpersons. It is sensible to burn a few trees in order to prevent the spread of a fire that would otherwise kill greater numbers. Presumably we would oppose an analogous practice if persons rather than trees were involved, for the rights of persons protect us from being sacrificed to the greater good. Of course, the permissibility of burning a few trees for the sake of greater numbers hardly entails that trees may be destroyed for no good reason. Utilitarianism, construed (*ex hypothesi*) as a moral theory without rights, does not condone the wanton killing of sentient creatures. Though trees may not have rights, it does not follow that they have no moral status whatever.

Now there may be little sympathy for believing that sheep or trees have rights, but the leap from sheep or trees to human nonpersons is certain to raise objections from human rights theorists. If the right to life is a human right, it should make no difference in these sorts of hypotheticals whether Karen Quinlan or (what I have been calling) a person is the single human whose organs are needed to save five persons. The transplants required to achieve a net saving of lives would violate her right to life, and thus would "trump" countervailing utilitarian considerations. It is only a slight exaggeration to suggest that the resolution of this hypothetical is the decisive basis on which the acceptance or rejection of my thesis depends. If one is willing to allow Karen Quinlan to be sacrificed to achieve a net saving of lives, while resisting that result when it is unquestionable that a *person* is involved, one has come a long way toward acceptance of the thesis that there are no human rights.

The suggestion that the above hypothetical represents a decisive test of my thesis is a slight exaggeration, primarily because of the uncertainty in predicting the outcomes of utilitarian calculations. Some utilitarians have claimed that the sacrifice of an innocent person to achieve a net saving of lives is impermissible *without* appeals to rights, and might make similar claims when Karen Quinlan is involved. Their reservations should be familiar to moral philosophers. They caution, e.g., that the sacrifice of innocent human beings sets a dangerous precedent for policies that promote disutility, or that no officials could be trusted to make such difficult determinations, etc. But *whatever* the outcomes of utilitarian calculations in such cases may be, my thesis (when coupled with the above theory of rights) requires that human nonpersons be treated accordingly. Thus my thesis does *not* relegate human nonpersons to the category of mere "things," with no moral status whatever. Their status is highly problematical, but no progress is made in this difficult determination by consulting treatises on human rights, which (at best) apply only to persons.

Philosophers have dreamed of specifying rights which human beings share regardless of their race, religion, sex or nationality. This dream is noble; most discriminations between human beings based on the above differences are unquestionably unjust. But when such philosophers attempted to answer the question of why all human beings possessed rights by specifying their ground or basis, they identified a characteristic(s) that is not shared by all human beings. Thus their projects are better understood as defenses of the rights of *persons* rather than of *human beings*. As so construed, their projects remain interesting and important. I have tried to show why philosophers should not lament the passing of *human* rights.[20]

Notes

1. For an indication of the difficulties that surround a failure to individuate rights, see Judith J. Thomson, "The Right to Privacy," *Philosophy and Public Affairs* 4 (1975): 295–314.

2. My argument against human rights fails if this assumption is false. There may be some temptation to construe human rights as "ideal directives" or "exhortations" to relevant parties to "do their best" for the values involved. See Joel Feinberg, *Social Philosophy.* (Englewood Cliffs, NJ: Prentice-Hall, 1973), pp. 71, 75, 86.

3. See Feinberg, "The Nature and Value of Rights," *Journal of Value Inquiry* 4 (1970):243–57.

4. Though I assume the adequacy of this theory of rights for present purposes, I believe it encounters difficulties. See my "Ronald Dworkin and the Right to Liberty," *Ethics* 90 (1979): 121–30.

5. It is difficult to avoid begging questions in drawing the distinction between persons and nonpersons. I do not suppose that nonpersons must lack what are sometimes called *special* rights, e.g., that they may be the intended beneficiaries of contractual duties. They lack only *general* rights. For an explication of this distinction, see H. L. A. Hart, "Are There Any Natural Rights?" *Philosophical Review* 64 (1955): 175–91.

6. Many of these proposals are refuted by Feinberg. See note 9, below.

7. See Mary Warren, "On the Moral and Legal Status of Abortion," *Monist* 57 (1973): 43–61.

8. Feinberg, *Social Philosophy,* p. 90.

9. *Ibid.,* p. 90.

10. *Ibid.,* p. 92.

11. *Ibid.,* p. 93.

12. *Ibid.,* p. 94.

13. *Ibid.*

14. Alan Gewirth, "The Basis and Content of Human Rights," *Nomos* 23 (1981): 119–47.

15. The fact that Gewirth employs a peculiar understanding of necessity becomes evident in his proposal to resolve conflicts of rights: "[O]ne right takes precedence over another if the good that is the object of the former right is more necessary for the possibility of action" (*ibid.,* p. 138). It is mysterious how necessity could admit of degrees.

16. Alan Gewirth, *Reason and Morality.* (Chicago: University of Chicago Press, 1978), p. 141.

17. Gewirth, "Basis and Content of Human Rights," p. 119.

18. Gewirth, *Reason and Morality,* p. 145. Elsewhere Gewirth "fudges" and predicts rights of all "normal" humans, p. 144.

19. See my own "On the Rights of Non-Persons," *Canadian Journal of Philosophy* 10 (1980): 607–22.

20. I would like to thank Kevin Michels, John Bronzon, and Tony Supino for much valuable assistance.

Why
There Are
Human Rights

ALAN GEWIRTH

At a time when respect for human rights is an almost universally acclaimed criterion of the moral legitimacy of societies, philosophers have been delivering critiques that call into question the very idea of human rights. I do not mention this correlation in order to deplore it; on the contrary, it reflects the philosophers' traditional function of subjecting received opinions to critical examination. It should be obvious that the issue is of first importance. If moral and political thinkers and publicists over the centuries have been mistaken in holding that all humans have certain moral rights, then some of the most significant aspects of public discourse, especially in the modern era, have been misguided. It is essential, therefore, to scrutinize carefully the contentions both of those who affirm and of those who deny the existence of human rights.

In *Reason and Morality*[1] and in a series of articles,[2] I have presented a theory of the basis and content of human rights. Central to the theory is an argument for the existence of human rights. The argument proceeds not assertorically but rather dialectically. I do not argue that because someone is human or has some humanly related property, such as rationality or capacity for agency or various needs, therefore he or she has rights. In my opinion, no such assertoric or straightforwardly naturalistic argument has been or can be successful.[3] Instead, I first point out that agency or action is the common subject matter of all morality and practice, and I then show that every actual or prospective agent logically must hold or accept that he and all other prospective agents have certain rights: namely, rights to the necessary conditions of

Alan Gewirth, "Why There Are Human Rights," *Social Theory and Practice,* 11, No. 2 (Summer, 1984), pp. 235–248. Reprinted with permission of *Social Theory and Practice.*

action and successful action in general. I call them *generic rights* because they are rights to have the generic features of action and successful action—freedom and well-being—characterize one's behavior.

The core of the argument is that if any agent were to deny that he has rights to these generic features or conditions, he would contradict himself. For he would then be in the position of holding that it is permissible for other persons to remove or interfere with his having what he must have in order to act. Thus he would be holding that he *need not have* what, as an agent, he has to hold that he *must have,* namely, the necessary conditions of action and successful action in general. For if he lacks these conditions, then he cannot act, either at all or with general chances of success in achieving the purposes for which he acts. Thus by this argument the existence of human rights is proved not directly or assertorically but rather dialectically, in terms of what logically must be claimed or accepted by every agent. I use, then, what I call a *dialectically necessary method.*

By the use of this method, the sense in which human rights have been shown to exist is not the same as the sense (or senses) in which material objects or mental states exist. Humans do not have human rights in the way in which they have legs or feelings. Instead, the existence of human rights is dialectically normative, in that every agent logically must accept a line of justificatory argument which establishes that he and all other actual or prospective agents have rights—that is, justified claims or entitlements—to the necessary conditions of action and successful action in general. Because every agent logically must accept the argument, the existence of human rights does indeed have a stringent rational justification, but only as agent-relative, that is, as having to be accepted by every agent; not as having an independent ontological status. Since, however, agency or action is the general context of all morality and practice, in that all moral and other practical precepts require actions of one sort or another, it follows that the existence of human rights has been shown to be normatively necessary and universal within the whole relevant context.

My theory has received considerable discussion and criticism. Some philosophers have said that my argument does not go through because agents need not *claim, hold,* or *accept* that they have any rights at all.[4] Other philosophers have said that my argument founders on the *"is-ought"* problem.[5] Still other philosophers have focused on the *distribution* of the generic rights; they have said that my argument has not established that the rights belong to *all* humans or to all humans equally.[6] I have elsewhere replied to most of these criticisms.[7]

Douglas N. Husak has presented a critique that focuses on the last, distributive question.[8] Declaring that "there is no sound argument establishing the existence of human rights" (p. 135), he has set forth a series of objections to my own argument. In view of the importance of the issues, I wish to offer the following clarifications in reply.

1. One objection concerns the linkage I have asserted between human rights and action. Husak says, "One might well wonder how the alleged human rights of freedom and well-being could be necessary conditions of purposive agency. Presumably a great part of the world's population is without these rights; is it therefore logically impossible for them to act—or to attain any of their purposes?" (p. 132).

Here, as in some of his other remarks, Husak has misunderstood my position. He has overlooked two main points in what I have said about the objects of human rights.

One point concerns their *substantive scope*. The objects of human rights are not only the necessary conditions of *action* but also the abilities and conditions needed for *successful action* in general. Thus I wrote that the generic rights "are generic in that they are rights to have the generic features of *successful* action characterize one's behavior" (*RM* 64; emphasis added); they are rights to "the necessary conditions not merely of one particular action as against another but of all successful action in general" (*RM* 77). These latter necessary conditions comprise both freedom and three different kinds of well-being. *Basic well-being* consists in having the essential preconditions of action, such as life, physical integrity, and mental equilibrium. *Nonsubtractive well-being* consists in having the abilities and conditions needed for maintaining undiminished one's general level of purpose-fulfillment and one's capabilities for particular actions; examples are not being lied to or stolen from. *Additive well-being* consists in having the abilities and conditions needed for increasing one's level of purpose-fulfillment and one's capabilities for particular actions; examples are education, self-esteem, and opportunities for acquiring wealth and income. The rights to these three levels of well-being are, respectively, *basic rights, nonsubtractive rights,* and *additive rights*. Not all of these rights, of course, have governments as their respondents or protectors. And the second and third classes of rights have as their objects the necessary conditions of successful action in general, not merely of action as such.

It was with a view to this complex substantive scope of the objects of human rights that I gave several answers to the objection that it is pointless for an agent to claim that he has these rights because, as an agent, he already has the generic features of action. One of my answers was directly pertinent to Husak's objection: "Not all actions are successful. Some actions do not manage to attain nonsubtractive and additive goods, and their agents may lack the abilities and conditions required for such attainment. Since well-being in its full scope consists in having these nonsubtractive and additive capabilities as well as the basic ones, the agent in claiming a right to well-being does not claim a right to what he necessarily has already" (*RM* 68).

Thus in these and other passages in *Reason and Morality,* I have already replied to Husak's objection. When he correctly says that "a great part of the world's population is without" human rights, this is not because they cannot act *at all* or achieve *any* of their purposes, but rather because they do not have the abilities and conditions required for *successful* action in general: such abilities and conditions as adequate health, education, income, and freedom from torture and other oppression. On my theory, such abilities and conditions of nonsubtractive and additive well-being are among the objects of human rights—something that Husak's objection fails to recognize.

A second point that Husak's objection overlooks is the *temporal scope* of the objects of human rights. Thus I wrote:

> Although these [i.e., freedom and basic well-being] necessarily pertain to every agent, a person is not always an agent. He claims the right to freedom and well-being not only as a present agent but also as a prospective agent; and in the latter

capacity he does not necessarily have freedom and well-being. There is always the possibility of interference with his agency and hence of his losing the freedom and well-being that agency requires. It is within this broader, prospective context that he, even as an agent, claims the right to have freedom and well-being (*RM* 68).

What has also been misunderstood in Husak's objection about "a great part of the world's population" being able "to act," then, is that the human rights are concerned with future or prospective as well as present agency: that persons *continue* to have the abilities and conditions—freedom and basic well-being—that are needed even for each particular action. Obviously, death, imprisonment, and starvation can operate to remove these elemental abilities and conditions. Hence, the human rights are rights to the necessary conditions of *prospective* as well as *present* agency (see also *RM* 111–112). Husak's objection has overlooked this complex substantive and temporal scope of the objects of human rights as I have dealt with them.

2. Husak's main objection bears on what he calls the "universality condition" for human rights: that such rights must be "shared by each and every human being" (p. 128). He says, "It is difficult to understand how agency can serve as the basis of human rights when, as Gewirth admits, capacities of agency vary among individuals" (p. 132). Involved in this objection are three distinct issues. They concern (a) the conceptual connection between human rights and the rights of agency; (b) the relation of human rights to humans who lack all capacity for agency; and (c) the relation between the equality of human rights and various humans' unequal capacities for agency.

2a. Do humans have human rights simply *qua* human or rather *qua* purposive agents? Since I hold that the human rights have as their objects the capacities for agency and successful agency, Husak says that on my account "we do not possess human rights simply in virtue of our humanity but rather in virtue of our capacity for purposive agency" (p. 133). He here overlooks that I have explicitly dealt with this issue: "When it is said that the right to be relieved from economic deprivation and the correlative duty pertain to all persons insofar as they are prospective purposive agents, this does not violate the condition that for human rights to be had one must only be human, as against fulfilling some more restrictive description. As was indicated earlier, all normal humans are prospective purposive agents; the point of introducing this description is only to call attention to the aspect of being human that most directly generates the rights to freedom and well-being" (*RM* 317. I shall discuss the qualification about "normal" below).

Thus there is no disconnection, as Husk says there is, between possessing rights "simply in virtue of our humanity" and possessing rights "in virtue of our capacity for purposive agency." For, so far as concerns the having of human rights, the salient aspect of being human is the capacity for purposive agency.

2b. But what of those humans who completely lack the capacity for purposive agency? Isn't this a clear case where being human does *not* confer rights to, or rights in virtue of, purposive agency? This indeed is Husak's central argument against the existence of human rights. He says, "The key premise in the argument is that no morally relevant characteristic(s) that could provide the basis or ground of such rights is possessed by all human beings" (p. 128). He goes on to apply this premise to a by now familiar example. "Since Karen Quinlan is not a purposive agent in any ordinary sense, agency could not provide a foundation for the rights of *all* human beings unless the capacity for purposive agency is given a most peculiar interpretation" (p. 132).

In dealing with this objection, we must keep in mind the dialectical character of my argument for rights. This is obscured in Husak's statement about "agency('s)" being able to "provide a foundation for the rights of *all* human beings." I do not argue directly from agency to human rights; rather, I argue from what every actual or prospective agent must *hold* or *accept* about his and all other agents' having rights. Now what directly emerges from this argument is that every agent logically must hold or accept that all other prospective agents, as well as himself, have the generic rights. But every agent logically must also recognize that when various entities, including not only other humans but also certain animals, have in lesser degree the practical abilities that enter into agency, such entities also have rights in correspondingly lesser degrees. I call this the *Principle of Proportionality*. This principle needs much clarification, which I have tried to provide (*RM* 120 ff.).

In its application to such a limiting case as that of Karen Quinlan, the Principle of Proportionality establishes that there are at least two respects in which she, as a human being, has[9] rights that are based upon agency. One bears on the "prospective" aspect I mentioned before. Insofar as there is any possibility that she may recover to the extent of being physically capable of action (and the medical research Husak refers to in his paper is relevant here), she has rights that such potential abilities of her agency be protected.

Second, insofar as Quinlan *was* a human agent, and is still a living human, she has the right to life and to any other goods that are conditions of agency which she is capable of having. Because of her coma, these goods are, of course, severely limited. But if, for example, she needs and can absorb nourishment, then, by virtue of her past membership in the class of agents and her present ability to benefit from action-enabling goods, she still has a human right to these goods. In this regard, her case differs from that of beasts who never were or will be agents in the senses I have indicated, although they too must be held to have certain rights in virtue of certain of their similarities to human purposive agents (*RM* 144–45).

2c. These considerations also bear on the less than completely limiting cases of humans who do have the capacities for purposive agency, but in reduced degrees. The issue here is that of the equality of human rights. Although Husak says he will not deal with this issue (p. 126), he in fact does so when, referring to my theory, he says: "Even if it were the case that all human beings were purposive agents in some limited sense, to grant rights in proportion to agency is not merely to grant varying degrees of the same human right; it is tantamount to countenancing different rights with distinct duties" (p. 133).

To begin with, let us note Husak's statement that "it is unclear what is meant by the claim that a given right is possessed equally or unequally" (p. 126). I have dealt with this point, albeit briefly, in discussing Aristotle's claim that "superior" agents "should have greater rights to freedom and well-being: more power to choose and control their own and other persons' participation in transactions and more means of fulfilling their purposes" (*RM* 120). Thus inequalities in the possession of rights bear crucially on the extent to which persons have the objects of the rights; and, so far as concerns the generic rights, these objects consist especially in the abilities and conditions that are proximately needed for agency and successful agency in general, as in my references, just given, to freedom and well-being.

Now I do hold that, in a certain respect, the human rights are distributed unequally among humans. But this inequality derives only from the fact that some humans either cannot exercise certain rights at all because they lack the relevant specific practical abilities or cannot exercise the rights without harming themselves or other humans in their capacities for agency. Thus the inequality of the possession of rights still entails that all humans possess rights based upon agency; but their possession of the rights varies insofar, and only insofar, as it bears on the possession of the exercise of the abilities of agency. For example, the reason why the freedom-rights of humans with severe mental deficiencies should be restricted is that, if it is not, they may use their freedom to inflict severe harm on themselves or other humans. And, with regard to the right to education, such humans may lack the ability to exercise the right.

I made this point in discussing the Principle of Proportionality: "Although children, mentally deficient persons, and animals do not have the generic rights in the full-fledged way normal human adults have them, members of these groups approach having the generic rights in varying degrees, depending on the degree to which they have the requisite abilities. The reason for this proportionality is found in the relation between the generic abilities of action and the having of purposes one wants to fulfill. *For the lesser the abilities, the less one is able to fulfill one's purposes without endangering oneself and other persons*" (*RM* 122; emphasis added). Thus the inequalities of human rights are based upon the degrees to which exercise of the rights is compatible with protecting the abilities of agency on the part of the humans affected.

In an important respect, therefore, these inequalities are themselves based upon a more fundamental equality of human rights. It is thus incorrect to say, as Husak does, that to allow such inequalities of possession of the objects of certain rights "is tantamount to countenancing different rights with distinct duties" (p. 133). For the unequal extents to which different humans have the objects of various rights are grounded on an equal concern for the abilities of agency of all humans. Just as the equality of human rights is compatible with some humans' being given more food or protection than other humans, when the former have a greater need for such objects in order to sustain their basic well-being, so too the lesser freedom allowed to some mentally deficient humans is justified by an equal concern for the basic well-being of them and of all other humans.

To establish that on my theory all humans do not have the same rights, Husak asks us to suppose "that Karen Quinlan and (what I have been calling) a person are in need of a life-saving transfusion, and there is only enough blood available to save one"

(p. 133). Husak assumes, of course, that in such a case the "person's" right to life should be fulfilled rather than Quinlan's right. But this does not prove that the two humans do not have the same right to life. For the identical problem would arise if there were only enough blood available to save the life of one of two "persons." The fact that a choice must be made when both lives cannot be saved does not establish that both "persons" do not have the same right to life. For a claim-right entails an "ought," which in turn entails "can." The fulfillment of "oughts" or duties and hence of the correlative rights is conditioned by any unavoidable limitations of relevant abilities. But here it is not the rights that are different but rather the abilities to fulfill the rights.

Nevertheless, Husak is correct in thinking that in the case he supposes, the "person's" life should be saved rather than Quinlan's. But this is because the person has more capabilities for action than does Quinlan, and the point of human rights is to protect and fulfill these capabilities. The Principle of Proportionality applies here.

3. It must be emphasized that, in my theory, inequalities or diminutions of rights are justified only when the capabilities for agency are lacking beyond a bare minimum. It is only in such cases that the Principle of Proportionality applies. In all other cases, where there are normal human agents, they have the human rights equally and in full.

Husak says that I "fudge" when I predicate rights of "all 'normal' humans" (p. 140). But there is no "fudging" here. By "normal" I mean actual or prospective agents who have "the practical abilities of the generic features of action: the abilities to control one's behavior by one's unforced choice, to have knowledge of relevant circumstances, and to reflect on one's purposes" (*RM* 122). It is indeed true that these abilities may vary in degree among different agents. But there are two considerations that establish that this variation does not ground any inequalities in the distribution of human rights.

One consideration is substantive. To be a normal human agent, one needs to have only the minimal rationality to which I referred above. Thus, for example, the practical abilities of agency include the ability to have knowledge of relevant circumstances; but this knowledge need not be especially profound or extensive; it is "knowledge of proximate particular circumstances, which ordinarily does not require any special expertise" (*RM* 260). This point goes back to Aristotle, who held that for action to be voluntary the agent must know "who he is, what he is doing, what or whom he is acting on. . . ."[10] Thus "normality" has a clear empirical meaning when applied to agents, and it is satisfied by all agents who have the minimal abilities in question.

The same minimalist consideration also applies to the rationality of the agent who traces or can trace the argument which concludes that he must hold or accept that he has the generic rights:

I shall henceforth refer to the agent who accepts or grasps such entailments as a *rational agent*. It is to be noted that the criterion of "rational" here is a minimal deductive one, involving consistency or the avoidance of self-contradiction in ascertaining or accepting what is logically involved in one's acting for purposes and in the associated concepts.

In addition to such deductive rationality, a certain minimal inductive rationality may also be attributed to the rational agent (*RM* 46).

I also emphasize at many other points the "minimal" character of the rationality required of the agent who is assumed to be tracing or following the argument (*RM* 28, 138, 217, 363). And I note the statistical "normality" of the capacity for this minimal rationality: "All normal human beings have the capacity to be rational in this strict sense, in that they have, at least in an elementary way, the empirical and logical abilities in question" (*RM* 138).

Thus, because the practical abilities needed for being a "normal" agent and hence for having the generic or human rights are of this minimal sort, the rights are had equally by all normal human agents, and variations in the degree of having the abilities do not justify any inequalities in the distribution of the rights.

A second consideration that establishes this equality of human rights, despite the inequality of various agents' practical abilities, is dialectical. The ground on which every actual or prospective agent logically must hold or accept that he has the generic rights is not that he has certain practical abilities (let alone superior abilities) but rather that he has purposes he wants to fulfill by acting. For if he had no purposes, he would claim no rights of agency. On the other hand, he would claim these rights even if he lacked superior intelligence or other superior practical abilities so long as he was a prospective purposive agent (see *RM* 109 ff.). It is hence by virtue of being a prospective agent who wants to fulfill his purposes that each agent, including even those with superior practical abilities, logically must hold that he has the generic rights.

It must be kept in mind that, beyond the minimal rationality and practical abilities just referred to, the whole argument for the existence and possession of human rights is dialectical, not assertoric. Thus what is established by the dialectical grounding of each agent's right-claim in his having of purposes or purposiveness is that the generic rights are had equally by all prospective purposive agents. For, in relation to the claim to have the generic rights, being such an agent "is an absolute quality, not varying in degree. The purposiveness in question does not itself vary in degree; it is not affected, for example, by whether one has more or fewer purposes in view, by whether one has them more or less intensely, by whether or not one organizes them under a few leading purposes, and so forth" (*RM* 123). Because of this generality of the purposiveness that grounds the generic rights-claims, the status of being an actual or prospective agent who has purposes he wants to fulfill serves to ground an equal distribution of the generic or human rights to all such agents. Here again inequalities of practical abilities do not justify inequalities of human rights because, once the minimal degree of normality and rationality is had, what grounds the claiming of rights is not the abilities themselves but rather the desire to achieve one's purposes, whatever they may be. And this desire is equally predictable of all normal human agents.

It is perhaps worth repeating here that the Principle of Proportionality applies only to the levels of approach to normal human agency, but not to any inequalities that are found within normal human agency itself. The class of normal human agents and the generic features of action are determined by general rational considerations, not by the dialectically necessary method. But once this class is determined, the dialectically necessary method then takes over (see *RM* 44, 123), and the method directly operates within this class in tracing what logically must be claimed or accepted by every normal agent. As we have seen, the claim to rights is based on the egalitarian consideration of the having of purposes by such agents.

The grounding of human rights in purposive agency, once it is understood in the ways indicated above, is superior to Husak's attempt to base rights on "personhood." He says: "Membership in the class of persons, however, is determined by moral criteria. By definition, persons possess a higher moral status (perhaps conferred by the enjoyment of rights) than nonpersons" (p. 127). There are at least two interrelated difficulties here. One is the vagueness of "moral criteria." *Which* moral criteria: Aristotle's, Nietzsche's, Kant's, Bentham's, Spencer's, Schweitzer's? Each of these would yield different classes of "persons," and hence different possessors of rights.

Second, if membership in the class of persons is determined by moral criteria, then what determines the content of moral criteria? It cannot be the rights (or needs, or other characteristics) of "persons," for this would be circular. And such nondeontological moral theories as utilitarianism have notorious difficulties in accounting for moral rights, and hence for membership in the class of "persons." Thus, to avoid begging the question, the class of those who are to be accounted right-holders must be delineated without reference to moral criteria, and then an argument must be given to establish that the members of this class do indeed have moral rights. This is what I have tried to do by dialectically deriving moral criteria, including criteria of the possession of moral rights, from agency and the claims that logically must be made or accepted by all agents. In this dialectical way, the existence of human rights is established and, with it, the understanding of how the humans whom Husak calls "nonpersons" also have moral rights.

I conclude, then, that Husak has not made out his case against the existence of human rights or against my argument for that existence. That there are human rights can be proved by a line of argument that avoids the difficulties he has tried to raise. The argument is not simple; it cannot be if it is to avoid these and other familiar difficulties. But, while welcoming criticism, I wish to urge that future critics of my argument try to take fuller account of its complexities than Husak has here succeeded in doing.

Notes

1. Alan Gewirth, *Reason and Morality.* (Chicago: University of Chicago Press, 1978). Page references in the text preceded by *RM* are to this book.

2. Many of these articles have been collected in Alan Gewirth, *Human Rights: Essays on Justification and Applications.* (Chicago: University of Chicago Press, 1982). Others of my relevant articles are cited below, notes 3 and 7.

3. See *Reason and Morality,* pp.159–61; *Human Rights: Essays on Justification and Applications,* pp. 22–24, 48–50, 54; and "The Epistemology of Human Rights," *Social Philosophy and Policy* 1 (1984): 5–8.

4. See Edward Regis, Jr., "Gewirth on Rights," *Journal of Philosophy* 78 (1981): 786–94; Loren Lomasky, "Gewirth's Generation of Rights," *Philosophical Quarterly* 31 (1981): 248–53; Alasdair MacIntyre, *After Virtue*. (Notre Dame, IN: University of Notre Dame Press, 1981), pp. 64–68; Martin P. Golding, "From Prudence to Rights: A Critique," in *Nomos XXIII: Human Rights*, J. R. Pennock and J. W. Chapman (Eds.). (New York: New York University Press, 1981), pp. 165–74; R. M. Hare, "Do Agents Have to Be Moralists?" in *Gewirth's Ethical Rationalism*, Edward Regis Jr. (Ed.). (Chicago: University of Chicago Press, 1984), pp. 52–58; Kai Nielsen, "Against Ethical Rationalism," in *Gewirth's Ethical Rationalism*, pp.59–83.

5. Jeffrey Paul, "Gewirth's Solution to the 'Is-Ought' Problem," *The Personalist* 60 (1979): 442–47; Paul Allen III, "A Critique of Gewirth's 'Is-Ought' Derivation," *Ethics* 92 (1982):211–26; W. D. Hudson, "The 'Is-Ought' Problem Resolved?," in *Gewirth's Ethical Rationalism*, Regis (Ed.), pp. 108–27.

6. See Richard B. Friedman, "The Basis of Human Rights: A Criticism of Gewirth's Theory," in *Nomos XXIII: Human Rights*, Pennock and Chapman, (Eds.), pp. 148–57; Arval A. Morris, "A Differential Theory of Human Rights," in *Nomos XXIII, ibid.,* pp. 158–64; Aaron Ben-Zeev, "Who Is a Rational Agent?," *Canadian Journal of Philosophy* 12 (1982): 647–62; James F. Hill, "Are Marginal Agents 'Our Recipients'?," in *Gewirth's Ethical Rationalism*, Regis, (Ed.), pp. 180–91.

7. My replies to the items listed in notes 4 to 6 above have appeared in the following places: (*Note 4*) to Regis: "Why Agents Must Claim Rights: A Reply," *Journal of Philosophy* 79 (1982):403–10; to MacIntyre: "Rights and Virtues," *Analyse und Kritik* (West Germany) 6 (1984): 28–48; to Golding: "Addendum: Replies to Some Criticisms," in *Human Rights* (above, n. 2), pp. 67–76; to Hare and Nielsen: "Replies to My Critics," in *Gewirth's Ethical Rationalism*, Regis, (Ed.), pp. 205–15. (*Note 5*) to Hudson: "Replies to My Critics," in *Gewirth's Ethical Rationalism*, pp. 222–225. (*Note 6*) to Friedman and Morris: "Addendum: Replies to Some Criticisms," in *Human Rights* (above, n. 2), pp. 76–78; to Ben-Zeev: "On Rational Agency as the Basis of Moral Equality: Reply to Ben-Zeev," *Canadian Journal of Philosophy* 12 (1982): 667–72; to Hill: "Replies to My Critics," in *Gewirth's Ethical Rationalism*, pp. 225–27.

8. Douglas N. Husak, "Why There Are No Human Rights," *Social Theory and Practice* 10 (1984): 125–41. Page references in the text with no other indication of source are to this article.

9. This was written before Karen Quinlan's death. Nevertheless, I have let the text stand unchanged because the principles here invoked remain the same.

10. Aristotle, *Nicomachean Ethics* III.1. 1111a2 ff.

Appendix A: Major International Human Rights Documents

Universal Declaration of Human Rights

Preamble

Whereas recognition of the inherent dignity and of the equal and inalienable rights of all members of the human family is the foundation of freedom, justice and peace in the world,

Whereas disregard and contempt for human rights have resulted in barbarous acts which have outraged the conscience of mankind, and the advent of a world in which human beings shall enjoy freedom of speech and belief and freedom from fear and want has been proclaimed as the highest aspiration of the common people,

Whereas it is essential, if man is not to be compelled to have recourse, as a last resort, to rebellion against tyranny and oppression, that human rights should be protected by the rule of law,

Whereas it is essential to promote the development of friendly relations between nations,

Whereas the peoples of the United Nations have in the Charter reaffirmed their faith in fundamental human rights, in the dignity and worth of the human person and in the equal rights of men and women and have determined to promote social progress and better standards of life in larger freedom,

Whereas Member States have pledged themselves to achieve, in co-operation with the United Nations, the promotion of universal respect for and observance of human rights and fundamental freedoms,

Whereas a common understanding of these rights and freedoms is of the greatest importance for the full realization of this pledge.

Now, Therefore,

The General Assembly

proclaims

This universal declaration of human rights as a common standard of achievement for all peoples and all nations, to the end that every individual and every organ of society, keeping this Declaration constantly in mind, shall strive by teaching and education to promote respect for these rights and freedoms and by progressive measures, national and international, to secure their universal and effective recognition and observance, both among the peoples of Member States themselves and among the peoples of territories under their jurisdiction.

Article 1

All human beings are born free and equal in dignity and rights. They are endowed with reason and conscience and should act towards one another in a spirit of brotherhood.

Article 2

Everyone is entitled to all the rights and freedoms set forth in this Declaration, without distinction of any kind, such as race, colour, sex, language, religion, political or other opinion, national or social origin, property, birth or other status.

Furthermore, no distinction shall be made on the basis of the political, jurisdictional or international status of the country or territory to which a person belongs, whether it be independent, trust, non-self-governing or under any other limitation of sovereignty.

Article 3

Everyone has the right to life, liberty and security of person.

Article 4

No one shall be held in slavery or servitude; slavery and the slave trade shall be prohibited in all their forms.

Article 5

No one shall be subjected to torture or to cruel, inhuman or degrading treatment or punishment.

Article 6

Everyone has the right to recognition everywhere as a person before the law.

Article 7

All are equal before the law and are entitled without any discrimination to equal protection of the law. All are entitled to equal protection against any discrimination in violation of this Declaration and against any incitement to such discrimination.

Article 8

Everyone has the right to an effective remedy by the competent national tribunals for acts violating the fundamental rights granted him by the constitution or by law.

Article 9

No one shall be subjected to arbitrary arrest, detention or exile.

Article 10

Everyone is entitled in full equality to a fair and public hearing by an independent and impartial tribunal, in the determination of his rights and obligations and of any criminal charge against him.

Article 11

1. Everyone charged with a penal offence has the right to be presumed innocent until proved guilty according to law in a public trial at which he has had all the guarantees necessary for his defence.
2. No one shall be held guilty of any penal offence on account of any act or omission which did not constitute a penal offence, under national or international law, at the time when it was committed. Nor shall a heavier penalty be imposed than the one that was applicable at the time the penal offence was committed.

Article 12

No one shall be subjected to arbitrary interference with his privacy, family, home or correspondence, nor to attacks upon his honour and reputation. Everyone has the right to the protection of the law against such interference or attacks.

Article 13

1. Everyone has the right to freedom of movement and residence within the borders of each state.
2. Everyone has the right to leave any country, including his own, and to return to his country.

Article 14

1. Everyone has the right to seek and to enjoy in other countries asylum from persecution.
2. This right may not be invoked in the case of prosecutions genuinely arising from non-political crimes or from acts contrary to the purposes and principles of the United Nations.

Article 15

1. Everyone has the right to a nationality.
2. No one shall be arbitrarily deprived of his nationality nor denied the right to change his nationality.

Article 16

1. Men and women of full age, without any limitation due to race, nationality or religion, have the right to marry and to found a family. They are entitled to equal rights as to marriage, during marriage and at its dissolution.
2. Marriage shall be entered into only with the free and full consent of the intending spouses.
3. The family is the natural and fundamental group unit of society and is entitled to protection by society and the State.

Article 17

1. Everyone has the right to own property alone as well as in association with others.
2. No one shall be arbitrarily deprived of his property.

Article 18

Everyone has the right to freedom of thought, conscience and religion; this right includes freedom to change his religion or belief, and freedom, either alone or in community with others and in public or private, to manifest his religion or belief in teaching, practice, worship and observance.

Article 19

Everyone has the right to freedom of opinion and expression; this right includes freedom to hold opinions without interference and to seek, receive and impart information and ideas through any media and regardless of frontiers.

Article 20

1. Everyone has the right to freedom of peaceful assembly and association.
2. No one may be compelled to belong to an association.

Article 21

1. Everyone has the right to take part in the government of his country, directly or through freely chosen representatives.
2. Everyone has the right of equal access to public service in his country.
3. The will of the people shall be the basis of the authority of government; this will shall be expressed in periodic and genuine elections which shall be by universal and equal suffrage and shall be held by secret vote or by equivalent free voting procedures.

Article 22

Everyone, as a member of society, has the right to social security and is entitled to realization, through national effort and international co-operation and in accordance with the organization and resources of each State, of the economic, social and cultural rights indispensable for his dignity and the free development of his personality.

Article 23

1. Everyone has the right to work, to free choice of employment, to just and favour-able conditions of work and to protection against unemployment.
2. Everyone, without any discrimination, has the right to equal pay for equal work.
3. Everyone who works has the right to just and favourable remuneration ensuring for himself and his family an existence worthy of human dignity, and supple-mented, if necessary, by other means of social protection.
4. Everyone has the right to form and to join trade unions for the protection of his interests.

Article 24

Everyone has the right to rest and leisure, including reasonable limitation of working hours and periodic holidays with pay.

Article 25

1. Everyone has the right to a standard of living adequate for the health and well-being of himself and of his family, including food, clothing, housing and medical care and necessary social services, and the right to security in the event of unemployment, sickness, disability, widowhood, old age or other lack of livelihood in circum-stances beyond his control.
2. Motherhood and childhood are entitled to special care and assistance. All children, whether born in or out of wedlock, shall enjoy the same social protection.

Article 26

1. Everyone has the right to education. Education shall be free, at least in the elementary and fundamental stages. Elementary education shall be compulsory. Technical and professional education shall be made generally available and higher education shall be equally accessible to all on the basis of merit.
2. Education shall be directed to the full development of the human personality and to the strengthening of respect for human rights and fundamental freedoms. It shall promote understanding, tolerance and friendship among all nations, racial or religious groups, and shall further the activities of the United Nations for the maintenance of peace.
3. Parents have a prior right to choose the kind of education that shall be given to their children.

Article 27

1. Everyone has the right freely to participate in the cultural life of the community, to enjoy the arts and to share in scientific advancement and its benefits.
2. Everyone has the right to the protection of the moral and material interests resulting from any scientific, literary or artistic production of which he is the author.

Article 28

Everyone is entitled to a social and international order in which the rights and freedoms set forth in this Declaration can be fully realized.

Article 29

1. Everyone has duties to the community in which alone the free and full development of his personality is possible.
2. In the exercise of his rights and freedoms, everyone shall be subject only to such limitations as are determined by law solely for the purpose of securing due recognition and respect for the rights and freedoms of others and of meeting the just requirements of morality, public order and the general welfare in a democratic society.
3. These rights and freedoms may in no case be exercised contrary to the purposes and principles of the United Nations.

Article 30

Nothing in this Declaration may be interpreted as implying for any State, group or person any right to engage in any activity or to perform any act aimed at the destruction of any of the rights and freedoms set forth herein.

International Covenant on Civil and Political Rights, 1966

Preamble

The States Parties to the present Covenant,

Considering that, in accordance with the principles proclaimed in the Charter of the United Nations, recognition of the inherent dignity and of the equal and inalienable rights of all members of the human family is the foundation of freedom, justice and peace in the world,

Recognizing that these rights derive from the inherent dignity of the human person,

Recognizing that, in accordance with the Universal Declaration of Human Rights, the ideal of free human beings enjoying civil and political freedom and freedom from fear and want can only be achieved if conditions are created whereby everyone may enjoy his civil and political rights, as well as his economic, social and cultural rights,

Considering the obligation of States under the Charter of the United Nations to promote universal respect for, and observance of, human rights and freedoms,

Realizing that the individual, having duties to other individuals and to the community to which he belongs, is under a responsibility to strive for the promotion and observance of the rights recognized in the present Covenant,

Agree upon the following articles:

PART I

Article 1

1. All peoples have the right of self-determination. By virtue of that right they freely determine their political status and freely pursue their economic, social and cultural development.
2. All peoples may, for their own ends, freely dispose of their natural wealth and resources without prejudice to any obligations arising out of international economic co-operation, based upon the principle of mutual benefit, and international law. In no case may a people be deprived of its own means of subsistence.
3. The States Parties to the present Covenant, including those having responsibility for the administration of Non-Self-Governing and Trust Territories, shall promote the realization of the right of self-determination, and shall respect that right, in conformity with the provisions of the Charter of the United Nations.

PART II

Article 2

1. Each State Party to the present Covenant undertakes to respect and to ensure to all individuals within its territory and subject to its jurisdiction the rights recognized in the present Covenant, without distinction of any kind, such as race, colour, sex, language, religion, political or other opinion, national or social origin, property, birth or other status.

2. Where not already provided for by existing legislative or other measures, each State Party to the present Covenant undertakes to take the necessary steps, in accordance with its constitutional processes and with the provisions of the present Covenant, to adopt such legislative or other measures as may be necessary to give effect to the rights recognized in the present Covenant.

3. Each State Party to the present Covenant undertakes:
   a. To ensure that any person whose rights or freedoms as herein recognized are violated shall have an effective remedy, notwithstanding that the violation has been committed by persons acting in an official capacity;
   b. To ensure that any person claiming such a remedy shall have his right thereto determined by competent judicial, administrative or legislative authorities, or by any other competent authority provided for by the legal system of the state, and to develop the possibilities of judicial remedy;
   c. To ensure that the competent authorities shall enforce such remedies when granted.

Article 3

The States Parties to the present Covenant undertake to ensure the equal right of men and women to the enjoyment of all civil and political rights set forth in the present Covenant.

Article 4

1. In time of public emergency which threatens the life of the nation and the existence of which is officially proclaimed, the States Parties to the present Covenant may take measures derogating from their obligations under the present Covenant to the extent strictly required by the exigencies of the situation, provided that such measures are not inconsistent with their other obligations under international law and do not involve discrimination solely on the ground of race, colour, sex, language, religion or social origin.

2. No derogation from Articles 6, 7, 8 (paragraphs 1 and 2), 11, 15, 16 and 18 may be made under this provision.

3. Any State Party to the present Covenant availing itself of the right of derogation shall immediately inform the other States Parties to the present Covenant, through the intermediary of the Secretary-General of the United Nations of the provisions from which it has derogated and of the reasons by which it was actuated. A further

communication shall be made, through the same intermediary on the date on which it terminates such derogation.

Article 5

1. Nothing in the present Covenant may be interpreted as implying for any State, group or person any right to engage in any activity or perform any act aimed at the destruction of any of the rights and freedoms recognized herein or at their limitation to a greater extent than is provided for in the present Covenant.

2. There shall be no restriction upon or derogation from any of the fundamental human rights recognized or existing in any State Party to the present Covenant pursuant to law, conventions, regulations or custom on the pretext that the present Covenant does not recognize such rights or that it recognizes them to a lesser extent.

PART III

Article 6

1. Every human being has the inherent right to life. This right shall be protected by law. No one shall be arbitrarily deprived of his life.

2. In countries which have not abolished the death penalty, sentence of death may be imposed only for the most serious crimes in accordance with the law in force at the time of the commission of the crime and not contrary to the provisions of the present Covenant and to the Convention on the Prevention and Punishment of the Crime of Genocide. This penalty can only be carried out pursuant to a final judgment rendered by a competent court.

3. When deprivation of life constitutes the crime of genocide, it is understood that nothing in this article shall authorize any State Party to the present Covenant to derogate in any way from any obligation assumed under the provisions of the Convention on the Prevention and Punishment of the Crime of Genocide.

4. Anyone sentenced to death shall have the right to seek pardon or commutation of the sentence. Amnesty, pardon or commutation of the sentence of death may be granted in all cases.

5. Sentence of death shall not be imposed for crimes committed by persons below eighteen years of age and shall not be carried out on pregnant women.

6. Nothing in this article shall be invoked to delay or to prevent the abolition of capital punishment by any State Party to the present Covenant.

Article 7

No one shall be subjected to torture or to cruel, inhuman or degrading treatment or punishment. In particular, no one shall be subjected without his free consent to medical or scientific experimentation.

Article 8

1. No one shall be held in slavery; slavery and the slave-trade in all their forms shall be prohibited.
2. No one shall be held in servitude.
3. a. No one shall be required to perform forced or compulsory labour;
   b. Paragraph 3 (a) shall not be held to preclude, in countries where imprisonment with hard labour may be imposed as a punishment for a crime, the performance of hard labour in pursuance of a sentence to such punishment by a competent court;
   c. For the purpose of this paragraph the term "forced or compulsory labour" shall not include:
      i. Any work or service, not referred to in sub-paragraph (b), normally required of a person who is under detention in consequence of a lawful order of a court, or of a person during conditional release from such detention;
      ii. Any service of a military character and, in countries where conscientious objection is recognized, any national service required by law of conscientious objectors;
      iii. Any service exacted in cases of emergency or calamity threatening the life or well-being of the community;
      iv. Any work or service which forms part of normal civil obligations.

Article 9

1. Everyone has the right to liberty and security of person. No one shall be subjected to arbitrary arrest or detention. No one shall be deprived of his liberty except on such grounds and in accordance with such procedures as are established by law.
2. Anyone who is arrested shall be informed, at the time of arrest, of the reasons for his arrest and shall be promptly informed of any charges against him.
3. Anyone arrested or detained on a criminal charge shall be brought promptly before a judge or other officer authorized by law to exercise judicial power and shall be entitled to trial within a reasonable time or to release. It shall not be the general rule that persons awaiting trial shall be detained in custody, but release may be subject to guarantees to appear for trial, at any other stage of the judicial proceedings, and, should occasion arise, for execution of the judgment.
4. Anyone who is deprived of his liberty by arrest or detention shall be entitled to take proceedings before a court, in order that that court may decide without delay on the lawfulness of his detention and order his release if the detention is not lawful.
5. Anyone who has been the victim of unlawful arrest or detention shall have an enforceable right to compensation.

Article 10

1. All persons deprived of their liberty shall be treated with humanity and with respect for the inherent dignity of the human person.

2. a. Accused persons shall, save in exceptional circumstances, be segregated from convicted persons and shall be subject to separate treatment appropriate to their status as unconvicted persons;

   b. Accused juvenile persons shall be separated from adults and brought as speedily as possible for adjudication.

3. The penitentiary system shall comprise treatment of prisoners the essential aim of which shall be their reformation and social rehabilitation. Juvenile offenders shall be segregated from adults and be accorded treatment appropriate to their age and legal status.

Article 11

No one shall be imprisoned merely on the ground of inability to fulfill a contractual obligation.

Article 12

1. Everyone lawfully within the territory of a State shall, within that territory, have the right to liberty of movement and freedom to choose his residence.

2. Everyone shall be free to leave any country, including his own.

3. The above-mentioned rights shall not be subject to any restrictions except those which are provided by law, are necessary to protect national security, public order (*ordre public*), public health or morals or the rights and freedoms of others, and are consistent with the other rights recognized in the present Covenant.

4. No one shall be arbitrarily deprived of the right to enter his own country.

Article 13

An alien lawfully in the territory of a State Party to the present Covenant may be expelled therefrom only in pursuance of a decision reached in accordance with law and shall, except where compelling reasons of national security otherwise require, be allowed to submit the reasons against his expulsion and to have his case reviewed by, and be represented for the purpose before, the competent authority or a person or persons especially designated by the competent authority.

Article 14

1. All persons shall be equal before the courts and tribunals. In the determination of any criminal charge against him, or of his rights and obligations in a suit at law, everyone shall be entitled to a fair and public hearing by a competent, independent and impartial tribunal established by law. The Press and the public may be excluded from all or part of a trial for reasons of morals, public order (*ordre public*) or national security in a democratic society, or when the interest of the private lives of the parties so requires, or to the extent strictly necessary in the opinion of the court in special circumstances where publicity would prejudice the interests of justice; but any judgment rendered in a criminal case or in a suit at law shall be

made public except where the interest of juvenile persons otherwise requires or the proceedings concern matrimonial disputes or the guardianship of children.

2. Everyone charged with a criminal offence shall have the right to be presumed innocent until proved guilty according to law.

3. In the determination of any criminal charge against him, everyone shall be entitled to the following minimum guarantees, in full equality:

   a. To be informed promptly and in detail in a language which he understands of the nature and cause of the charge against him;

   b. To have adequate time and facilities for the preparation of his defence and to communicate with counsel of his own choosing;

   c. To be tried without undue delay;

   d. To be tried in his presence, and to defend himself in person or through legal assistance of his own choosing; to be informed, if he does not have legal assistance, of this right; and to have legal assistance assigned to him, in any case where the interests of justice so require, and without payment by him in any such case if he does not have sufficient means to pay for it;

   e. To examine, or have examined, the witnesses against him and to obtain the attendance and examination of witnesses on his behalf under the same conditions as witnesses against him;

   f. To have the free assistance of an interpreter if he cannot understand or speak the language used in court;

   g. Not to be compelled to testify against himself or to confess guilt.

4. In the case of juvenile persons, the procedure shall be such as will take account of their age and the desirability of promoting their rehabilitation.

5. Everyone convicted of a crime shall have the right to his conviction and sentence being reviewed by a higher tribunal according to law.

6. When a person has by a final decision been convicted of a criminal offence and when subsequently his conviction has been reversed or he has been pardoned on the ground that a new or newly discovered fact shows conclusively that there has been a miscarriage of justice, the person who has suffered punishment as a result of such conviction shall be compensated according to law, unless it is proved that the non-disclosure of the unknown fact in time is wholly or partly attributable to him.

7. No one shall be liable to be tried or punished again for an offence for which he has already been finally convicted or acquitted in accordance with the law and penal procedure of each country.

Article 15

1. No one shall be held guilty of any criminal offence on account of any act or omission which did not constitute a criminal offence, under national or international law, at the time when it was committed. Nor shall a heavier penalty be imposed than the one that was applicable at the time when the criminal offence was committed. If, subsequent to the commission of the offence, provision is made by law for the imposition of a lighter penalty, the offender shall benefit thereby.

2. Nothing in this article shall prejudice the trial and punishment of any person for any act or omission which, at the time when it was committed, was criminal according to the general principles of law recognized by the community of nations.

Article 16

Everyone shall have the right to recognition everywhere as a person before the law.

Article 17

1. No one shall be subjected to arbitrary or unlawful interference with his privacy, family, home or correspondence, nor to lawful attacks on his honour and reputation.
2. Everyone has the right to the protection of the law against such interference or attacks.

Article 18

1. Everyone shall have the right to freedom of thought, conscience and religion. This right shall include freedom to have or to adopt a religion or belief of his choice, and freedom, either individually or in community with others and in public or private, to manifest his religion or belief in worship, observance, practice and teaching.
2. No one shall be subject to coercion which would impair his freedom to have or to adopt a religion or belief of his choice.
3. Freedom to manifest one's religion or beliefs may be subject only to such limitations as are prescribed by law and are necessary to protect public safety, order, health, or morals or the fundamental rights and freedoms of others.
4. The States Parties to the present Covenant undertake to have respect for the liberty of parents and, when applicable, legal guardians to ensure the religious and moral education of their children in conformity with their own convictions.

Article 19

1. Everyone shall have the right to hold opinions without interference.
2. Everyone shall have the right to freedom of expression; this right shall include freedom to seek, receive and impart information and ideas of all kinds, regardless of frontiers, either orally, in writing or in print, in the form of art, or through any other media of his choice.
3. The exercise of the rights provided for in paragraph 2 of this article carries with it special duties and responsibilities. It may therefore be subject to certain restrictions, but these shall only be such as are provided by the law and are necessary:
   a. For respect of the rights or reputations of others;
   b. For the protection of national security or of public order (*ordre public*), or of public health or morals.

Article 20

1. Any propaganda for war shall be prohibited by law.
2. Any advocacy of national, racial or religious hatred that constitutes incitement to discrimination, hostility or violence shall be prohibited by law.

Article 21

The right of peaceful assembly shall be recognized. No restrictions may be placed on the exercise of this right other than those imposed in conformity with the law and which are necessary in a democratic society in the interests of national security or public safety, public order (*ordre public*), the protection of public health or morals or the protection of the rights and freedoms of others.

Article 22

1. Everyone shall have the right to freedom of association with others, including the right to form and join trade unions for the protection of his interests.
2. No restrictions may be placed on the exercise of this right other than those which are prescribed by law and which are necessary in a democratic society in the interests of national security or public safety, public order (*ordre public*), the protection of public health or morals or the protection of the rights and freedoms of others. This Article shall not prevent the imposition of lawful restrictions on members of the armed forces and of the police in their exercise of this right.
3. Nothing in this article shall authorize States Parties to the International Labour Organization Convention of 1948 concerning Freedom of Association and Protection of the Right to Organize to take legislative measures which would prejudice, or to apply the law in such a manner as to prejudice, the guarantees provided for in that Convention.

Article 23

1. The family is the natural and fundamental group unit of society and is entitled to protection by society and the State.
2. The right of men and women of marriageable age to marry and to found a family shall be recognized.
3. No marriage shall be entered into without the free and full consent of the intending spouses.
4. States Parties to the present Covenant shall take appropriate steps to ensure equality of rights and responsibilities of spouses as to marriage, during marriage and at its dissolution. In the case of dissolution, provision shall be made for the necessary protection of any children.

Article 24

1. Every child shall have, without any discrimination as to race, colour, sex, language, religion, national or social origin, property or birth, the right to such measures of

protection as are required by his status as a minor, on the part of his family, society and the State.

2. Every child shall be registered immediately after birth and shall have a name.

3. Every child has the right to acquire a nationality.

Article 25

Every citizen shall have the right and the opportunity, without any of the distinctions mentioned in Article 2 and without unreasonable restrictions:

a. To take part in the conduct of public affairs, directly or through freely chosen representatives;

b. To vote and to be elected at genuine periodic elections which shall be by universal and equal suffrage and shall be held by secret ballot, guaranteeing the free expression of the will of the electors;

c. To have access, on general terms of equality, to public service in his country.

Article 26

All persons are equal before the law and are entitled without any discrimination to the equal protection of the law. In this respect, the law shall prohibit any discrimination and guarantee to all persons equal and effective protection against discrimination on any ground such as race, colour, sex, language, religion, political or other opinion, national or social origin, property, birth or other status.

Article 27

In those States in which ethnic, religious or linguistic minorities exist, persons belonging to such minorities shall not be denied the right, in community with the other members of their group, to enjoy their own culture, to profess and practice their own religion, or to use their own language.

PART IV

Article 28

1. There shall be established a Human Rights Committee (hereafter referred to in the present Covenant as the Committee). It shall consist of eighteen members and shall carry out the functions hereinafter provided.

2. The Committee shall be composed of nationals of the States Parties to the present Covenant who shall be persons of high moral character and recognized competence in the field of human rights, consideration being given to the usefulness of the participation of some persons having legal experience.

3. The members of the Committee shall be elected and shall serve in their personal capacity.

Article 29

1. The members of the Committee shall be elected by secret ballot from a list of persons possessing the qualifications prescribed in Article 28 and nominated for the purpose by the States Parties to the present Covenant.
2. Each State Party to the present Covenant may nominate not more than two persons. These persons shall be nationals of the nominating State.
3. A person shall be eligible for renomination.

Article 30

1. The initial election shall be held no later than six months after the date of the entry into force of the present Covenant.
2. At least four months before the date of each election to the Committee, other than an election to fill a vacancy declared in accordance with Article 34, the Secretary-General of the United Nations shall address a written invitation to the States Parties to the present Covenant to submit their nominations for membership of the Committee within three months.
3. The Secretary-General of the United Nations shall prepare a list in alphabetical order of all the persons thus nominated, with an indication of the States Parties which have nominated them, and shall submit it to the States Parties to the present Covenant no later than one month before the date of each election.
4. Elections of the members of the Committee shall be held at a meeting of the States Parties to the present Covenant convened by the Secretary-General of the United Nations at the Headquarters of the United Nations. At that meeting, for which two thirds of the States Parties to the present Covenant shall constitute a quorum, the persons elected to the Committee shall be those nominees who obtain the largest number of votes and an absolute majority of the votes of the representatives of States Parties present and voting.

Article 31

1. The Committee may not include more than one national of the same State.
2. In the election of the Committee, consideration shall be given to equitable geographical distribution of membership and to the representation of the different forms of civilization and of the principal legal systems.

Article 32

1. The members of the Committee shall be elected for a term of four years. They shall be eligible for re-election if renominated. However, the terms of nine of the members elected at the first election shall expire at the end of two years; immediately after the first election, the names of these nine members shall be chosen by lot by the Chairman of the meeting referred to in Article 30, paragraph 4.
2. Elections at the expiry of office shall be held in accordance with the preceding articles of this part of the present Covenant.

Article 33

1. If, in the unanimous opinion of the other members, a member of the Committee has ceased to carry out his functions for any cause other than absence of a temporary character, the Chairman of the Committee shall notify the Secretary-General of the United Nations, who shall then declare the seat of that member to be vacant.

2. In the event of the death or the resignation of a member of the Committee, the Chairman shall immediately notify the Secretary-General of the United Nations, who shall declare the seat vacant from the date of death or the date on which the resignation takes effect.

Article 34

1. When a vacancy is declared in accordance with Article 33 and if the term of office of the member to be replaced does not expire within six months of the declaration of the vacancy, the Secretary-General of the United Nations shall notify each of the States Parties to the present Covenant, which may within two months submit nominations in accordance with Article 29 for the purpose of fulfilling the vacancy.

2. The Secretary-General of the United Nations shall prepare a list in alphabetical order of the persons thus nominated and shall submit it to the States Parties to the present Covenant. The election to fill the vacancy shall then take place in accordance with the relevant provisions of this part of the present Covenant.

3. A member of the Committee elected to fill a vacancy declared in accordance with Article 33 shall hold office for the remainder of the term of the member who vacated the seat of the Committee under the provisions of that article.

Article 35

The members of the Committee shall, with the approval of the General Assembly of the United Nations, receive emoluments from United Nations resources on such terms and conditions as the General Assembly may decide, having regard to the importance of the Committee's responsibilities.

Article 36

The Secretary-General of the United Nations shall provide the necessary staff and facilities for the effective performance of the functions of the Committee under the present Covenant.

Article 37

1. The Secretary-General of the United Nations shall convene the initial meeting of the Committee at the Headquarters of the United Nations.

2. After its initial meeting, the Committee shall meet at such times as shall be provided in its rules of procedure.

3. The Committee shall normally meet at the Headquarters of the United Nations or at the United Nations Office at Geneva.

Article 38

Every member of the Committee shall, before taking up his duties, make a solemn declaration in open committee that he will perform his functions impartially and conscientiously.

Article 39

1. The Committee shall elect its officers for a term of two years. They may be re-elected.
2. The Committee shall establish its own rules of procedure, but these rules shall provide, *inter alia,* that:
   a. Twelve members shall constitute a quorum:
   b. Decisions of the Committee shall be made by a majority vote of the members present.

Article 40

1. The States Parties to the present Covenant undertake to submit reports on the measures they have adopted which give effect to the rights recognized herein and on the progress made in the enjoyment of those rights:
   a. Within one year of the entry into force of the present Covenant for the States Parties concerned;
   b. Thereafter whenever the Committee so requests.
2. All reports shall be submitted to the Secretary-General of the United Nations, who shall transmit them to the Committee for consideration. Reports shall indicate the factors and difficulties, if any, affecting the implementation of the present Covenant.
3. The Secretary-General of the United Nations may, after consultation with the Committee, transmit to the specialized agencies concerned copies of such parts of the reports as may fall within their field of competence.
4. The Committee shall study the reports submitted by the States Parties to the present Covenant. It shall transmit its reports, and such general comments as it may consider appropriate, to the States Parties. The Committee may also transmit to the Economic and Social Council these comments along with the copies of the reports it has received from States Parties to the present Covenant.
5. The States Parties to the present Covenant may submit to the Committee observations on any comments that may be made in accordance with paragraph 4 of this article.

Article 41

1. A State Party to the present Covenant may at any time declare under this article that it recognizes the competence of the Committee to receive and consider communications to the effect that a State Party claims that another State Party is not fulfilling its obligations under the present Covenant. Communications under this article may be received and considered only if submitted by a State Party which has made a declaration recognizing in regard to itself the competence of the Committee. No communication shall be received by the Committee if it concerns a State Party which has not made such a declaration. Communications received under this article shall be dealt with in accordance with the following procedure:
   a. If a State Party to the present Covenant considers that another State Party is not giving effect to the provisions of the present Covenant, it may, by written communication, bring the matter to the attention of that State Party. Within three months after the receipt of the communication, the receiving State shall afford the State which sent the communication an explanation or any other statement in writing clarifying the matter, which should include, to the extent possible and pertinent, reference to domestic procedures and remedies taken, pending, or available in the matter.
   b. If the matter is not adjusted to the satisfaction of both States Parties concerned within six months after the receipt by the receiving State of the initial communication, either State shall have the right to refer the matter to the Committee, by notice given to the Committee and to the other State.
   c. The Committee shall deal with a matter referred to it only after it has ascertained that all available domestic remedies have been invoked and exhausted in the matter, in conformity with the generally recognized principles of international law. This shall not be the rule where the application of the remedies is unreasonably prolonged.
   d. The Committee shall hold closed meetings when examining communications under this article.
   e. Subject to the provisions of sub-paragraph (c), the Committee shall make available its good offices to the States Parties concerned with a view to a friendly solution of the matter on the basis of respect for human rights and fundamental freedoms as recognized in the present Covenant.
   f. In any matter referred to it, the Committee may call upon the States Parties concerned, referred to in sub-paragraph (b), to supply any relevant information.
   g. The States Parties concerned, referred to in sub-paragraph (b), shall have the right to be represented when the matter is being considered in the Committee and to make submissions orally and/or in writing.
   h. The Committee shall, within twelve months after the date of receipt of notice under sub-paragraph (b), submit a report:
      i. If a solution within the terms of sub-paragraph (e) is reached, the Committee shall confine its report to a brief statement of the facts and of the solution reached;

    ii. If a solution within the terms of sub-paragraph (e) is not reached, the Committee shall confine its report to a brief statement of the facts; the written submissions and record of the oral submissions made by the States Parties concerned shall be attached to the report.

        In every matter, the report shall be communicated to the States Parties concerned.

2. The provisions of this article shall come into force when ten States Parties to the present Covenant have made declarations under paragraph 1 of this article. Such declarations shall be deposited by the States Parties with the Secretary-General of the United Nations, who shall transmit copies thereof to the other States Parties. A declaration may be withdrawn at any time by notification to the Secretary-General. Such a withdrawal shall not prejudice the consideration of any matter which is the subject of a communication already transmitted under this article; no further communication by any State Party shall be received after the notification of withdrawal of the declaration has been received by the Secretary-General, unless the State Party concerned has made a new declaration.

Article 42

1. a. If a matter referred to the Committee in accordance with Article 41 is not resolved to the satisfaction of the States Parties concerned, the Committee may, with the prior consent of the States Parties concerned, appoint an *ad hoc* Conciliation Commission (hereinafter referred to as the Commission). The good offices of the Commission shall be made available to the States Parties concerned with a view to an amicable solution of the matter on the basis of respect for the present Covenant;

   b. The Commission shall consist of five persons acceptable to the States Parties concerned. If the States Parties concerned fail to reach agreement within three months on all or part of the composition of the Commission the members of the Commission concerning whom no agreement has been reached shall be elected by secret ballot by a two-thirds majority vote of the Committee from among its members.

2. The members of the Commission shall serve in their personal capacity. They shall not be nationals of the States Parties concerned, or of a State not party to the present Covenant, or of a State Party which has not made a declaration under Article 41.

3. The Commission shall elect its own Chairman and adopt its own rules of procedure.

4. The meetings of the Commission shall normally be held at the Headquarters of the United Nations or at the United Nations Office at Geneva. However, they may be held at such other convenient places as the Commission may determine in consultation with the Secretary-General of the United Nations and the States Parties concerned.

5. The secretariat provided in accordance with Article 36 shall also service the commissions appointed under this article.

6. The information received and collated by the Committee shall be made available to the Commission and the Commission may call upon the States Parties concerned to supply any other relevant information.

7. When the Commission has fully considered the matter, but in any event not later than twelve months after having been seized of the matter, it shall submit to the Chairman of the Committee a report for communication to the States Parties concerned.

   a. If the Commission is unable to complete its consideration of the matter within twelve months, it shall confine its report to a brief statement of the status of its consideration of the matter.

   b. If an amicable solution to the matter on the basis of respect for human rights as recognized in the present Covenant is reached, the Commission shall confine its report to a brief statement of the facts and of the solution reached.

   c. If a solution within the terms of sub-paragraph (b) is not reached, the Commission's report shall embody its findings on all questions of fact relevant to the issues between the States Parties concerned, and its views on the possibilities of an amicable solution of the matter. This report shall also contain the written submissions and a record of the oral submissions made by the States Parties concerned.

   d. If the Commission's report is submitted under sub-paragraph (c), the States Parties concerned shall, within three months of the receipt of the report, notify the Chairman of the Committee whether or not they accept the contents of the report of the Commission.

8. The provisions of this Article are without prejudice to the responsibilities of the Committee under Article 41.

9. The States Parties concerned shall share equally all the expenses of the members of the Commission in accordance with estimates to be provided by the Secretary-General of the United Nations.

10. The Secretary-General of the United Nations shall be empowered to pay the expenses of the members of the Commission, if necessary, before reimbursement by the States Parties concerned, in accordance with paragraph 9 of this article.

Article 43

The members of the Committee, and of the *ad hoc* conciliation commissions which may be appointed under Article 42, shall be entitled to the facilities, privileges and immunities of experts on mission for the United Nations as laid down in the relevant sections of the Convention on the Privileges and Immunities of the United Nations.

Article 44

The provisions for the implementation of the present Covenant shall apply without prejudice to the procedures prescribed in the field of human rights by or under the constituent instruments and the conventions of the United Nations and of the specialized agencies and shall not prevent the States Parties to the present Covenant from having recourse to other procedures for settling a dispute in accordance with general or special international agreements in force between them.

Article 45

The Committee shall submit to the General Assembly of the United Nations through the Economic and Social Council, an annual report on its activities.

PART V

Article 46

Nothing in the present Covenant shall be interpreted as impairing the provisions of the Charter of the United Nations and of the constitutions of the specialized agencies which define the respective responsibilities of the various organs of the United Nations and of the specialized agencies in regard to the matters dealt with in the present Covenant.

Article 47

Nothing in the present Covenant shall be interpreted as impairing the inherent right of all peoples to enjoy and utilize fully and freely their natural wealth and resources.

PART VI

Article 48

1. The present Covenant is open for signature by any State Member of the United Nations or member of any of its specialized agencies, by any State Party to the Statute of the International Court of Justice, and by any other State which has been invited by the General Assembly of the United Nations to become a party to the present Covenant.
2. The present Covenant is subject to ratification. Instruments of ratification shall be deposited with the Secretary-General of the United Nations.
3. The present Covenant shall be open to accession by any State referred to in paragraph 1 of this article.
4. Accession shall be effected by the deposit of an instrument of accession with the Secretary-General of the United Nations.
5. The Secretary-General of the United Nations shall inform all States which have signed this Covenant or acceded to it of the deposit of each instrument of ratification or accession.

Article 49

1. The present Covenant shall enter into force three months after the date of the deposit with the Secretary-General of the United Nations of the thirty-fifth instrument of ratification or instrument of accession.
2. For each State ratifying the present Covenant or acceding to it after the deposit of the thirty-fifth instrument of ratification or instrument of accession, the present Covenant shall enter into force three months after the date of the deposit of its own instrument of ratification or instrument of accession.

Article 50

The provisions of the present Covenant shall extend to all parts of federal States without any limitations or exceptions.

Article 51

1. Any State Party to the present Covenant may propose an amendment and file it with the Secretary-General of the United Nations. The Secretary-General of the United Nations shall thereupon communicate any proposed amendments to the States Parties to the present Covenant with a request that they notify him whether they favour a conference of States Parties for the purpose of considering and voting upon the proposals. In the event that at least one third of the States Parties favours such a conference, the Secretary-General shall convene the conference under the auspices of the United Nations. Any amendment adopted by a majority of the States Parties present and voting at the conference shall be submitted to the General Assembly of the United Nations for approval.
2. Amendments shall come into force when they have been approved by the General Assembly of the United Nations and accepted by a two-thirds majority of the States Parties to the present Covenant in accordance with their respective constitutional processes.
3. When amendments come into force, they shall be binding on those States Parties which have accepted them, other States Parties still being bound by the provisions of the present Covenant and any earlier amendment which they have accepted.

Article 52

Irrespective of the notifications made under Article 48, paragraph 5, the Secretary-General of the United Nations shall inform all States referred to in paragraph 1 of the same article of the following particulars:

a. Signatures, ratifications and accessions under Article 48;
b. The date of the entry into force of the present Covenant under Article 49 and the date of the entry into force of any amendments under Article 51.

Article 53

1. The present Covenant, of which the Chinese, English, French, Russian and Spanish texts are equally authentic, shall be deposited in the archives of the United Nations.
2. The Secretary-General of the United Nations shall transmit certified copies of the present Covenant to all States referred to in Article 48.

International Covenant on Economic, Social, and Cultural Rights, 1966

Preamble

The States Parties to the present Covenant,

Considering that, in accordance with the principles proclaimed in the Charter of the United Nations, recognition of the inherent dignity and of the equal and inalienable rights of all members of the human family is the foundation of freedom, justice and peace in the world,

Recognizing that these rights derive from the inherent dignity of the human person,

Reocgnizing that, in accordance with the Universal Declaration of Human Rights, the ideal of free human beings enjoying freedom from fear and want can only be achieved if conditions are created whereby everyone may enjoy his economic, social and cultural rights, as well as his civil and political rights,

Considering the obligation of States under the Charter of the United Nations to promote universal respect for, and observance of, human rights and freedoms,

Realizing that the individual, having duties to other individuals and to the community to which he belongs, is under a responsibility to strive for the promotion and observance of the rights recognized in the present Covenant,

Agree upon the following articles:

PART I

Article 1

1. All peoples have the right of self-determination. By virtue of that right they freely determine their political status and freely pursue their economic, social and cultural development.
2. All peoples may, for their own ends, freely dispose of their natural wealth and resources without prejudice to any obligations arising out of international eco-

nomic co-operation, based upon the principle of mutual benefit, and international law. In no case may a people be deprived of its own means of subsistence.

3. The States Parties to the present Covenant, including those having responsibility for the administration of Non-Self-Governing and Trust Territories, shall promote the realization of the right of self-determination, and shall respect that right, in conformity with the provisions of the Charter of the United Nations.

PART II

Article 2

1. Each State Party to the present Covenant undertakes to take steps, individually and through international assistance and co-operation, especially economic and technical, to the maximum of its available resources, with a view to achieving progressively the full realization of the rights recognized in the present Covenant by all appropriate means, including particularly the adoption of legislative measures.

2. The States Parties to the present Covenant undertake to guarantee that the rights enunciated in the present Covenant will be exercised without discrimination of any kind as to race, colour, sex, language, religion, political or other opinion, national or social origin, property, birth or other status.

3. Developing countries, with due regard to human rights and their national economy, may determine to what extent they would guarantee the economic rights recognized in the present Covenant to non-nationals.

Article 3

The States Parties to the present Covenant undertake to ensure the equal right of men and women to the enjoyment of all economic, social and cultural rights set forth in the present Covenant.

Article 4

The States Parties to the present Covenant recognize that, in the enjoyment of those rights provided by the State in conformity with the present Covenant, the State may subject such rights only to such limitations as are determined by law only in so far as this may be compatible with the nature of these rights and solely for the purpose of promoting the general welfare in a democratic society.

Article 5

1. Nothing in the present Covenant may be interpreted as implying for any State, group or person any right to engage in any activity or to perform any act aimed at the destruction of any of the rights or freedoms recognized herein, or at their limitation to a greater extent than is provided for in the present Covenant.

2. No restriction upon or derogation from any of the fundamental human rights recognized or existing in any country in virtue of law, conventions, regulations or custom shall be admitted on the pretext that the present Covenant does not recognize such rights or that it recognizes them to a lesser extent.

PART III

Article 6

1. The States Parties to the present Covenant recognize the right to work, which includes the right of everyone to the opportunity to gain his living by work which he freely chooses or accepts, and will take appropriate steps to safeguard this right.
2. The steps to be taken by a State Party to the present Covenant to achieve the full realization of this right shall include technical and vocational guidance and training programmes, policies and techniques to achieve steady economic, social and cultural development and full and productive employment under conditions safe-guarding fundamental political and economic freedoms to the individual.

Article 7

The States Parties to the present Covenant recognize the right of everyone to the enjoyment of just and favourable conditions of work, which ensure, in particular:

   a. Remuneration which provides all workers, as a minimum with:
      i. Fair wages and equal remuneration for work of equal value without distinc-tion of any kind, in particular women being guaranteed conditions of work not inferior to those enjoyed by men, with equal pay for equal work;
      ii. A decent living for themselves and their families in accordance with the provisions of the present Covenant;
   b. Safe and healthy working conditions;
   c. Equal opportunity for everyone to be promoted in his employment to an appropriate higher level, subject to no considerations other than those of seniority and competence;
   d. Rest, leisure and reasonable limitation of working hours and periodic holidays with pay, as well as remuneration for public holidays.

Article 8

1. The States Parties to the present Covenant undertake to ensure:
   a. The right of everyone to form trade unions and join the trade union of his choice, subject only to the rules of the organization concerned, for the promo-tion and protection of his economic and social interests. No restrictions may be placed on the exercise of this right other than those prescribed by law and which are necessary in a democratic society in the interests of national security or public order or for the protection of the rights and freedoms of others;

   b. The right of trade unions to establish national federations or confederations and the right of the latter to form or join international trade union organizations;
   c. The right of trade unions to function freely subject to no limitations other than those prescribed by law and which are necessary in a democratic society in the interests of national security or public order or for the protection of the rights and freedoms of others;
   d. The right to strike, provided that it is exercised in conformity with the laws of the particular country.
2. This article shall not prevent the imposition of lawful restrictions on the exercise of these rights by members of the armed forces or of the police or of the administration of the State.
3. Nothing in this article shall authorize States Parties to the International Labour Organization Convention of 1948 concerning Freedom of Association and Protection of the Right to Organize to take legislative measures which would prejudice, or apply the law in such a manner as would prejudice, the guarantees provided for in that Convention.

Article 9

The States Parties to the present Covenant recognize the right of everyone to social security, including social insurance.

Article 10

The States Parties to the present Covenant recognize that:

1. The widest possible protection and assistance should be accorded to the family, which is the natural and fundamental group unit of society, particularly for its establishment and while it is responsible for the care and education of dependent children. Marriage must be entered into with the free consent of the intending spouses.
2. Special protection should be accorded to mothers during a reasonable period before and after childbirth. During such period working mothers should be accorded paid leave or leave with adequate social security benefits.
3. Special measures of protection and assistance should be taken on behalf of all children and young persons without any discrimination for reasons of parentage or other conditions. Children and young persons should be protected from economic and social exploitation. Their employment in work harmful to their morals or health or dangerous to life or likely to hamper their normal development should be punishable by law. States should also set age limits below which the paid employment of child labour should be prohibited and punishable by law.

Article 11

1. The States Parties to the present Covenant recognize the right of everyone to an adequate standard of living for himself and his family, including adequate food,

clothing and housing, and to the continuous improvement of living conditions. The States Parties will take appropriate steps to ensure the realization of this right, recognizing to this effect the essential importance of international co-operation based on free consent.

2. The States Parties to the present Covenant, recognizing the fundamental right of everyone to be free from hunger, shall take, individually and through international co-operation, the measures, including specific programmes, which are needed:

   a. To improve methods of production, conservation and distribution of food by making full use of technical and scientific knowledge, by disseminating knowledge of the principles of nutrition and by developing or reforming agrarian systems in such a way as to achieve the most efficient development and utilization of natural resources;

   b. Taking into account the problems of both food-importing and food-exporting countries, to ensure an equitable distribution of world food supplies in relation to need.

Article 12

1. The States Parties to the present Covenant recognize the right of everyone to the enjoyment of the highest attainable standard of physical and mental health.

2. The steps to be taken by the States Parties to the present Covenant to achieve the full realization of this right shall include those necessary for:

   a. The provision for the reduction of the stillbirth-rate and of infant mortality and for the healthy development of the child;

   b. The improvement of all aspects of environmental and industrial hygiene;

   c. The prevention, treatment and control of epidemic, endemic, occupational and other diseases;

   d. The creation of conditions which would assure to all medical service and medical attention in the event of sickness.

Article 13

1. The States Parties to the present Covenant recognize the right of everyone to education. They agree that education shall be directed to the full development of the human personality and the sense of its dignity, and shall strengthen the respect for human rights and fundamental freedoms. They further agree that education shall enable all persons to participate effectively in a free society, promote understanding, tolerance and friendship among all nations and all racial, ethnic or religious groups, and further the activities of the United Nations for the maintenance of peace.

2. The States Parties to the present Covenant recognize that, with a view to achieving the full realization of this right:

   a. Primary education shall be compulsory and available free to all;

   b. Secondary education in its different forms, including technical and vocational secondary education, shall be made generally available and accessible to all by every appropriate means, and in particular by the progressive introduction of free education;

c. Higher education shall be made equally accessible to all, on the basis of capacity, by every appropriate means, and in particular by the progressive introduction of free education;

d. Fundamental education shall be encouraged or intensified as far as possible for those persons who have not received or completed the whole period of their primary education;

e. The development of a system of schools at all levels shall be actively pursued, an adequate fellowship system shall be established, and the material conditions of teaching staff shall be continuously improved.

3. The States Parties to the present Covenant undertake to have respect for the liberty of parents and, when applicable, legal guardians, to choose for their children schools, other than those established by the public authorities, which conform to such minimum educational standards as may be laid down or approved by the State and to ensure the religious and moral education of their children in conformity with their own convictions.

4. No part of this article shall be construed so as to interfere with the liberty of individuals and bodies to establish and direct educational institutions, subject always to the observance of the principles set forth in paragraph 1 of this Article and to the requirement that the education given in such institutions shall conform to such minimum standards as may be laid down by the State.

Article 14

Each State Party to the present Covenant which, at the time of becoming a Party, has not been able to secure in its metropolitan territory or other territories under its jurisdiction compulsory primary education, free of charge, undertakes, within two years, to work out and adopt a detailed plan of action for the progressive implementation, within a reasonable number of years, to be fixed in the plan, of the principle of compulsory education free of charge for all.

Article 15

1. The States Parties to the present Covenant recognize the rights of everyone:
   a. To take part in cultural life;
   b. To enjoy the benefits of scientific progress and its applications;
   c. To benefit from the protection of the moral and material interests resulting from any scientific, literary or artistic production of which he is the author.

2. The steps to be taken by the States Parties to the present Covenant to achieve the full realization of this right shall include those necessary for the conservation, the development and the diffusion of science and culture.

3. The States Parties to the present Covenant undertake to respect the freedom indispensable for scientific research and creative activity.

4. The States Parties to the present Covenant recognize the benefits to be derived from the encouragement and development of international contacts and co-operation in the scientific and cultural fields.

PART IV

Article 16

1. The States Parties to the present Covenant undertake to submit in conformity with this part of the Covenant reports on the measures which they have adopted and the progress made in achieving the observance of the rights recognized herein.
2. a. All reports shall be submitted to the Secretary-General of the United Nations, who shall transmit copies to the Economic and Social Council for consideration in accordance with the provisions of the present Covenant.
   b. The Secretary-General of the United Nations shall also transmit to the specialized agencies copies of the reports, or any relevant parts therefrom, from States Parties to the present Covenant which are also members of these specialized agencies in so far as these reports, or parts therefrom, relate to any matters which fall within the responsibilities of the said agencies in accordance with their constitutional instruments.

Article 17

1. The States Parties to the present Covenant shall furnish their reports in stages, in accordance with a programme to be established by the Economic and Social Council within one year of the entry into force of the present Covenant after consultation with the States Parties and the specialized agencies concerned.
2. Reports may indicate factors and difficulties affecting the degree of fulfillment of obligations under the present Covenant.
3. Where relevant information has previously been furnished to the United Nations or to any specialized agency by any State Party to the present Covenant, it will not be necessary to reproduce that information, but a precise reference to the information so furnished will suffice.

Article 18

Pursuant to its responsibilities under the Charter of the United Nations in the field of human rights and fundamental freedoms, the Economic and Social Council may make arrangements with the specialized agencies in respect of their reporting to it on the progress made in achieving the observance of the provisions of the present Covenant falling within the scope of their activities. These reports may include particulars of decisions and recommendations on such implementation adopted by their competent organs.

Article 19

The Economic and Social Council may transmit to the Commission on Human Rights for study and general recommendation or as appropriate for information the reports concerning human rights submitted by States in accordance with Articles 16 and 17, and those concerning human rights submitted by the specialized agencies in accordance with Article 18.

Article 20

The States Parties to the present Covenant and the specialized agencies concerned may submit comments to the Economic and Social Council on any general recommendation under Article 19 or reference to such general recommendation in any report of the Commission on Human Rights or any documentation referred to therein.

Article 21

The Economic and Social Council may submit from time to time to the General Assembly reports with recommendations of a general nature and a summary of the information received from the States Parties to the present Covenant and the specialized agencies on the measures taken and the progress made in achieving general observance of the rights recognized in the present Covenant.

Article 22

The Economic and Social Council may bring to the attention of other organs of the United Nations, their subsidiary organs and specialized agencies concerned with furnishing technical assistance any matters arising out of the reports referred to in this part of the present Covenant which may assist such bodies in deciding, each within its field of competence, on the advisability of international measures likely to contribute to the effective progressive implementation of the present Covenant.

Article 23

The States Parties to the present Covenant agree that international action for the achievement of the rights recognized in the present Covenant includes such methods as the conclusion of conventions, the adoption of recommendations, the furnishing of technical assistance and the holding of regional meetings and technical meetings for the purpose of consultation and study organized in conjunction with the Governments concerned.

Article 24

Nothing in the present Covenant shall be interpreted as impairing the provisions of the Charter of the United Nations and of the constitutions of the specialized agencies which define the respective responsibilities of the various organs of the United

Nations and of the specialized agencies in regard to the matters dealt with in the present Covenant.

Article 25

Nothing in the present Covenant shall be interpreted as impairing the inherent right of all peoples to enjoy and utilize fully and freely their natural wealth and resources.

PART V

Article 26

1. The present Covenant is open for signature by any State Member of the United Nations or member of any of its specialized agencies, by any State Party to the Statute of the International Court of Justice, and by any other State which has been invited by the General Assembly of the United Nations to become a party to the present Covenant.
2. The present Covenant is subject to ratification. Instruments of ratification shall be deposited with the Secretary-General of the United Nations.
3. The present Covenant shall be open to accession by any State referred to in paragraph 1 of this article.
4. Accession shall be effected by the deposit of an instrument of accession with the Secretary-General of the United Nations.
5. The Secretary-General of the United Nations shall inform all States which have signed the present Covenant or acceded to it of the deposit of each instrument of ratification or accession.

Article 27

1. The present Covenant shall enter into force three months after the date of the deposit with the Secretary-General of the United Nations of the thirty-fifth instrument of ratification or instrument of accession.
2. For each State ratifying the present Covenant or acceding to it after the deposit of the thirty-fifth instrument of ratification or instrument of accession, the present Covenant shall enter into force three months after the date of the deposit of its own instrument of ratification or instrument of accession.

Article 28

The provisions of the present Covenant shall extend to all parts of federal States without any limitations or exceptions.

Article 29

1. Any State Party to the present Covenant may propose an amendment and file it with the Secretary-General of the United Nations. The Secretary-General shall there-

upon communicate any proposed amendments to the States Parties to the present Covenant with a request that they notify him whether they favour a conference of States Parties for the purpose of considering and voting upon the proposals. In the event that at least one third of the States Parties favours such a conference, the Secretary-General shall convene the conference under the auspices of the United Nations. Any amendment adopted by a majority of the States Parties present and voting at the conference shall be submitted to the General Assembly of the United Nations for approval.

2. Amendments shall come into force when they have been approved by the General Assembly of the United Nations and accepted by a two-thirds majority of the State Parties to the present Covenant in accordance with their respective constitutional processes.

3. When amendments come into force they shall be binding on those States Parties which have accepted them, other States Parties still being bound by the provisions of the present Covenant and any earlier amendment which they have accepted.

Article 30

Irrespective of the notifications made under Article 26, paragraph 5, the Secretary-General of the United Nations shall inform all States referred to in paragraph 1 of the same article of the following particulars:

a. Signatures, ratifications and accessions under Article 26;
b. The date of the entry into force of the present Covenant under Article 27 and the date of the entry into force of any amendments under Article 29.

Article 31

1. The present Covenant, of which the Chinese, English, French, Russian and Spanish texts are equally authentic, shall be deposited in the archives of the United Nations.

2. The Secretary-General of the United Nations shall transmit certified copies of the present Covenant to all States referred to in Article 26.

Appendix B: Selected Bibliography on Human Rights

Books and Anthologies

Benn, S. I., and R. S. Peters (Eds.), *The Principles of Political Thought*. (New York: Free Press, 1959).

Bloch, Ernst, *Natural Law and Human Dignity*, Dennis J. Schmidt (Trans.). (Cambridge, MA: The MIT Press, 1986).

Brown, Peter G., and Douglas MacLean (Eds.), *Human Rights and U.S. Foreign Policy*. (Lexington, MA: Lexington Books, 1979).

Brownlie, Ian (Ed.), *Basic Documents on Human Rights* (2nd ed.). (New York: Oxford University Press, 1981).

Campbell, Tom (Ed.), *Human Rights: From Rhetoric to Reality*. (New York: Blackwell, 1986).

Chomsky, Noam, and Edward Herman, *The Political Economy of Human Rights*. 2 vols. (Boston: South End Press, 1979).

Claude, R. P., *Comparative Human Rights*. (Baltimore: Johns Hopkins University Press, 1976).

Cranston, Maurice, *What Are Human Rights?* (New York: Taplinger Publishing Co., 1973).

Dominguez, J. I., *Enhancing Global Human Rights*. (New York: McGraw-Hill, 1979).

Downie, R. S., and E. Telfer (Eds.), *Respect for Persons*. (New York: Schocken Books, 1970).

Dworkin, Ronald, *Taking Rights Seriously*. (Cambridge, MA: Harvard University Press, 1977).

Feinberg, Joel, *Rights, Justice and the Bounds of Liberty; Essays in Social Philosophy*. (Princeton, NJ: Princeton University Press, 1980).

Flathman, Richard E., *The Practice of Rights*. (Cambridge: Cambridge University Press, 1976).

Forsythe, David P., *Human Rights and World Politics*. (Lincoln: University of Nebraska Press, 1983).

Frankel, Charles, *Human Rights and Foreign Policy*. (New York: Foreign Policy Association, 1978).

Frey, R. G. (Ed.), *Utility and Rights*. (Minneapolis, MN: University of Minnesota Press, 1984).

Gewirth, Alan, *Reason and Morality.* (Chicago: University of Chicago Press, 1978).

Gewirth, Alan, *Human Rights: Essays on Justification and Applications.* (Chicago: University of Chicago Press, 1982).

Glaser, Kurt, and Stefan T. Possony, *Victims of Politics: The State of Human Rights.* (New York: Columbia University Press, 1979).

Goldinger, M. (Ed.), *Punishment and Human Rights.* (Cambridge, MA: Schenkman, 1974).

Gotesky, R., and E. Lazslo (Eds.), *Human Dignity: This Century and the Next.* (New York: Gordon and Breach, 1970).

Hart, H. L. A., *The Concept of Law.* (Oxford: Clarendon Press, 1964).

Henkin, Alice, *Human Dignity.* (New York: Aspen Institute for Humanistic Studies, 1979).

Henkin, Louis, *The Rights of Man Today.* (Boulder, CO: Westview, 1978).

Hohfeld, Wesley, *Fundamental Legal Conceptions As Applied in Judicial Reasoning,* Walter Wheeler Cook (Ed.). (New Haven, CN: Yale University Press, 1966).

Howard, H. E., and M. K. Munitz (Eds.), *Ethics and Social Justice.* (Albany, NY: State University of New York Press, 1970).

Humphrey, John P., *Human Rights and the United Nations: A Great Adventure.* (Dobbs Ferry, NY: Transnational Publishers, 1984).

Joyce, James A., *The New Politics of Human Rights.* (New York: St. Martin's, 1979).

Kamenka, Eugene, and Alice Erh-Soon Tay (Eds.), *Human Rights.* (New York: St. Martin's Press, 1978).

Kommers, D. P., and G. D. Loescher (Eds.), *Human Rights and American Foreign Policy.* (Notre Dame, IN: University of Notre Dame Press, 1979).

Laqueur, W., and B. Rubin (Eds.), *The Human Rights Reader.* (New York: New American Library, 1979).

Leiser, Burton, *Values in Conflict: Life, Liberty, and the Rule of Law.* (New York: Macmillan, 1981).

Lyons, David (Ed.), *Rights.* (Belmont, CA: Wadsworth, 1979).

Machan, T., *Human Rights and Human Liberties: A Radical Reconsideration of the American Political Tradition.* (Chicago: Nelson Hall, 1975).

Melden, A. I. (Ed.), *Human Rights.* (Belmont, CA: Wadsworth, 1970).

Melden, A. I., *Rights and Persons.* (Berkeley: University of California Press, 1977).

Meyers, Diana, *Inalienable Rights: A Defense.* (New York: Columbia University Press, 1985).

Milne, A. J. M., *Human Rights and Human Diversity.* (Albany, NY: State University of New York Press, 1986).

Mower, Alfred G., *The United States, the United Nations, and Human Rights: The Eleanor Roosevelt and Jimmy Carter Eras.* (Westport, CN: Greenwood Press, 1979).

Nanda, V. P., et al. (Eds.), *Global Human Rights: Public Policies, Comparative Measures, and NGO Strategies.* (Boulder, CO: Westview, 1981).

Nelson, Jack, and V. M. Green (Eds.), *International Human Rights: Contemporary Issues.* (Stanfordville, NY: Human Rights Publishing Group, 1980).

Newberg, Paula (Ed.), *The Politics of Human Rights.* (New York: New York University Press, 1980).

Nickel, James W., *Making Sense of Human Rights: Philosophical Reflections on the Universal Declaration of Human Rights.* (Berkeley: University of California Press, 1987).

Owen, David, *Human Rights.* (New York: Norton, 1978).

Paul, Ellen F., J. Paul, and Fred D. Miller (Eds.), *Human Rights.* (Oxford: Basic Blackwell, 1984).

Pennock, J. R., and J. W. Chapman (Eds.), *Nomos XXIII: Human Rights.* (New York: New York University Press, 1981).

Pollis, A., and P. Schwab (Eds.), *Human Rights: Cultural and Ideological Perspectives.* (New York: Praeger, 1979).

Raphael, D. D. (Ed.), *Political Theory and the Rights of Man.* (Bloomington, IN: Indiana University Press, 1967).

Robertson, A. H., *Human Rights in the World Today.* (New York: Humanities Press, 1972).

Rubin, B., and E. Spiro (Eds.), *Human Rights and U.S. Foreign Policy.* (Boulder, CO: Westview, 1979).

Said, A. A. (Ed.), *Human Rights and World Order.* (New York: Praeger, 1978).

Shue, Henry, *Basic Rights: Subsistence, Affluence, & U.S. Foreign Policy.* (Princeton, NJ: Princeton University Press, 1979).

Sidorsky, David (Ed.), *Essays on Human Rights: Contemporary Issues and Jewish Perspectives.* (Philadelphia, PA: Jewish Publication Society, 1979).

Sumner, L. W., *The Moral Foundations of Rights.* (Oxford: Oxford University Press, 1987).

Swidler, A. (Ed.), *Human Rights in Religious Traditions.* (New York: Pilgrim Press, 1982).

Thompson, Kenneth (Ed.), *The Moral Imperatives of Human Rights: A World Survey.* (Washington, DC: University Press of America, 1980).

Tuck, Richard, *Natural Rights Theories.* (Cambridge: Cambridge University Press, 1979).

Van Dyke, V., *Human Rights, The United States, and the World Community.* (New York: Oxford University Press, 1970).

Veatch, Henry B. *Human Rights: Fact or Fancy?* (Baton Rouge, LA: Louisiana State University Press, 1985).

Vincent, R. J., *Human Rights and International Relations.* (New York: Cambridge University Press, 1986).

Vogelgesang, Sandy, *American Dream, Global Nightmare: The Dilemma of U.S. Human Rights Policy.* (New York: Norton, 1980).

Waldron, Jeremy (Ed.), *Theories of Rights.* (Oxford: Oxford University Press, 1984).

Wellman, Carl, *A Theory of Rights.* (Totowa, NJ: Rowman and Allanheld, 1985).

Werhane, Patricia, A. R. Gini, and D. T. Ozar (Eds.), *Philosophical Issues in Human Rights: Theories and Applications.* (New York: Random House, 1986).

White, Alan R., *Rights.* (Oxford: Clarendon Press, 1984).

Reference Works and Bibliographies

Friedman, Julian, and Marc J. Sherman (Eds.), *Human Rights: An International Comparative Law Bibliography.* (Westport, CN: Greenwood Press, 1985).

Garling, Margaret, *The Human Rights Handbook.* (London: Macmillan, 1979).

Gastil, Raymond D., *Freedom in the World: Political Rights and Civil Liberties.* (New York: Freedom House, 1978).

Humana, Charles, *World Human Rights Guide.* (New York: Facts on File, 1986).

Human Rights: A Topical Bibliography, The Center for the Study of Human Rights, Columbia University. (Boulder, CO: Westview Press, 1983).

Human Rights in International Law: Basic Texts, Directorate of Human Rights, Council of Europe, Strasbourg. (Croton, NY: Manhattan Publishing Co., 1985).

Human Rights Organizations and Periodical Directory. (Berkeley, CA: Meiklejohn Civil Liberties Institute, 1983).

Human Rights: Status of International Instruments. (New York: United Nations Publications, 1987).

Martin, Rex, and James W. Nickel, "A Bibliography on the Nature and Foundations of Rights, 1947–1977," *Political Theory,* 6:3 (August 1978), pp. 395–413.

Indexes